The Excellence of Play

4th edition

Edited by Janet Moyles

Open University Press

Open University Press
McGraw-Hill Education
McGraw-Hill House
Shoppenhangers Road
Maidenhead
Berkshire
England
SL6 2QL

email: enquiries@openup.co.uk
world wide web: www.openup.co.uk

and Two Penn Plaza, New York, NY 10121-2289, USA

First published 2015

A catalogue record of this book is available from the British Library

ISBN-13: 978-0-33-526418-6 (pb)
ISBN-10: 0-33-526418-2 (pb)
eISBN: 978-0-33-526419-3

Library of Congress Cataloging-in-Publication Data
CIP data applied for

Typesetting and e-book compilations by
RefineCatch Limited, Bungay, Suffolk

Fictitious names of companies, products, people, characters and/or data that may be
used herein (in case studies or in examples) are not intended to represent any real
individual, company, product or event.

Praise for this book

Janet Moyles's 'The Excellence of Play' has become a corner-stone of Early Childhood Education and Care and provides evidence that young children learn best by playing, exploring, experimenting – in short having exciting, adventurous, creative experiences which are meaningful and interest them. The ideas and examples in the chapters from Janet and her co-writers (many of them 'new') are a source of utter delight. Please, please someone, make this book compulsory reading for MPs and policy wonks.

Tricia David, Emeritus Professor, Canterbury Christ Church University

'The Excellence of Play' is now in its 4th edition and this is testimony to how thought-provoking an edited collection it continues to be. This much anticipated new edition does not disappoint: there are chapters written by foremost authors in the field and a vast array of perspectives on play are gathered together in one volume. In summary, this book is a valuable contribution to the field of Early Childhood Studies and should be considered essential reading for students and practitioners alike. On reading this book, one is left in no doubt about the primacy of play in young children's lives and the important role of adults in supporting their play.

Dr. Deborah Albon, London Metropolitan University

This book explores play from differing perspectives, which combine to provide a thought-provoking and comprehensive account of its value. The rigorous introduction examines and explains the relevance of the different chapters, written by experts in their fields, placing them in historical, cultural, psycho-social, curricular and pedagogical contexts.

This new edition of a classic text offers encouragement as well as information to all working with young children and their families. It provides grounded evidence for the importance of play, spelling out the complex but crucial contribution it makes to self-regulation, motivation and well-being, which are under threat in current conditions. Readers will be equipped to affirm and disseminate the importance of ensuring that future generations benefit from meaningful play.

Wendy Scott, President TACTYC

Play absorbs children; it fascinates them. It also fascinates and intrigues teachers, researchers and theorists, as the fourth edition of this book demonstrates. Its contributors do justice to the delights, complexities, puzzles and imponderables of play and make a powerful case against the undue "schoolification" of childhood and for the "playification" of schooling.

Colin Richards, HMI (retired) Emeritus Professor of Education, University of Cumbria

Contents

PART 5

Play is universal

List of figures, tables and photographs

Figures

Tables

Photographs

Notes on contributors

Dr Angela Anning is Emeritus Professor of Early Childhood Education, University of Leeds, where she was involved in primary teacher education, childhood studies and professional development. Her research interests are in the professional knowledge of those working in early childhood services, multi-agency teamwork, early childhood curricula and art education/children's drawing. She has published extensively in the field of early childhood services and education.

Karen Barr is Senior Lecturer in Early Years at Sheffield Hallam University, where she leads an Early Years Teacher Status pathway for undergraduates on Childhood Studies and Early Childhood Studies degrees. She has worked with children in schools, out-of-school clubs and nurseries in various practitioner and management roles. Her most recent publication is on young children's growth and development, in J. Kay (ed.) (2012) *Good Practice in the Early Years* (Continuum).

Marisol Basilio is a developmental and educational psychologist, working as a research assistant at the University of Cambridge. She is currently writing up her PhD concerned with the role of pre-verbal communicative tools in the early emergence of self-regulatory skills. Marisol first worked at Cambridge as a visiting scholar in 2009 and then in 2011 with a fellowship sponsored by UNESCO. She also collaborates with the LEGO Foundation as an educational psychology consultant.

Penny Borkett is Course Leader for the Foundation Degree in Early Years at Sheffield Hallam University. She was previously the Coordinator of a Sure Start Children's Centre and is currently involved in research that focuses on encouraging learners to develop their critical reflection skills. Her most recent publication is 'Diversity and inclusion in the early years', in J. Kay (ed.) (2012) *Good Practice in the Early Years* (Continuum).

Helen Bradford is an early years specialist who has worked first as a practitioner and now at the Faculty of Education, University of Cambridge, where she leads early years English as well as child development and well-being. She has written widely on early years education. Her research centres on young children writing. For her doctoral degree, she is currently investigating two-year-old children and their writing behaviours.

Dr Pat Broadhead was Professor of Playful Learning at Leeds Beckett University. Her research focuses on play and learning in early years settings and how open-ended play materials inspire children to engage in intellectually challenging and cooperative play. She has published widely, the most recent being: Broadhead, P. and Burt, A. (2011) *Understanding Young Children's Learning Through Play: Building Playful Pedagogies* (Routledge).

Dr Chris Brown is the John Adams Career Development Research Fellow in the Faculty of Policy and Society, Institute of Education, London. His interests include the processes through which research is brought to the attention of policy makers and what might be required in order to improve this. His current role involves helping schools and government(s) develop as research-engaged organisations, and to identify and scale up best practice.

Professor Tina Bruce CBE is a Froebel-trained teacher. She trained at the University of Manchester to teach children with hearing impairments and became Director of the Centre for Early Childhood Studies at Roehampton. She has written many books and articles, and was awarded International Woman Scholar in Education by the University of Virginia Commonwealth. She is a Vice-President of BAECE and a Trustee of the Froebel Trust.

Liz Chesworth has spent the past 20 years working within the field of early childhood education. She has taught in primary schools and children's centres, and is now a senior lecturer at Leeds Beckett University leading the BA (Hons) Early Childhood Education leading to QTS. She is currently completing her PhD, which considers play in a reception class from the perspectives of children, parents and teachers.

Dr Aline-Wendy Dunlop is Emeritus Professor in the School of Education, Faculty of Humanities and Social Sciences, University of Strathclyde, Glasgow. She is the Scottish coordinator for a European-funded International Research Staff Exchange Project on Educational Transitions, and chairs Autism Network Scotland. Her current research is on educational transitions across the lifespan, autism, family engagement in education, practitioner beliefs and practices, and arts-related childhood experiences.

Dr Peter Elfer is Principal Lecturer in Early Childhood Studies and Convenor of the Masters Programme in Early Childhood Studies at the University of Roehampton, London. His research and long-standing interest is in the play and well-being of babies and children under three. He has published a number of academic papers and co-written, with Elinor Goldschmied and Dorothy Selleck (2011) *Key Persons in the Early Years*, 2nd edn (Routledge).

Dr Hilary Fabian has taught in primary schools and the university sector. Her MSc dissertation in Education Management explored staff induction; her PhD thesis, books and journal publications reflect her research into transitions, particularly children start-ing school, children transferring between schools, and the way in which the process for children and adults is managed.

Dr Jan Georgeson is Research Fellow in Early Education Development in the Institute of Education at Plymouth University. After working as a teacher of children with special educational needs in a range of secondary, primary and preschool settings, Jan developed a strong interest in the diversity of early years settings. Her EdD is in Educational Disadvantage and Special Educational Needs. She researches and teaches on Early Childhood Studies courses.

Dr Kathy Goouch is a lecturer and researcher at Canterbury Christ Church University. Her knowledge and experience of teaching and research span the fields of literacy and early years, and her publications reflect these twin interests, with the central theme of play weaving through both. Her current research project is attempting to understand the nature of the relationships in baby rooms in nurseries.

Dr Justine Howard is Senior Lecturer in the School of Human and Health Science at Swansea University and the Programme Director of the Masters in Developmental and Therapeutic Play. She is a Chartered Psychologist and has worked as a play specialist, and retains close links with practice via research and consultancy. She has published extensively on the topic of play and is co-author of *Play and Learning in the Early Years: From Research to Practice* (Sage, 2010).

Helen Jameson is a teacher with more than 30 years' experience in a wide variety of settings. Her postgraduate research in learning through play, with David Whitebread at the University of Cambridge, led to their paper on 'The impact of play on the oral and written storytelling of able 5–7 year olds'.

Dr Peter King originally qualified as a secondary school teacher before his career path took him into the area of children's play and playwork. He is currently a lecturer at Swansea University, teaching on the Masters Childhood Studies and Developmental and Therapeutic Play courses. His interests are around all aspects of children's play, particularly the concept of choice and how this is addressed in policy construction and implementation.

Neil Kitson, a psychologist and teacher, was a lecturer at the University of Leicester for 12 years, where he developed his research in the field of drama and explored the power-ful role that play has in the development of young learners. Following advisory work in Northamptonshire, he has recently taken up a role with Warwick University Centre for Educational Studies and is an advisor to the Department for Education.

Val Melnyczuk is a qualified early years teacher and is currently employed as an Associate Lecturer with the Open University. Until recently she ran her own early years training company, N4K Ltd, and prior to that was an Early Years Consultant for Cheshire LA, a Children's Centre teacher and an EYP assessor.

Dr Janet Moyles (Editor) is Professor Emeritus at Anglia Ruskin University and is now mainly working in an author/editor capacity. One of her passions is children's learning through play and practitioner roles. She has undertaken several studies observing, documenting and analysing children's play in the context of education, and has produced a range of practitioner- and research-based books around play and children's learning, as well as directing several research projects.

Dr Jane Murray worked as an early years teacher before moving to become Senior Lecturer at the University of Northampton. She writes and publishes in education and early childhood, teaches students at levels 4–7, supervises PhD students, and researches locally, nationally and internationally. Jane is currently based at the University's Centre for Education and Research. Her PhD focused on young children's engagements in research behaviour.

Dr Celia O'Donovan has worked in education for more than 30 years as university lecturer, researcher, trainer and inspector. She has a particular interest in the link between movement and brain development, and has written two practical books for early years practitioners and teachers, as well as articles. She has collaborated with Val Melnyczuk on early years training projects and conferences.

Dr Jayne Osgood is Professor of Education at London Metropolitan University. She is a sociologist of education focusing specifically on the early years and is particularly concerned to research issues of inequality relating to gender, social class and 'race', and to critically engage with policy as it affects the workforce, families and children in this context. As a feminist she is committed to developing and applying critical feminist theorisations to her work.

Rod Parker-Rees was a nursery and reception class teacher but is now Associate Professor in Early Childhood Studies at Plymouth University, UK. He has particular interests in early communication and social interactions, playfulness, informal learning and the history of childhood. He has co-edited several key texts and he has edited *Meeting the Child in Steiner Kindergartens*. He is an editor of *Early Years: An International Research Journal*.

Dr Jane Payler is a Senior Lecturer in Early Years Education at the University of Winchester, and Chair of TACTYC. Jane has taught, examined, researched, published and practised in early years education and care for more than 20 years. Prior to that, she worked in the NHS as a Health Education Officer. Her publications and research include inter-professional practice, professional development, and young children's learning experiences.

Dr Sally Peters is an Associate Professor at the University of Waikato, Hamilton, New Zealand, and an Associate Director of the Faculty of Education's Early Years Research Centre. Her main research interests involve several main threads, including educational and other transitions, working theories and key competencies. Sally has been involved in a range of research projects, all of which involved working collaboratively with teachers.

Linda Pound is an early years consultant, trainer and writer who has been head of an inner-city nursery school, an LA inspector and a university lecturer. Linda writes extensively for a range of audiences on a range of topics related to early childhood care and education.

Dr Kathy Ring has extensive experience in the field of early years education. She now combines her part-time role as a Senior Lecturer at York St John University with independent consultancy. Kathy has written extensively about young children's use of drawing as a tool for thinking and learning, and continues to research and write about this area.

Dr Sue Rogers is Professor of Early Years Education at the Institute of Education, London. Her research interests include play, curriculum and pedagogy in early childhood, young children's perspectives and child–adult interaction. She has published widely in the field of early childhood education, including *Rethinking Play and Pedagogy: Concepts, Contexts and Cultures* (2010, Routledge) and *The Role of the Adult in Early Years Settings* (2012, Open University Press, with Janet Rose).

Dr Helen Tovey is a Principal Lecturer in Early Childhood Studies in the School of Education at the University of Roehampton. Previously head of Somerset Nursery School, Wandsworth, Helen is recognised nationally as an authority on the development of outdoor environments, publishing widely in this area, including *Playing Outdoors, Spaces and Places, Risk and Challenge* (2007, OUP) and *Bringing the Froebel Approach to your Early Years Practice* (2012, Routledge).

Lynne Truelove is a Senior Lecturer in Early Years at Sheffield Hallam University, where she teaches on the Early Years Foundation Degree and Early Years Teacher Status (EYTS) courses. She worked extensively with nursery children before working with adults as a local authority quality assurance assessor. Lynne is currently studying for a doctorate and is researching the impact of the early years assessment process on trainees, mentors and assessors.

Dr David Whitebread is a Senior Lecturer at the University of Cambridge. He is a developmental psychologist and early years education specialist. He is currently directing research projects investigating the role of play in children's development of meta-cognition and self-regulation, and their impact upon learning. His publications include *Teaching and Learning in the Early Years*, 3rd edn (2008, RoutledgeFalmer) and *Developmental Psychology and Early Childhood Education* (2012, Sage).

Dr Elizabeth Wood is Professor of Education at the University of Sheffield and Director of Research in the School of Education. Her research interests include play in early childhood and across the lifespan, specifically children's agency in their play activities, their cultural repertoires, and how they blend traditional and digital forms of play. She is currently leading an AHRC-funded network and has also carried out research on teachers' professional knowledge and practice.

Maulfry Worthington is currently writing up her doctoral research (VU University, Amsterdam) into the genesis of children's mathematical graphics in three- to four-year-old children's spontaneous pretend play. She has conducted extensive research (individually and jointly with Elizabeth Carruthers) and published widely, including *Children's Mathematics: Making Marks, Making Meaning* (Sage, 2006). Maulfry co-founded the international Children's Mathematics Network: www.childrens-mathematics.net.

Dr Nicola Yelland is Professor and Director of Research in the College of Education at Victoria University, Melbourne, Australia. Her teaching and research is related to the use of ICT in school and community contexts. Her multidisciplinary research focus has enabled her to work with early childhood teachers to enhance the ways in which ICT can be incorporated into learning contexts. She has published widely in the area.

Preface

ELIZABETH WOOD

Over a period of 25 years the four editions of *The Excellence of Play* have paralleled three areas of development in play scholarship. First, play has become embedded in curriculum policies for early childhood education in many nations, across the global north and south. This has drawn attention to the educational benefits of play, specifically to learning, pedagogy, curriculum and assessment practices, and the different ways and contexts in which play is used to transmit valued cultural knowledge. Second, new ways of theorising play have contested some of the established psychological truths and certainties that dominated play scholarship through the nineteenth and twentieth centuries. Challenging insights from feminist, critical, queer, post-structural and post-modern theories continue to provoke much debate, and have foregrounded issues of agency, power, free versus structured play, and the ways in which children construct knowledge that is valued within the context of play. Third, new methodologies and research approaches, including digital modes of data collection and analysis, have continued the tradition of close observation of children at play as a means of understanding their voices, meanings, intentions, patterns of activity and play themes, and the variations among players. Children's participation in research, and as researchers, is fundamental to adults co-constructing these insights and to respecting children as experts in their own lives.

These three areas of development are woven through each of the five sections, showing development over time, and the continued fascination that play holds as a field of scholarship in its own right. The contributors bring their own interests and insights, revealing that play is the ultimate mash-up in terms of the diverse influences that children bring to their play, and the complex demands it makes of them and of us as researchers. Though it appears to be chaotic, unpredictable and transient, play contains complex themes and narratives that develop over time, as children engage with monsters and sharks, witches and wizards, superheroes and villains, celebrities and popular culture. Underlying those themes we can also discern children's deep engagement with existential issues of life and death, of ethics and identities, and of multiple possibilities for being/becoming.

These are some of the fundamentals of play that readers will engage with throughout this book. In the opening chapter, Anning lays the historical groundwork for understanding the tensions that have beset play, including its tenuous place in the curriculum, and the dilemmas practitioners face in reconciling the conflicting imperatives of getting children 'ready for school' and 'learning through play'. The issues of transition and readiness are explored in more detail by Fabian and Dunlop in Chapter 15, and Peters in Chapter 24, foregrounding cultural variations in home and school practices. Moyles addresses the problems of definition, and the different attributes that make play a unique process in children's learning and development. These attributes are explored in the second section, 'Play is learning'. O'Donovan and Melnyczuk discuss emerging links between current research in brain development and approaches to play. Cognitive neuroscience is a relative theoretical newcomer to the field of play, but similar principles are being advocated here – namely the importance of sensory experiences, and meaningful interactions between children and adults. Barr and Truelove examine play and learning from different cultural perspectives, and invite us to reflect on key challenges and opportunities for developing respectful, inclusive provision. An understanding of play and diversity continues to be a missing dimension in policy narratives, particularly family beliefs and practices, and different cultural repertoires for play. Drawing on feminist theories, Osgood expands this principle by exploring the various ways and means by which children negotiate, resist, celebrate, indulge and transgress gendered ways of being/becoming through their play in early childhood contexts. Here we have some interesting tensions between claims about the universal nature and benefits of play, and the variations that are evident in play as dimensions of diversity intersect to create spaces in which children's agency is highlighted. As my own research has shown, play can be a challenging space because children do not always 'play nicely' as they engage with issues of status, power and identities, contest adults' rules in creative ways, and create their own ways of getting under the radar of the adult gaze (Wood, 2013a).

A long-standing empirical challenge for play research has been to establish causal links between play and the specific areas of learning to which it contributes. But because play is so eclectic, these causal links have been elusive, and there has been a tendency to separate areas of learning and development in the attempt both to prove the value of play and justify its place in curriculum frameworks. But this atomisation and fragmentation of play has been problematic in that children experience their material, social and relational worlds in complex and dynamic ways. In the second section, the focus on play and learning brings together a range of theoretical perspectives to explore the unity between the affective, physical, cognitive and social/relational aspects of learning. Drawing on naturalistic observation methods, Elfer argues that babies' play is the external expression of internal experience, of thinking *and* emotion. Parker-Rees proposes two alternative ways of understanding play and learning as 'hunting for knowledge' and a 'gathering of awareness', including ways of getting to know people, social customs and cultural values. Whitebread, Jameson and Basilio build on a substantial body of research that demonstrates the ways in which play impacts upon self-regulation, metacognitive and representational processes. They propose that its effects emerge most clearly in tasks and aspects of development that involve problem solving and creativity. Broadhead and Chesworth focus on the complex dynamics of *friendship-in-development* and *friendship-in-action* in the context of children's cooperative play. Intellectual and emotional unity are evident as children co-create their identities, and bring thematic and culturally based interests to their play. The principle of children as agents in their learning and development is extended in Murray's chapter, which focuses on a different methodological position for involving children as researchers, not just as participants. This becomes a more ethical proposition when adults seek to recognise the sophisticated ways in which children naturally behave as researchers to construct knowledge through their play.

The relationships between play, pedagogy and curriculum remain contested spaces within and beyond the UK (Wood, 2013b). The research reported in these chapters provokes critical engagement with the ways in which play has been captured in policy frameworks as a means of identifying curriculum goals or learning outcomes that are the valued 'products' of early childhood education. Indeed, the taming of play is aligned with the taming of children and of practitioners as their practices must align with these goals and outcomes (Wood, 2014). In contrast, the more complex characteristics of play require deep and ethical engagement with children as knowledge makers and users, in order to understand their co-created play repertoires.

The theme of Part 3, 'Playful pedagogies', foregrounds some of the tensions and debates identified in the previous sections. The topic of adults' roles in children's play remains contentious, notably because of professional uncertainty about the style and purposes of adult involvement. Howard and King argue for re-establishing teachers as play professionals, drawing on substantial research to underpin practition- ers' confidence in facilitating a range of play practices. Similarly, Goouch supports the fundamental principle that adults can be most useful to children's learning and development if they serve the immediate intentions of children who are playing, rather than depending upon predetermined adult agendas. However, as Rogers and Brown argue, practitioners continue to face competing imperatives to meet curriculum require- ments and to acknowledge children's individual and collective interests through freely chosen play. The narrow ways in which play is framed in some curricula frameworks offers few solutions to these dilemmas. In contrast, Rogers and Brown explore the ways in which an innovative approach to action research and reflective practice can address some of these challenges. The principal aim of their research is to improve outcomes for children from specific disadvantaged groups through pedagogic change focusing on interactive, reciprocal and responsive pedagogic relationships in the context of play.

Georgeson and Payler address the work/play debate through two studies that aim to understand how children use cues in interactions and in the environment to distin- guish between these different contexts. They raise questions about whether and how practitioners should make distinctions between work and play, a recurring debate that has at least three potential pitfalls. First, children often make the distinction that work is adult-led and that play is child-chosen. Second, some policy frameworks promote play that is 'planned and purposeful', with the implicit message that adults' plans and purposes are privileged as the means for achieving curriculum goals (Wood, 2014). Third, play is sometimes disguised as work, with similar intentions.

The issue of play and transitions also remains contentious, and, as Fabian and Dunlop argue, a personalised approach requires an understanding of learning through play, and of children's family and community contexts. Pedagogic progression is narrowly conceptualised as the transition from play to formal adult-led activities, in spite of the research reported in this book and elsewhere that play increases in complexity and challenge. Furthermore, children often display similar dispositions in work and play – engagement, interest, attention, motivation, persistence, creating and solving problems, and self-regulation. So the potential for integrated pedagogical approaches remains an area for continued exploration beyond the preschool phase. Themes of professional knowledge, empowerment, personalisation and agency recur in this section, with the implication that early childhood practitioners must take responsibility for solving the problems that are created (intentionally or otherwise) by national policy frameworks.

In the fourth section, 'Playful curricula', the contributors articulate what professional agency looks like as practitioners develop their practice in ways that are multimodal, interactive, reciprocal and responsive. Ring argues that the availability of intelligent materials – materials that have transformational properties – enables children to gain the expertise needed to become fluent and flexible thinkers. For Pound, music is a multimodal form of expression that promotes playfulness and joyful learning. Tovey argues eloquently for outdoor play, addressing concerns about risk, hazard and safety, and highlighting the multiple benefits of enabling children to explore, act on and transform aspects of the natural environment. Yelland also takes us into the controversial territory of digital play. It is somewhat ironic that these two areas – outdoor and digital play – attract diametrically opposed arguments; the first because outdoor play poses too may hazards for children's health and safety, and the second because sedentary play is the cause of childhood obesity and a fear of nature. Like Tovey, Yelland provides research-informed arguments for new technologies as a means of promoting children's engagement with ideas and concepts that enable them to make meaning and to communicate their understandings. Children are not rejecting the physical in favour of the digital, but are blending traditional and new forms of play in multimodal ways, with new possibilities for learning and development.

In the following two chapters, Worthington and Bradford focus, respectively, on children's emergent mathematics, and language and literacy, both using socio-cultural theories to explore the interrelationships between children's funds of knowledge and experience in home and education settings. Both chapters draw attention to ongoing debates about the ways in which children develop everyday concepts, and the extent to which these connect with school instruction, leading to scientific, or formal, concepts. We return to ongoing debates about the proactive/responsive nature of adults' involvement in play, and the extent to which they structure play to support particular ways of knowing. Kitson makes the case for adult intervention in fantasy role play, taking the Vygotskian perspective of leading children ahead of their development. This reminds us of the fundamental question of where pedagogic work should take place – within or beyond the context of children's freely chosen play activities?

In the final section, 'Play is universal', the contributors articulate diversity and plurality within the dominant narrative of play as a universal activity of childhood. Barr and Borkett focus on some of the socio-cultural theories that relate to working with children from diverse communities and discuss how the role of effective communication with parents in understanding. The work of Peters in New Zealand exemplifies the potential for play to support children's learning, but also highlights the need for teachers to understand subtleties and variations in play across transitions from home to preschool and school. In the Endpiece, Bruce brings together some of the key themes of the book, and articulates her 12 principles of play, drawing on traditional and contemporary perspectives.

Taken together, the contributors all convey their deep interest in children's play, and a concern to engage readers with different theoretical perspectives, research evidence and international policy contexts. But there is no orthodoxy here, rather an open-minded, intellectual endeavour to advance play scholarship in ways that can inform different areas of professional knowledge and practice. While rigorous research can expose some of the conflicting imperatives that practitioners face, providing solutions is more problematic, especially in the contexts of policy frameworks that often promote diminished forms of play and privilege narrow ways of understanding what 'school readiness' means for children. This is where the professional knowledge, reflection, dialogue, criticality and action research must remain integral to the professional development of the early childhood workforce.

To this end, I have proposed four key questions that can support critical engagement with conflicting imperatives, particularly ongoing uncertainties about adults' roles in play (Wood, 2014: 147), as follows.

1   What are the goals for the pedagogy?
2   What assumptions are in the mind of the practitioner (beliefs about learning, about play, about the child)?
3   What is the purpose of the play and what is the purpose of the interaction?
4   What are the assessed outcomes of the pedagogical interaction for the child, and for the practitioner?

The first two questions require some critical engagement with where pedagogic work should take place – through play, or through other means such as direct instruction, which might foreground the adults' intentions in playful ways. Question 3 is particularly important, as it requires us to think carefully about *whose* purposes should take precedence – those of the playing child/children or those of the adult? If the purpose of the interaction is to turn the play towards adults' intentions then the mood and spirit of play may be lost, and children may become less willing to involve and accept adult involvement in their freely chosen activities. The fourth question serves as a reminder that the outcomes of play may be highly significant for children but may not align easily with curriculum goals. Children play for the sake of play, to become more skilled at their play, and (hopefully) to transfer the qualities of playfulness and playful learning to other areas of their lives. The educational challenge is to harness the excellence of play, without taming or negating those very qualities that make play so life enhancing for all of us.

We know that we can neither trust nor rely on policy makers to do justice to the complexities of play, however well intentioned their pronouncements and however glossy their curriculum guidance materials. Nor should the early childhood community rely on outdated and emotive positions from which to defend play. Rather, the intellectual agenda should be to understand children as players, as playful knowledge makers and as expert narrators of their play lives.

References and further reading (in bold)

Wood, E. (2013a) Free play and free choice in early childhood education: troubling the discourse. *International Journal of Early Years Education*. Available online at: 2.9.12 DOI: 10.1080/09669760.2013.830562.

Wood, E. (2013b) Contested concepts in educational play: a comparative analysis of early childhood policy frameworks in New Zealand and England. In J. Nuttall (ed.) *Weaving* Te Whāriki: *Aotearoa New Zealand's Early Childhood Curriculum Framework in Theory and Practice*, 2nd edn. Wellington, New Zealand: NZCER Press.

Wood, E. (2014) The play-pedagogy interface in contemporary debates. In L. Brooker, S. Edwards and M. Blaise (eds) *The Sage Handbook on Play and Learning in Early Childhood Education***. London: Sage.**

PART 1
Play is fundamental

'Children must be allowed to follow their inborn drives to play and explore, so that they can grow into intellectually, socially, emotionally and physically strong and resilient adults.'

P. Gray (2014) *Free to Learn: Why unleashing the instinct to play will make our children happier, more self-reliant and better students for life.* New York: Basic Books.

1

Play and the legislated curriculum

Angela Anning

Summary

This chapter explores changes in the subject-based National Curriculum for five to seven year olds introduced in UK schools in the 1980s, and the Foundation Stage Curriculum for birth to five year olds introduced into early childhood settings in 2000. Tensions arise between beliefs of practitioners in the value of educational play, and governments' demands for 'raising standards' and achieving 'school readiness'. Three key dilemmas in interpreting theory and research that might reconcile play with legislated curricula are discussed: how children learn through play in educational settings; how play is shaped into appropriate curriculum models; and how to implement a pedagogy of play.

Introduction

Policy: the legislated curriculum

Every education system functions within a social context underpinned by a particular set of values and political imperatives. So it has been with educational reforms in the legislated curriculum for early years education in the UK.

There was no statutory curriculum for children in England until the 1988 Educational Reform Act (except for the anomaly of statutory religious education). Curriculum content was inherited from custom and practice and the values underpinning elementary schooling: to prepare a skilled workforce and law-abiding citizens. Literacy and numeracy were prioritised each morning and other subjects subsumed into 'topic work' in the afternoons. Play for 'infants' (5–7 year olds) – natural materials (sand and water), construction (block play), small figure play and role play, and 'make and do' messy areas – was around the periphery of classrooms and mainly unsupervised by teachers.

In 2000 the idea of defining a statutory curriculum for 'preschool' children (three to five year olds) was introduced to a sceptical early years workforce steeped in a play-based approach to learning.

A National Curriculum for five to eleven year olds: broad and balanced curriculum

The 1988 version of a Primary National Curriculum in England included ten foundation subjects, of which three – English, mathematics and science – were designated core subjects. Pupil progression was tracked cumulatively along detailed lists of attainment targets in each subject and assessed at the end of each Key Stage (at seven and eleven years). There were parallel initiatives with variations in content in Northern Ireland, Scotland and Wales.

The role of play within subject learning was not an issue of concern for the predominantly secondary-based designers of the National Curriculum. The ideologies underpinning the model were based on concepts of value for money in a market-led economy, raising 'standards', a return to disciplined behaviour, competence in 'traditional' school subjects and preparation of a workforce capable of underpinning economic recovery. With minor tinkering, the Programmes of Study of the National Curriculum continued to hold sway for 30 years. Some 'policy' non-statutory bolt-ons such as citizenship and personal/social/health education were shoehorned into a crowded curriculum in response to moral panics about 'bad behaviour' and 'obesity'.

The National Curriculum was designed to be broad and balanced, but teachers of five to seven year olds (Key Stage 1 – KS1) were initially resistant to a *subject-based* curriculum, despite evidence that showed their habitual way of teaching separated literacy and numeracy, music and physical education from 'the rest', and delivered the arts and humanities through topic work. KS1 teachers reluctantly abandoned their preferred cross-curricular or thematic approaches.

Learning through play remained a significant feature of their espoused theories. They brought with them to curriculum planning and delivery the history of the importance of structured learning activities from Montessori and Froebel, of exploratory and dramatic play from Steiner and Isaacs, and of healthy outdoor play from the Macmillan sisters. Translating these ideologies into practice was problematic. The play-based curriculum-in-waiting was still lurking around the edges of classrooms – sand and water trays, construction kits, wet areas for messy activities, role-play areas (usually domestic play based). But the teachers tended to focus on seated activities – mostly reading, writing and arithmetic – defined as 'work', with groups (usually by ability) of children symbolically in the centre of classrooms. Teaching assistants took responsibility for prescribed creative or craft-based tasks, or play activities based on a current topic. Children were in no doubt that, whatever Susan Isaacs' views on play being the child's work, their teachers held a different view. Children were kept 'busy' using play activities or rewarded with time to play when they had completed their 'work'. Trainee teachers on school placements found it hard to make sense of the gap between the rhetoric and reality of their teacher-mentors' talk about the centrality of play in young children's learning.

The Primary National Strategies: concern for raising standards

Despite the optimism of the educational reforms of the 1980s, there were growing concerns about improving standards in primary schools. From the late 1990s Primary

National Strategies, the Literacy and Numeracy Hours, designed to raise standards, were funded by successive Conservative and Labour governments. Conforming to the strategies squeezed the time in primary classrooms available to deliver the breadth of the National Curriculum. The Strategies included guidance on both content and prescribed ways of delivering content. So, for the first time, UK governments determined not only curriculum content but also the pedagogy of classrooms. Although the Strategies were non-statutory, schedules used by the dreaded inspectors from the Office for Standards in Education (OfSTED) looked for evidence of their implementation. OfSTED reports were accessible to parents on the internet. The added pressure of the publication at school level of results for seven year olds in Standard Assessment Tasks (SATs) in language and mathematics (tests in science were soon dropped), left teachers of young children in England in no doubt that what mattered was that their pupils progressed in the basics of reading, writing and mathematics.

By the beginning of the twenty-first century, doubts had been raised about the efficacy of the National Curriculum. In primary schools the curriculum was seen to be 'overcrowded' (particularly with the 'obligatory' literacy and numeracy strategies) and fragmented (as teachers struggled to deliver the ever expanding content). Assessment was perceived to be driving timetables and shaping modes of teaching into a return to whole-class teaching at KS1 with a didactic style of pedagogy and a reduction in practical small-group activities. Learning through play was sidelined and play resources locked away in storerooms. Children's choice of play was limited to perhaps a (tongue in cheek) 'golden hour' for the whole class on a Friday afternoon, or snatched ten minutes of playing for individual children when they had finished all their work *and* been 'good'. For many KS1 children this happy convergence of criteria – finishing work and being good – to be 'allowed' to play never happened.

The statutory school starting age in the UK is the term after the child's fifth birthday. Most European countries start formal schooling at six and in other international contexts at seven. In order to fund 'nursery education' on the cheap, both Conservative and Labour governments promoted the idea of an *early start to school* being beneficial; four year olds were admitted to reception classes where parents expected that children would start 'proper school work' immediately and teachers felt pressurised to do so. Concerns grew about the appropriateness of four year olds being offered a 'too formal too soon' curriculum, a lack of outdoor space for learning, play and exercise, and a high ratio of children to adults.

Every Child Matters: catering for 'the whole child'

In the new millennium, New Labour policy changed to broadening children's learning experiences, often beyond the conventions of a school day and a prescribed curriculum, reflecting a wider government agenda for the reform of services for children. The new mantra was 'joined-up thinking' to encourage education, health, welfare and family support services to work together in multi-agency teams (Anning *et al.*, 2010). A seismic change in conceptualising children's services was under way. In 2004 The Children Act legislated for a new framework, *Every Child Matters*, for children's services, including schools, catering for children from birth to the end of secondary schooling, and taking a holistic view of children's development. Central to the principles of *Every Child Matters* were five outcomes: being healthy, staying safe, enjoying and achieving, making a positive contribution, and economic well-being. This overarching framework, and the notion of schools hosting 'extended services' as a form of social rescue, including offering before- and after-school childcare to encourage parents to work, sat uneasily with pressure on primary schools to drive up standards in 'the basics' and to deliver a demanding subject-based curriculum.

A Foundation Stage curriculum for birth to three year olds: getting ready for school

In an attempt to rationalise preschool education and childcare services, the Labour government introduced a raft of reforms in England. These included: dramatically expanding childcare; universal entitlement for all three and four year olds to part-time preschool education; a unified set of standards and inspection regime delivered by OfSTED for both childcare and education settings; an ambitious anti-poverty initiative, Sure Start, to deliver universal, integrated services to families with children under five in the most disadvantaged communities of England (Anning and Ball, 2008); and by 2008 a roll-out of 1,700 Children's Centres as the hub of services for families with young children.

The unthinkable concept of introducing a statutory curriculum for under-5s was introduced. The Foundation Stage (FS) consisted of six areas of learning: personal, social and emotional development; communication, language and literacy; mathematical development; knowledge and understanding of the world; physical development and creative development. A total of 69 Early Learning Goals were linked to a baseline assessment system on the first three areas of learning administered by reception class teachers as children entered KS1 at five years. An unwieldy *Foundation Stage Profile*, designed to record children's progression across all aspects of learning in early years settings, was introduced in 2003.

All settings (including childminders and childcare group settings – mostly privately funded), preschool playgroups (in the voluntary sector), reception classes in primary schools, Children's Centres and nursery schools (in the maintained sector) claiming to offer education to three and four year olds, and thus to qualify for government funding as providers of preschool education, had to demonstrate that they were delivering the FS curriculum. For a childcare workforce used to an unstructured play-based curriculum as the bedrock of their daily activities this was a huge cultural shift. Concerns grew that the 'teaching and learning' of two and three year olds was poor, and in 2002 a framework to support practitioners working with children under three, *Birth to Three Matters*, was published. The framework was organised around the concepts of a strong child, a skilful communicator, a competent learner and a healthy child.

As the distinction between preschool education and childcare became increasingly blurred, the two frameworks and the national standards for daycare and childminding for under-eights were combined into a Statutory Framework for the Early Years Foundation Stage in 2007, with reduced assessment requirements. There was a clear statement about the value of play: 'Play underpins the delivery of all the EYFS . . . Play underpins all development and learning for young children' (paras 1.16 and 1.17).

One of the last flagship anti-poverty initiatives of the Labour government was a scheme to offer free nursery places to 'vulnerable' two year olds living in socio-economic disadvantage. Early evaluations reported that provision for the two year olds was patchy, with low levels of staff qualifications and poor-quality provision in many of the settings.

The Coalition government policy: tightening the grip on 'standards'

The Coalition government was elected in 2010. It operated in a climate of economic austerity. Sometimes it was difficult to disentangle ideological from economic imperatives in policies. Public services were ravaged by funding cuts while being subjected to a raft of performance-related measures to demonstrate value for money. Universal services delivered by Children's Centres were decimated and surviving centres charged with focusing on improving health, well-being, educational and return-to-work outcomes for the most vulnerable/at-risk families.

At the same time, the Coalition sought to decentralise and deregulate services. Schools could opt out of local authority control to be Free Schools or Academies. Head teachers were given more autonomy and allegedly reduced bureaucracy.

In September 2014 a new National Curriculum was introduced with a strong emphasis on traditional subject-based learning (ironically statutory only for the remaining 'state' schools under local authority control in England). The curriculum was championed by an idiosyncratic Education Secretary, Michael Gove, who derided 'play-based learning, project work and an anti-knowledge ideology'. 'Subject' knowledge was defined in daunting detail; for example, in English the itemising of synthetic phonics knowledge as the foundation for the teaching of reading and set lists of spelling for each year group.

A revised Foundation Stage curriculum for birth to five year olds introduced in 2012 specified three prime (Communication and Language; Physical Development; Personal, Social and Emotional Development) and four specific (Literacy; Mathematics; Understanding of the World; Expressive Arts and Design) areas of learning (DfE, 2012). By now there were wider variations in the Foundation Stage curricula between England and the other countries of the UK, with Wales giving the greatest emphasis on play for its Foundation Phase for three to sevens.

A highly prescriptive Early Years Outcomes document (http://www.gov.uk/government/publications/early-years-outcomes) was not well received by practitioners in England; instead they continued to use sections of *Development Matters* material produced by Early Education (http://www.early-education.org.uk, accessed 1 March 2014). Between 24 and 36 months children are assessed as meeting, exceeding or emerging in relation to 17 Early Learning Goals. In parallel, health visitors assess all two year olds in the Healthy Child Programme review. Local authorities return the data to the government. School and early years settings are monitored for how much 'value' they add to these baseline scores. At the time of writing it is not clear how these policy changes will impact on the role of play in early childhood settings, but a fair prediction would be that opportunities for play will be further marginalised.

Meanwhile there are societal anxieties beyond educational settings about the well-being of our children. Time and space for children to play unsupervised outside the home has drastically reduced. As parents become increasingly anxious about the safety of their children and more risk averse, children are over-regulated into 'safe' hobbies where adults dictate the activities – sports clubs, art and theatre groups, learning zones in museums. Now that half of our children live in cities there are concerns about their separation from the natural world. There are questions about the impact of hours of screen-based games play on young children and of their lack of physical exercise.

Play, curriculum and pedagogy in early childhood education

I have reviewed the role of play in recent policies governing the legislated curricula for birth to seven year olds in the UK. I have referred frequently to the tensions felt by practitioners responsible for delivering curricula between their espoused theories about the centrality of play to young children's learning and their theories in action. There is deep confusion about how to conform to government policies *and* implement learning through play. How can we help practitioners find a way through this minefield?

Learning through play

The first source of confusion is that research into how children learn through play rarely connects with research into how children learn in educational settings.

Our understanding of how children learn has been transformed in the last decade. Yet we still have little empirical research on the efficacy of play-based learning in educational contexts. Consequently early years professionals are accused of arguing based on ideologies rather than evidence for the value of learning through play.

Early years educators argue the case for educating 'the whole child' and for the importance of recognising links between the emotions, the intellect and the body in learning. There *is* evidence to substantiate their beliefs. Recent research into brain development and functions has alerted us to what many early years educators know instinctively: the importance of the biological basis of learning processes (Gopnik, Melzoff and Kuhl, 1999).

The biological basis for learning

We know that information comes to the brain via the five senses: sight, hearing, touch, smell and taste. Information is taken on board visually, auditorily or kinaesthetically (i.e. physically experienced or related to feelings). For young children, sensory experiences are strong and powerful. You have only to observe an 18 month old's raw responses to unfamiliar tastes and noises to have this confirmed. There is a processing system to prevent information overload, a sort of switchboard system, within the brain. Information that invokes an emotional response, or with content relating to self-preservation, ranks high in the editing process for selective attention.

All information is processed through the left or right hemispheres of the brain. Both are capable of similar functions but they have particular propensities. The left brain emphasises language, logic, mathematical formulae, linearity and sequencing: in general, analytical aspects of thinking. The right hemisphere emphasises forms and patterns, spatial manipulation, images, things of the imagination, rhythm and musical appreciation. The right hemisphere appears to have the capacity to process faster more holistic aspects of thinking and learning. When the right side of the brain is processing data, it triggers pleasurable responses and chemicals are released that give the learner a sense of heightened awareness and well-being. This positive feedback encourages the learner to repeat the action and is a *strong motivation to want to learn*.

Research by neuroscientists and psychologists helps us to understand what we instinctively know about the power of self-initiated play as a vehicle for young children's learning. In a 'flow' state, absorbed by an activity they have chosen, children persevere on difficult tasks and set themselves challenges. These insights have not legitimated proper attention being paid to resourcing and supporting such play-based activities in *educational settings*. This is partly because 'flow' state play bouts are fast moving and fluid, and their outcomes are hard to predict and measure. We do not have the protocols to measure such learning, whereas in adult-structured play episodes based on curriculum content we can observe and tick off outcomes more easily.

The socio-cultural context of learning

We now acknowledge that context and societal expectations have a profound impact on how people behave. Learning behaviours are socially mediated by families, communities and cultural mores. This paradigm shift is called socio-cultural research and scholarship (Anning *et al.*, 2009). If we view play through a socio-cultural lens, we have to acknowledge that the formal contexts of many early childhood settings, where priorities are determined by target setting and individual progression through a prescribed curriculum, cannot be conducive to collaborative or individual's 'flow state' play.

Socio-dramatic play among groups of children in informal contexts is characterised by fluidity, spontaneity and changes in direction. Constructing narratives in the mind – storying – is a fundamental way for children to make sense of the world and is central to dramatic play (Paley, 2005). Socio-dramatic and rough-and-tumble play offer children opportunities to test out who they are and who they might become; to negotiate turn taking; to self-regulate behaviours; to feel the heady power of groups working in harmony and to reconcile differences when conflict arises; and to take risks and feel strong emotions (Broadhead and Burt, 2012). It is also crucial to the development of a 'theory of mind' – that is, the ability to infer mental states in others and ourselves. When we observe young children engrossed in this kind of play, we know that the experiences they are having are the building blocks of self-regulation and resilience in young adults (essential tools for citizenship), but such play episodes do not fit neatly with a culture of target setting, timetabling and adult control in primary schools, and increasingly in many Foundation Stage settings.

Multi-modality in learning

We are also aware now of the importance of multi-modality in children's representation, symbolic actions and meaning making in their play. Kress (1997) used detailed observations of his own children's journeys towards literacy at home to explore their use of drawing, cutting and sticking, making models and marks, gestures and play with everyday materials to make 'worlds' in which to act out complex narratives. He argued that 'children act multi-modally, both in the things they use, the objects they make, and in the engagement of their bodies; there is no separation of body and mind' (1997: 97).

Pahl (1999) extended these kinds of detailed observations and analysis of children's meaning making in the context of a nursery class. She was the kind of teacher/researcher who encouraged children to move resources and objects to different spaces and places in the nursery to support their elaborate play narratives. Many early years practitioners find such 'spontaneous' play behaviour with objects and artefacts difficult to manage. An emphasis on teaching 'subjects', metaphorically boundaried by the tradition of workshop areas and timetables for language and literacy, mathematical development and knowledge and understanding of the world, discourages this kind of fluidity of meaning making. For practitioners the results of allowing freedom for children to explore such connections over space and time can be quite literally too messy.

A play curriculum in educational contexts

The second source of confusion is how play can be shaped in educational contexts into a curriculum that accommodates both the deep learning potential of young children and the imperatives of schooling.

An important premise is that early years professionals have a grasp of models of play from which they can design curricula appropriate to their settings. One such model is Smilansky's (Smilansky and Shefatya, 1990), but there are others referenced in this book. Smilansky categorised four types of play behaviour: functional (offering opportunities to explore the environment); constructive (exploring and manipulating the material world); dramatic (at early stages exploring pretend and role play, and later involving others in socio-dramatic play); and games with rules (table-top games and physical games – both involving rules and procedures).

The challenge for practitioners is to translate conceptual models into practical activities. Early years professionals are bound by the imperatives of managing large groups of children in buildings shared with other services or classes. There have to be routines and protocols holding activities together. But taking a model such as Smilansky's, it is possible for adults to structure environments, resources and daily routines so that children have an entitlement to routine and self-regulated access to (using this model as an example) four types of play, some of which would be outdoors, for at least part of the day. It would be left to the professional judgement of practitioners to structure this entitlement. The last thing we want is a formal prescription of hourage for typologies of play! The constraints will be access, time, choice and the pragmatics of noise levels and resource management.

Access

As I have argued in the first half of this chapter, *access* to play activities for many young learners is constrained by adult rules, and the need to measure and record educational outcomes. For children the switch from a domestic culture of play, based on real-life problem solving, to the 'peculiar' school tasks of worksheets, sorting plastic shapes and playing in waist-high containers of sand and water, can be traumatic, particularly where children's cultural norms of learning may be profoundly different from 'educational' versions (Brooker, 2002). Teachers are often so socialised into perceiving these school-based activities as 'normal' that they neglect to explain to children their purposes and involve them in the reasoning behind and negotiations about what are 'fair' and 'safe' practices.

Time

The amount of time adults and children spend on activities indicates how much they value them. Currently in FS settings there is confusion about a split of children's time being spent on 'child-initiated' activities and 'adult-initiated' tasks. The *Researching Effective Pedagogy in the Early Years* (REPEY) project (Siraj-Blatchford *et al.*, 2002) argued that, in effective FS settings, adult- and child-initiated activities are split 50/50 per cent of the time. Proficient early years professionals make pragmatic judgements about a strategic mixture of 'free flow' (where children move seamlessly through spaces, including outdoors, engaged in self-chosen activities) and drawing together small groups for particular purposes for adult-directed activities. However, in many Year R classes, bored four year olds spend too much time seated at tables doing adult-directed tasks and squatting uncomfortably on carpets in front of whiteboards. Even so, Year 1 teachers grumble that Year R teachers are not 'getting them ready' for the start of formal schooling, and now even two year olds will be assessed for their potential as 'pupils'.

Choice

Children's *choice* of play activities demands equal sensitivity. It is unrealistic to argue that education contexts can offer the same freedoms to children's play choices as in home or out-of-school settings' contexts. But the shaping of children's self-initiated play into 'sanitised' versions for educational purposes is not helpful. Children's play scripts reflect their cultural and gendered preferences. Children are skilled in subverting the overt purposes of 'educational' play to their own agendas. A predominantly female workforce often comes into conflict with boys' choices of play content, but banning boys from superhero and conflict play is not helpful. It generates ill feeling between boys and authority figures right at the start of their education.

The strategy of using 'play outdoors' as a safety valve for boisterous, physical play for girls and boys is increasingly being employed, but I worry that outdoor play, overseen by teaching assistants, is in danger of becoming a 'dumping ground' for therapeutic and energetic play, when for me the outdoor spaces for learning should be integral to all subjects and areas of experience.

A pedagogy of play

A third source of confusion is that adults are unsure about their role in supporting children's play.

The holy grail of early years education is to construct 'a pedagogy of play'. The *Effective Provision of Pre-School Education* (EPPE) project, with its central notion of 'sustained shared thinking' (Siraj-Blatchford *et al.*, 2002) has made a significant contribution to the debate, but for me there are fundamental problems yet to be unpicked. The discourse about a pedagogy of play often foregrounds cognitive gains (particularly in language and mathematical development) as 'potentially instructive play', and sidelines physical, social and affective outcomes of play. Time-consuming and detailed observations of play on sticky notes are often at a superficial level, and frequently do not feed back into reflective practice or inform curriculum planning. Finally adults are flummoxed when they intervene inappropriately in children's play episodes and cause them to grind to a halt.

Wood (2010) argues that we need to differentiate between distinct but complementary pedagogic roles and know when best to deploy them. Four complementary and equally valid roles in promoting learning through play are as follows.

1   *Engaging playfully with learners:* adults adopting spontaneous playful interactions and dialogue with children in episodes such as functional play and games with rules.

2   *Modelling play and learning behaviours:* adults teaching skills such as using appropriate cutting and sticking techniques in constructing puppets and how to structure language for a puppet show.

3   *Observing and reflecting on play:* adults tuning in to evidence of deep and meaningful learning evidenced in children's self-initiated and socio-dramatic play as the basis for reflection and planning.

4   *Becoming a play partner:* adults negotiating entry into play episodes with individual or groups of children.

Conclusion

Early years professionals in England have fought long and hard to try to hold on to cherished beliefs about the importance of play in children's learning. Many four year olds in Year R and five year olds at the start of KS1 have fewer and fewer opportunities for self-initiated and sustained play; two to four year olds in a range of early years settings are now subject to a formal curriculum. This is likely to result in more adult-structured, goal-orientated activities, particularly in phonics, writing and mathematics. We need well-trained early years professionals to demonstrate high-quality learning through play and be advocates to policy makers and parents for informed and evidence-based arguments for its value. We need them to argue with clarity about how children learn through play, how educational and childcare settings support such learning and how adults intervene appropriately in promoting learning through play as all the chapters in this book promote and demonstrate.

Questions to promote reflection

1   What were the processes by which different versions of National and Foundation Stage Curricula were introduced into early years settings in England?

2   How did these shifting government initiatives impact on your setting or classroom?

3   How might new research into how young children learn influence the way you argue for the importance of learning through play in your setting?

4   What might a robust pedagogy of play in early childhood education look like?

References and further reading (in bold)

Anning, A. and Ball, M. (2008) *Improving Services for Young Children: From Sure Start to Children's Centres.* London: Sage.

Anning, A., Cottrell, D.J., Frost, N., Green, J. and Robinson, M. (2010) *Developing Multi-professional Teamwork for Integrated Children's Services*, 2nd edn. Maidenhead: Open University Press.

Anning, A., Cullen, J. and Fleer, M. (2009) *Early Childhood Education: Society and Culture*, 2nd edn. London: Sage Publications.

Broadhead, P. and Burt, A. (2012) *Understanding Young Children's Learning through Play.* Abingdon: Routledge.

Brooker, L. (2002) *Young Children Learning Cultures.* Buckingham: Open University Press.

Department for Education (DfE) (2012) Available online at: https://www.education.gov.uk/publications/standard/AllPublications/Page1/DfE-00023-2012 (accessed 12 March 2014).

Gopnik, A., Melzoff, A. and Kuhl, P. (1999) *How Babies Think: The Science of Childhood.* London: Weidenfeld and Nicolson.

Kress, G. (1997) *Before Writing: Rethinking the Paths to Literacy.* London: Routledge.

Pahl, K. (1999) *Transformations: Meaning Making in Nursery Education.* Stoke-on-Trent: Trentham Books.

Paley, V.S. (2005) *A Child's Work: The Importance of Fantasy Play.* Chicago: Chicago University Press.

Siraj-Blatchford, I., Sylva, K., Muttock, S., Gilden, R. and Bell, D. (2002) *Researching Effective Pedagogy in the Early Years*, Research Report 365. London: HMSO.

Smilansky, S. and Shefatya, L. (1990) *Facilitating Play.* Silver Spring, MD: Psychological and Educational Publications.

Wood, E. (2010) Developing integrated pedagogical approaches to play and learning. In P. Broadhead, J. Howard and E. Wood (eds) *Play and Learning in the Early Years: From Research to Practice.* London: Sage Publications.

2
Starting with play: taking play seriously
Janet Moyles

Summary

While the majority of policy makers involved in early childhood education and care still seem to underestimate play, this chapter will argue that play is a fundamental, innate characteristic of childhood. Play's excellence lies in its capacity to motivate children and engender positive, long-lasting learning dispositions. Play has been observed in almost every culture in the world and it has influenced learning over centuries.

This chapter will discuss the challenges of defining play and the many different attributes of play that make it a unique process in children's learning and development. It will offer a broad background to play and learning theories, and the links with practice and practitioner reflection.

Introduction

The challenges facing practitioners in resolving dilemmas between policy and play practices (Chapter 1) are both very real and very frustrating, as the comments below show.

> There is a continual dilemma between practitioners' wish to support more play-focused learning and the downward pressures from school leadership and targets. Many young children still experience a very adult-directed environment and there is a lack of pedagogical knowledge of child development and play in some early years teachers in schools.
>
> (LEA advisor)

> Reception classes have moved on from opportunities to socialise, learn playfully and engage in new experiences to a preparation for compulsory education . . . an extension of formal schooling . . . I have a very able five year old . . . but have noticed that since entering reception he is overly competitive, easily upset, loses confidence very quickly when he doesn't understand something instantly and requires immediate gratification.
>
> (Parent)

> There is still a lack of understanding and knowledge of how children learn and play . . . Reception classes tend to be too formal for the needs and abilities of young children . . . many boys start the system as failures.
>
> (Nursery nurse)

> I feel strongly that within reception classes children are being short-changed and that a lack of understanding by teachers and OfSTED of play-based approaches is primarily the cause of this.
>
> (Reception class teacher)

It's infuriating to me that, a quarter of a century on from the publication of *Just Playing?* (Moyles, 1989) and more than 20 years since the first edition of *The Excellence of Play*, we should still be questioning the value of play in children's learning and development, especially since so much has been researched and written about the nature and value of play in the education and holistic development of young children in the intervening years. Some might say that it's a good thing we're still exploring how children learn and the best ways to support that learning, but it seems to me that continually having to challenge 'the system' and fight for play when the fight should have already been won, takes energy that would best be expended on developing more effective and playful pedagogies. One has only to think of the pedagogical qualities valued in, for example, the Reggio Emilia and Te Whāriki approaches to realise the full potential of play-based, child-initiated early childhood curricula.

Yet society, through government, seems to believe that children can learn only when they are formally taught and the earlier that occurs the better, whereas there is much evidence to the contrary. A simple way to counteract this is to stop and ask ourselves, is what I know now and understand only what I was directly taught? As Gray (2014) points out, most of the knowledge and understanding we use in our everyday lives was decidedly *not* that which we were formally taught.

Politicians, parents and practitioners alike must remember that children have the *right* to play, enshrined in international law, irrespective of their individual or special needs, disability, language, culture, background, gender or behaviour:

> Research evidence highlights that playing is . . . central to children's spontaneous drive for development, and that it performs a significant role in the development of the brain, particularly in the early years.
>
> (UNCRC, 2013: para. 9F)

With fewer occasions for play outside early education, it is even more important that children today have opportunities for quality play within their early education environments. For each child to be able to play in their own way, their individual needs and dispositions have to be taken into account. Treating children equally does not mean treating them all the same. The rich cultural heritages that children bring with them often become manifest in their play, and are part of understanding and catering for the 'unique child'. One wonders how this unique child can be 'falling behind' at age four!

Children in the UK start formal schooling at a younger age than almost any others around the world, yet seem to have increasingly fewer and fewer opportunities to play, as the respondents above rue. The Early Years Foundation Stage (EYFS) (DfES, 2013) has scant mention of play in its 29-page document. We seem hell-bent on preventing children from engaging in play experiences despite the fact that we know play is an integral and essential part of a healthy childhood (and adulthood). According to Gray (2014: 12), the dramatic decline in opportunities for children to play 'has been accompanied by an equally dramatic increase in childhood mental disorders' and we are aware, too, of the ever increasing problem with childhood obesity. The difficulty appears to lie with acknowledging that issues such as 'school readiness' and 'assessment' have very formal connotations for those with little knowledge of children's mental and physical early development, remembering as they frequently do only those experiences from their own later childhoods – 'Doing tests never did me any harm' – so it must be fine to assess very young children, even two year olds. This attitude underestimates the pressure that such tests place not only on such young children, however kindly conducted, but on practitioners and parents who rightly aspire to the best for their children. As Katz remarks, in referring to what she calls the 'push down' phenomenon, 'this concept seems to result in doing earlier and earlier to young children what probably should not be done to them later either!' (2014: 216). Assessing children through observation of their play experiences is a far more reliable and valid way of understanding their individual strengths and needs, albeit a very skilled and analytic process.

Some of the challenges of play arise from the fact that 'teaching' is perceived by most parents, policy makers and practitioners to be a formal activity – and has been for well over a century. We need now to think of pedagogy – and playful pedagogy at that (Moyles, 2010) – rather than just 'teaching', and embrace a diverse range of deeper learning and teaching practices if we are to serve twenty-first century children and support them into a confident and competent adulthood. These involve practitioners letting go of sometimes long-established values in relation to schooling and recognising what it is that children achieve in deep, meaningful play. Let's face it, education and learning start long before children enter 'schooling': these earlier life and learning experiences are brought into settings and should be the firm basis for curriculum and pedagogy.

In this chapter, I shall first approach the vexing issue of defining play before turning respectively to play as a learning process and playful, reflective pedagogies.

Determining what is play: catching bubbles

Grappling with the concept of play can be analogous to trying to seize bubbles, for every time there appears to be something to hold on to, its ephemeral nature disallows it being grasped. Activities can look like play without actually being play – for example, children may be 'playing' with letters to make up words but if this is a teacher-driven activity, it may be playful teaching but it may not be play in the eyes of the child.

But do we need a definition in order to be able to value play? Surely simply observing what children experience in play ought to be sufficient in itself to convince intelligent adults that it is eminently worthwhile? The nearest we perhaps get to determining what is play is to say:

> In play, everything is possible with reality often disregarded and imagination and free-flow thinking taking precedence. Play is a highly creative process, using

body and mind; it is flexible and often free from externally imposed goals . . . It has positive, often pleasurable, effects on the players and frequently involves deep commitment and deep level learning. Play develops and changes over time . . . from basic repetitive and pleasurable actions and vocalisations to highly intellectual and collaborative processes. Above all play offers children freedom, choice and control over some aspects of their lives, experiences they are rarely afforded in an inevitably adult-led world. Play is a context in which children's voices can be clearly heard.

(Moyles, 2013: 2)

and we could add, heeded, if we're prepared as practitioners to listen!

Play is nature's way of enabling the development of a range of concepts, skills, dispositions, knowledge of the world and other people, their own capabilities and values that it would be difficult for children to acquire in any other way because of their lack of life experiences. At age five, children have lived only 60 months (just 1,825 days) in the world. We need to remember this, and just how many different experiences children need to extend and enhance their cognitive functioning – a narrow diet of synthetic phonics or number crunching, for example, is a limited and limiting experience, and also has little meaning to most young children.

Yet, in many ways, play can represent a seemingly long route to learning – for example, a child kicking a ball up against a wall over and over again, or a baby throwing a spoon on the floor repeatedly. This may seem like a waste of time to those observing, but isn't it true that nature does not tolerate waste? Play must have been 'invented' by nature for some good purpose: as an aid to effective, pleasurable, joyful, intense learning. We can all learn in different ways but, if you're like me, being told something involves only a fraction of my learning: doing things for myself and finding out – as children do in their play – is a far superior way to learn, especially when experiences are new.

It is obvious when one observes children engaged in self-initiated play that they are learning from the experience, even if it can't be quantified (Smith, 2005). Play is an observable behaviour but it is also a process: being playful is a worthwhile disposition because it means that we (adults as well) can take risks and make mistakes in a safe, meaningful environment. The process of play equates well with learning processes in so far as it can act as a powerful scaffold for children's learning, enabling metacognition (learning about how to understand one's own learning and play). It allows children to cope with not knowing something long enough in order to know – they can rehearse, practise, revise, replay and re-learn: play is a non-threatening way to cope with new learning and still retain one's self-esteem and self-image (Moyles, 2005). Have you ever stopped to think why children are so much more adept at technology than adults? Because they are prepared to play with it over and over again and learn without fear of failure! The development in children of such positive dispositions to learning will serve them well into adult life where things are unlikely to always go smoothly and without challenges! Positive dispositions regulate how we play and learn, and should not be underestimated: 'Most problems in life cannot be solved with formulae and memorised answers . . . learnt in school. They require judgement, wisdom and creative ability that come from life experiences . . . embedded in play' (Gray, 2014).

Play and work

Let's get rid of another myth: play takes just as much effort as 'work' – often more. It's about perspective and the deeply embedded puritanical feeling that one can enjoy play but not work. It's known that many adults play at their work and, indeed, where work is playful, greater job satisfaction is reported. We all need to think which aspects of our work we enjoy: is it those that actually seem rather more playful?

Although it may not always feel like it, playfulness resides in us all, even if it's hard to surface at times. We know that adults play, and need to play, in similar ways to children. On the whole, however, we do it more covertly, lest we be thought of as 'childish'. But when presented with new equipment or ideas, the main way we learn about the new phenomenon and whether we can cope is to play. The more we can accept this basic principle, the more likely we are to value and accommodate children's play. As Elkind asserts, 'Play is not a luxury but rather a crucial dynamic of healthy physical, intellectual and social-emotional development at all ages' (2008: 4).

Play behaviours, types and patterns

The unique behaviours outlined previously make play both a process and a product and, according to Isenberg and Quisenberry (n.d.), 'these features make play both a process and a product. As a *process*, play facilitates individual understanding of skills, concepts, and dispositions; as a *product*, play provides the vehicle for children to demonstrate their understanding of skills, concepts, and dispositions.' There are also strong play links with positive emotions, such as curiosity, which generally improve motivation and facilitate learning; negative emotions (anxiety, panic, stress, for example) generally detract from motivation (Santrock, 2003).

Others prefer 'definitions' based on functional types of play such as those outlined by many play theorists and researchers, including those elsewhere in this book. These types include: physical, language, exploratory, constructive, fantasy and social play: one can easily recognise the overlaps here as well as the tremendous potential learning in play experiences.

One observed episode of role play in the home area of a reception classroom (no need for a cameo, as readers will all have seen this type of play) showed children doing the following (examples in brackets):

- making choices (choosing equipment and who to play with)
- generating decisions (deciding on who should play which role)
- negotiating (ensuring that everyone was happy with the assigned role)
- pursuing their own interests (each child showed specific interests in different elements of the role play)
- using their own ideas and imaginations (several children contributed individual ideas, which were adopted by the group)
- showing independence in thought and action (sticking by decisions and persuading others into that frame of mind)

- exhibiting intrinsic motivation and persistence (persisting in the play for over an hour and pursuing a specific storyline)
- being physically and intellectually active in a sustained way (children did not stop thinking about the situation and moving themselves and props as relevant)
- operating from a basis of what makes sense to them (children used many experiences from home and previous role play to support their story)
- being confident and prepared for challenges (children were able to argue their viewpoint with others involved in the play)
- experimenting, exploring and investigating ideas and objects (what could be used for bathing the baby)
- setting their own goals and targets (deciding when they would go shopping and what they would buy for dinner)
- operating in an open frame of mind in which everything is possible, and engaged in 'what if' situations (speculating on whether there might be a ghost in the house – it was near to Halloween)
- learning new behaviours, and practising and consolidating established ones (counting out the knives, forks, spoons, plates and dishes, and offering a running commentary on what they were doing)
- acquiring new skills and interests (developing the theme of the play over several days)
- using skills and knowledge already acquired for different purposes (fetching a book and reading it to the baby, comparing sizes of clothes for 'baby')
- showing themselves, in an age-appropriate way, to be socially adroit and linguistically competent (continually narrating what they were doing together and to practitioners)
- using a range of social and interpersonal skills (sharing, cooperating and turn taking)
- performing in a literate and numerate way (several examples above!)
- functioning symbolically (making one thing represent another), and
- 'working' hard at something they are developing themselves!

Practitioners could use this list to generate information about the value of play activities in their own settings as there is more than enough evidence of children exhibiting the kinds of powerful expressions of understanding, skills and dispositions to learning. For a majority of academics, writers and practitioners working within early years contexts there is no 'proof' of play's excellence greater than their own ongoing observations and analysis of children's play. We all know in our hearts and minds that, for all of us, especially young children, 'Learning should be self-directed and joyful' (Gray, 2013: 26); achieving such ideals is more difficult, but through play and playful pedagogies is certainly possible.

Play as a learning process: prove it!

While the links between play, development and learning have yet to be unconditionally established, those who have researched play have overwhelmingly found the benefits of play. Whether it's children's self-regulation and executive functioning, the promotion of language development and comprehension, literacy or creativity and problem solving, the growing evidence is strong (Golinkoff *et al.*, 2013).

Brain studies research (see Chapter 3) is extremely complex, but it is not difficult to establish at a simple level that the human mind is a pattern collector: young children are natural seekers of pattern and meaning. Play fosters personal meaning: when children perceive experiences as personally relevant, their neural connections proliferate, and knowledge, skills and understanding become part of long-term memory. Meaningless concepts (e.g. isolated facts) are irrelevant and are not transferred to long-term memory. Brain research also demonstrates that play is a scaffold for development, a vehicle for increasing neural structures and a means by which all children practise skills they will need later (Christie, 2001). Findings from neuroscience indicate the flexibility of mind promoted by play, including the ability to use creative, adaptable thinking (Shonkoff and Phillips, 2000). Recent research also provides evidence that learning is something that happens through the connections made within the brain as a result of external stimuli received through the senses (see, for example, Jong *et al.*, 2009).

This neuroscientific knowledge facilitates thinking about how we unpick the early relationships between play and learning, especially through thought, problem solving and creativity. It also leads to questions about children's perceptions of formal learning contexts and how children begin to make sense of the sometimes meaningless activities presented to them.

It is clear that there is a vast difference for children between 'performance' and 'internalisation' of learning; by the former, I mean being able to 'jump through hoops' (tasks set, such as being able to recognise the sounds of letters or manipulate abstract numbers), and by 'internalisation', the ability of children to take their learning on board and make it their own. The latter requires significant understanding on the part of children, which can be gained only by first-hand, playful and meaningful experiences. The complexity of children's pretend play, for example, and the connections with early literacy, mathematical thinking and problem solving are evidenced in research (see, for example, Chapters 20 and 21). Roskos and Christie (2000) also give evidence that children's engagement in pretend play significantly and positively correlates with competencies such as text comprehension and metalinguistic awareness, and with an understanding of the purposes of reading and writing. As Howard (2009) suggests, 'Children respond positively and quickly when adults convey an acceptance of play. For example, it is known that children for whom play is a regular and fulfilling occurrence in the classroom complete teacher-directed tasks more quickly' (Howard, 2009: 156).

Each unique young child learns and develops differently, as Siegler (2005) suggests: 'Perhaps the most consistent phenomenon that has emerged in contemporary studies of children's learning is the great variability that exists within the thinking of each individual' (p.772). These differences are also related to the cultural backgrounds in which children grow and develop. All of us learn in a myriad of different ways – for example, through modelling others' behaviours and skills, observing, being physical, looking at books, talking, from the internet – and through our own efforts and creativity. In the present day, we need creative people more than ever. As Gray (2013) writes:

we don't need people to follow directions . . . (we have robots for that), or to perform routine calculations (we have computers for that), or to answer already-answered questions (we have search engines for that). But we do need people who can ask and seek answers to new questions, solve new problems and anticipate obstacles before they arrive. These all require the ability to think creatively. The creative mind is a playful mind.

When children have fun learning, they want to pursue it for its own sake. This suggests that we need to consider much more playful and creative pedagogies in the early years, if we are to support children effectively now and into adulthood.

Playful pedagogies

So, what is pedagogy? In the government-funded SPEEL project (Moyles, Adams and Musgrove, 2002) colleagues and I defined pedagogy as:

> . . . both the behaviour of teaching and being able to talk about and reflect on teaching. Pedagogy encompasses both what practitioners actually DO and THINK and the principles, theories, perceptions and challenges that inform and shape it. It connects the relatively self-contained act of teaching and being an early years educator, with personal cultural and community values . . . curriculum structures and external influences. Pedagogy in the early years operates from a shared frame of reference . . . between the practitioner, the young children and his/her family.
>
> (p. 5)

'Practice' we defined as 'all the pedagogue does within the teaching and learning context on a daily, weekly and longer term basis . . . Practice includes planning, evaluating and assessing children's play and other learning experiences both indoors and outdoors' (Moyles *et al.*, 2002: 5).

   In Stewart and Pugh (2007: 9), pedagogy is defined as 'the understanding of how children learn and develop, and the practices through which we can enhance that process. It is rooted in values and beliefs about what we want for children, and supported by knowledge, theory and experience.' The fundamental issue is how practitioners perceive themselves as 'playful' or otherwise in handling children's play experiences and in being playful pedagogues (Moyles, 2010).

   Playful pedagogies are essentially those in which the teacher or practitioner recognises different strategies for play and encourages playfulness, including interacting in playful ways with the children (Goouch, 2008) to shape curriculum content and outcomes without 'formal' approaches. The practitioner's style respects, values and trusts the children's contributions to their own learning, and allows for children's ownership of the activities. Within a playful pedagogy the play may be co-constructed between adults and children, and the adult acts as a sensitive co-player in line with the children's own intentions and meanings. Playful pedagogies are creative and innovative for both teaching and learning. Hirsh-Pasek *et al.* (2009) stress that traditional research on playful pedagogy points continually to better outcomes and deeper learning for young children. Elsewhere, I have identified pure play, playful learning and playful teaching (Moyles, 2010): pure play (within the total control of children); playful learning (child or adult initiated or inspired, which engages the child in playful ways of learning); playful teaching (which utilises the child's natural and innate joy in play activities but can be directed).

Practitioner reflection on play and learning

Practitioner reflection is about having a questioning approach to personal and professional values and pedagogical practices, and is related to deep learning. Practitioners work within the constraints of government and institutional systems but are free to question their own actions on behalf of children. For many children, out-of-home 'schooling' can last for as much as 16 years, and all teachers have a responsibility to ensure that the time is spent as profitably and enjoyably as possible. Some of the constraints under which practitioners perceive they work (e.g. OfSTED, formalised assessments, leader issues) are very real but others can be due to confusions about play, work and learning, which we have tried to dispel in this book.

Children who are in classrooms and settings where the opportunity to play is restricted or pushed to the periphery by the emphasis on structured, academic curricula and testing, often find moments in which they can exercise their desire to play and often become 'behaviour problems' as a result (Kuschner, 2012: 103).

Reflecting on our provision for learning and teaching is a vital way in which practitioners can ensure that the years children spend institutionally can be as profitable and enjoyable an experience as possible, with full opportunities for learning through play and playful experiences. Observing and reflecting on children's competencies in their play-based learning can be an eye-opener for some of us, enabling a recognition that suitable environmental provision, and interaction and collaboration in children's play offer opportunities to assess progression, differentiation needs and the curriculum's relevance to each child.

Reflecting, too, on the inviting nature of the play and learning environment, with adults drawing attention to children's values and interests, co-constructing activities and engaging in meaningful conversations about children's thinking and feeling (Rogers, 2014), are vital to our understanding of dealing with each child's needs.

Above all, we need to reflect on the insidious belief in society at large (especially politicians) that only what is taught is what children learn. Any observation and documentation will show just how much children learn through their own play and indirect teaching and support. We must constantly ask ourselves what sense formal activities have for children and could they be more playfully and meaningfully presented. How do children perceive themselves in an educational and care context? If we don't trust children to understand themselves and others through their play, they begin to see themselves as inadequate and powerless, leading to dependency and greater vulnerability.

Conclusion

Kuschner (2012: 103) asks, 'Why does the life force of play survive even under such inhospitable circumstances as slavery, war, illness and rigid classroom curriculum?'

Play survives because young children innately know what is necessary for their healthy development. And so do effective practitioners. The evidence is here in this book, and the reflective practitioner will use this as verification and justification for play provision.

Questions to promote reflection

1   Are you a playful pedagogue? Give examples from your own practice. Could anyone challenge your interpretation?
2   What example do you have of a practitioner's ability to provide sufficient opportunities for children to raise their own questions and voice their ideas in play contexts?
3   How can you create a climate of acceptance by respecting children's play choices, recognising the cultural context in which play occurs and providing many play options?
4   If we've lost sight of children's competence in the light of perceived external pressures, how can we redress the balance to gain the excellence of play?

References and further reading (in bold)

Christie, J. (2001) Play as a learning medium. In S. Reifel (ed.) *Theory in Context and Out*, Vol. 3. Westport, CT: Ablex.

Department for Education and Skills (DfES) (2013) *Early Years Foundation Stage.* London: DfES.

Elkind, D. (2008) *The Power of Play: How Spontaneous, Imaginative Activities Lead to Happier, Healthier Children.* Cambridge, MA: De Capo Lifelong.

Golinkoff, R., Hirsh-Pasek, K., Russ, S. and Lillard, A. (2013) Probing play: what does research show? *American Journal of Play*, 5(1): xi.

Goouch, K. (2008) Understanding playful pedagogies, play narratives and play spaces. *Early Years: An International Journal of Research and Development*, 28(1): 93–102.

Gray, P. (2013) *Free to Learn.* New York: Basic Books.

Gray, P. (2014) Give childhood back to children. Available online at: http://www.independent. co.uk/voices/comment/give-childhood-back-to-children-if-we-want-our-offspring-to-have-happy-productive-and-moral-lives-we-must-allow-more-time-for-play-not-less-are-you-listening-gove–9054433.html (accessed 25 January 2014).

Hirsh-Pasek, K., Golinkoff, R., Berk, L. and Singer, D. (2009) *A Mandate for Playful Learning in Preschool: Presenting the Evidence.* New York: Oxford University Press.

Howard, J. (2009) Play, learning and development in the early years. In T. Maynard and N. Thomas (eds) *An Introduction to Early Childhood Studies.* London: Sage.

Isenberg, J.P. and Quisenberry, N. (n.d.) *Play: Essential for All Children.* Available online at: http://365waystounplugyourkids.com/play_Essential_for_kidsl.htm (accessed 26 January 2014).

Jong, T. de, Gog, T. van, Jenks, K., Manlove, S., Hell, J. van., Jolles, J., Merrienboer, J. van, Leeuwen, T. van and Boschloo, A. (2009) *Explorations in Learning and the Brain: On the Potential of Cognitive Neuroscience for Educational Science.* New York: Springer.

Katz, L. (2014) International perspectives on the Early Years Foundation Stage. In J. Moyles, J. Payler and J. Georgeson (eds) *Early Years Foundations: An Invitation to Critical Reflection*. Maidenhead: Open University Press.

Kuschner, D. (2012) What is the state of play? *International Journal of Play*, 1(1): 103–104.

Moyles, J. (1989) *Just Playing? The Role and Status of Play in Early Childhood Education*. Buckingham: Open University Press.

Moyles, J. (2005) Introduction. In J. Moyles (ed.) *The Excellence of Play*, 2nd edn. Maidenhead: Open University Press.

Moyles, J. (2010) Practitioners reflection on play and playful pedagogies. In J. Moyles (ed.) *Thinking About Play: Developing a Reflective Approach*. Maidenhead: Open University Press.

Moyles, J. (2013) *Play and Early Years: Birth-to-Seven-Years*. Cardiff: Play Wales.

Moyles, J., Adams, S. and Musgrove, A. (2002) *SPEEL: Study of Pedagogical Effectiveness in Early Learning*, Research Report 363. London: DfES.

Rogers, S. (2014) Enabling pedagogy: meanings and practices. In J. Moyles, J. Payler and J. Georgeson (eds) *Early Years Foundations: An Invitation to Critical Reflection*. Maidenhead: Open University Press.

Roskos, K. and Christie, J.F. (eds) (2000) *Play and Literacy in Early Childhood: Research from Multiple Perspectives*. Mahwah, NJ: Erlbaum.

Santrock, J. (2003) *Children*, 7th edn. Boston: McGraw-Hill.

Shonkoff, J. and Phillips, D. (eds) (2000) *From Neurons to Neighborhoods: The Science of Early Childhood Development*. Washington: National Academy Press.

Siegler, R. (2005) Children's learning. *American Psychologist*, 60(8): 769–778.

Smith, P.K. (2005) Play: types and functions in human development. In B. Ellis and D. Bjorklund (eds) *Origins of the Social Mind: Evolutionary Psychology and Child Development*. New York: Guilford Press.

Stewart, N. and Pugh, R. (2007) *Early Years Vision in Focus, Part 2: Exploring Pedagogy*. Shrewsbury: Shropshire County Council.

United Nations Convention on the Rights of the Child (UNCRC) (2013) *General comment No: 17 on the right of the child to rest, leisure, play, recreational activities, cultural life and the arts* (Article 31).

3

Brain development and play

Celia O'Donovan and Val Melnyczuk

Summary

This chapter describes the links between current research in brain development and approaches to play in young children (from birth to seven years). Infancy and childhood are the starting points for the continuum that is human life and early experiences shape a child's future. The implications of early brain development studies on play in young children are considered, and a series of cameos illustrate what is happening both from the child's point of view and that of the adult practitioner in a number of play scenarios. Underpinning the chapter is the idea that children need to experience the world through their senses and to be given opportunities to develop according to their potential supported by sensitive interactions from adults. Practitioners with a basic grounding in how young children's brains work will have a better chance of creating appropriate play opportunities that will develop cognitive, affective and psycho-motor skills.

Introduction

Our aim will be to bring fresh eyes to the ways in which children's brain development can be supported by adults in their lives (parents, carers, practitioners). It is essential that those caring for babies and young children have a working knowledge of how the brain develops and works in order that they can create appropriate play opportunities to develop optimum cognitive, affective and psycho-motor skills.

All children deserve the best start in life and this means ensuring that those who care for them, whether it be parents, carers, early years practitioners or teachers, need to have at their disposal certain information that will allow them to provide what all children need: stability, continuity, affection and opportunity. Recognising the importance of the early years in a child's brain development is vital, for it is in this way that appropriate strategies can be planned. In the past, babies and young children had, in many ways, more opportunities for physical activity and free play, and babies were cared for by mothers in the home. Those days have gone. We are now much better informed about how the brain is wired and develops, but we seem to have lost many of the practices that actually stimulated and created essential neural connections. It is strange that, as we have become more aware of the effects of the environment and experience on the growing brain, we have moved further away from allowing children the time to play and develop at their own pace. The emphasis would now appear to be on learning in an adult-guided way and then being measured according to a prescriptive scale (see Chapter 1).

Current research in brain development can provide us with the evidence we need to support play as an essential part of life, but it is only with the dedication, commitment and understanding of those caring for babies and young children that we can feel we are reaping the benefits of what science is telling us.

Babies and young children should not be sidelined from the rest of humanity (see also Chapters 6 and 7). They represent potential and the future. Every baby becomes an adult, and it is our responsibility to ensure that they are treated as human beings and given opportunities to thrive as opposed to being just minded and contained. Every human being needs to feel loved, appreciated and stimulated. With the right kinds of stimulus, brain connections are made and pathways made more efficient, enabling an optimum development for the individual.

We often talk about school readiness – what do we mean by this? It is not the ability to sit still and be taught. It is rather the ability to integrate socially as a well-balanced, secure and playful individual, and it is only through free play and experience that a child can reach this stage.

What have we learned from research so far?

Much research has now been carried out in this area both by neuroscientists and specialists in play theory. The aim of most of the research has been to demonstrate the value of play in the development of young children. Spinka *et al.* (2001: 141) have determined that 'play is training for the unexpected'. It is spontaneous and contains elements of surprise. Play, then, in evolutionary terms, gives the individual the chance to practise skills in a way that is less dangerous than actually doing them. As Graham Music (2011: 125) says, 'Feeling secure and at ease allows the possibility of play, and play in itself can facilitate development.' Whitebread's Report for the European Union (2012) highlights that:

> . . . in play the individual can try out new behaviours, exaggerate, modify, abbreviate or change the sequence of behaviours, endlessly repeat slight variations of behaviours, and so on. It is this characteristic of play, it is argued, that gives it a vital role in the development of problem-solving skills in primates, and the whole gamut of higher-order cognitive and social-emotional skills developed by humans.
>
> (p. 15)

> Three key factors emerge from the research concerning the support for play in these environments. These relate to the level of stimulation, the quality of interactions with adults, and the degree of independence or autonomy offered to the children concerning their play.
>
> (p. 27)

In the past 30 years, we have made great strides in understanding the way in which the brain develops from conception on through life. In particular, we have learned about the impact of early experience on brain wiring and the idea of neuroplasticity. Research has shown that functions of both motor and cognitive areas of the brain can be greatly enhanced by specific types of play and interaction. A child's first language is movement. Physical movement from birth is vital in allowing primitive reflexes, having their origin in the brain stem, to be inhibited. These reflexes, if allowed to persist, can lead to a poorly integrated central nervous system and problems with balance and coordination that will lead to difficulties with learning later on. Today's children often do not receive the natural kinds of stimuli that were common in previous times. Rocking movements, tummy time, opportunities to crawl are all crucial in allowing the vestibular system and the cerebellum to develop. Repeating movements allows them to become automatised through the cerebellum. So babies need the chance to kick, stretch and roll before they can crawl and walk. They need to be exposed to all types of sensory stimulation since they experience the world through their senses. As the child becomes older and begins to develop some degree of physical control, different parts of the brain come into play. Panksepp's laughing rats (2004: 283–293) show us the importance of physical play for brain development. Not only do rats enjoy rough-and-tumble play but the density of their cortical area increases, and they are better able to learn and make decisions. We must guard against taking too much from animal research, but it is clear that there are many similarities in the ways in which mammalian brains are organised and develop.

Another brain area that is crucially affected by play and interaction with the environment and others is the limbic system. This area is responsible for emotional development, and has connections both downwards to the brain stem and upwards to the cortex. It is therefore linked to both the evolutionary need for survival and the decision-making potential of the rational brain. It is particularly open to change and remains plastic as the young child encounters different experiences and feelings. It is in this context that attunement and attachment are so important to the baby and young child. These early experiences shape the limbic system pathways and, through them, children learn theory of mind and then empathy. Efficient brain connections and pathways established in the early years through positive interactions and opportunities have a significant impact on an individual's resilience and emotional stability throughout life.

In the beginning . . .

As we know from brain scanning and research into babies' brains, the primitive part – the so called 'reptilian brain' – is fully formed at birth in order to ensure a baby can breathe and survive from the moment of entry into the world. The remaining parts of the brain then develop over the lifetime of the person, with significant growth spurts and development taking place in the first three years of life continuing throughout childhood and adolescence. The baby's brain is developed by stimulation and experience, and literally grows in size as connections are made. Some development is genetic but is triggered by the environments to which children find themselves exposed. Love and attachment are the key influences in helping a baby's brain to develop, and play at this stage is essential for the limbic (emotional) brain to grow. Initially the adult who is nurturing the child will make eye contact, mirror actions from the baby such as poking their tongue out, talk to the baby, and comment on actions or routines being performed such as bathing, feeding, changing a nappy and so on. These everyday care routines are vital opportunities for the baby and adult to form a strong attachment, and for the baby's brain to make positive connections through their emotional experiences. As the baby grows, playing games such as peek-a-boo, singing rhymes, lullabies or songs, and looking at books together are all vitally important for the development of language and for the brain to grow normally. Humans learn through experience and repetition in order to develop patterns (or templates) within the brain to store information and abilities to function in familiar and unfamiliar situations. Sensory stimulation increases a child's ability to remember, so very young children need to be exposed to situations where more than one of their senses may be developed, i.e. songs and music, movement, visual stimulation and smell. Talking to the baby before they are able to form words to talk back, but acknowledging their responses, is an essential stage of communication and language development:

> Experience is changing the brain from the very beginning. Everything a baby sees, hears, tastes, touches, and smells influences the way the brain gets hooked up.
>
> (Gopnik *et al.*, 2001: 181)

Reading to babies and young children is also an important way to help their brains to develop. Children need opportunities to learn about books, and this shared experience with a trusted adult can strengthen the attachment relationship and develop the child's emotional brain while also stimulating language development. This does not mean that babies or very young children should be expected to read the words, but the experience of being read to, sharing pictures and making up stories is vital for cognitive development. As the old adage goes, read a story, tell a story, write a story. A language-rich environment feeds in to this important sequence, enabling a child to become not only a reader but a writer too (see also Chapter 21). This is an example of what 'school readiness' should apply to.

Alongside cognitive development the baby needs to explore their own physicality – where they are in space by kicking and reaching out – so they need to have time lying on their back on the floor or in a large cot to explore the limits of their own body. Once babies have developed neck muscles sufficiently to hold their heads up (around five to seven months), they also need tummy time where, under the watchful eye of a caring adult, they can explore the world from a different perspective and can strengthen their arm muscles by pushing themselves up from the floor and then reaching out for toys or other suitable objects. This exercise should be seen as the baby's early muscle development required for gross and fine motor skills as the child grows. The cross pattern coordination needed when crawling helps break up primitive reflexes, and develops the connections in the brain that are required for skills such as reading and writing. Conditions such as dyslexia or dyspraxia may develop if these early stages are missed.

Imitation is how we learn

> When we study children, we are studying ourselves; when we see how they develop, we are seeing how we became what we are.
>
> (Gopnik *et al.*, 2001: 206)

Crucial to babies' development are the people around them, from whom they learn a great deal by observing and imitating. Observation is a two-way path: practitioners and parents observe the children in their care, but the children observe, often with great clarity, the adults around them. Witness a child using a brick to represent a mobile phone and chatting (even without words) to the person on the other end; or the baby who tries to swipe the page of a magazine imitating the actions of an adult using a tablet. This is how babies and young children learn, through close observation, imitation, repetition and experimentation. The environment of an early years setting needs to reflect this by being a place where adults are good role models, where the use of language is appropriate and sensitive, where a child can explore and experiment appropriate to their age and stage of development, where they can be challenged and challenge themselves, but be safe both physically and emotionally, supported by caring, loving adults.

Young children watch to see the reaction of the adults around them and from this they learn about emotions and also about themselves. Two year olds in particular try to test their environment and also the adults caring for them! At this age the child is learning who they themselves are and what it is to be independent from their carer, so they challenge the knowledge they have so far gained in order to confirm or alter their understanding and therefore make more connections within the brain. This makes the brain of a two year old far busier than that of an adult.

Experimentation can be seen as the child's way of questioning the world and exploring a series of hypotheses they hold to test their theory of how the world works. In this way, children learn about the world around them and so develop and enhance their brains (see Cameo 1).

Cameo 1

A nine-month-old baby sitting in a high chair tests her knowledge of a cup – she drops a plastic drinking cup on to the floor and it is returned in the same state (i.e. unbroken). Then the child drops a china mug that has been inadvertently left within her reach and sees it shatter into several pieces.

Experiences such as this challenge a child's current knowledge of an object. This moves learning on and leads to further experimentation and hypothesising. In Cameo 1, imagine the reaction of the adult. What might the baby learn from the two different emotional reactions to a seemingly similar physical action?

Over time as the child experiments further and hones his or her understanding of the world around them, the brain realises they do not need all the connections that have been made and so prunes some of the 'dead wood', leaving the important and useful connections to grow stronger as the child develops into adulthood. These stronger connections mean the brain has less plasticity so new concepts and skills can become more difficult to learn. It also means, however, that we have greater knowledge and understanding of the way our environment, community and people within it operate, so we are less surprised by things that happen and may be in a better position to predict the reactions of both people and objects in a given situation. A teenager may be as impulsive as a two year old because, in this stage of their lives, the brain is still undergoing change and growth with the rational part of the brain unable to fully control impulses.

Development of the neo-cortex and the huge number of connections made in this part of the brain allow humans to think about their own reactions and emotions and those of others. Metacognition enables humans to heal their emotions by thinking of different ways to react to a situation or how someone else may have treated them. Babies learn to regulate their emotions through the responses of the adults in their lives, especially those with whom they have an attachment. A young baby learns to be patient when hungry because the attachment figure has consistently responded to their cries of hunger; so when a parent or practitioner says to a one year old, 'Your food is coming: it won't be long', the baby knows that this has been an experience in the past and is able to curtail any worry until the food arrives. If a baby has not been responded to in this way then they will not be able to control emotions and will become very distressed until the hunger is satisfied.

The world for a child under the age of four years is literal: they have learned about object permanence, but they cannot yet put themselves into the place of another and understand or imagine experiences not encountered themselves. In Cameo 2, Anna will not understand why Misha looks for his teddy under the chair because she knows the teddy is in the pushchair behind the tree and so thinks Misha knows this too. This is because she has not yet developed 'theory of mind' and cannot think that Misha doesn't know the teddy has been moved. Children who have autism may never develop theory of mind and their world remains very literal.

Cameo 2

Misha (29 months) and Anna (32 months) are making dens in the garden. Misha hides his teddy under the chair and then goes inside. Anna takes the teddy from under the chair and puts it into the pushchair behind the tree.

When Misha comes back outside where does he look for his teddy?

Playing without interference

Humans need time and space to play in their own way at their own pace in order to learn (see Chapter 2). How do you feel when someone is rushing you along, suggesting things that you aren't interested in, when you are focused on learning how your new phone works? We learn only when we are in the right frame of mind and able to be receptive to learning. We can function at an easier, repetitive stage where we consolidate knowledge or a skill when we are feeling tired or fed up, but to really learn we have to be in the optimum state of mind for learning. When children are ready to learn they often thrive by being left to their own devices to explore and play in their own way under a watchful but slightly distant adult eye. We are often afraid to let children make mistakes, to have their own ideas and to enter into mild conflict with another child, but it is only through these encounters that they will develop the skills they need to cope with life. Brains need to build up a bank of experiences against which the baby/child/adolescent/adult can test a situation and know how to respond and react, as in Cameo 3.

Cameo 3

Carla is sitting unaided, deriving great pleasure from meaningful play with the carefully selected objects in the treasure basket. She is engrossed in the activity, examining, exploring and discarding objects in her own time, at her own pace and concentrates for long periods, showing great interest in the objects. As she mouths and holds them, her brain is comparing the object to what she may already know, her eyes confirming the size, shape and texture that touch is telling her. She is building up data about the objects against which she can experiment further on a subsequent encounter.

The adult's role is to provide the objects and a nurturing environment that indicates to the baby that it is OK to explore and play.

With space, time and support, children can play together or alongside one another testing, watching and manipulating heuristic materials in their own ways without interference from adults. This kind of play allows children to repeat actions, explore different and familiar objects, building on their databank with information regarding shapes, sizes, weights and properties of materials, what they themselves can do, what the objects are capable of and what the limitations are. These experiences, learning about the properties of objects and materials, are the basis of mathematical and scientific knowledge without which children will find it difficult to move to abstract thought when asked to predict what might happen in a scientific experiment or to solve a problem that is written on a page (see Chapters 19 and 20). Throughout life we need hands-on, practical experiences to learn new concepts and consolidate prior knowledge. As the young children learn through physical and emotional experiences so this continues throughout life; this is why all children need to participate in practical experiences such as cooking, woodwork, painting, science experiments, practical mathematics, role play and debating. It is important to add to this the practical experience of manipulating objects and materials such as playdough, clay, shaving foam, paint, sand, water and so on and, crucially, a sensitive adult who respects the child's own exploration but is on hand to teach new skills and also to develop children's thinking by providing language. Without language would we be able to think? We may think in pictures or images, especially when remembering, but could we discuss our thoughts with others if we did not have a shared language and cultural experience? (See Cameo 4.)

> **Cameo 4**
>
> For a little while, I watched, puzzled, as four-year-old Jack (in a reception class) with great care repeatedly took a teaspoon full of sand from the sand tray and deposited it into the water tray. I asked what he was doing; his reply gave me an insight into his thinking: 'I put some water into the sand and I'm trying to take it out again.' So simple, so logical and so insightful; his actions and reply told me far more about his stage of development than any formal test could have done.

As England's *Birth to Three Matters* (DfES, 2002) recognised, babies are social beings from the very start and love to interact with other humans, being able to recognise the form of a human face from the moment of birth. They also recognise the sound of mother's voice and maybe other sounds heard while in the womb. Babies are receptive to the sounds in all languages in their first 12 months but soon learn to recognise the sounds within the language in which they find themselves immersed, and lose the ability to distinguish less familiar sounds as they grow; their brain becomes attuned to their home language and they are less receptive to others. Children growing up in a dual (or more) language environment are advantaged by being surrounded by more than one language, enabling them to retain the ability to recognise sounds that are unique to different languages. Without language we would not be able to communicate. We are adept at using signs and symbols to stand for words and can communicate in a basic way through gesture and facial expression (think of holidays in countries other than our own) but this can be a frustrating and limiting experience. Young children who are acquiring language can become frustrated, too, when their expressive language is misunderstood by the adults around them or they have not yet learned the words to express their developing thinking. Children need to be in a language-rich environment, hearing complex language to challenge their thinking, but also simple language when they need to follow an instruction or explanation. From a very young age, children should be encouraged to develop metacognition (thinking about thinking) and this can only really take place in environments where skilful adults encourage children to express their thoughts and take time to listen to them. So children should be given time to wonder and encouraged to ask why the sky is blue, where the clouds go at night, what would happen if a tiger came to tea or where a butterfly goes to sleep.

Are we afraid of losing control?

Adults can be very bossy. We often think we know best and we can be very demanding. Why does the world have to be the way adults want it to be? Is it because we are afraid of losing control? Is it a power thing? In a setting where young children are, whether it be a nursery, at home, in a school or anywhere that adults require order, the uninitiated may be horrified on walking into a room full of children under three flitting from place to place, avoiding bumping into things by a whisker, laughing, talking, being boisterous, maybe jumping or standing on one leg as they lean across the sand tray to reach a tool from the far side. Might the adult exclaim that the children are being unruly, chaotic and out of control, and wouldn't it be better if these children were sitting down quietly being taught by an adult? So, is child-centred learning wrong? Does it lead to a slip in the ranking on the PISA scales? Or is it that the adults do not fully understand what child-initiated learning means, or how to encourage and develop it? (See also Chapter 22.)

Throughout the centuries children have learned skills, knowledge, cultural expectations, language, negotiation tactics, their place in the pecking order, and everything they need to know to be a responsible adult from their parents, siblings, peers, grandparents and other people in their lives. We are now questioning this and allowing children less time to play with children of different ages, mess about in puddles and streams, fall out with their friends and make up again in their own way and in their own time. How does a child learn how to be sociable, negotiate their place, learn from their own mistakes, take chances or risk things if an adult is constantly telling them what to do and how to view the world from an adult perspective? How irritating! For the most part children enjoy rough-and-tumble play; they learn a lot from it. If they don't enjoy it they do not participate but may enjoy watching other children play in this physical way. Fathers often play in a rough-and-tumble way with their young children and, from the age of about three years, children may enjoy playing in this manner with their peers. It is often feared by adults (parents, practitioners, teachers) that play fighting will lead to real fighting; however, research (Smith, 2010) has shown that rarely does this happen in children of primary school age, and that the participants are well aware of the difference between play fighting in rough-and-tumble play and real fighting: the former is fun and enjoyable, the latter is not. Over-protective adults can limit a child's development physically, cognitively and emotionally by preventing physical exploration, which may begin as tummy time but develops through to rough-and-tumble play as the child grows.

When adults know children well and trust them to trust themselves they may interfere less in the children's play in whatever form this may take. It is often fear of consequences from parents, law enforcement officials, social workers and so on that causes practitioners and teachers to control the children in their care and to inhibit their learning by encouraging them to sit instead of move, to be quiet rather than exuberant, to be placid rather than inquisitive, to limit brain development rather than develop it, to teach children that being yourself if you are energetic, physical, noisy is not acceptable. A free-for-all is not being advocated here, and it is important for children to learn when some behaviours are inappropriate and to accept the conventions and norms of society, but inhibiting children's natural development in order to comply with pressure from authority should be challenged. Research through longitudinal studies by Schweinhart and Weikart (1997) and others has shown that children who are inhibited in their play are more likely to find themselves in trouble with the authorities in adulthood; play is the way children learn to be good citizens.

How does play impact on brain development?

It is clear, then, that providing appropriate play opportunities and interactions of a stimulating kind can help the child's developing brain to make connections that will enable successful cognitive, social and psycho-motor skills throughout life. The brain is malleable throughout life, but there are critical or sensitive periods in childhood when neural pathways proliferate, and it is vital that during these periods children experience an optimal input of a sensory, physical, social and emotional nature in order that the pathways are used and not lost. Unused pathways wither and die. Play deprivation shows that the brain can actually decrease in size and brain function can deteriorate to significant levels, as explored by Whitebread (2012):

> The many studies of the severely deprived children discovered in Romanian orphanages following the breakup of the Soviet Union reported a range of severe cognitive and emotional deficits including abnormal repetitive or brief play behaviours, together with deficient growth and functioning in a number of key brain regions.
>
> (p. 28)

Conclusion

How do we move forward to provide children with the opportunities they require to equip them for their lives? What can we do to restore play to its rightful and important place in children's lives? Who will be brave enough to say that play is what children need to learn, to develop their brains, to become the responsible, intelligent, creative adults of the future? Will it be you?

Questions to promote reflection

1   Do you understand as much about the development of a child's brain as you do of their physical development?
2   What are the 'milestones' for brain development? How do you know a child has reached/achieved them?
3   Are you a reflexive practitioner who allows a child to learn or an adult who fears losing control? Which would you rather be?

References and further reading (in bold)

Department for Education and Skills (DfES) (2002) *Birth to Three Matters*. London: HMSO.
Gopnik, A., Meltzoff, A. and Kuhl, P. (2001) *How Babies Think*. Phoenix/London: Orion Books.
Graham Music (2011) *Nurturing Natures*. Hove and New York: Psychology Press.
Panksepp, J. (2004) *Affective Neuroscience*. Oxford: Oxford University Press.
Schweinhart, J. and Weikart, D.P. (1997) High/Scope Preschool Curriculum Comparison Study. *Early Childhood Research Quarterly*, 12(2): 117–143.
Smith, P.K. (2010) *Children and Play*. Chichester: Wiley/Blackwell.
Spinka, M., Newberry, R.C. and Bekoff, M. (2001) Mammalian play: can training for the unexpected be fun? *Quarterly Review of Biology*, 76(2): 141–176.
Whitebread, D. (2012) *The Importance of Play*. Written for Toy Industries of Europe (TIE).

4

Play and the achievement of potential

Karen Barr and Lynne Truelove

Summary

This chapter discusses the value of play in relation to early intervention strategies designed to ensure that all children have the opportunity to reach their full potential. It begins with the current policy context in the early years sector in England, and examines how play is used with children who exceed developmental expectations, with examples of how individual interests are captured and then used to provide effective and tailored opportunities for play. The importance of parental involvement in contributing to their child's development through play is discussed, followed by an examination of styles of assessing and documenting children's learning. Children's contribution to documenting their own achievements through play is explored. The chapter also considers the concepts of inclusion and special educational needs within play-based pedagogical practices, and concludes with a discussion of how play environments can be inclusive so that all children can achieve their full potential.

Introduction

Play is an invaluable vehicle through which children can make satisfying achievements of which they are proud. Children learn and develop when they engage in playful activities relevant to them that provide an appropriate level of challenge. When early years practitioners work in partnership with parents in their children's learning, this impacts positively on children's well-being and development. Careful observations illuminate our understanding of how children learn through engagement with play-based experiences, and provide a means of ascertaining how best to respond or, at times, offer interventional support, so that children have opportunities through inclusive provision to achieve their potential as learners and individuals.

This chapter considers key elements of early years practice that contribute to children's achievement through play. These are:

- the policy context for early intervention
- respectful assessment and documentation of achievement

- children's ownership of their learning
- playful and inclusive provision for all children.

The policy context for early intervention

Early years practitioners are increasingly using early intervention strategies to ensure that all children reach their full potential. The culture of early intervention seems to have become a central component of practice as recent knowledge and understanding of brain development has influenced how we nurture babies and young children. Committed early years practitioners strive to support the children in their care, and in this section we consider recent significant political context that surrounds the practice issue of early intervention and that contributes to 'play and the achievement of potential'.

When elected to power in 2010, the Coalition government began to reform education and childcare in the UK for children from birth to five years. At the time, Frank Field's independent review on poverty and life chances called for local and national governments to recognise the vital importance of the earliest years of life, from pregnancy to five years. Early intervention is not only good for people but good for the economy, as improved behaviour results in higher educational attainment, fewer violent crimes and better employment opportunities (Field, 2010). Comparably, the costs of 'late intervention', such as public expenditure on unemployment benefits, tackling crime and treating poor health, are extremely high. Moving away from Field's focus on children in poverty, the message of using early intervention strategies has wider implications for *all* children to achieve their potential. Indeed, early intervention strategies are thought to develop a bedrock of social and emotional development that promotes happiness, health and achievement throughout children's lives (Allen, 2011). An independent report on the Early Years Foundation Stage (EYFS) strongly recommended that the early identification of children's needs should be prominent in the framework about to be revised (Tickell, 2011). The government policy document *Supporting Families in the Foundation Years* (DfE, 2011) announced a commitment to giving all children the best start in life with an opportunity to fulfil their potential, while acknowledging the wider economic and social benefits for society. When the revised EYFS (DfE, 2012) was introduced in September 2012, the theme of early intervention was visible in the form of two main changes, which include a statutory 'progress check' of children when aged two years and a simplified EYFS profile assessment at five years. Such statutory obligations mean that dedicated opportunities now exist for all children to have their individual learning and development needs carefully assessed and catered for. As children's learning is regarded as developing through playful engagement with their environment and with others, the EYFS (DfE, 2012: 5) echoes the Coalition's policy statement in that 'every child deserves the best possible start in life and the support that enables them to fulfil their potential'. The next section considers the role of 'play' in realising that aim.

Early intervention strategies

The EYFS statutory progress checks carried out when a child is aged between two and three, and later at the age of five years old, require practitioners to identify a child's strengths and any areas where they are not progressing as expected (DfE, 2012). These early intervention strategies are aimed at identifying any significant emerging concerns, additional needs and disabilities, and through close partnership working with the parents/carers. This process should lead to the implementation of a targeted plan to support the child's learning and development requirements. Individual Education Plans (IEPs) in such circumstances generally involve the Special Educational Needs Coordinator (SENCo). However, practitioners have an opportunity at any point to develop Individual Play Plans (IPPs) themselves in partnership with parents and carers to use play as a means to support children of any ability and age to achieve their potential. Individual Play Plans were developed by Sayeed and Guerin (2000) as an extension to the IEP, with an added emphasis on the adult's role in supporting play through participation and interaction. Yet IPPs could be a useful tool for practitioners planning for children's individualised next steps, and IPPs' formats can be developed to suit each type of early years provision and pedagogical approach to practice.

Another example of pedagogical documentation is the Individual Learning Journey. Cameo 1 illustrates how this format was used to support a young child who attended a Children's Centre in a northern city in England.

Cameo 1: Gifted and talented play provision

When Asha aged three years 11 months began attending the Children's Centre, practitioners quickly noted her advanced language skills in both English and her home language. Additionally, her letter, number, shape and colour recognition skills were well above age-related expectations. Asha's mother was keen to explain how her daughter spent time at home with family members, formally learning numbers, letters and colours in English, and using the computer. Asha's key person, Michelle, soon realised that Asha was gifted and talented, yet identified that Asha's social skills might be developed further as she had not had many opportunities to play with other children at home.

Over the next few weeks, Michelle used both formal and informal conversations to learn more about Asha's home life, while observing her in the centre. By the end of her first term in the centre, at 37 months old, Asha was assessed at the 40–60-month level in all the prime and specific areas of the EYFS. Michelle reflected that Asha would be able to achieve further potential through play, and so began sensitive discussion with Asha's mother about the value of play rather than formal learning methods, while planning Asha's next steps in learning together.

My learning journey

EYFS: End of Term Learning & Development summary

A Unique Child

Name: Date: Age:

How do I Learn?

Playing and exploring; Finding out and exploring; Playing with what they know; Being willing to have a go

Active Learning; Being involved and concentrating; Enjoying and achieving what they set out to do; Keeping on trying

Creating and thinking critically; Having their own ideas; Making links; Choosing ways to do things

What did I Learn?

Personal, Social and Emotional Development; Self-confidence and self-awareness; Making relationships; Managing feelings and behaviour

Self-confidence and self-awareness					
0–11	8–20	16–26	22–36	30–50	40–60
Making relationships					
0–11	8–20	16–26	22–36	30–50	40–60
Managing feelings and behaviour					
0–11	8–20	16–26	22–36	30–50	40–60

What did I Learn?

Communication and Language; Listening and attention; Understanding; Speaking

Listening and attention					
0–11	8–20	16–26	22–36	30–50	40–60
Understanding					
0–11	8–20	16–26	22–36	30–50	40–60
Speaking					
0–11	8–20	16–26	22–36	30–50	40–60

What did I Learn?

Physical Development; Moving and Handling; Health and self-care

Moving and handling					
0–11	8–20	16–26	22–36	30–50	40–60
Health and self-care					
0–11	8–20	16–26	22–36	30–50	40–60

Figure 4.1 Pedagogical documentation illustration (1)

EYFS: End of Term Learning & Development Summary (Specific Areas)

A Unique Child		
Name:	**Date:**	**Age:**

What did I Learn?
Literacy: Reading and Writing

Reading					
0–11	8–20	16–26	22–36	30–50	40–60

Writing					
0–11	8–20	16–26	22–36	30–50	40–60

What did I Learn?
Mathematics: Numbers and Shape, Space & Measure

Numbers					
0–11	8–20	16–26	22–36	30–50	40–60

Shape, Space & Measure					
0–11	8–20	16–26	22–36	30–50	40–60

What did I Learn?
Understanding the World: People & Communities, The World and Technology

People & Communities					
0–11	8–20	16–26	22–36	30–50	40–60

The World					
0–11	8–20	16–26	22–36	30–50	40–60

Technology					
0–11	8–20	16–26	22–36	30–50	40–60

What did I Learn?
Expressive Arts & Design: Exploring & Using Media & Materials and Being Imaginative.

Exploring & Using Media & Materials					
0–11	8–20	16–26	22–36	30–50	40–60

Being Imaginative					
0–11	8–20	16–26	22–36	30–50	40–60

If age/stage highlighted ▓▓▓ there are no development matters statements for that age/stage

Figure 4.1 *(Continued)*

Family contribution and my next steps in learning

Future steps needed to support my learning and development		
Physical Development	**Language & Communication**	**Personal Social & Emotional**

Characteristics of Learning:

To be reviewed again by:
Signed key person:

Families comments and contribution

Signed:

Figure 4.2 Pedagogical documentation illustration (2)

Michelle and Asha's mother agreed on the following play activities for Asha and documented them in an Individual Learning Journey, along with a rationale for each choice.

Activity 1. To provide wooden shapes and plastic bears of different sizes
Rationale – these play activities of ordering and sorting aimed to embed Asha's understanding of size differentiation through spontaneous and adult-initiated play. Opportunities were made available daily in the continuous provision and in group times when one practitioner worked with a small group of children. These activities were

intended to enable Asha to experience either on a one-to-one basis with an adult, or in a social group of her peers and encounter specific mathematical language about size.

Activity 2. Talk about 'time' and provide clocks in the role play and maths area in the setting

Rationale – this activity was to provide indoor play opportunities for Asha to experience language and activities around the concept of 'time' both from self-chosen activities in two areas that observations showed to be favourite areas for Asha. In group times and through spontaneous conversations, practitioners used talk about time to engage Asha and extend her vocabulary and understanding of this concept.

Activity 3. Play 'What time is it Mr Wolf?' outside

Rationale – this exciting outdoor activity provided a structured group game where Asha could be supported by practitioners to follow the format of the questioning and chasing with 'Mr Wolf' and experience the social aspect of group collusion, while using language about 'time'.

Activity 4. Count everyday objects, such as, fruit and flowers in the garden

Rationale – this calmer and quieter activity builds on Asha's interest in the garden and her sense of pride when counting with adults. The naturalistic setting of the garden provides more spontaneous and fun opportunities to count rather than more formal and adult-structured instances that Asha was accustomed to at home.

Activity 5. Use 'Bee Bot' (programmable robotic toy that moves on inputted instruction) to explore number, length and making predictions

Rationale – this technology-based activity aims to offer a new play opportunity to extend Asha's advanced mathematical knowledge and understanding. Using this toy within the context of a practitioner-led small group activity also aimed to provide Asha with opportunities to take turns, share and converse with her peers.

Asha's mother was intrigued by the potential of play-based learning and its possible applications at home. Furthermore, she highly valued the collaborative partnership with Michelle as she saw her daughter develop increasing confidence and social skills through play. Asha's learning continued positively throughout her time in the nursery as planned play activities were adjusted according to her changing interests and her developing skills. Michelle's commitment to supporting Asha's achievement of potential as a gifted and talented child in this way meant that, by the time Asha left the nursery to start school, she was a happy, confident and sociable child who loved to learn through play.

Respectful assessment and documentation of achievement

The story of Asha's learning and achievement highlights the value of adopting a respectful approach to assessment and responsive planning that enables children to take their next steps in development. While recognising areas of learning in which Asha would benefit from specific support through personalised planning, practitioners identified Asha's strengths and made provision to build on these. Often, adults feel pressurised to get children to achieve expected 'norms' of development for their age, when in fact no two children develop in exactly the same way or at the same rate. Of course, part of an adult's role in pedagogy is to enable children to reach their full potential, but it is important to appreciate that each child is unique; thus achievement in different areas of development varies between each child and may happen out of sequence with the goals suggested in the EYFS.

One of the risks of using an outline of expected goals for young children is that a 'deficit model' of assessment is adopted. This means that a child's achievement is predominantly assessed in terms of what they cannot do – in other words, by looking for gaps in their development. A key question here might be whether children should be viewed as human beings or human 'becomings', or both (Uprichard, 2008). If we view children as complete beings in their own right, although they are still growing and developing, we accept and value them for who they are now, irrespective of their abilities, as well as respecting their potential. Indeed, as adults we can view ourselves as both beings and becomings in that we continue to develop personally and professionally during adulthood. It can be a challenge to balance the responsibility of ensuring that children receive specialised support through early intervention strategies to maximise opportunities for development, with the need to respect each child's uniqueness and view them as whole individuals, worthy of respect for who they are rather than what they can or cannot do. However, by applying a 'credit model' of assessment, which means starting from what the child can do, adults can enable children to build on their current achievements and continue to develop in their own unique ways. This can be challenging when using the development charts in the guidance document, *Development Matters in the Early Years Foundation Stage* (Early Education, 2012), or other development charts from various sources. A 'checklist' approach is sometimes taken in which practitioners mark off when a child has reached an expected milestone. Moreover, it is not unusual, particularly when the time to complete statutory summary assessments draws near. However, effective pedagogy involves assessing children's achievements in ways that are authentic and relevant to children's interests. For example, in order to understand a child's problem-solving skills adults can engage with and observe children during play activities that children have chosen to do themselves, such as constructing sculptures from recyclable materials, or by listening to their negotiation skills during role play in the home corner. In this way, achievement can be observed when children are intrinsically motivated and thus more likely to perform at their best. Thorough observations and engagement with children at appropriate times during play enable practitioners to get to know children well and develop a deeper understanding of their interests and abilities. In order for observation and assessment to feed in to effective curriculum planning, a holistic view of children's interests as well as their achievements is needed if they are to feel motivated to engage with experiences offered. Occasions where it has not been possible for practitioners to ascertain children's achievements in this way perhaps highlight issues around time constraints due to insufficient adult–child ratios. Practitioners need to be supported appropriately to carry out this part of their role if they are to know the children in their care and be confident in observing children's achievements during genuine play and learning experiences.

It is important to recognise achievements beyond those suggested in the EYFS development charts. The authors of *Development Matters* acknowledge that the charts detail possible journeys that children might take, and suggest that practitioners use them to make 'best-fit' judgements (Early Education, 2012: 3) about whether concerns should be addressed, rather than use them merely as checklists. Nevertheless, time and budget pressures on settings can sometimes lead to less effective practice taking place. This should be resisted if respectful approaches to enabling children's achievement are to prevail.

Learning stories and dispositions

It is useful to look at further ways of recognising and promoting children's development by taking account of alternative pedagogic practices of observation and assessment. One such example, and one that extols a credit model of assessment, was developed by Carr (2001), in which 'learning stories' are recorded and used to observe children's development of tools or required tendencies that enable them to learn. This method was designed to be used in conjunction with the New Zealand early years curriculum policy, *Te Whāriki*. Carr (2001: 23) advocates focusing on five key 'dispositions' for learning, which are:

- taking an interest
- being involved
- persisting with difficulty or uncertainty
- communicating with others
- taking responsibility.

All children can develop these dispositions in their own unique ways and at different levels. Practitioners who notice these dispositions can support children to develop them further, rather than checking off anticipated milestones. The EYFS development charts do in fact draw upon elements of these dispositions, so it is possible to use this type of assessment in conjunction with other EYFS documentation and develop a holistic approach to understanding and recording children's achievement. Such dispositions enable children to develop resourcefulness and motivation to continue learning and achieving by engaging in experiences that interest and challenge them. By developing these skills for learning, children gain more control over their own achievements.

Children's ownership of their learning

Documenting children's achievement is a useful means of reflecting on playful learning experiences offered and how they enable children to achieve. Furthermore, it is a necessary part of implementing the EYFS curriculum policy and identifying where early intervention from within the setting or from specialist agencies might be appropriate. Nevertheless, it is important to reflect on who else the documentation is produced for, or even who primarily it should be for. When children can access and be involved in creating their own records, this is invaluable in empowering them to reflect on their own achievements, feel a sense of pride and remember what they have done. Through constructive and sensitive dialogue with children about the learning documented, adults can support children to reflect on what their next steps might be. In this way, children are able to participate in planning playful learning experiences that are relevant to them and thus have more ownership of their learning. If children are to be viewed as people in their own right, surely they should be supported to take this ownership and be in charge of their own achievement.

In order for children to understand their learning journey records, they must include information that is accessible to children, particularly visual modes of communication such as drawings and photographs. Careful attention needs to be paid as to how involved children are in deciding what should be included. Bath (2012) highlights problems in early years settings where children feel confused and excluded when they are not involved in creating their own development records, even when they are entitled 'My Learning Journey'. She discusses research carried out with children on their experiences of the EYFS, in which some children did not recognise this document as their own. For example, when one child was shown his record, he evidently did not consider a photograph of himself sat in a group at story time as particularly significant to his own learning journey, saying 'I didn't even choose a story. I don't like stories' (p. 198). In other examples, children could not access the information contained at all where records were made in writing that children were unable to read. However, children in some settings were clearly able to reflect on their records – for instance, one child could recall and explain the processes explored through playing with a pulley, which had been photographed and included in his Learning Journey. When children are able to situate themselves within the context of their record they can draw meaning from it. Records that are meaningful to children have much more pedagogical value than those created purely for adults such as practitioners and OfSTED inspectors.

Some settings encourage children to create photograph books to take home and share with their families. Another useful practice is to create displays or albums that children can access freely and share with peers or adults in order to remember and celebrate what they have done. At a nursery in the north of England, children are encouraged to display their own artwork on a large child-height board in order to celebrate their achievements. The children can do this independently as the materials needed to attach their work are accessible next to the board. This enables children to make their own choices about what to include, and can offer practitioners an insight into which achievements have significant meaning to children, even if they do not have the language needed to discuss their work verbally.

Observations are a key way of understanding children's achievements. Detailed written recordings are an essential way of capturing what children do, but are not necessarily accessible to children. However, where adults talk to children about what they have seen and recorded, children often respond and provide deeper insight into their thinking and actions. This can be added to the record in order to include children's perspectives on their own learning. Visual methods such as photographs of what children are doing, which are discussed with children and their thoughts transcribed, are most useful, yet it need not only be the adult who takes the photographs. When children are encouraged to photograph the things that are important to them, including their own creations, they can document their own learning in collaboration with the adults involved.

The Reggio approach to documenting achievement

In preschools in Reggio Emilia, children are viewed as co-researchers in collaboration with adults. Practitioners create 'mini stories' in the form of written observations, video recordings, photographs and pieces of children's artwork that they have created individually as well as collaboratively with their peer group. Quick decisions must be made in order to decide how best to capture the essence of the learning that is taking place and the context in which this occurs. Vea Vecci, an artist and pedagogue in Reggio Emilia, explains that this is a skill that takes time to develop as the documenter 'must be highly alert, *antennae vibrating*' (Vecci, 2010: 134). Being so alert to children's thinking and capturing the atmosphere of the learning that is happening leads to a deeper understanding of children's learning and creation of documentation that is more meaningful to children. Moreover, the documentation process in Reggio Emilia settings is concerned with searching for meaning in the way that children learn (Rinaldi, 2006), rather than looking to assess children's achievement of pre-set outcomes that are determined by adults. In this way, an emergent curriculum in which experiences are planned in response to what is documented and interpreted can be developed and tailored according to what captures the children's imagination and builds on what they have already achieved.

Collaborating with parents

The emergent curriculum is planned in collaboration between practitioners and parents in regular meetings after the preschool day finishes, in order to gain parents' unique perspectives on children's interests and learning. Challenges in achieving a similar level of parental involvement in English settings include often having a longer working day and less available time to meet with parents outside the hours that practitioners spend with children. Nevertheless, working in partnership with parents to enable children to achieve their full potential is an essential part of a practitioner's role within the EYFS. This is true for children across the early years age range and, as Asha's story illustrates, parents offer insight that might otherwise be unknown. Dialogue with parents is especially useful where children may not have the language needed to share their home experiences with practitioners – for example, babies and very young children. What children can achieve in the home environment is often different to what they can achieve in nursery or school, as levels of confidence and opportunities to interact with different people vary. Thus, in order to gain a fuller picture of children's achievements and ensure that appropriate, playful opportunities are available and shared between home and the setting, positive relationships between parents and practitioners are invaluable.

Playful and inclusive provision for all children

In order for children to benefit fully from experiences offered, opportunities for every child to engage with the environment, resources and people should be created. Making provision that is tailored for individual children should not mean singling them out, but rather ensuring that they feel a sense of belonging and are not excluded from participating in experiences in the setting. Where specific resources are offered – for example, a visual timetable so that children with learning difficulties can see and feel reassured about what happens next during the day – everyone can benefit from this as a point of reference. Signs, symbols and pictures that are used to label where particular resources are kept will help all children to access the things that they need in their play. If a child's IPP includes additional support from an adult to develop social skills when playing with other children, the child's peers are also likely to benefit from interaction with the adult and develop inclusive attitudes and skills in socialising with one another.

The term 'special educational needs' (SEN) is often applied to children who require additional support to reach their full potential. This is a contested term, partly as it can be argued that everyone's support needs vary due to our uniqueness. The danger in labelling children as having SEN is that this singles them out as different, which appears to contradict the notion of the 'unique child' theme within the EYFS. Additionally, we all have 'needs' but there are connotations of 'neediness' where someone is deemed to be in need of special treatment. This seems out of line with principles of respecting and valuing all children equally. One dilemma surrounding the use of this term is that, in order for settings to receive additional funding to provide further support for children deemed to have SEN, this label is accorded. The term 'inclusion' is also contestable, as what one person feels is inclusive another might view as exclusive. In order to understand what works best for each child and group of children and their parents, constant dialogue and renegotiation of practice is essential.

Inclusion is broadly about creating an environment in which all children are valued, treated respectfully, feel that they belong and have real opportunities to achieve their potential. While specific provision might be made for children at times, inclusive settings adopt an anti-discriminatory approach to fostering an inclusive setting ethos and making play accessible in varied ways to all children. Two key models of disability are the 'medical model' and the 'social model'; the former views disability as a flaw in an individual that needs to be corrected. This resonates with a deficit model of assessment in which a child is seen as lacking in ways that have to be fixed. Conversely, the social model views the environment as being at fault when a disabled person is prevented from participating fully and therefore issues within the environment should be addressed, thus viewing children as whole people irrespective of differences in the way they learn or access provision. Practitioners need to be vigilant in ensuring that environments are respectful and inclusive in order to uphold all children's rights to achieve their full potential, and remove barriers to children's participation when they arise. This requires constant reflection in order to continue developing practice. Contexts and people change all the time, so reflective, proactive approaches are essential.

Effective communication between the child's home and the setting is key to understanding factors that might affect a child's capacity to achieve their full potential. This allows for early identification of issues at home such as illness, economic difficulties or relationship breakdowns, where interventional support can be offered on a temporary or longer-term basis. Inclusive settings are aware of issues that might affect families who use their service and are proactive in removing barriers without singling children out. For example, where a family is living in poverty and perhaps the children do not come to nursery with wellington boots in the snow or rain, or a warm coat due to affordability, the setting might provide spares available for all children to access outdoor play experiences rather than miss out on opportunities by having to go inside early due to the cold or wetness. This provision can actually benefit all children if the weather changes suddenly during the day or if, in the morning rush to drop children off, items are forgotten. The beauty of an inclusive approach rather than making special arrangements that stigmatise individuals is that often everyone benefits from provision that enables participation. As families' circumstances change, engagement with them can enable practitioners to develop a deeper understanding of potential inclusion issues and respond appropriately by adapting provision that everyone can use.

Conclusion

Policy contexts impact on the way that practitioners enable children to achieve through play, yet constant reflection is essential if challenges and dilemmas are to be addressed so that respectful pedagogies uphold children's right to gain ownership of and achieve their potential. Engagement with alternative practices supports reflection and illuminates possibilities to enhance opportunities to understand children's development. Receptiveness to ideas is key to improving practice, and dialogue with families offers insight into ways in which practice can be renegotiated to make inclusive provision for play. In doing this, the potential for play to enable children's achievement can be realised.

Questions to promote reflection

1   How would you decide whether intervention strategies are appropriate for individual children?
2   How do you involve parents in their children's learning?
3   How do you document children's learning and what involvement do children have in this process?
4   What opportunities are there to make provision for play more inclusive in your setting?

Acknowledgements

The authors extend their thanks to the Children's Centre and Michelle for sharing the example of practice for one cameo. Grateful thanks are also extended to the child's parents for granting permission to share this information.

References and further reading (in bold)

Allen, G. (2011) *Early Intervention: The Next Steps. An Independent Report to Her Majesty's Government.* London: HM Government.

Bath, C. (2012) 'I can't read it; I don't know': young children's participation in the pedagogical documentation of English early childhood education and care settings. *International Journal of Early Years Education*, 20(2): 190–201.

Carr, M. (2001) *Assessment in Early Childhood Settings: Learning Stories*. London: Paul Chapman.

Department for Education (DfE) (2011) *Supporting Families in the Foundation Years*. London: Crown.

Department for Education (DfE) (2012) *The Early Years Foundation Stage: Setting the Standards for Learning, Development and Care for Children from Birth to Five*. London: Crown.

Early Education (2012) *Development Matters in the Early Years Foundation Stage (EYFS)*. Available online at: http://www.foundationyears.org.uk/files/2012/03/Development-Matters-final-print-amended.pdf (accessed 6 April 2014).

Field, F. (2010) *The Foundation Years: Preventing Poor Children Becoming Poor Adults. The Report of the Independent Review on Poverty and Life Chances*. London: DfE.

Rinaldi, C. (2006) *In Dialogue with Reggio Emilia*. Abingdon: Routledge.

Sayeed, Z. and Guerin, E. (2000) *Early Years Play. A Happy Medium for Assessment and Intervention*. Abingdon: Fulton.

Tickell, C. (2011) *The Early Years: Foundations for Life, Health and Learning. An Independent Report on the Early Years Foundation Stage to Her Majesty's Government*. London: Crown Publishing.

Uprichard, E. (2008) Children as beings and becomings: children, childhood and temporality. *Children and Society*, 22(4): 303–313.

Vecci, V. (2010) *Art and Creativity in Reggio Emilia: Exploring the Role and Potential of Ateliers in Early Childhood Education*. London: Routledge.

5

Reimagining gender and play

Jayne Osgood

Summary

Drawing on recent feminist theorising, which works with the material and affective, this chapter attempts to (re-)position children as active in processes of developing and transgressing gendered identities through play. By drawing on observations of young children at play, with a particular focus on a three-year-old girl, Sylvie, the closely monitored and regulated gendered boundaries within early childhood are re-examined to consider how we might think differently through our adult practices. Framed by the work of Braidotti (2013), I conceptualise the becoming child as a series of multiple becomings set within an early childhood assemblage comprising objects, emotions, sensory incidents, social interactions and un/intentional events. Approaching gender and play through this lens opens up opportunities to observe the various ways and means by which children negotiate, resist, celebrate, indulge and transgress gendered ways of being through their play (with people and things), through verbal, non-verbal, physical becomings in early childhood contexts. This refocusing enables new ways of observing, sensing and engaging with the everydayness of young childhoods lived at home and in the nursery, and offers a means to re-engage with debates about the persistence of gender inequity in society more broadly. This approach invites us to question our world-views and make space to reconfigure the becoming child.

Introduction

Play remains a central focus in the field of early childhood education and care, and there continues to be debate about its various forms and potentialities as testified in this book. There is a wealth of literature that offers guidance on how best to facilitate play, to regulate and assess the value of play, and so on. However, I would suggest that there is less debate about stepping back (as adults: practitioners, parents, researchers) and critically observing the generative possibilities that play affords young children to develop and transgress gendered identities through play that occurs in the 'in-between spaces'. There has intermittently been a preoccupation in early childhood to put and/ or keep gender on the agenda. But this gender agenda has tended to take the form of intervention and regulation (MacNaughton, 2000; Holland, 2003). In its place, I would like to put forward the idea that it is imperative for children to play *with* gender, to allow space and opportunities for children to negotiate, resist, celebrate and queer gendered ways of being through their play with people and things. This requires a de-centring of the adult subject and calls upon a need to view the becoming child as a series of successive becomings (Braidotti, 2013), as having rights to explore and transgress (Robinson, 2013), and to pay attention to their engagements with matter (Lenz Taguchi, 2010).

This chapter focuses attention on reconfiguring play so that we (adults: practitioners, parents, researchers) might reach fuller understandings of children as gendered beings who actively and consciously or unconsciously play with gender within and through early childhood encounters and contexts. By highlighting interwoven events in the lives of young children's play such as rough and tumble, superhero and nature, I will illustrate the means by which the becoming child encounters a series of multiple becomings. These becomings are formed within early childhood assemblages comprising objects, emotions, sensory incidents, social interactions and un/intentional events (Renold and Mellor, 2013). Applying such a lens to seek new understandings of the gendered lives of children in early childhood education provides an opportunity to challenge our taken-for-granted assumptions about childhood, gender and our (adult) roles in making space to play.

This chapter builds upon the work of key feminist theorists such as Butler (1990; 1993), who theorises gender as performative and highlights the significance of everyday routines, performances and interactions that shape gendered behaviours and contribute to the formation of gendered identities. Recognising that gender is socially constructed, fluid and shifting, and hinges upon the context in which it is performed is important when considering how gender is negotiated by young children in the context of early childhood settings – particularly through play. Taking Butler's ideas as a starting place and extending them by considering the work of Braidotti (2013), it is possible to consider post-humanist ideas around embodied experience that stress that play in early childhood forms an *assemblage* – made up of objects, feelings, sensory encounters, interactions and events.

> She's usually so girly, with her sparkly shoes and fairy wings and the next minute you see her throwing herself across the room . . . And she can be *so* loud sometimes [laughs]. She certainly surprises us every day.

This quote from an early years teacher provides reflection on unexpected displays of gender variance that challenge normative ideas that abound in early childhood. The three-year-old girl in question, Sylvie, in many senses can be understood to embody hegemonic forms of femininity through her investments in wearing princess outfits, and other aesthetic investments in hyper-femininity – a desire for long, flowing hair, and pretty clothes, and a seeming obsession with all things pink. Yet, observations of Sylvie (at nursery, at home and in other contexts) – engaging with matter and through interactions with her peers – reveal that she also readily performs masculine-femininity (Halberstam, 1998). Her place within the early years assemblage is shifting and reworked on a minute-by-minute basis.

Physical 'rough-and-tumble' play is a common feature of early childhood, and is typically associated with rowdy boys taking up space in the heterosexual matrix through displays of hegemonic masculinity (Davies 1989; Epstein 1998; Walkerdine 1993). It is variously tolerated and regulated by parents and practitioners. However, observations of Sylvie illustrate that gendered becomings are generated relationally by objects and senses of all kinds. Through her boisterous physical displays and through the material production of femininity that rupture molar lines (Deleuze and Guattari, 2004), we see that agency is exercised in surprising ways that transgress what might otherwise be read as heteronormativity. By allowing space for such play and further space for critical engagement it becomes possible to reach different conclusions about gender and the becoming child.

Despite her usual choice of 'girly' clothes and displays of complicity with what it is to 'do girl', Sylvie engages in subversive acts that challenge and unsettle, and allow us to see her de-territorialised from striated spaces. Borrowing from Deleuze and Guattari (2004), girls can become constructed as hyper-feminine based upon simplistic gendered assumptions about the minority, marginal or excluded position of women and girls in society more generally. This in turn invokes a notion of deficiency and establishes the foundation for territorialisation into striated spaces. As Tamboukou (2008: 360) explains, 'striated spaces are hierarchical, rule intensive, strictly bounded and confining, whereas smooth spaces are open, dynamic and allow for transformation to occur'. Through un/conscious subversive acts, Sylvie is seeking de-territorialisation from striated spaces of gender conformity or heteronormativity to the smooth spaces described by Tamboukou (op cit.) to play with gender in fluid, dynamic ways, and as this occurs through her daily interactions with people and matter. As such, we witness the important transformations that occur in respect of our understandings of young femininity as enacted by this three year old.

I will attempt to illustrate moments where such de-territorialisation occurs in the routine events of Sylvie's life lived at home, in the nursery and elsewhere. As is the case for many young children, dressing up is a key feature of Sylvie's childhood at nursery and home. She regularly arrives at nursery dressed in any one of an array of outfits, from fairy princess, to Easter bunny, to superhero; and quite often a hybrid of several outfits. Observing her arrival to nursery on one occasion, she was dressed as Sportacus, a fictional character from the children's television show *LazyTown*. The name is a portmanteau of the ancient figure Spartacus and the word 'sport', which represents the character's athleticism. Sportacus describes himself as a 'slightly above-average hero'. There is also a young female character in *LazyTown*, Stephanie, who dresses from head to toe in pink and is equally as athletic as Sportacus – it is Stephanie that Sylvie most readily identifies with through her play; this perhaps explains the puzzlement at Sylvie's enactment as the male superhero upon arrival at nursery. Often Sylvie is greeted with coos of excitement, most typically by the practitioners, at the fairy wings/sparkly slippers/princess dress that she might be wearing. On this particular day, the arrival of Sylvie-Sportacus (albeit with sparkly slippers peeping out from beneath the spandex superhero costume) was greeted with bemused stares and questioning looks. One of Sylvie's peers, Stanley, was eagerly awaiting her arrival so that she might join him in playing dress-up. He was dressed in a red flamenco dress, over the top of his combat trousers, T-shirt adorned with a truck, and heavy boots. He had reserved a similar dress in yellow for Sylvie to wear. On hearing that Sylvie had arrived, Stanley held the dress aloft, but upon recognising that Sylvie was already in a costume, and that therefore the yellow flamenco dress was redundant at this moment, Stanley retreated towards a far corner of the room – apparently dejected, confused and taking time to reconsider his play options. En route Stanley quickly became engaged with another storyline being enacted by his peers nearby; this illustrates the ebb and flow that so readily characterises children's play in early childhood settings. Often play(ing) is subverted or dying in one place but erupting elsewhere. As Sellers (2010) highlights, children feed off their collective imaginings for/with/in their storyline, and feed off imaginings of games and children nearby. We see how the forces of play and interrelationships affect and are affected by other play and relationships and the physical materiality of the setting.

It is interesting to note the momentary affects that Sylvie's transgression of gendered expectations evoked, particularly as Stanley was adorned in a brightly coloured, frilly dress and was, therefore, also complicit in transgressing binary gendered ways of being, but also how quickly Stanley is able to overcome the space of misunderstanding and to merge/fade away into another storyline. This in-between event is useful as it provides opportunities to go beyond heteronormative understandings of how young children negotiate gender through hyper-feminine and hyper-masculine performances. While Sylvie and Stanley are unsettling gendered ways of being, the various reactions and dis/engagements to their embodied states is noteworthy. Both Stanley and Sylvie play with gender through various subversive and complicit acts, in multiple ways and through enactment with objects (dressing-up costumes, role play, weaponry, dance, and so on); how gender is understood through the lived performances of bodies and the gendered inscriptions that act to frame and contain 'boy' and 'girl' in early childhood are brought into sharp focus. Taking up the post-humanist invitation to decentre the subject and to make the familiar strange allows us to transcend what we think is being signified (Jones, 2013). This emergent assemblage simultaneously regulates and ruptures molar lines, where agency is exercised in ways that trouble what is thought of as normal. Below are further visual representations of the contradictory, multiple, inconsistent and shifting embodied performances with matter that challenge gendered inscriptions, which act to contain and limit the possibilities to 'do girl' in early childhood: Viking, swimming costume, sword-wielding girl (Photograph 5.1); and bunny ears-caped crusader – Spider-Man/superhero, lip balm, fairy-wand girl (Photograph 5.2). I want to retain a focus on space, time, matter, interrelationships and the chaotic, rhizomatic nature of children's play, and the possibilities to reconfigure gendered understandings by identifying de-territorialising moments.

Mummies and daddies?

Domesticity and family life provide a re-emergent, familiar and customary focus of Sylvie's play. Sylvie is often found playing with dolls at nursery, often in the 'home corner', seemingly taking on the role of mummy in providing care and nurturance; however, closer attention to the minute occurrences within her enactments provide alternative means of engaging with conceptualisations of gender in early childhood.

Photograph 5.1 Viking, swimming costume, sword-wielding girl

Photograph 5.2 Spider-Man/superhero, lip balm, fairy-wand girl

Sylvie is also 'doctor' to sickly babies; the dolls are deployed by Sylvie and her peers as ventriloquists' dummies, and engage in conversations with one another about a whole array of topics – some of which are thought taboo (Robinson, 2013) – and are deployed in magical, superhero and other fantasy games. Doll-play takes many forms that diverge from those that are readily anticipated, if and when read through the heterosexual matrix (Butler, 2005) characterised by heteronormativity – girls playing with dolls can be read as problematic and limiting to what girls can 'do' through their play. Yet microscopic mapping of play reveals a far more complex and multi-layered assemblage at work. This ebb and flow of doll-play highlights the interrelationships between a multiplicity of materialities and highlights the performative aspects of matter (i.e. how things function within a particular context and in relation to the bodies they encounter (see Lenz Taguchi, 2010).

In an attempt to continue to recast humans and human agency within heterogeneous assemblages alongside other entities (Deleuze and Guattari, 2004), I draw attention to other play events. At home Sylvie is the proud owner of a four-storey, bubblegum-pink dolls' mansion (a gift from her grandparents). From psychological and sociological perspectives this space/object might be read as highly feminised and, therefore, interpreted as providing the means by which gender-stereotypical behaviours and heteronormativity might become reinforced. Like the doll-play described above, a close examination of play with/in and stemming from the dolls' house reveals complexity, uncertainty, ambiguity and transgression. Sylvie plays with the dolls' house differently, on different occasions and with different playmates. As Renold and Mellor (2013) remind us, dominant systems of power (class, race, gender, age, and so on) are omnipresent – they are the mechanics that provide the 'conditions of possibility' for certain subjectivities to emerge, while others are less possible. In early childhood these conditions are deeply embedded at the molar level of sexed subjectivities – i.e. dominant ideas about what it is to be/do boy/girl, but where gender circulates in multiple ways at the molecular level, through and across bodies. So when at home with her older brother the conditions of possibility for Sylvie to play with the dolls' house in particular ways are mediated differently to the play that occurs with the nursery dolls' house with her nursery peers, or when she has 'playdates' at home with her cousins, for example. At home, Sylvie mostly plays with her older brother (Noah, aged six). Sylvie and Noah rarely play with the dolls' house but on the few occasions that they do, fears that it might reinforce heteronormativity are called into question. Typically the chimney stacks are removed – adorned with key rings and LEGO figures so that they become transformed into spaceships at the centre of subterfuge and battle, which are flown around the adjoining rooms as the storyline is narrated, to Sylvie's room, to Noah's room, to the sitting room, then it fades away and morphs into an alternate storyline. Upon coming to rest on various surfaces in Sylvie's bedroom (steps, bookshelf, chest of drawers, bed) the spaceships come to land on the fire engine. Soon the dolls' house is reassembled (the spaceships revert to chimney stacks, albeit with the weaponry still attached) and a fire-rescue scenario is embarked upon. The fire engine (complete with six fire-fighters) sets out on a rescue mission to save the family inhabiting the dolls' house but this storyline then merges into another and another. As Sellers (2010) usefully illustrates through a Deleuzian lens, children's play is full of activity and energy, and the physical territory of the game as well as the surrounding environment, including natural resources and material artefacts, are already chaotically becoming with/in/through the multiplicity of storylines. Sylvie is at the forefront of orchestrating and narrating these play tales with the imaginative (gendered, aged) input of her brother.

Liberal-feminist fears and anxieties that a large pink dolls' house might limit and contain gendered ways of be(com)ing appear unfounded. Concerns to closely manage or excessively regulate young children's lives, particularly girls so as to protect or empower them, are rendered obsolete when a close examination is undertaken to reach alternative understandings. By taking a step back to more closely observe the assemblages, moments of de- and re-territorialisation, it is possible to see the becoming child reworking and negotiating gendered ways of being, and transgressing what is thought knowable, doable and/or acceptable. This raises important questions about what happens when young children transcend or complicate practitioners'/parents' gendered expectations (Blaise, 2013; Jones, 2013; Renold and Mellor, 2013) – what do we (adults: practitioners, parents, researchers) have a responsibility to do? I would suggest that we have a responsibility to observe the transgressions, deconstruct and reconfigure alternative readings (and which present a challenge to dominant ideas encapsulated in the EYFS and developmentalism that implicitly promote ideas around normativity and biological determinism, which justifies the measurement and regulation of childhood; see Osgood (2014) for further discussion). Instead we need to make space for children to play with gender. Braidotti (2013) stresses that sensory encounters – that is, movement and touch – are important ways of being in the world, but that they are inextricably embedded in wider social, political and economic contexts – shaped by hierarchies and injustices. However, this refocusing on the minute happenings within particular early childhood assemblages, which I have outlined, provides the means of engaging in everyday happenings within early childhood that recognise young children as agents and relationally interdependent to the worlds in which they are located and the assemblages of which they form part.

Rossholt (2012) draws attention to children's bodies as more than simply inscribed by external, societal discourses (about how to do child, do gender and do play, for example). Rather children participate in the material production of themselves and others as doing bodies. It is to these corporeal, material and affective practices that I want to draw further attention, by focusing on Sylvie's engagement with objects, subjects, matter on a recent trip to the woods. Upon discovering a makeshift treehouse in the woods, Sylvie became very purposeful, unusually disaffected by getting dirty, intent on further constructing the dwelling, wielding sticks in boisterous fashion and entering hunter-gatherer mode. Following Jones (2013), I raise a number of post-humanist-inspired questions about play, nature and gender: what does becoming a treehouse make possible? What are its foundations and connections with other things? What does it transmit? What intensities does it induce, condone or negate? I go on to explore some of these in the next section.

Nature's playground

A further key area of debate surrounding play and the early years arises from a concern that children are losing touch with nature, spend too much time indoors, are overly engaged with the virtual world and that there is therefore an urgent need for them to reconnect (Save Childhood Movement, 2014; see also Chapter 18). This is promoted in the plethora of books that promote 'nature's playground' through supported or structured outdoor pursuits for young children (for an example, see Danks and Schofield, 2005). And there has been a steady growth in popularity of Forest Schools implanted from the Scandinavian context. Forest Schools are framed by naturalist discourses that promote the idea that children develop in rich natural environments with few pressures, and are consequently less stressed, more confident (especially in the area of taking calculated risks), have better communication skills, are more creative and demonstrate emotional well-being. It rests on the belief that children can be active and learn through movement and use all senses. Taylor (2013), in her recent book, offers a critical assessment of the conflation of nature and childhood, which promotes ideas of purity and innocence. Rather she recasts childhood as messy and implicated; situated and differentiated; and entangled in real-world relations rather than protected in a separate space. Braidotti (2006) urges us to take account of the vitality of non-human bodies and life forms, and their intersections with discursively produced and politically governed human bodies. She promotes a nomadic subjectivity that seeks multiple belongings. Haraway (2004) stresses that:

> We must find another relationship to nature besides reification, possession, appropriation, and nostalgia ... all the partners in the potent conversations that constitute nature must find a new ground for making meanings together.
>
> (p. 158)

Such feminist re-theorisations of nature emphasise the relation between human and more-than-human worlds, and are increasingly being taken up by scholars working in the field of early childhood to reach new understandings – of childhoods as relational and formed of assemblages (for example, Lenz Taguchi, 2010; Jones, 2013; Renold and Mellor, 2013), and how we (as practitioners, parents, researchers) can recognise this relationality and support children to grapple with the challenges of the assemblages of which they form part and that are inevitably shaped by inheritance and coexistence. Taylor (2013) suggests that this encourages inquisitiveness about the asymmetries of relations related to the conditions of possibility (i.e. gender), and would support children in reflecting upon how best to deal with differences and to situate themselves within the worlds in which they live.

Photographs 5.3–5.6 show 'Sylvie in the woods' and could be read as reinforcing dominant naturalistic discourses that celebrate the freedom of nature and the innocence of childhood, which Taylor and Giugni (2012) usefully unsettle. However, the woods are a small oasis in central London, with red buses visible through the trees, a café, and manicured lawns and playground within a few hundred metres. Furthermore, romanticised ideas of childhood innocence and escape to nature are further troubled when a closer examination of the event is undertaken. Sylvie was required to negotiate her engagements with the objects, people and wider conditions of possibility when she encountered a family inside the treehouse. Two children in the hut were considerably older girls (approximately seven and ten years old) and they appeared to have taken temporary ownership of the treehouse. Sylvie was faced with negotiating access into the house, negotiating shared (mis-)understandings of the rules of the game, and

5.3

5.4

5.5

5.6

Photographs 5.3–5.6 Sylvie in the woods

subsequently engaging with matter to demonstrate her competence as a worthy and useful member of this temporary community. She became immersed in collecting sticks to further strengthen the structure in an attempt to make it watertight. There followed a lengthy role play, where she took on the hunter-gatherer role and collected 'food for supper'. Within the treehouse stumps were designated specific functions including a sink, toilet and beds, and one entrance was nominated for adults, another for children. Through this unstructured and serendipitous event Sylvie was afforded space to play, and play with her gendered, aged and embodied relational interdependence to people and matter.

This event demonstrates that when children are afforded space to explore the worlds in which they live in supported and enabling ways, they are able to generate knowledge about the people, places and the events in which they are immersed. This includes conscious or unconscious recognition of the relational interdependence that human beings have with places, spaces and matter, and the shared contribution that this interdependence generates (Taylor and Giugni, 2012). Children's knowledge of, and relationship with their environments, and with the world more generally, become critical. This is precisely what the events in Sylvie's world, outlined in this chapter, have sought to demonstrate. Her critical engagement with the places, people and objects in her world enables negotiation and transgression.

Conclusion

Considerations such as these will clearly have implications for the learning opportunities that connect with these issues – including the approaches taken by adults (practitioners, parents, researchers), the learning materials, resources and research methodologies that are selected, and the 'politics' associated with them. It may also include attention being given to the kind of environments that are created, accessed and provided with and for children's learning. Following Sellers (2010), such informed professional, adult choices should recognise that

> Young children's understandings are equitably expert to those of adult worlds; children are embodied within *their* life-living experiences of their negotiating [their] childhood(s) in ways that adults cannot be, yet also in ways similar to adults working from/with/in their experiences, past and present of life and living.
>
> (p. 557)

So, approaching the becoming child through the lens applied in this chapter highlights that *everything* surrounding children matters. How children come to understand themselves (as gendered be(com)ings) is inextricably about the experiences, activities and events, whether direct or indirect, that occur within environments that aid children's learning and development. Play (and the in-between chaotic lines of flight that characterise children's play) occurs through un/conscious engagements with people, places, objects, matter and emotions. It is incumbent that we – as adults privileged to be involved in early childhood in some sense or another – recognise this and make space for children to play (with their multiple be(com)ings). The generative possibilities of spontaneous play characterised by the ebb and flow of ideas, innovation, creativity and imagination allow children to explore and transgress, and to make the familiar strange. It is our responsibility to make space for this and crucially to learn from their expertise and experiences as children living and negotiating childhood.

Notes

Sylvie is my daughter. I chose to focus on these events from her childhood-lived as they afforded the opportunity to explore her becomings through and within early childhood assemblages at home, at nursery and in other contexts. She has given her informed consent to be the focus of this chapter.

'Stanley' is a pseudonym; his informed consent and that of this parents has been given.

'Becoming' in a Deleuzo-Guattarian sense is markedly different from psychological and sociological perspectives of being and becoming, which view the child as always being in states of development towards an ultimate end-point of actualised adulthood. The Deleuzo-Guattarian imaginary of becoming affords opportunities to view children as embodied be(com)ings.

Questions to promote reflection

1 In what ways do you enable children to play *with* gender, or allow space and opportunities for children to negotiate, resist and celebrate gendered ways of being through their play with people and things?

2 What kinds of environments, recognising gender issues, are created in your setting that can be accessed by all children, and provide for the children's learning and becoming?

3 What occasions have you observed in your setting where it is possible to see the becoming child reworking and negotiating gendered ways of being and transgressing what is thought knowable, doable and/or acceptable?

4 What instances have you seen of young children negotiating gender through hyper-feminine and hyper-masculine performances? How have you responded?

5 On what occasions have you been able to observe the various ways and means by which children negotiate, resist, celebrate, indulge and transgress gendered ways of being through their play? How have you reacted?

References and further reading (in bold)

Blaise, M. (2013) Activating micropolitical practices in the early years: (re)assembling bodies and participant observations. In R. Coleman and J. Ringrose (eds) *Deleuze and Research Methodologies*. Edinburgh: Edinburgh University Press.

Braidotti, R. (2006) *Transpositions: On Nomadic Ethics*. Cambridge: Polity Press.
Braidotti, R. (2013) *The Posthuman*. Cambridge: Polity Press.
Butler, J. (1990) *Gender Trouble: Feminism and the Subversion of Identity*. London: Routledge.
Butler, J. (1993) *Bodies That Matter*. London: Routledge.
Butler, J. (2005) *Undoing Gender*. London: Routledge.
Danks, F. and Schofield, J. (2005) *Nature's Playground: Activities, Crafts and Games to Encourage Children to Get Outdoors*. London: Francis Lincoln.
Davies, B. (1989) *Frogs and Snails and Feminist Tales: Preschool Children and Gender*. Sydney: Allen and Unwin.
Deleuze, G. and Guattari, F. (2004) *A Thousand Plateaus*. London: Athlone Press.
Epstein, D. (1998) *Failing Boys? Issues of Gender and Underachievement*. Buckingham: Open University Press.
Halberstam, J. (1998) *Female Masculinity*. Durham: Duke University Press.
Haraway, D. (2004) Otherworldly conversation; terrain topics; local terms. In D. Haraway (ed.) *The Haraway Reader*. London: Routledge.
Holland, P. (2003) *We Don't Play with Guns Here: War, Weapon and Superhero Play in the Early Years*. Buckingham: Open University Press.
Jones, L. (2013) Becoming child/becoming dress. *Global Studies in Childhood*, 3(3): 289–296. Available online at: http://www.wwwords.co.uk/gsch/content/pdfs/3/issue3_3.asp (accessed 10 April 2014).
Lenz Taguchi, H. (2010) *Going Beyond the Theory/Practice Divide in Early Childhood Education: Introducing an Intra-active Pedagogy*. London: Routledge.
MacNaughton, G. (2000) *Rethinking Gender in Early Childhood Education*. London: Paul Chapman.
Osgood, J. (2012) *Narratives from the Nursery: Negotiating Professional Identities in Early Childhood*. London: Routledge.
Osgood, J. (2014) Playing with Gender: making space for post-human childhood(s). In J. Moyles (ed.) *Early Years Foundations: Critical Issues*. Maidenhead: Open University Press.
Renold, E. and Mellor, D. (2013) Deleuze and Guattari in the nursery: towards an ethnographic, multi-sensory mapping of gendered bodies and becomings. In R. Coleman and J. Ringrose (eds) *Deleuze and Research Methodologies*. Edinburgh: Edinburgh University Press.
Robinson, K.H. (2013) *Innocence, Knowledge and the Construction of Childhood: The Contradictory Nature of Sexuality and Censorship in Children's Contemporary Lives*. London: Routledge.
Rossholt, N. (2012) Food as touch/touching the food: the body in-place and out of place in preschool. *Educational Philosophy and Theory*, 44(3): 323–334.
Save Childhood Movement (2014) *Manifesto for the Early Years: Putting Children First*. Available online at: http://www.savechildhood.net (accessed 1 April 2014).
Sellers, M. (2010) Re(con)ceiving young children's curricular performativity. *International Journal of Qualitative Studies in Education*, 23(5): 557–577.
Tamboukou, M. (2008) Machinic assemblages: women, art education and space. *Discourse*, 29(3): 359–375.
Taylor, A. (2013) *Reconfiguring the Natures of Childhood*. London: Routledge.
Taylor, A. and Giugni, M. (2012) Common worlds: reconceptualising inclusion in early childhood communities. *Contemporary Issues in Early Childhood*, 13(2): 108–119.
Walkerdine, V. (1993) Beyond developmentalism? *Theory and Psychology*, 3: 451–469.

PART 2
Play is learning

'Most children's learning potential is limitless: only their lack of experience and accumulated knowledge limits their abilities. It is through play that children acquire this experience and actively construct patterns identified and learnt through play to make sense of the new experience or absorb the new information.'

Moyles, J. (2012) *The A to Z of Play in Early Childhood.* Maidenhead: Open University Press: 28.

6

Babies at play: musicians, artists and scientists

Peter Elfer

Summary

Working professionally with babies and young children is one of the most complex and difficult jobs, despite its joys and satisfactions. Yet, for all the acknowledgement of the early years as crucial to well-being over the lifespan, work with babies is given the least recognition and status. This chapter is partly about the innate brilliance and creativity of babies, but it is also about the difference it makes to babies to have the presence of an adult who is genuinely interested and admiring of a baby's brilliant investigations and overtures. Adults can only do this consistently well if they, too, feel valued and admired in their role.

Introduction: babies as brilliant thinkers

When I think about babies' finely tuned sensitivity to the people and things around them, I always seem to return to a description by Alvarez (1992), a child psychotherapist who has long experience of working with children who are autistic. She concludes:

> By demonstrating the baby's sensitivity to the form and quality of experience, observation and research have changed the conventional picture of the infant. He is no longer just a . . . passionately loving and destructive creature, finding and losing love and nurture. He is also, when the conditions allow, a little music student listening to the patterning of his auditory experience, a little art student studying the play and pattern of light and shade and its changes . . . a little scientist working to yoke his experiences together and understand them.
>
> (p. 76)

Alvarez uses the words both 'baby' and 'infant'. These words are often used interchangeably, although formally 'infant' means 'without spoken language'. So, in this sense, we might think of the word infant meaning roughly birth to first birthday. In this chapter, I use the term babies to mean from birth to around 18 months, when most babies are actively using words, walking and exploring. In much writing about young children, 'early childhood' often seems to really mean two, three and four year olds – and the months and years before do not get the same level of attention.

Real eyes and realise

The pun of looking with 'real eyes' and 'realise-ing' how much there is to see is useful in thinking about observation. This chapter draws its inspiration from the founding observations of Froebel (1782–1852) and his beautifully detailed naturalistic observations of babies and young children. The term 'naturalistic' means observations that see the baby 'holistically', in ordinary and everyday situations and interactions. Many of the pioneers who came after Froebel drew on the power of naturalistic observations, yet while these pioneers understood their observations in different ways, what they had in common was their deep respect for babies and their understanding of babies' immense capacities for playful creativity and understanding.

I have spent much of the last 20 years observing in baby rooms in nurseries; the work that goes on in these rooms is exciting, often joyful, but also extraordinarily complex. I have learned an enormous amount from the people who spend their days in these rooms – the babies and toddlers as well as the staff. Summing up my experience in a few points, I would say:

- the complexity and challenge of the work is desperately underestimated (Goouch and Powell, 2012; McDowall Clark and Bayliss, 2012)
- there is an immense responsibility in keeping the babies free from injury
- the delicate work of building sensitive partnerships with family members – work can be deeply pleasurable and satisfying, but long periods of crying can be exhausting.

The work of the baby room can easily become isolated from that of the rest of the nursery, and seen as little more than feeding, holding and nappy changing. If that is the view of those outside the baby room, it can quickly undermine those inside.

Another point is that, because the staff are so close, they often do not seem to see how much they matter to individual babies. This is true not only for the babies' emotional well-being but also for their liveliness and engagement in their playful explorations. I hope the three babies, Alex (7 months), Amy (13 months) and Ellen (18 months), through observations below, can demonstrate this last point. Before turning to these observations, though, I want to briefly remind ourselves of the insights and understandings we have inherited from some of the well-known early childhood pioneers.

Sitting on shoulders

Babies and toddlers are sometimes seen sitting on the shoulders of family adults. The height helps them to see much more and they often seem excited by the distance from the ground and the new perspectives this gives them. We, too, can enrich our perspectives about play by sitting on the shoulders of the pioneers. Here, I mention just five: Froebel, Piaget, Vygotsky, Goldschmied and Trevarthen. My aim is to offer only the briefest of reminders of some of the powerful insights they have given us as resources for our own thinking about babies' play.

Froebel's observation of babies' smiles intimates:

> ... the first smile, which instantly distinguishes the young human being from any other creature. It shows that the child has reached the stage where he is becoming conscious and aware of himself. It is an essentially human characteristic . . . it is the way in which the child, while as yet without any means of expression, first enters into communication with other minds. The first smile is therefore the expression of an independent human mind . . .
>
> (Lilley 1967: 75)

It is through such careful detailed observations that the greatest advances have been made in our ability to understand and respond to babies as 'people' with feelings and powerful capacities (Goldschmied and Jackson, 2004). In Froebel's time, it was rare for babies to be cared for outside of the family. Now provision for babies in nurseries is commonplace and raises the question of how Froebel's ideas might apply in these settings.

Goldschmied was the pioneer for the 'key person' in nurseries, based on the importance for the baby of interactions with mainly one or two named practitioners (Elfer, 2012). For Froebel, such adults meant primarily mothers, but we now know that nursery practitioners can take this role, too (Howes, 1999). Froebel also believed that babies and young children learn from birth through experiencing natural environments. The treasure basket and the idea of heuristic play (both developed by Goldschmied over a lifetime of work with under-threes) are now well accepted. Goldschmied was careful to point out that children were always dependent upon the key person's or parents' 'calm presence', 'containing' the infant's anxiety to release curiosity as he or she explores new and unfamiliar items (EGFAPT, 2013).

When considering Piaget (1896–1980), his description of sensorimotor exploration, meaning literally to experience (via the senses) through action is indisputable. Alex (seven months), in the cameos below, was doing this for much of his time in nursery, moving things to his mouth and 'sensing' their properties by weight, taste, size and fit. Amy (13 months) and Ellen (nearly 18 months) also did this, although not nearly as much.

The senses act as the babies' mobile laboratory, fully equipped as they are to explore and investigate any objects that they come across. Vygotsky enabled us to understand the crucial importance of the social context of young children's thinking and learning, and the role of others who can include both adults and other babies:

> Selby and Bradley (2003) sat trios of babies between 6 and 10 months of age . . . at equal distances from one another in a triangle. Complex and subtle expressive behaviours and exchanges established mini dramas between the interactants, demonstrating a far greater capacity for sociable encounters than has been expected for infants . . .
>
> (cited in Trevarthen, 2005: 78–79)

Much of Trevarthen's work has demonstrated the central role of emotions in interactions including trust, admiration, pride and shame, whether in babies' interactions together or a baby and practitioner's interactions in a nursery (2005: 84). What does Trevarthen mean by 'pride' and 'shame' here? He refers to the importance of attachment theory and the significance of an attachment with special people (family adults or nursery key person) acting as a secure base to enable infants to feel safe to explore. However, he also shows how feeling safe, on its own, does not explain why young children are so motivated to explore:

> . . . discovery of meaning is not something the child wants to do on his or her own . . . Meaning is made by emotions that may turn to address others, to share the fun of discovering and doing.
>
> (2005: 63)

It is these emotions that include both pride and shame. When a baby's gestures, vocalisations or physical explorations are admired by others, there is, of course, pride; however, there can be feelings of shame, too. Babies are not born with shame but come to feel it in their interactions with others. When a practitioner moves away from a baby or toddler having settled them into an activity, it may be with a feeling of relief to attend to other pressing demands. But what feelings does her departure evoke in the baby? For a while, the baby may manage to remain alone, engaged in the activity, but she may also feel how any one of us might feel when we are doing something and those around us turn away – that what we are engaged in is not of interest, is not taken seriously, understood or admired. Treasure baskets and heuristic play are important resources for babies and toddlers provided by an attentive practitioner. Even more important is the practitioner him/herself as a resource of calm presence and the conveyor of genuine interest, curiosity and admiration.

In the next section, the naturalistic observations of Alex, Amy and Ellen are taken from a study of babies and young children in different kinds of nursery (Elfer, 2009). Each of the children in the study was observed between four and seven times, for around an hour, at two-weekly intervals. What did these careful observations tell us about each baby's explorations and ideas?

Three babies exploring, thinking and feeling

Cameo 1: Alex (seven months)

Alex was in the baby room (for between six and nine babies) of a small private nursery. When I first met Alex, he seemed small in contrast to the other babies and rather vulnerable. The staff seemed to have the pace and timing of their handling and rocking of the babies just right, but in the first three or four observations Alex always seemed to be crying or on the brink of crying. However, as the observations progressed, he seemed to settle a little, although always showing his struggle between anxiety (needing to be held and soothed) and curiosity (mouthing and handling, reaching, stretching and crawling). Sometimes, particularly towards the end of the day, anxiety got the better of him. At other times, curiosity prevailed!

Great attention was paid to the physical environment of the baby room. Resources were chosen to offer varied sensory experiences, with soft rugs and materials, and objects made of natural materials and with different properties. Alex spent a great deal of his time sucking and mouthing objects (see Cameo 2).

Cameo 2

Alex is sitting on Mikela's lap, facing outwards. In his hands is a wooden cylinder containing a rattle. Using both hands, he presses it to his mouth and gums, working it round his mouth. It is fumbled, pressed between his two half-open, half-fisted hands, neither big enough to grasp it firmly . . .

This kind of oral and manual exploration was seen many times. Sometimes it was for comfort but, in others, Alex had an expression of such intense concentration that even if the motivation were to comfort himself or soothe his teething gums, his desire to understand what it was that he had in his hands seemed extraordinary.

There were other examples of this intense exploratory endeavour (see Cameo 3).

Cameo 3

Strapped into a low wooden chair, Alex seems quite happy to be pulled up into a semi-circle of other babies. Then his demeanour seems to move up a gear, sitting upright, as if his body is electrified, alert, constantly in a state of small but energetic movements, almost like reflexes. As he looks around, alternately focusing and scanning, he sometimes seems to reach for imaginary objects . . . he turns, and reaches in a similar sudden rapid grasp towards his neighbour, almost out of reach in the adjacent chair, then to the neighbour on the other side. His limbs are working all the time, sometimes in unison with his gaze, sometimes as if completely independently.

One might think there is nothing unusual about this kind of exploration in a seven month old. It is easy to see Alex as a perfect example of Piaget's notion of sensorimotor exploration. Yet there may be more to Alex's intense reaching and stretching than only the sensorimotor exploration of objects.

Winnicott (1896–1971) helped us to understand how babies have no concept yet of singularity – of how people and objects are entities with discrete boundaries. Babies do not yet understand what *is* the object and what *is not* the object. Similarly, they do not know what is themselves and what is not themselves, where they begin and where they end, what is 'me' and what is 'not me' (Schmidt Neven, 1997: 93). By stretching his arm as far as it will go, Alex gains a sense of the limit of his arm. He is discovering where he begins and where he feels he ends. This is significant psychologically as well as physically. All of us, throughout our lives, are stretching to see what might be reached and what are our limits, not necessarily in a physical sense, but mentally too, to explore the 'new idea' that for a while we are sure is there but may feel just out of reach.

Many of Alex's explorations could not have happened without the practical assistance of the staff. They were hard working in attending to the babies' physical needs throughout the day and soothing them when they were upset. When Alex's key person, Mehta, was available, his familiarity with her helped him to a new level of exploration, reducing his levels of anxiety and distress. Others managed this for Alex, too. I saw a very experienced member of staff change his nappy, giving him all her attention as she spoke to him in a low, melodic voice that could almost have been singing. I had rarely seen him more still and attentive before his legs burst into a kind of ecstatic dance in both delight and response to her.

Yet Mehta and other staff were often not very available to Alex in a sustained way. The staff were always responsive to distress, soothing a baby and supporting her or him to engage in another episode of playful exploration. But once a baby was occupied, staff put the baby down to attend to another baby or have a short break. As staff did this, I saw what they often did not see. As soon as they turned away from one baby, that baby's exploratory activity, whatever it was, declined and sometimes stopped altogether.

The staff's presence was vital to babies' explorations through practical assistance and as an emotionally secure base, but it was vital in a third way, too. It was clear babies wanted staff's *interest* in their clever ideas and investigations. It is important for all of us to feel that our endeavours attract the interest of others and sometimes even admiration. Alex really seemed to need and to flourish when staff were closely interested in him and admired his explorations.

Cameo 4: Amy (13 months)

Amy attended her nursery centre, a large maintained nursery school with extended day care, from 8.30 am to 6 pm three days each week. When I started the observations, it soon became apparent that the staff in the room worked closely together by sharing all the different tasks with different children rather than through a key person approach. In the first observation, a member of staff had started giving Amy her lunch but then left to attend to another child. Amy then sought attention from Jack who was sitting nearby, attracting his attention by touching his arm whenever she was ready for another spoonful. She would sit in her high chair, seeming to enjoy her lunch and without crying or signs of distress, but always moving and stretching as if her body was full of longing to be interacting with the adults around her. She often looked towards Jack, although his attention was often needed elsewhere, her face full of anticipation as she looked up to him. But she also looked with eagerness to other staff and to the other children.

When Jack left to fetch his own lunch, Amy did not cry but continued to reach and stretch with her body. When Jack returned within minutes to sit beside her, she again looked up at him intently. However, she soon seemed to begin to lose some of her energy and vitality and, after lunch, Jack did settle her to sleep.

As the observations progressed, I saw this pattern of intense interest and engagement occur mostly when an adult was nearby and interested, but some collapse in Amy's spirits, even when she was clearly not tired, when adults suddenly left her. The staff were always responsive to her but they gave this attention collectively, with no consistent person ever spending continuous time with Amy.

On one occasion, a practitioner watched attentively while Amy played with two coloured balls. The difference Sonia's attention makes to Amy's play is clear (Cameo 5).

Cameo 5

When Amy clasps a ball in each hand, she seems to love to bang them together, smiling and looking at Sonia as if for recognition. Sonia watches what Amy is doing making brief comments . . . Amy seems sustained by Sonia's interest . . . Suddenly Amy coughs loudly and Sonia comments, 'Oh dear, oh dear!' Amy looks at Sonia with intense curiosity . . . She seems to think for a minute and then forces a tiny little artificial cough and watches Sonia intently . . .

They played a little longer before Sonia turned away to talk to another member of staff. Amy then turned away too, but still played with the plastic balls. When Sonia turned back, Amy also seemed to renew her interest in the interaction. There were many more examples of Amy's attention seeming to mirror adults' attention to her.

On another occasion, Sarah helped Amy to stand at a table, which supported her and where she could play with some wooden shapes. She stood, half leaning on the table and half attentive to the shapes. Her fingering of the wooden pieces seems absent minded, as if she needed Sarah to concentrate on her more. But Sarah was soon called away and Amy then dropped down from the table and crawled to sit with another member of staff who had just arrived on duty. That person too attended to her briefly but then left to be with a small circle of children. Amy followed, crawling right into the middle of the circle, looking pleased as she positioned herself in the centre of the group. With neither children nor adults now responsive to her, she crawled away again.

Only just embarking on her second year, Amy shows what capabilities she has already developed. Physically, she is adept at crawling. Walking will quickly follow and this will give her many additional advantages. The staff obviously care greatly about Amy and are interested in her ideas. However, the way the staff work means that Amy is also learning that no one member of staff will spend very much continuous time with her. Amy is very good at communicating what a difference individual staff attention can make to her explorations and thinking; however, it sometimes seems as if the most important resource of all for the children – the consistent, sustained individual attention of a staff member – is barely understood.

Cameo 6: Ellen (18 months)

Ellen was one of 18 children aged 12 to 48 months, in two mixed-aged, interconnecting rooms in a voluntary nursery with an active key person approach. Her key person was Shabana with Sara as back-up. In the first observation, she cried as her father left her in Shabana's arms but was not so distressed that she could not be comforted. When she was more settled, a different practitioner helped her sit up at the 'drawing table', talking to her about what she might do. I noticed that Ellen soon got down when that person had gone. Finding a plastic ball, about the size of a grapefruit, she tapped it against her mouth several times before quite suddenly throwing it, watching it drop and roll away. As she walked the perimeter of the room, she encountered me and picking up a teddy, gave it to me without waiting for me to respond, perhaps offering me something to occupy me in a way that had been done to her many times?

In a subsequent observation, Ellen was left in Sara's arms: she continued to hug her, kissing the top of her head and then taking her to the water tray, before sitting at a nearby table to talk with other practitioners and children. Some readers may be surprised at Sara's open expression of physical affection; however, this nursery has done much work on child protection and safeguarding as part of their overall attachment approach. They are vigilant to keep under continual review, working in close partnership with families, what kind of physical affection – and when – is appropriate and important for individual children.

Cameo 7

Ellen stands at the water tray, holding the edge, but turning back to look at Sara, her expression a mixture of curiosity about what Sara was saying and confusion (about why Sara was not attending to her?). Frequently, she would turn back to the tray but always very briefly, before turning her head right back again, to look with curiosity and bewilderment at Sara's interactions with others. It felt very much as if she could not believe that Sara was not attending to her. After five or ten minutes, with almost no interest in the water trough, Ellen's lips pucker into something that approaches, but is not quite, a lip movement to make a raspberry sound.

Perhaps 'projecting' things (the plastic ball and the raspberry) is Ellen's way of expelling difficult feelings and showing us this? Ellen then switched to painting and Sara helped her with the apron but, otherwise, she was left to paint alone. For the next ten or fifteen minutes she worked steadily, experimenting with different techniques, ways of holding the brush and strokes, exactly expressing the creativity of the artist that Alvarez describes (see also Chapter 16).

Towards the end of the observations, when I had been observing Ellen for more than two months, there was an interesting interaction between us (Cameo 8).

Cameo 8

> . . . she notices me watching and looks back with interest. Then very definitely she brings a beaker to me. I take it, holding it in mid-air between us so that she can take it back if she wishes. But she moves away . . . Playing alone again, it was some 15 minutes before she suddenly noticed the beaker still by my chair, now with a 'plate of toast' put there by another child. She collects this with an air of confidence, carries it to the other side of the room and sits pretending to eat and drink. She catches my eye watching her and seems to think it is a game of peek-a-boo. She smiles a broad smile, the most response I have seen from her, and I cannot resist but to join in . . . She smiles again broadly but then breaks off as if returning her attention to concentrate on drinking and eating . . .

Ellen was clearly attached to Shabana and to Sara. The sadness she often expressed, as she had to leave her father in the mornings, seemed better soothed by them than by other staff. Ellen would also ask where Shabana was if she had to leave the room. Yet while Shabana or other practitioners would offer practical assistance to Ellen in response to their understanding of her actions and interests, this was not accompanied by much sustained attention or interest in what she was doing. Both Shabana and Sara are proud of her and Sara expressed this openly. Analysis of her activities showed many schemas, particularly around containment, as well as her mark making. Yet once undertaking an activity, she often seemed only partly engaged with it or abandoned it shortly after the adult who had helped her get started moved away.

In the episode towards the end of the observations, when she bought me the beaker and later played peek-a-boo, I wondered if she had come to notice my close 'noticing of her'. As an observer in a busy nursery, all of my time is available to be able to notice in such a focused and interested way. It is much more difficult for the staff with so many practical tasks to attend to.

Noticing practitioners noticing babies

Alex, Amy and Ellen give many examples of babies' impressive capabilities. Other writers have written much more detailed descriptions of how babies and toddlers show their thinking through their music, art and investigations – see, for example, Dorothy Selleck's beautiful chapter on under-threes (Selleck, 2001). What I have been more concerned to do is to focus attention on *both* what each baby or toddler might be doing *and* how this is influenced by particular attentive adults. I have illustrated how the explorations of babies and toddlers can be energised by the interest, curiosity and admiration of closely familiar adults.

Providing this individualised attention, with its careful thinking and emotion components, is immensely difficult work (Elfer, 2013). There is currently a great deal of anxiety about child protection and safeguarding in early years settings. However, many practitioners are understandably reluctant to be too emotionally or physically responsive to any young child, especially a baby or toddler, for fear it is misunderstood.

Vigilance about safety and safeguarding is clearly a vital part of early years work. But so too is consistent and emotionally attuned responsiveness. Babies and young children communicate their needs by evoking in the adults around them powerful feelings of wanting to understand and respond – to soothe, comfort, protect and collaborate with fun. It is very difficult to be passive in response to a baby or toddler, and few family adults would try. Nursery staff, however, are caught between the desire to respond and the pressure to be seen to be 'not too involved'. The demand of inspectors for increasing amounts of written documentation does not help. In the absence of strong leadership and support, it is understandable that many staff may sometimes avoid, even consciously, the overtures of babies for fear of being seen as too responsive (Elfer, 2012; 2013).

Fortunately there is some exciting research work to understand better how best to support the practitioners doing the most emotionally and intellectually complex of all early years work: work with babies and toddlers. Goouch and Powell (2012) have looked at new ways of supporting baby room practitioners through a social networking site. Page (2011) has focused more directly on the desire of mothers that nursery practitioners should love their babies, what practitioners may feel about this and the notion of 'professional love'. In collaboration with child psychotherapists, I have been developing forms of professional reflection groups for nursery practitioners that aim to be more thoughtful about the diversity and meanings of babies' play and the emotional complexities of managing emotionally close interactions with them (Elfer and Dearnley, 2007; Elfer, 2012).

Conclusion

There is a strong and shared desire among the early years community to be seriously respectful and supportive of babies as individuals with great individual creativity in which emotion plays a central role in their investigations. However, to put this into widespread effect, we must be much more serious in our collective efforts to find new ways to talk about the emotions that play a central role in how practitioners notice and respond to the play and creativity of babies and toddlers.

Questions to promote reflection

1   Do any episodes of play from your own early childhood stand out for you? If yes, what were they like and in what ways did adults help or hinder your playful ideas?
2   As an adult, can you think of being in the company recently of a baby or toddler under 18 months? What was that baby or toddler doing and communicating to you about what she (or he) was doing?
3   What difference did you feel your presence made to their thinking and exploration?
4   Do you think your unique ideas and ways of supporting their play are understood and recognised by those other adults around you?

References and further reading (in bold)

Alvarez, A. (1992) *Live Company: Psychoanalytic Psychotherapy with Autistic, Borderline, Deprived and Abused Children*. London: Routledge.

Elfer, P. (2009) 5000 hours: facilitating intimacy in the care of children under three attending full time nursery. Unpublished doctoral dissertation, University of East London, UK.

Elfer, P. (2012) Emotion in nursery work: work discussion as a model of critical professional reflection. *Early Years: An International Journal of Research and Development*, 32(2): 129–141.

Elfer, P. (2013) Emotional aspects of nursery policy and practice – progress and prospect. *European Early Childhood Education Research Journal*. Available online at: http://www.tandfonline.com/doi/full/10.1080/1350293X.2013.798464 (accessed 8 April 2014).

Elfer, P. and Dearnley, D. (2007) Nurseries and emotional well being: evaluating an emotionally containing model of professional development. *Early Years: An International Journal of Research and Development*, 27(3): 267–279.

Elinor Goldschmied Froebel Archive Project (EGFAPT) (2013) *Elinor Goldschmied (1910–2009) Discovered Treasure*. Funded and published by the Froebel Trust.

Goldschmied, E. and Jackson, S. (2004) *People Under Three: Young Children in Daycare*, 2nd edn. London: Routledge.

Goouch, K. and Powell, S. (2012) *The Baby Room: Research: Summary 1*. December. Esmée Fairbairn Foundation.

Howes, C. (1999) Attachment relationships in the context of multiple caregivers. In J. Cassidy and P.R. Shaver (eds) *The Handbook of Attachment: Theory, Research and Clinical Applications*. London: Guildford Press.

Lilley, I. (1967) *Friedrich Froebel. A Selection from His Writings*. Cambridge: Cambridge University Press.

McDowall Clark, R. and Bayliss, S. (2012) 'Wasted down there': policy and practice with the under-threes. *Early Years: An International Journal of Research and Development*, 32(2): 229–242.

Page, J. (2011) Do mothers want professional carers to love their babies? *Journal of Early Childhood Research*, 9: 310–323.

Schmidt Neven, R. (1997) *Emotional Milestones from Birth to Adulthood: A Psychodynamic Approach*. London: Jessica Kingsley.

Selleck, D. (2001) Being under 3 years of age: enhancing quality experiences. In G. Pugh (ed.) *Contemporary Issues in the Early Years: Working Collaboratively for Children*, 3rd edn. London: Paul Chapman.

Trevarthen, C. (2005) Action and emotion in development of cultural intelligence: why infants have feelings like ours. In J. Nadel and D. Muir (eds) *Emotional Development*. Oxford: Oxford University Press.

7

Learning from play: hunting and gathering

Rod Parker-Rees

Summary

We are all familiar with models of development and education that focus attention on the pursuit of knowledge. This form of learning may seem well matched to a curriculum that specifies what individual learners need to acquire but, by creating an artificial separation between the 'work' of the hunt for knowledge and the 'play' of social gatherings, it distorts our understanding of how we come to know about our environment. In this chapter I will make a case for greater recognition of the role of playful, enjoyable, social processes in gathering or letting in the contextual information that transforms knowing into understanding.

Introduction

I believe that two different kinds of learning can be supported by play. One of these can be characterised as 'getting in' information; this is learning that results from purposeful engagement with our environment. If this learning is thought of as a form of hunting for understanding, 'working it out' or abstracting it, the other kind of learning can be thought of as a form of gathering, of 'picking things up' as we go along, without necessarily knowing in advance what we might come across or even noticing what we have noticed. This 'letting in' of information is an intuitive process by which we 'get to know' extraordinarily complex webs of relationships between objects, events and people without needing to trouble our conscious awareness. Perhaps we should think of gathering more in terms of social processes, the getting-together of people rather than the collecting of resources, because relaxed, social gatherings are particularly conducive to this letting in of knowledge about other people, customs and cultural values.

Cameo 1: Rosie plays with pens and lids

Six-month-old Rosie is sitting at the kitchen table with her mother. On the table is a pack of fat felt-tip pens and some paper. Rosie holds a pen lightly in her left hand as she picks another up in her right hand and begins to 'draw' on the paper – she clearly knows what pens are for – but the pen still has its lid on. Her mum reaches out, 'Shall we take the lid off?' Rosie murmurs assent, but when mum has to take a firmer hold, with two hands, to get the lid off, she shrieks with frustration – 'Wait, wait, wait, wait – Oh it's hard. There you go, go on, you do it then – on there – Oh', Rosie now pants with excitement, waving the freed pen but also making an exaggerated expression with wide open mouth – 'Oh – funny face.' Rosie tries to put the pen back in its box, mum holds out the lid, 'There's the lid', and Rosie immediately tries to fit the pen into the lid as mum carefully adjusts its position, 'Push it back in, clever girl.' As soon as the pen and the lid are connected Rosie yanks the pen out of mum's hand and waves it about triumphantly. Mum gasps to share her delight and Rosie immediately puts the lid end back in mum's hand, which her mum immediately recognises as a cue to grip the lid so that Rosie can pull the pen free – 'Take it off – oh!', and then try to put it back in: 'Put it back in.' This takes several attempts, with mum moving the lid to meet the pen as Rosie concentrates fixedly on controlling its movement, making little gasps of effort with each stab. After six near misses, mum uses her other hand to guide the pen into the lid, 'Ooooooh come on, do it?' – she is clearly giving no more help than is needed, so that Rosie remains in control. Rosie flashes eye contact and then murmurs 'Aaaah' (echoing mum's 'Oooooh') as the pen and lid finally make contact, 'Yeeaah!', but she immediately pulls the pen out again, *'Oop!'* Rosie says, 'eh, eh, Geh! Geh!' as she manoeuvres the pen and mum echoes, 'Try again?' – 'Eh – *There!*' – 'Aah oooh oh, deh!' 'There!' as the pen and lid are again fitted together. Again, Rosie immediately snatches the pen back out of the lid but with her eyes still fixed on the opening of the lid she quickly brings the pen back, saying 'Deh – aDEH – oh-oh-oh' as she again joins the dance of fitting pen to lid. Both Rosie and her mum are accompanying the effort with extended sounds, which rise in intensity until both reach a simultaneous peak as Rosie again manages to pull the pen, with its lid, out of mum's hand. Rosie gazes for a few seconds at the point where pen and lid meet – 'Done!' before she puts the lid back into mum's hand again, 'Deh' – 'Take it off? – off', and then again concentrates on fitting them together again, with mum's help – but the lid slips from mum's hand and falls to the floor just as the pen makes contact with the paper. Rosie switches her attention to making a mark – 'Oooh – Deh! Dere.'

Rosie is clearly engaging actively with her world, making sense of the made sense that surrounds her, with a particular, earnest focus on exploring the way in which the pen and its lid can be put together and taken apart.

This process of getting in information about our environment by actively experimenting with it and noting how our actions affect what we perceive is central to our understanding of how play supports learning. The repetition and variation that characterise playful activity allow us (at any age) to jiggle and adjust, to finesse the fit between our personal idiosyncrasies and the public possibilities our environment offers us. Whether fitting a pen into its lid, wiggling a piece from an inset puzzle until it slips into its place or exploring how we can fit our principled practice into a prescribed policy framework, play enables us to adjust our fit with our environment.

While Rosie is playing with the pen and its lid, and getting in information about the way they fit together, her absorbed engagement is kept afloat by a sea of cultural support. Everything about her environment is unnatural, everything has been made to afford possibilities for certain kinds of action: the kitchen provides a safe, comfortable place for focused interactions; the table and highchair ensure that Rosie and her mother are able to see eye to eye, and also that everything is conveniently reachable; the pens and lids have been designed to be held by small hands and to snap together in a satisfying (if rather challenging) way; her mother provides sensitive, responsive assistance to scaffold her efforts at manipulation and uses her voice both to provide a running commentary and to echo and acknowledge Rosie's shifting moods. While Rosie does not seem to be consciously aware of the circles of support that surround her as she plays, focusing more on 'in and out', 'tightness' and fine motor control, she is nevertheless letting in a mass of information about her place in a cultural world of made things and in a relationship with her mother.

This relationship of active, intersubjective engagement between adult and child seems to be uniquely human (Parker-Rees, 2007). Where other animals may have opportunities to learn by imitation of adults, human infants are constantly exposed to a *pedagogical* social environment – a world in which adults are willing to give up time to enter into the intricate, sophisticated sort of partnership seen in Rosie's mum's sensitive support for her engagement with cultural tools, practices and values. Human children are not left to blossom untended in a natural environment; they are projects, nurtured, shaped and made by the social and cultural environment that surrounds them and that they also influence – not only in terms of the sheer volume of 'stuff' that parents accumulate but also the new behaviours children train their parents to adopt. Tronick (2005: 311) insists that we should see this negotiation of roles as co-creation rather than co-construction, because co-construction 'implies a pre-existing plan' whereas co-creation 'emphasizes that the meaning made is a process in which each individual's meaning is changed and created into a new meaning' – social conversations do not have predetermined aims or intended outcomes but we enjoy them because they allow participants to get to know one another in rich and subtle ways.

Our first experiences are always dyadic. While we are still in our mother's womb we are gathering information about her as well as about our own processes, so our first environment is intensely mutual and social. Trevarthen has shown how this mutuality develops into 'primary intersubjectivity' as both babies and parents delight in the reciprocity of 'liking', of co-creating a match in the timing, rhythm and dynamics of their movements, sounds and gestures. The pleasure of being liked fuels sustained bouts of gooey wallowing in one another's attention, providing an affective predisposition to enjoy this kind of interaction in social play and in conversations with friends (Parker-Rees, 2007; see also Chapter 9).

Trevarthen noted that this short period of primary intersubjectivity gives way, when babies are about four months old, to a period when developing motor skills and active exploration of objects fuel an explosion of 'hunting' or exploratory play. But even when babies are most absorbed in their 'little scientist' engagement with their physical environment they depend on the 'intentionally supportive teaching behaviours that more experienced partners offer' (Trevarthen, 2005: 84). Rosie may not be consciously aware of her mother's role in getting the lid where it needs to be, or of the way her vocalisations and dynamics are matched, but everything about her mother's support will be gathered up with how she *feels* about this experience, tuning her expectations about how the world will meet her.

As infants become more adept and experienced in their handling of objects they need to devote less of their attention to the physical processes of manipulation and exploration, allowing them to 'look up' and notice how other people respond to things and events. This ability to read through another person's activity and gather information about their attitude to aspects of their experience is described by Trevarthen as 'secondary intersubjectivity', and by Hobson (2002: 102) as a 'relatedness triangle', and it illustrates how hard-won direct knowledge can provide a foundation that makes us more able to let in more intuitive perceptions about other people. We have to know, ourselves, what it feels like to use an object before we can really draw inferences from how another person uses it. The 'to and fro' between preoccupation with relationships and fascination with things in the first year illustrates the intricate ways in which active theory finding and more receptive 'tuning in' to underlying complexities can support and enable each other.

As infants are helped to co-create hypotheses, event representations, scripts and theories about how the world can be expected to behave, they free up more of their attention for gathering more subtle, less tidily organisable 'local colour', which in turn allows them to refocus their interests.

Getting to know people

The close, familiar and intensely supportive environment of home usually provides a manageable, contained frame within which infants can be helped to develop their ability to engage with the complexities of cultural life. Among family a child is richly and deeply familiar to people who are also richly and deeply familiar to her. Of course the degree of familiarity will vary but, relatively speaking, a child can count on being known and understood better by family than by strangers. Meeting strangers, and finding one's place in new and unfamiliar groups is therefore both potentially exciting and a special challenge.

Among family a child is known for who they are, but among strangers they may be reduced to a shell of visible signs, while all they can know about unfamiliar people is what their shells reveal to them. As adults, especially as urban adults, we must learn how to interact with people who do not know us and whom we do not know. This is always more demanding than interacting with familiar people and for young children it may be particularly challenging. But it can also be exciting to have opportunities to play with peers 'on a level' – an experience that is refreshingly different from playing with familiar adults or siblings. What children gather from being in new, unfamiliar situations is likely to colour the way they feel about entering into unexpected, novel and strange situations later in life. As they learn to engage with unfamiliar people they need plenty of time and space to circle around one another, check one another out, notice when they have been noticed, play alongside one another, and risk entering into imitation and shared play.

Although every unfamiliar person may be no more than a shell of appearances to begin with, each comes trailing clouds of a home culture, bearing exotically different ideas about what is fun, what is naughty, what is interesting and what is special. Without resorting to profiles or checklists, children begin to size one another up – especially if they are given time and space to play freely around one another.

Hobson (2002), Rochat (2004), and Carpendale and Lewis (2006) argue that our awareness of a self, which lifts us out of the undifferentiated melee of infant egocentrism, results from our gradual discovery of differences between the selves of others. As we let in information about the 'person patterns' or regularities in other people's behaviour, we notice ways in which they are like and unlike one another and, as a result, we can begin to notice ways in which we are like and unlike them. Of course, we will have been told what we are like for a considerable time before this, especially if we have older brothers or sisters, but it is only when other people's ways of talking about us meet up with our own dawning awareness of our differentiated selves that we can really be said to bob to the surface of the social flow and into our own conscious awareness.

This co-creation of a self requires active pursuit of awareness of patterns in what usually happens and what people can be expected to do, but it also requires less purposeful 'boundary work' to let in the much more intricate social awareness that informs our understanding of individual identities.

An important part of the self we construct for ourselves will be determined by our own style of meeting other people. Some of us are particularly adept at tuning in to other people's interests and concerns; like neighbouring areas of watercolour on wet paper these people have particularly permeable boundaries, which enable them to meet others and expertly absorb information about them. Others find meeting people more of a challenge and may need prolonged exposure before they get the hang of a new acquaintance's personal ways and patterns. For these people, social playfulness may be a particularly important way of softening personal boundaries so that the colours can run into one another. Adults may need the support of special social contexts (and often alcohol), to help them to relax into the unstructured, meandering forms of interaction that enable us to get to know one another. Children, just beginning to tune in to the nuances of social interaction, also need extensive opportunities for relaxed, unhurried and undirected play, but there is considerable variation in the extent to which early years settings can meet these needs.

Hedegaard (2009: 72) points out that the forms of practice afforded by settings both shape and restrict children's activities and 'become conditions for their development'. In some countries, such as Norway, Sweden and Denmark, preschool provision reflects what the OECD (2006) has described as a 'social pedagogy' tradition, where 'greater emphasis is placed on learning to live together and supporting children in their current developmental tasks and interests' (OECD 2006: 60), but in other countries, including the UK, the US, France and the Netherlands, the 'schoolification' (OECD 2006: 61) of preschool practice reflects a 'pre-primary' approach to early education with a greater emphasis on identifying *what* children should learn. How children play in different settings both reflects these cultural differences and contributes to different perceptions of the nature of play. Where, for example, children's play is separated out from the work of learning into designated playtimes and playgrounds, this is bound to affect the ways children play. The release of children into the playground for a short playtime, like opening a fizzy drink, can result in a rather frantic, wild form of play that scares civilised adults into further efforts to limit and manage it (see also Chapter 18). Early years practitioners who have themselves experienced the UK education system will have experienced many years of being released into playgrounds for short doses of playtime, and even if this is not the way they manage play in their settings, they may see this sort of binge-playing as the 'true' essence of play, so that calmer, quieter play feels rather flat by comparison. Where children are given greater opportunities to manage their own activity, however, binge playing may be relatively rare. In the celebrated preschools of Reggio Emilia, for example, children show that, given the chance, they enjoy exploring ideas, and developing their skills and knowledge. In Steiner kindergartens where children are allowed time and space to play with older and younger peers, they are able to exercise and develop their abilities through casual interactions, observations and opportunities to 'let in' knowledge about their social world within a reassuring framework of consistent routines, rhythms and structures (Parker-Rees, 2011).

The following observation (Cameo 2) took place in a Steiner kindergarten; 13 children were present for this session: eight boys and five girls, aged between 3:8 and 5:4.

Cameo 2: Warren finds his place

Carol is crawling into Warren's sanctuary – a secluded spot behind a large wooden crate of logs – Warren calls out 'Stop that you naughty rascal!' – clearly enjoying the game – but Carol says 'I'm your dog' and starts spitting at him. Warren says, 'Those dogs are such a idiot' to Damien, who is sitting with him in their corner, watching Mark and Tim, older boys, who are throwing balls into a basket on the roof of the house they have built out of clothes horses, planks and pieces of cloth. Tim comes to get a big piece of hollow log from the crate – Warren shouts, 'Stop taking our hockey balls!' – Tim smiles and says, 'Now I've got a new game – watch', and he shows Warren how he can use the hollow log as a new target.

Patrick, another older boy, plays at 'attacking' Warren and Damien – 'Can I be a snow-lion or a snow-tiger? They're both really strong.' Warren responds with, 'Who do you think you are looking at, tomato-head?' Carol has joined in and is poking at Warren with a walking stick. Patrick attacks again, 'I'm a tyrannosaurus rex!', but Warren is safe behind his wooden crate – 'can't hurt me anyway!'

Xavier and Patrick are again 'attacking' Warren and Damien – the mood turns when the bigger boys take Warren's bucket of 'hockey balls', which upsets him. He asks for his wooden crate back so he can retreat behind it into his corner.

Warren, Otto and Damien are negotiating with Mabel over the balls. Warren says, 'He [Otto] is the middle one, so he's big AND little.' He then persuades Otto and Damien to join him in another cosy spot, tucked under a big shelf in an alcove, 'Come down here and I'll tell you something.' He has to work at this as their attention is taken up by watching other children, but he persists and finally manages to tell them, 'We're like numbers, you [Damien] are three, you [Otto] are four and I'm five.' It was clearly important to him that he should share this observation with them.

Leo declaims in a very stagey voice, 'I am not dead. One bite shall not kill ME! I am not an ordinary panda.' Banging on the table seems to remind him of a judge's gavel – 'Silence in court! Silence and die!' In the same voice, he asks Patrick, 'How many people have you shot since you have been a marshal?' Patrick replies, 'A thousand he has shot.'

Warren, Otto and Damien are still tucked under their shelf, but are now 'armed' with various sticks and logs, which they brandish at anyone who approaches. Tim peers into their hideaway. Leo and Patrick are talking light-sabres and superheroes – 'I jumped and it was such a force!'

When Otto tells his friends that Patrick is a baddy, Patrick replies, 'I don't care, I've got a light-sabre – just chop my leg.' Otto 'chops' at his leg with his penknife (a short piece of log) and Patrick says, 'You chopped your own penknife!' Patrick then steals one of the hockey balls and Warren shouts, 'He's absolutely foggy!' and laughs.

Warren is doing more gathering or 'letting in' than hunting or 'getting in' here. He clearly enjoys watching what the older boys are doing and being cosy with the younger boys – protecting them and explaining things to them. The older boys seem to recognise his need to tuck himself away, but they also include him in their play by occasionally pretending to 'attack' – Warren certainly seems to enjoy their attention. He is allowed to find his own ways of managing his need for security, and he is given time to make his own decisions about when and how far he will emerge.

In this Steiner kindergarten the protective environment of structure, routines and 'a place for everything', the adults' consistent reminders about a shared understanding of 'how we do things' and the mix of children of different ages all combine to enable everyone to get to know one another in particularly satisfying ways.

Meaning for us, for them, for you and for me

As they gather awareness of the subtle differences between other people's unique ways of performing common roles, children co-create a web of relationships between the kinds of meanings that tangle around objects, ideas and events. Everything acquires multiple meanings:

- 'meaning for us' – the *lingua franca* that emerges out of shared frameworks, contexts, experiences and stories

- 'meaning for them' – which allows us to refine our understanding of how others, 'babies', 'old people' or 'teachers', for example, may have different patterns of responses

- individual versions of 'meaning for you' – which can be noticed in terms of particular people's ways of engaging with a shared culture, and which build into awareness of differences in personality, character and temperament

- 'meaning for me' – which is particularly intense, rich and deeply buried in personal experience, but which can rise to the surface of awareness when we notice differences between our own meanings and those of other people.

Curriculum models have to focus on common, shared ideas rather than the messy tangle of relationships which complicate and colour the meanings in any particular setting. But the bare, snow-capped peaks of abstract 'meanings for us (all)' cannot hover, unsupported, in mid-air. They have to be grounded in the warmer, richer lowlands and valleys that teem with an irreducible ecosystem of lived relationships. The webs of personal associations that weave knowledge into understanding are much too complex and individual to be mapped on to a sequence of learning activities. Early years provision must allow children to gather in the rich variety of social and cultural meanings that swarm around them, as well as encourage them to strip out the clearer, simpler ideas that can be shared with all.

Effective early years environments appear to be characterised by a blurring of divisions between 'work' and 'play', where people can find their own ways of fitting in and of contributing to the co-creation of shared understandings. Sawyer (1997) argued that both the unplanned flow seen in children's pretend play and in playful adult conversation can be understood as improvisation (see also Chapter 22). Both forms of interaction allow participants to get to know one another by combining emergent frames of common elements and rules with opportunities to notice individual differences in how these are creatively performed. In many 'work'-focused environments, however, playfulness is discouraged because it tends to slow things down, and may make it harder to keep to a planned agenda or curriculum. The challenge, then, is to manage social environments so that focused, coordinated 'hunting' activities are securely rooted in looser, more playful activities that allow people to gather intricate, intuitive knowledge about how things have different meanings for different people. Such environments are 'convivial, playful, cooperative and non-judgemental, as well as being purposeful and professional' (Claxton 2000: 48). They feel more enjoyable and exhilarating and provide the conditions in which old ideas can be reinvigorated with new interpretations, allowing them to adapt to changing cultural circumstances.

The greatest challenge to maintaining a balance between the purposeful pursuit of knowledge and the more relaxed getting of wisdom seems to be a lack of trust in intuitive processes. When practitioners know that they will be held accountable for what they know about children's progress, they are likely to pursue recordable, 'hard' facts rather than trust to the more relaxed processes we rely on when getting to know friends and colleagues. When practitioners are unsure about their status in the eyes of parents they are more likely to adopt cooler, more 'professional' relationships, which are more about giving and getting information than about the co-creation of a supportive community. Yet practitioners also know that they can learn more about children from joining them in chat, sharing meal times with them or going out with them on a social outing than from hunting down and capturing the 'facts' required to complete a formal assessment. They know that relationships built on friendly chat with parents make it much more likely that subsequent conversations about their children will flow smoothly, contributing to the emergence of a shared understanding. They also know that tightly structured business-like staff meetings will run more smoothly when colleagues also have opportunities to get to know one another through more relaxed, informal gatherings (Parker-Rees, 2000).

The *Statutory Framework for the Early Years Foundation Stage* (DfE, 2012: 6) stipulates that, 'Each area of learning and development must be implemented through planned, purposeful play and through a mix of adult-led and child-initiated activity', making it difficult for early years practitioners to feel comfortable about relaxing their control and allowing space for children to enjoy one another's company as they play. As long as play continues to be seen as an obstacle to getting work done, rather than as an essential component of any form of social interaction, playfulness, in adults as well as in children, will continue to be discouraged. 'Hunting' play, where practitioners can show that the hunt is 'planned, purposeful' and likely to result in the capture of predetermined learning outcomes, may be acceptable. The forms of play that allow children to gather less immediately impressive, albeit essential, resources may still be given little encouragement or support, and may have to be squeezed in around the margins and concealed from public view.

Conclusion

Rogoff (2003) reminds us that 'humans develop through their changing participation in the sociocultural activities of their communities, which also change' (p. 368), and we can hope that playful early years practitioners and playful children will continue to change the landscape until convivial, enjoyable, relaxed playfulness can be recognised as a necessary part of all forms of social interaction.

Questions to support reflection

1   Think about one particular child you care for (not a member of your family) and one adult friend. How well do you know each of them? How well do they know you? How did you get to know them? What might help you get to know them better?

2   In your experience, what are the main differences between how you feel about work meetings and how you feel about more playful gatherings? In what ways might work meetings benefit from being a bit more playful?

3   What can you do to improve your skills in getting to know children, parents, colleagues?

4   What is the balance between 'hunting' play and 'gathering' play in different children's activities in different parts of your setting and at different times?

References and further reading (in bold)

Carpendale, J. and Lewis, C. (2006) *How Children Develop Social Understanding*. Oxford: Blackwell.

Claxton, G. (2000) The anatomy of intuition. In G. Claxton and T. Atkinson (eds) *The Intuitive Practitioner: On the Value of Not Always Knowing What One is Doing*. Buckingham: Open University Press.

Department for Education (DfE) (2012) *Statutory Framework for the Early Years Foundation Stage*. Runcorn: Department for Education.

Hedegaard, M. (2009) Children's development from a cultural-historical approach: children's activity in everyday local settings as foundation for their development. *Mind Culture and Activity*, 16(1): 64–82.

Hobson, P. (2002) *The Cradle of Thought: Exploring the Origins of Thinking*. London: Macmillan.

OECD (2006) *Starting Strong II: Early Childhood Education and Care*. Paris: OECD Publications.

Parker-Rees, R. (2000) Time to relax a little: making time for the interplay of minds in education, *Education 3–13*, 28(1): 29–35.

Parker-Rees, R. (2007) Liking to be liked: imitation, familiarity and pedagogy in the first years of life. *Early Years*, 27(1): 3–17.

Parker-Rees, R. (ed.) (2011) *Meeting the Child in Steiner Kindergartens: An Exploration of Beliefs, Values and Practices*. London: Routledge.

Rochat, P. (2004) Emerging co-awareness. In G. Bremner and A. Slater (eds) *Theories of Infant Development*. Oxford: Blackwell.

Rogoff, B. (2003) *The Cultural Nature of Human Development*. Oxford: Oxford University Press.

Sawyer, K. (1997) *Pretend Play as Improvisation: Conversation in the Preschool Classroom*. New York: Lawrence Erlbaum Associates.

Trevarthen, C. (2005) Action and emotion in development of cultural intelligence: why infants have feelings like ours. In J. Nadel and D. Muir (eds) *Emotional Development*. Oxford: Oxford University Press.

Tronick, E.Z. (2005) Why is connection with others so critical? The formation of dyadic states of consciousness: coherence governed selection and the co-creation of meaning out of messy meaning making. In J. Nadel and D. Muir (eds) *Emotional Development*. Oxford: Oxford University Press.

8

Play beyond the Foundation Stage

David Whitebread, Helen Jameson and
Marisol Basilio

Summary

This chapter argues for the power of playful approaches and activities in supporting
children's self-regulation and narrative skills, which underpin their developing abilities
to write in both fictional and non-fictional genres. Despite the recent support for playful
approaches in the Foundation Stage, other current developments in primary education
have increased the downward pressure to use exclusively formal teaching methods,
particularly in the area of literacy, to ever younger children. By contrast, evidence is
presented of the potential benefits of playful approaches being extended to older and
more able children.

Introduction

Recent research related to learning within developmental psychology has established
the overwhelming significance of the development of children's cognitive and emotional
self-regulation and their skills in symbolic representation, involving language and other
semiotic systems. In this chapter it is argued that both free and guided play experiences
provide a powerful context for these crucial areas of development throughout the
primary years. The research reported in this chapter is consistent with the view that
play impacts upon self-regulation, metacognitive and representational processes, and
as a consequence its effects emerge most clearly in tasks and aspects of development
that involve problem solving and creativity.

Age, ability and learning through play

The importance of play in early years contexts now seems to be accepted, and indeed
encouraged, for children up to the age of five years. In contrast, however, play is being
squeezed out of the curriculum for five year olds onwards. The emphasis on formal
learning in KS1 denies the fact that these children are still in the early years of their
development. The change in language following the introduction of the National
Curriculum regarding the group of children in school aged between five and seven

years from 'infants' (with its connotations of babyhood) to KS1 (a much more formal title) again emphasises the move away from regarding these children as still relatively young and in need of a less formal, play-based curriculum.

The only areas where slightly older children are still encouraged to play are those where there is evidence of special educational need or early deprivation. In 2001 the English Government announced it would be giving six million pounds to set up and run 150 toy libraries in deprived areas. This followed research by London University's Institute of Education, tracking 2,800 children between the ages of three and seven, which concluded that children who have high-quality play equipment at home outperform those who don't, and that these educational advantages stay with children at least through primary school.

Anyone visiting a special school, be it for severe learning difficulties (SLD) or emotional and behavioural difficulties (EBD), cannot fail to notice all of the extra play equipment available to the children, and the extra time and emphasis placed upon play. This is despite the fact that many of the children in these schools are still required to follow (or at least pay lip service to) the National Curriculum. The assumption seems to be that able children from Year 1 onwards, who are doing well in school, do not 'need' to play as much as their less able or educationally less 'successful' peers.

This appears to be a dominant view even among many in the teaching profession. As Eyles (1993) reported, when considering the importance of play, it is clear that most of the teachers she interviewed believed that:

> ... time spent on play activities should decrease with the increased age of the children ... and many children in Year 2 classes did not seem to be involved in any identified play experiences in the classroom ... By Year 2 the overwhelming opinion (of the children) was that they did not play! Where 'play' did take place with the older age-group it was always referred to as 'not work' and therefore learning was not taking place during the activity.
>
> (p. 45)

Twenty years on, the transition from a play-based curriculum to a no-play curriculum has changed from being a gradual slope to a sheer cliff. This dramatic change in pedagogy occurs when children are a year younger, at the start of Year 1.

Given the opportunity, all children, regardless of age, often choose to play and even adults still like to play (as can be demonstrated in our culture by the phenomenal sales of adult computer games, board games and puzzles, along with the large number of adults taking part in sports, historical re-enactments and activities such as paint-balling and ten-pin bowling – see also Chapter 2). Despite this, the assumption remains that play is indicative of immature functioning, a developmental 'stage' that children go through and, if successfully transcended, they will then be ready for formal schooling, with little need for any more play in order to learn.

A number of related pressures are currently reinforcing this trend towards squeezing playfulness out of the school curriculum beyond the Foundation Stage, and making it difficult for teachers of children of five years and older to justify the inclusion of playful opportunities and approaches in their classrooms. Furthermore, there is a general perception that parents prefer more formal approaches. This is backed up, for example, by research commissioned by the American Toy Institute (2000) in the USA, which found that 72 per cent of parents thought it very important for their children to start (academic) learning early, while 54 per cent believed there was already enough play time in schools.

This is all exacerbated in the UK by the extraordinarily young age at which children start formal schooling. Our formal approach in Year 1 is in stark contrast to that of most other industrialised countries around the world, where children are commonly six or even seven years old before they start formal school (Whitebread and Bingham, 2014).

There is now a growing body of research giving us increasingly firm evidence as to whether this debate over formal versus playful education and/or the appropriate age for formal schooling to start really matters in the long term. A longitudinal study by Marcon (2002), for example, demonstrated that, by the end of their sixth year in school, children whose preschool model had been academically directed achieved significantly lower marks in comparison to children who had attended child-initiated, play-based preschool programmes.

Play and creativity

With the apparent paradox between the emphasis on play-based learning for the Foundation Stage and for educationally disadvantaged children, combined with the sudden introduction of a more formal approach for Year 1 onwards, we have been keen to investigate whether, in fact, for older (Year 1 and above) and more able children, playful approaches to learning may be beneficial. This possibility has seemed to be worth investigating given the powerful range of evidence and theory from psychological research supporting the developmental significance of play, particularly in relation to problem solving and creativity.

Psychologists have been researching and developing theories about the nature and purposes of children's play since the middle of the nineteenth century. It has been suggested as a mechanism for letting off steam, for providing relaxation, for relieving boredom, for practising for adult life, for living out our fantasies, and much more. That it is important in children's development, however, has never been in doubt. As Moyles (1989) demonstrated, for every aspect of human development and functioning, there is a form of play.

It is only in the past 20–30 years, however, that its significance for thinking, problem solving and creativity has been fully recognised. The human being, of course, has a much greater length of immaturity than any other animal, plays more and for longer, and is supreme in flexibility of thought. The more recent neuroscientific evidence has supported this (see, for example, Pellis and Pellis, 2009; see also Chapter 3).

Play is about developing flexibility of thought. It provides opportunities to try out possibilities, to put different elements of a situation together in various ways, to look at problems from different viewpoints. This is very close to Craft's (2000) more recent definition of creativity as 'possibility thinking'. Sylva et al. (1984) demonstrated this in a series of experiments where children were asked to solve practical problems. Typically in these experiments, one group of children was given the opportunity to play with the objects involved, while the other group was 'taught' how to use the objects in ways that would help solve the problem. Consistently, the two groups subsequently performed at a similar level, in terms of numbers of children completing the task with total success, when they were individually asked to tackle the problem. However, in the 'taught' group there tended to be an 'all or nothing' pattern of responses, with the children either succeeding immediately by accurately recalling and following their instructions, or giving up following an initial failure. By contrast, the children who had the experience of playing with the materials were more inventive in devising strategies to solve the problem and persevered longer if their initial attempts did not work. The same proportion of children as in the 'taught' group solved the problem almost immediately, but many of those who didn't succeed immediately solved the problem at a second or third attempt, or came close to solving the problem, by trying out different possibilities.

Play and self-regulation

Observation of children at play gives some indication of why it might be such a powerful learning medium. During play children are usually totally engrossed in what they are doing. It is quite often repetitive and contains a strong element of practice (see Endpiece). Two further elements, which have been highlighted by psychological research and theory, also contribute to an understanding of its vital significance in learning and creativity. These relate to its role in children's developing sense of control and self-regulation of their own learning and in their developing powers of symbolic representation. Within all kinds of physical, constructional and social play, children have been shown to develop their skills of intellectual and emotional 'self-regulation' – that is, they learn to be aware, and in control of their own physical, mental and behavioural activity (Whitebread and Coltman, 2007; Whitebread, 2010). A growing number of empirical educational studies have shown that early play experiences enhance young children's self-regulation (e.g. Ponitz et al., 2009) and that educational interventions supporting children's self-regulation are the most effective in supporting children's development as learners (Hattie, 2009). A key mechanism by which this is achieved relates to young children's use of self-commentary or 'private speech'. Berk et al. (2006) reported a series of observational studies of two- to six-year-old children in which they recorded incidences of 'private speech'. They found particularly high levels of private speech and verbal self-regulation among these young children during open-ended, make-believe or pretend play.

Play and symbolic representation

Play also has a pivotal contribution to the development of symbolic representation. Human thought, culture and communication is all founded on the unique human aptitude for using various forms of symbolic representation or psychological tools, which would include drawing and other forms of visual art, visual imagination, language in all its various forms, mathematical symbol systems, musical notation, dance and drama, and so on. Play, crucially, is recognised as the first medium through which children explore the use of symbol systems (most obviously through pretence). So, as an adult, when you have had an interesting experience upon which you wish to reflect, or a problem to solve, or a story to write, you have the intellectual tools to do this in your mind. Lacking these tools, children require the support of real situations and objects with which the ideas are worked out through play.

The precise ways in which play, thinking, learning, development and creativity influence one another have been the subject of extensive research (see Craft, 2000, and Lillard, 2002, for useful reviews). Of particular relevance to our own research, which we report in the final part of this chapter, are two empirical studies related to children's storytelling, both carried out as long ago as the 1980s. Pellegrini (1985) showed that the verbal narratives of preschoolers who especially enjoyed pretending were more elaborate and cohesive than those of age mates who preferred other forms of play. Dyachenko (1980, cited in Karpov, 2005) showed that five to six year olds' ability to retell a story was significantly enhanced by the use of representational objects such as sticks, paper cut-outs, etc., and that their ability to retell a story without the use of these objects was subsequently enhanced.

The role of 'guided play'

An important implication of the Vygotskian notion of the 'zone of proximal development' for education is that there is a crucial role for the teacher in participating and intervening in children's play. Smith (1990), in an extensive review, examines the evidence relating to the issue of free play and 'structured' play. He concludes that there is a role in learning for both kinds of play; sensitive adult intervention can usefully enhance the intellectual challenge for children, mainly by opening up new possibilities and opportunities.

In the remainder of this chapter, we review two studies that we have carried out exploring the impact of what might be termed guided play in relation to children's narrative writing. As Nicolopoulou and Ilgaz (2013) have shown, while there remains controversy in the psychological literature over the precise role of pretence play in some areas of development, the evidence of its role in the development of children's narrative skills is very clear.

A study of pretend play and narrative writing

In the first study, we replicated the study by Sylva *et al.* (1984) in which the impact of play on practical problem solving in young children was investigated. However, given the prominence placed upon developing reading and writing skills in the contemporary primary school curriculum, we were interested to see if the same kind of pattern observed between play and taught conditions would emerge in relation to the rather different area of children's narrative writing. The sample chosen for this research (Whitebread and Jameson, 2003) consisted of Years 1 and 2 children (aged five to seven years) in an independent school. We were particularly interested to study a very specific sample group of children who were all (with the exception of two 'intellectually average' children) of at least 'above average' intellectual ability (as measured by Ravens Progressive Standard Matrices IQ Test). In fact, the average IQ of the group was 131, which is within the top 2 per cent of the population as a whole. Every child in the group had a reading age at least six months above his/her chronological age. All of the children in the sample were of a white British ethnic origin with English as their first language. All of the children had had experience of nursery/preschool education and many opportunities to play during school time up until the end of their Foundation year; however, none of them had experience of playing with Storysacks or story props prior to the start of the research. All of the children had a great deal of experience of stories being read to them at school and also of being asked to write stories themselves. This sample would normally be expected, according to the generally held views discussed earlier, to have the least 'need' for play; consequently we were intrigued to have the opportunity to discover if play would actually have any beneficial effect upon their storytelling and writing.

Following the general structure of the original Sylva *et al.* (1984) study, 35 of this group of able five to seven year olds were asked to produce oral and written stories after they had been read a story and had experience of story props under 'play', 'taught' and 'control' conditions.

In order to engage in the 'play' condition Storysacks were used. In English schools, there has been an increasing use in recent years of Storysacks (originally devised by Griffiths, 1997). These consist of sets of toys and artefacts relating to items and characters in a story and were used for three stories appropriate to the age range. The children were read each of the stories and then had follow-up activities that varied according to a 'play', 'taught' or 'control' condition. The order of stories and conditions was varied for different sub-groups within the sample in order to control for the differential effects of the three stories, and for ordering effects between the three conditions.

The children were read the stories in groups of 10–15, using a picture-book version. In the 'play' condition, the group was then allowed ten minutes to play with the story props in groups of five without any intervention from the teacher. In the 'taught' condition, the teacher then worked with the group for ten minutes discussing and modelling with the story props other possible stories, but did not allow the children to handle the props. In the 'control' condition, the children were shown photocopied sheets of the story characters with their names, but no further help or guidance was offered. All the groups were then asked to write their own stories containing one or more of the characters in the story they had just heard. It was emphasised that this should be different from the original story.

These written stories were analysed according to the time taken to write them, the number of words they contained, their English National Curriculum level, using national government guidelines (QCA, 2001), and the number of points of information, beginnings, conflicts and resolutions that were the same or different from those in the original story. An assessment of the children's confidence in creating their alternative stories was also carried out.

The results of the analysis of the children's written stories arising from the three conditions showed that in the 'play' condition the children included more conflicts and resolutions than the control group. Also, more of these conflicts and resolutions were different from those in the original story, and their stories were of higher quality (as measured by NC levels) than in either of the 'taught' or 'control' conditions. In the 'taught' condition, although the children included more conflicts and resolutions in their written stories than in the 'control' condition, they spent less time writing their stories than in the other two conditions, and they included more 'same' points in relation to the original story than the 'play' condition and fewer 'different' points than either of the other two conditions. They also included more 'same' resolutions than either of the other two conditions.

It was extremely interesting to observe that, despite investigating a completely different area of learning to the original Sylva study our findings, like theirs, clearly showed the value and importance of play in enabling children to develop their creative problem-solving abilities. The results of our analysis of various aspects of the stories showed a high level of congruence with each other and supported the theory that children who were not given an opportunity to play, and had only the experience of watching the teacher (control and taught groups), felt that they had to model the teacher as closely as possible in order to be able to complete the task. This inhibited the children's creativity and for many of them also appeared to increase their anxiety and fear of failure.

Considering that the only difference between the independent variables was an isolated ten-minute opportunity to play or be taught, it was impressive just how significant these results were. In a curriculum that is increasingly pressed for time to fit everything in, it is reassuring to note that just ten minutes spent playing has such a significant effect on both confidence and creativity (among other things). That these results were obtained with a highly able group of five to seven year olds clearly indicates that abandoning playful approaches to learning at the start of Year 1 is likely to lower rather than enhance the quality of early learning and development.

A study of constructional and pretence play and narrative skills

Following on from this earlier study, we are currently carrying out a fuller study with children in Years 1, 3 and 5. Working closely with teachers, we are developing a playful approach to teaching narrative and writing skills. This includes playful activities during regular literacy lessons when children have opportunity to use different LEGO sets, including constructional and pretence (e.g. minifigures) elements, to create collaboratively and express their ideas before writing about them. Some examples of these activities are:

- building a scene from a book
- creating a storyboard (on separate LEGO plates)
- building characters and settings of their own story
- acting out parts of a story, building a new ending for a well-known story, among other things.

In these activities teachers allow a high degree of freedom for children to choose what they will be representing with LEGO, and how to go about carrying out the task with their group (including the choice of working on a table or on the carpet). All the activities require children to be imaginative and creative, and involve a hands-on experience of building a concrete, 3-D LEGO model. These characteristics promote a playful context in which children are engaged and relaxed, which differs from normal teacher-directed instructional approaches to writing.

The degree of choice that children have in the activities together with the collaborative building experiences afford powerful learning opportunities for working in the key areas outlined in the first part of this chapter: self-regulatory skills, mastery of symbolic representational systems (including dialogic or 'talking' skills) and creativity. This approach fits into the idea of 'guided play' because teachers play an important role in setting up the activity and capitalising on the high levels of engagement observed to promote effective learning opportunities. For example, one aspect that teachers have devised as part of this approach is to connect the experiences of building stories and ideas using LEGO and specific instruction about writing by modelling and reflecting about the process. From this approach LEGO is seen not just as a toy, but as an external representational system that children use to create and convey ideas. These ideas are then adapted and translated into the more complex writing system. This experience gives children the opportunity to create, plan and edit ideas before putting them into writing. Further, it provides a scaffolding stage for children who struggle with writing, allowing them to contribute with their ideas to the group in a way that is motivating and more accessible to them.

This project is currently under way. By the end of the school year, the 108 participating children will have been working with this methodology for a full academic year. Measures at the beginning of the year have already been collected and will be collected again at the end of the year. These include children's writing attainments (according to National Curriculum levels) and narrative skills using *Expression, Reception and Recall Of Narrative* (ERRNI) (Bishop, 2004), as well as creativity measures included in the *Torrance Tests of Creative Thinking* (Torrance, 1972), self-regulation and metacognition using a developmentally appropriate problem-solving task that requires building a train track from a plan (Bryce and Whitebread, 2012), among others. Quantitative data measuring the impact of this playful approach will be analysed using pre- and post- assessments, which will be compared to a non-intervention group.

We have also gathered qualitative data by recording classroom activities and particularly children working in groups. We have interviewed some of the children and the teachers to understand their own views about this learning experience. Early evidence from these sources shows that this playful approach has been extremely well received by both teachers and children. Teachers especially emphasise the high level of engagement in the classroom and the creativity that children display while working collaboratively to represent their ideas in LEGO. Some of the interviewed children have provided highly elaborate accounts of why working with LEGO is helping with their writing. Children have stated that having their model built as part of planning a piece of writing in front of them, during the process of writing, is helpful because they can remember all the details that they want to include in the story without having to 'think them all over again'. They have mentioned that working with LEGO, in comparison with drawing a story, is 'more fun', and it is easier because, unlike drawing, 'you don't have to be good at it'. They have expressed that, because LEGO creates a 3-D representation, they can see the elements of their models from different angles and perspectives. Some children have developed pretence play strategies, for example, to write descriptive accounts by moving the minifigures and imagining that they can see through their eyes, and describing the scene from that point of view.

Conclusion

The two studies outlined here support the increasing body of evidence concerning the role of play, particularly pretend or symbolic play, which might involve objects or other children, in providing a context in which children can develop their representational skills, and their skills and dispositions as self-regulated learners. The first author of this chapter and others have written elsewhere concerning the now considerable body of evidence relating the development of self-regulation to children's success as problem solvers, creative thinkers and learners, and the implications for the classroom environment, for learning activities and for teacher–child interactions. Particularly at this time, with the pressures on primary education that we have discussed, it is critical that the procedures and practices these authors have promoted, and most importantly that support children's imaginative play, are well understood by practitioners not only in the Foundation Stage, but across the primary age range, and form the foundation for their practice.

Questions to promote reflection

1 Up to what age is it valuable for children to play in school?
2 What kinds of behaviours might we observe which indicate that children are developing their skills as learners during constructional or pretence play?
3 What are the relative contributions to children's learning of free, child-initiated and 'guided' play?
4 Why might play enhance children's development as writers?

References and further reading (in bold)

American Toy Institute (2000) *The Power of Play Factsheet*. ATI.

Berk, L.E., Mann, T.D. and Ogan, A.T. (2006) Make-believe play: wellspring for development of self-regulation. In D.G. Singer, R.M. Golinkoff and K. Hirsh-Pasek (eds) *Play=Learning: How Play Motivates and Enhances Children's Cognitive and Social-emotional Growth*. Oxford: Oxford University Press.

Bishop, D.V. (2004) *Expression, Reception and Recall of Narrative Instrument*. London: Harcourt Assessment.

Bryce, D. and Whitebread, D. (2012) The development of metacognitive skills: evidence from observational analysis of young children's behavior during problem-solving. *Metacognition and Learning*, 7(3): 197–217.

Craft, A. (2000) *Creativity Across the Primary Curriculum*. London: Routledge.

Eyles, J. (1993) Play – a trivial pursuit or meaningful experience. *Early Years*, 13(2): 45–49.

Griffiths, N. (1997) *Storysacks: A Starter Information Pack*. Storysacks Ltd.

Hattie, J. (2009) *Visible Learning: A Synthesis of Over 800 Meta-analyses Relating to Achievement*. London: Routledge.

Karpov, Y.V. (2005) Three- to six-year-olds: sociodramatic play as the leading activity during the period of early childhood. In Y.V. Karpov, *The Neo-Vygotskian Approach to Child Development*. Cambridge: Cambridge University Press.

Lillard, A. (2002) Pretend play and cognitive development. In U. Goswami (ed.) *Blackwell Handbook of Childhood Cognitive Development*. Oxford: Blackwell.

Marcon, R.A. (2002) Moving up the grades: relationship between pre-school model and later school success. *Early Childhood Research and Practice*, 4(1): 517–530.

Moyles, J. (1989) *Just Playing? The Role and Status of Play in Early Childhood Education*. Milton Keynes: Open University Press.

Nicolopoulou, A. and Ilgaz, H. (2013) What do we know about pretend play and narrative development? *American Journal of Play*, **6(1): 55–81.**

Pellegrini, A.D. (1985) The narrative organisation of children's fantasy play. *Educational Psychology*, 5: 17–25.

Pellis, S. and Pellis, V. (2009) *The Playful Brain: Venturing to the Limits of Neuroscience*. **Oxford: Oneworld Publications.**

Ponitz, C.C., McClelland, M.M., Matthews, J.S. and Morrison, F.J. (2009) A structured observation of behavioral self-regulation and its contribution to kindergarten outcomes. *Developmental Psychology*, **45(3): 605–619.**

Qualifications and Curriculum Authority (QCA) (2001) *English Tasks Teacher's Handbook*. London: QCA/DfES.

Smith, P.K. (1990) The role of play in the nursery and primary school curriculum. In C. Rogers and P. Kutnick (eds) *The Social Psychology of the Primary School*. London: Routledge.

Sylva, K., Bruner, J. and Genova, P. (1984) The role of play in the problem-solving of children aged 3–5 years. In J. Bruner, A. Jolly and K. Sylva (eds) *Play: Its Role in Development and Evolution*. Harmondsworth: Penguin.

Torrance, E.P. (1972) Predictive validity of the Torrance Tests of Creative Thinking. *Journal of Creative Behavior*, 6(4): 236–262.

Whitebread, D. (2010) Play, metacognition and self-regulation. In P. Broadhead, J. Howard and E. Wood (eds) *Play and Learning in the Early Years*. London: Sage.

Whitebread, D. and Bingham, S. (2014) School readiness, starting age, cohorts and transitions in the Early Years. In J. Moyles, J. Payler and J. Georgeson (eds) *Early Years Foundations: Critical Issues,* **2nd edn. Maidenhead: Open University Press.**

Whitebread, D. and Coltman, P. (2007) Developing young children as self-regulated learners. In J. Moyles (ed.) *Beginning Teaching Beginning Learning*, 3rd edn. Maidenhead: Open University Press.

Whitebread, D. and Jameson, H. (2003) The impact of play on the oral and written storytelling of able 5–7 year olds. Paper presented at the 33rd Annual Meeting of the Jean Piaget Society, Chicago, USA.

Whitebread, D., Bingham, S., Grau, V., Pino Pasternak, D. and Sangster, C. (2007) Development of metacognition and self-regulated learning in young children: the role of collaborative and peer-assisted learning. *Journal of Cognitive Education and Psychology*, **3: 433–555.**

9

Friendship, culture and playful learning

Pat Broadhead and Liz Chesworth

Summary

This chapter illustrates how friendship is linked to identity development through playful cultural explorations and then to challenging, intellectual engagements between cooperating peers who are friends. These engagements are a crucial site for young children's learning. Consequently, nurturing friendships carries pedagogical responsibilities for educators. We show how open-ended and flexible play resources can stimulate and sustain friendships because of their potential for joint engagement in intellectual challenges at a level that children determine for themselves. Four cameos reveal how such resources allow children to bring their interests and cultural experiences into their early years setting and to jointly engage in playful explorations with peers, both with newly emerging friends and with well-established friends.

Introduction

Many texts discuss the importance of social skills and of children's activities within 'peer groups'. However, relatively little is said about friendship as an integral and developing part of their playful engagements with peers and even less about its promotion within a pedagogy of playful learning. The chapter shows also how the Early Years Foundation Stage has relatively little to say on these matters; however, there are some positive messages to consider.

Friendship is more than the 'development of social skills' or 'being active within a peer group'. Through cameos and related reflections, this chapter reveals how friendships are an expression of culture and identity that, within the right environment, children can become extremely skilled at exploiting and enjoying in support of their own learning. Friendships can frame and nurture intellectually challenging learning experiences when the resources available are sufficiently flexible so as to allow cooperating children to select and engage, over long periods, with resources that have the potential to chime with their lived, cultural experiences, both at home and in their setting.

Working extensively in partnership with practitioners, Pat Broadhead (PB) has researched how children become sociable and cooperative in their play in early years settings and has illustrated links with learning (Broadhead, 1997; 2001; 2004). This research was based on observations of children in traditionally available activities where they were likely to interact, such as sand, water, role play, large and small construction and small world. Observations were followed by joint reflections, informed by the practitioner's knowledge of individual children, their interests and play preferences. Findings revealed that intellectually challenging play flourished in the more open-ended areas of sand, water and large construction. Open-ended play materials were introduced (cardboard boxes, beautiful fabrics, hats, wheels, tyres, etc.) and further study confirmed the potential of such materials for intellectual challenge between cooperating peers, but notably when the children knew one another well; hence the growing interest in friendship as linked with playful learning. A recent study with early years teacher Andy Burt (Broadhead and Burt, 2012) examined open-ended play resources in greater depth, and Cameos 1, 2 and 3 arise from this joint research.

Liz Chesworth's (LC's) research focused upon the playful experiences of five children in their reception year of school. Filmed recordings of child-initiated classroom experiences were used as prompts to elicit perspectives of play from the children, their parents and two practitioners. During the eight-month data-collection period, Liz spent at least one day a week participating in the life of the classroom while filming episodes of play and watching the filmed material with the children and their teachers. A key priority was to establish and sustain reciprocal relationships with the children to enable their active participation in the research. The video software package allowed the children to take the lead in deciding which play activities were watched and discussed. The children's responses to viewing their play often focused upon themes relating to friendships and relationships. Friendship was also frequently included in parents' and practitioners' perspectives of play. Cameo 4 was taken from this study. It shows stills of Chloe and Harry playing in the water, and provides the children's commentary on the play that Chloe selected for viewing and discussion with Liz.

Play and friendship in the Early Years Foundation Stage

The revised statutory framework for the Early Years Foundation Stage (EYFS) (DfE, 2012) acknowledges that play is essential for children's development, and identifies 'play and exploration' as one of three characteristics that underpin effective learning. Furthermore, the EYFS Profile, the statutory assessment that takes place at the end of the EYFS, requires practitioners to provide a short, written description of how each child demonstrates these characteristics within the learning process. However, the EYFS also places considerable emphasis upon school readiness and during the reception year 'it is expected that the balance will gradually shift towards more activities led by adults, to help children prepare for more formal learning, ready for Year 1' (DfE, 2012: 6). Hence, while the EYFS offers opportunities for play, there are pedagogical challenges associated with a curriculum that promotes playful approaches while at the same time emphasising the role of the EYFS in preparing children for formal education (Chesworth, 2014). In some cases, play seems to be presented as a vehicle for curriculum delivery by adults rather than an opportunity for children to understand the world around them in the company of similarly and collaboratively engaged peers. The revised framework's underpinning principles include the identification that 'children learn to be strong and independent through positive relationships' (DfE, 2012: 3), but the document makes no reference to friendship development. The Early Learning Goal for 'Making Relationships' in the Personal, Social and Emotional Area of Learning and Development sets an expectation that the majority of children should, by the end of the EYFS, be able to play cooperatively, taking turns with others (DfE, 2012: 8). This somewhat narrow interpretation of cooperative play does not acknowledge the capacity of young children to set and solve increasingly complex problems together when working with trusted and familiar peers; the intellectual dimension and potential for shared experiences of cognitive challenge that arise from friendship-based interactions is lacking, as is the sense of helping children to understand their own characters and personalities in relation to the development of their relationships with other children.

Why friendship is important for children in an early years setting

Learning is a social process and play is a principle activity for children in relation to building knowledge and understanding of the world in all its aspects (Vygotsky, 1978). Younger children learn best when *actively* engaged alone and with peers and while making meaning in a well-resourced environment that acknowledges children's intellectual and cultural interests (Yelland *et al.*, 2008). The environment should allow the child to immerse in their learning both socially and culturally within their 'zone of proximal development', this being the learning space into which they may move with assistance from expert others (Vygotsky, 1978).

While the educator is an important 'expert other' who scaffolds learning, peers and friends are also expert others and scaffolders (Gallimore and Tharp, 1990). When children play with those whom they know well, the high levels of familiarity allow them to expose one another to personal knowledge, skills and abilities and, through language, to ways of thinking about the problems and creative experiences with which they are engaged. Children's play is more complex and intellectually challenging when they are playing with friends (Howes, 1994); cooperative play is more sustained when engaged in by friends (Hartup, 1996). It may be that, through their friendships, children begin to recognise cultural similarities in the extent to which 'others' are like themselves in terms of shared interests and goals. They practise, repeat, explore and experiment, sharing and gaining skills, exchanging knowledge and ideas, and setting goals and targets for joint endeavour. The cooperation deepens their knowledge and pleasure, but only if the environment allows them the time and space for these endeavours. Children have to function in a world determined by adults, but as Corsaro (2000) states, they are still active agents of their own socialisation and, as such, create their own childhood culture as well as bringing with them the culture of home. Play is the means by which they construct and reconstruct their social and cultural worlds. As the forthcoming cameos reveal, this is heightened when the resources to hand are flexible enough to accommodate the breadth of culture and interests that children bring to their play both individually and collectively.

Friendship-in-development

Friendships are 'made', implying the passage of time. Educators often say, 'We are all friends here.' The adult is trying to denote a sense of community to children, a sense of togetherness and shared responsibility. However, the danger is of conveying a false sense of community to a child who has not yet made any friends, perhaps because they are new to the setting (see also Chapter 15). Young children are in the process of learning what a friend is, which is why they ask, 'Are you my friend?' or 'You're my friend, aren't you?' As well as seeking to make a social relationship, the child is building their concept of 'friend', of how friends behave, of what friends do and of why they might want a friend. All this has to be learned and an early years setting is, potentially, an excellent place for learning about friends and friendship, and for making and keeping friends.

Friendship is not a contrivance to manage human behaviour; it is a state of being, and by no means necessarily a permanent state. As children become older, they have core friends and contingency friends that they fall back on; we are a social species and children without friends are seldom happy children (Factor, 2009). At the core of friendship is the making of choices, the seeking of direction, individually and together. The forthcoming cameos aim to show that flexible and open-ended play resources, along with the time to explore and experiment with peers who become friends, is at the heart of a playful pedagogy that is rewarding and learning-rich for children and educators.

Cameos and reflections

This section presents four cameos. The first three are taken from PB's research and the fourth from LC's research. Cameo 1 focuses on friendship-in-development. Nadia and Roxanna are each making choices in their own small but important ways as they explore and experiment as new children. A raised stage area has been provided to offer an indoor, open-ended play resource. There are also props, fabric, costumes and music.

Cameo 1

Nadia and Roxanna are older three year olds who have been in the early years unit for three weeks. Nadia is already confidently exploring the environment and interacting with adults. She plays alongside other children but not with them. Roxanna is often observed walking around the unit. She watches children and watches adults interact with other children but seldom approaches adults or children. She may go to a table to draw or play but does not seem to want to interact.

Today, a tape of Abba is playing by the stage area. Nadia goes to it immediately, climbs on the stage and begins to dance, smiling at others on the stage but not speaking. Roxanna approaches and watches from the floor as Nadia dances; Roxanna smiles but does not make eye contact with Nadia. Nadia does not seem to notice and continues to dance. Roxanna copies Nadia's actions and Nadia looks at her, studies her for a moment, smiles and makes eye contact. Both girls smile and the eye contact is intermittent over a brief period. Nadia stops dancing and goes outside. Roxanna follows her and watches but does not go through the door.

Nadia returns a few minutes later and goes back to the dancing. Roxanna sees her immediately and goes over to be near her (but not on the stage), and copies her dance movements. Eye contacts and smiles begin again and are more pronounced and more frequent. Nadia stops and goes outside again. Roxanna follows her and this time follows Nadia outdoors. She watches as Nadia begins to run around the area pulling a piece of rope behind her. Roxanna gets a piece of rope and runs after Nadia, following her and laughing.

Did Nadia return in order to renew the contact with Roxanna? Had she expected Roxanna to follow her outside? What gave Roxanna sufficient confidence to exit the door the second time? We cannot know if this is the beginning of a friendship between these two new, young entrants but the play resource has allowed them to recognise that they share a common interest in music and dancing. As they venture outside together, the chance to run and drag a piece of rope (a common activity for young children whether at home or school) again allows them a mutual interest that does not ask too much of them in terms of language or intellectual challenge at this very early stage of joint playful engagement in an unfamiliar environment. Nadia and Roxanna have the potential of many months in the setting before them.

Friendship-in-action

Cameos 2 and 3 explore links between friendship and cooperation, intellectual engagement and playful learning. These cameos are drawn from filmed material, recorded across a two-month period. They focus on Hughie and Josh, both of whom are reception-aged children and good friends. They are outdoors where a wide range of open-ended play materials are available. Cameos 2 and 3 together illustrate the progression in their play from small to a large-scale design, and the incorporation of greater amounts of open-ended materials in the second cameo because their 'vision' of home seems enlarged. Cameo 3 also reveals that Hughie has other interests born of home experiences that he wants to re-enact in the setting.

Cameo 2

Hughie and Josh have made a small enclosure, about two metres square, with plastic milk crates. Hughie has a small wooden box, a pine cone and a stone on the wall that forms one edge of the enclosure, and is arranging and rearranging them carefully. Josh is moving in and out of the enclosure collecting various items from inside the unit and outdoors – a fork, a bucket, a spade, some leaves – returning with them to the enclosure. Josh says something to Hughie about 'the toilet'; it appears serious and relates to the area around the collection of objects that Hughie is engaged with; Hughie focuses on this area for much of the play. Hughie then spends time collecting soil with a spoon from a pile just outside the enclosure and placing it carefully in an aerosol top, taking it to his collection of objects on the wall. Josh fetches water from an outside tap in the bucket he found earlier. He then goes and 'sits' on the toilet, quite absorbed; Hughie laughs at him as if sharing a joke and Josh laughs. It seems amicable and jointly understood as humour. Hughie has found a piece of paper, which he takes to his collection of objects. Josh pours the water he has fetched into the 'toilet'; Hughie watches and then appears to clean the toilet. There are two 'doors' in the construction and Josh, who often leaves and returns to the enclosure, is careful to 'open' and 'close' these by moving the crate to one side and back again, imitating a door's movement. Josh goes to dig in the soil as Hughie returns to the corner where the action is taking place. He carefully manipulates small piles of soil and looks carefully at stones and pieces of paper. Josh has found a woodlouse in the soil and examines it carefully but does not say anything to Hughie; Hughie remains preoccupied and busy around the 'toilet'. Their interactions are brief and infrequent but their goals are shared and connected.

The film was played back to Josh and Hughie. PB asked Hughie if this was their house. He nodded, saying, 'That's the toilet. I'm putting bleach down the toilet to make it clean.' Hughie then said, 'I'm still cleaning the toilet.' Josh remarked, 'I flush the toilet.' Hughie responded, 'I need a stick to clean the toilet', and then 'I got the paper to wipe inside the toilet.' Hughie looked at PB and explained, 'That's the sink there.' As they watch the film, they have a quiet conversation with one another about 'wiping your bum when you go to the toilet'. They smile as they talk to each other, but it is also clear that they both share an understanding of the seriousness of this to them. Josh (who was the one who often left and re-entered the enclosure through the 'doors') says, 'The crates keep falling down so you have to be careful.'

It is evident that Hughie and Josh have shared preoccupations around toilets, a common theme among young children, especially boys, as they master the responsibilities of changing toilet habits at this stage in their lives; it seemed an integral part of their identity. Andy, the teacher, watched the film, and was able to confirm an ongoing interest in designing and playing together in a space that represented 'home'. In the May cameo (Cameo 2), the domestic-related activities seemed of more importance than the space in which they were played out, which was quite small. By July (Cameo 3), their design skills had developed, as had their skills and confidence in creating and inhabiting a larger space. Hughie shows wider interests in designing and an example of this is built in to this cameo.

Cameo 3

When filming begins, the play space is well developed, although Hughie continues to add to the design. The boys have used milk crates to create an entrance hall or corridor about three metres long with a 'door' at the entrance. The corridor leads into a large enclosure roughly measuring six square metres, occupying a large space in the playground and representing a house/home. The entrance to the enclosure for Hughie and Josh, and for other children who come and go and engage with the boys in a range of ways, is always via the 'door' at the end of the corridor; everyone understands the rules around entering and leaving. The enclosure has 'rooms', although these are not boundaried. There is a bed made from a box; Hughie and Josh get into it for conversations. There is a kitchen where cooking is ongoing; there are discussions about watching TV both in bed and elsewhere in the enclosure. Josh becomes preoccupied with a construction that looks like a window (they have hung a plastic container about one metre square on the wall). Josh spends time cleaning this area, whereas Hughie leaves the enclosure regularly to fetch other resources to develop the area. He seems to be working to an internal image of what he wants, although of course it is difficult to be sure of this. Josh's main preoccupations, when not with Hughie, are with the 'window' and cleaning.

Their enclosure play ended through the intervention of other children. They were building an 'obstacle course' around the playground for a long line of children to follow (10–15 children were engaged in following the course). The course builders needed more materials and began to take them from Josh and Hughie's enclosure. At first they tried jointly to resist but when Hughie saw what they were doing, he stopped his resistance and began to watch the course builders. Josh continued to defend his resources a little longer but as he noticed Hughie's loss of resistance he looked at what Hughie was looking at and allowed the materials to be taken.

Hughie's interest in design and construction had been evident at other times in his play, where he often took the lead in deciding what to build and what to use. One day he worked with a student teacher to build a telescope; he had visited a real telescope the previous weekend with his mum and dad, and chatted about this to the student teacher. Josh watched but did not seem to know what Hughie had in mind – until it was finished – and they could look through a wide tube, balanced on some tyres, into the sky. Josh suddenly understood what Hughie was trying to achieve, and smiled. The fact that Josh stayed interested suggested that he understood that Hughie had good ideas that were worth taking an interest in.

With the passage of time, the boys are building on a bigger and more complex scale. Hughie seems less interested in domestic themes but happy to engage in them alongside Josh, who engages in domestic aspects more extensively when Hughie moves back to design and development of the structure. Hughie seems to enjoy design but it is also notable that he engages far less than Josh with other children who are entering and playing in the space. Josh has several conversations with other children, explaining what he is doing, encouraging them to join him. The open-ended play materials allow each of them to pursue their interests in joint endeavour. Neither boy seems particularly concerned about the requirement to end their play because of other children's interventions. Hughie in fact seemed very interested in what they were doing and, after initial resistance, Josh capitulates, perhaps because he notes Hughie's interest and apparent unconcern, perhaps because he knows, from his many daily experiences in accessing these materials, that he and Hughie can replicate their play again and again if they wish. The materials are always available even if designs are dismantled.

One comment Andy, the teacher, made as he watched the film was that the mother of the girl leading the construction of the 'obstacle course' was in the armed services. She may have seen such a course or heard her mother speak of using one; potentially another example of culture and identity influencing play and problem solving.

Cameo 4 is from LC's research and focuses on a play episode involving Chloe and Harry, who were frequently observed playing together. The episode occurred towards the end of the eight-month research period and illustrates how the enduring relationship between two friends can promote playful collaboration. The discussion focuses upon the children's responses to viewing their play, but also includes some interesting perspectives from Chloe's mother and her teacher.

Cameo 4

For several weeks the children have been able to freely access water from a large water butt. Here, Chloe and Harry engage in a series of playful explorations focused upon the flow of water. The children's responses to the filmed footage present play as an inherently collaborative experience in which they develop their ideas with friends and bring complexity to the play. Chloe stops the film at key times when she wishes to make a point. Chloe, Harry and Liz watch the film on a laptop in the book area.

Stills from recorded footage: Chloe and Harry engage in a series of playful explorations

Chloe's narrative (as told to LC):

Chloe: [Pauses the film. Looks directly at LC] Oh it hasn't started yet. Here I'm waiting for Harry and Pippa. [Whispers] They was inside. Working with Mrs Dearling. [Pauses] They come out soon and we'll go over to the water, won't we.

Harry: Yeah I, I was inside.

Harry: Chloe look, it's time for the brush to go. I dropped my brush, and then it went down. [Raises arm and moves it to resemble the brush's movement]
Liz: Oh, in there? [Pointing at gutter]
Harry: Yes, it went zooming down. [Laughs and glances at Chloe]
Chloe: [Pauses the film] Yes, it went too far. It was actually his fault. He shouldn't have poured the water 'til I'd done it properly. [Places hand on hip and looks at Harry, frowning. Harry giggles. Chloe's frown dissolves. She laughs with Harry]

Chloe: Look, Harry!

Chloe: [Laughing] Oh look, the water went all the way down, right down there. Yeah, I liked that it went all the way down.
Harry: Yeah, I didn't know that was going to happen.
[Chloe and Harry look at each other and laugh]
Chloe: Yeah the floor [pauses] the ground got soaked. The water's gonna come out of them. Them gutters.

Harry: It's going down here!
Jordan: You've made it all wet. Are you allowed?

Chloe: [Pauses film] Yeah, this is where we play the game where we tip water out. It goes all the way down. Down to there. [Points outside the window towards the bottom of the playground]
Liz: Have you played that game before, Chloe?
Chloe: No, that's our first time. But we'll play it again now, we're gonna do it for well, 7 weeks.
Harry: Yeah but next we'll tip the whole water out won't we?
Chloe: Yeah, we're gonna get a lot of water so it goes down there and makes a puddle again. No bigger than a puddle actually. [Extends both arms]
Harry: Yeah shall we go and play it now, Chloe?

Chloe's comment that the play 'hasn't started yet' reveals that she is waiting for Harry and Pippa to begin the play because '. . . they was inside, working with Mrs Dearling'. This play episode has been conceived as a shared experience from the outset and Chloe has no intention of beginning until her friends can join her outside. Chloe makes no further comment about her mark making with the chalk (see the first photo in the cameo); the pursuit appears to carry little significance for her beyond acting as a holding activity to occupy her time until her friends arrive. Chloe understands the system; she knows that children are sometimes called to 'work' with teachers. She accepts this and delays her play to await the arrival of her friends.

The children's commentary on their play suggests that their explorations with water are firmly embedded within a social context. It appears that their mutual engagement and shared interests sustain the play, even when there is some minor conflict over the 'rules of the game' that Chloe identifies when she alludes to Harry being at fault as he emptied his bucket before she did. The conversation that takes places between Chloe and Harry as they watch the recording illuminates how they co-construct ideas and consequently bring complexity to their play. The children's friendship enables them to develop their joint interest in the flow of water, and their discovery that water flows down the playground slope acts as a provocation to consider further possibilities. Hence, what begins as a relatively simple game becomes reframed as a more sophisticated investigation into the movement of water. The act of watching the play reignites their fascination and acts as a further prompt, in which Chloe and Harry reconsider their explorations and begin to plan for future possibilities. It seems likely that the two friends' subsequent investigations will bring further complexity and new possibilities to their play.

Chloe's teacher, Lynne, also noted the friendship between the pair, commenting, 'she's obviously very comfortable with particular children. She's quite confident; she likes to play with Harry.' Likewise, Chloe's mother, Hannah, immediately picked up on Harry's presence, saying, 'Oh look, she's with Harry again . . . well, she's marrying Harry!' Through piecing together the perspectives of Chloe, Lynne and Hannah, we are able to view the children's activities within the context of an established friendship that perhaps enables the pair to endure the minor disagreements regarding the rules of their game in order to sustain their playful investigation. Thus, at the heart of this cameo we see a sense of togetherness (Van Oers and Hannikainen, 2001) that underpins the children's playful collaboration.

Conclusion

Friendships do not occur in isolation but within the blending of home and school life. Friendships are linked with identity development and cultural preferences and, as such, are integral to young children's learning processes with play as a key medium. To understand this we need to engage methodologically with children's own perspectives on play. LC's research has developed this further to locate teachers' and parents' perspectives alongside the children's own views on their play.

School-based friendships need pedagogical support and open access to resources that promote collaboration. Children are powerfully self-determining in their play and may move play away from teacher intention. However, this often deepens the intellectual challenges of the play.

Open-ended resources of the type described here stimulate flexible and creative thinking in cooperating peers, and friendship is a key element of cooperation and play extension.

The current curriculum stance on playful learning and playful pedagogies is somewhat ambiguous, but there are positive messages if your pedagogical intentions for play are strong. Children can deepen the intellectual quality of their play in the right environment.

Questions to promote reflection

1 How do you see friendships as contributing to the social and intellectual life of the classroom?
2 In what ways does your practice enable children to draw on the culture of home within their play in school?
3 Consider examples of occasions when you have seen children use similar, open-ended play resources, and identify the outcomes when they manipulated materials in ways you were not anticipating.
4 Consider which children might be the expert others in the cameos. How do adults operate here as expert others given that only Cameo 3 includes an adult (the student teacher)?

References and further reading (in bold)

Broadhead, P. (1997) Promoting sociability and co-operation in nursery settings. *British Educational Research Journal*, 23(4): 513–531.

Broadhead, P. (2001) Investigating sociability and cooperation in four and five year olds in reception class settings. *International Journal of Early Years Education*, 9(1): 23–35.

Broadhead, P. (2004) *Early Years Play and Learning: Developing Social Skills and Cooperation.* London: RoutledgeFalmer.

Broadhead, P. and Burt, A. (2012) *Understanding Young Children's Learning Through Play: Building Playful Pedagogies*. London: Routledge.

Chesworth, L. (2014) A deeper understanding of play. In A. Brock (ed.) *The Early Years Reflective Practice Handbook*. Oxford: Routledge.

Corsaro, W. (2000) Early childhood education, children's peer cultures, and the future of childhood. *European Early Childhood Education Research Journal*, 8(2): 89–102.

Department for Education (DfE) (2012) *Statutory Framework for the Early Years Foundation Stage.* Available online at: http://www.gov.uk/government/publications/early-years-foundation-stage-framework (accessed 22 March 2014).

Factor, J. (2009) 'It's only play if you get to choose.' Children's perceptions of play and adult interventions. In C. Dell Clark (ed.) *Transactions at Play. Play and Culture Studies*, 9. New York: University Press of America: 129–146.

Gallimore, R. and Tharp, R. (1990) Teaching mind in society: teaching, schooling and literate discourse. In L.C. Moll (ed.) *Vygotsky and Education: Instructional Implications and Applications of Socio-historical Psychology*. Cambridge: Cambridge University Press.

Hartup, W.W. (1996) The company they keep: friendships and their developmental significance. *Child Development*, 67: 1–13.

Howes, C. (1994) *The Collaborative Construction of Pretend*. Albany, NY: State University of New York Press.

Van Oers, B. and Hannikainen, M. (2001) Some thoughts about togetherness: an introduction. *International Journal of Early Years Education*, 9(2): 101–124.

Vygotsky, L. (1978) *Mind in Society: The Development of Higher Psychological Processes*. London: Harvard University Press.

Yelland, N., Lee, L., O'Rourke, M. and Harrison, C. (2008) *Rethinking Learning in Early Childhood Education*. Berkshire: Open University Press.

10

Young children as researchers in play

Jane Murray

Summary

The *Young Children As Researchers* (YCAR) study (Murray, 2012) found that when young children lead play they sometimes behave similarly to professional adult researchers and, although this is often unacknowledged, there are ways for adults to recognise such behaviour. This chapter discusses young children's rights to play and research, and definitions of play and research, alongside their marginalisation from both. Links are made between young children's epistemic play and research, exemplified by YCAR findings revealing children as capable researchers during play. The YCAR has messages for practitioners wishing to recognise children's self-directed research in play as a valuable tool for constructing understanding.

Introduction

As an early years teacher, I encountered many young children questioning, planning, acquiring information, analysing and interpreting, solving problems, exploring and reporting novel ideas and artefacts they had created. The children engaged in these activities every day, resulting in their own constructions of knowledge and understanding; most happened when the children were engaged in play they were leading themselves. There were clearly similarities between the research activity encountered in my university work and the behaviours presented by my Foundation Stage children as part of their everyday naturalistic play.

In recent years, interest in children as researchers has increased but it has tended to focus on older children and young people (Cammarota and Fine, 2008) or it has required children and young people to adopt adults' agenda and research methods. Research is often part of everyday life for children in schools but tends to be limited to participation in adults' projects or by-products of learning. Recognised research roles of children younger than eight years old have generally been limited to co-researcher or researched, and methodologies designed by adults tend to prevail (Clark and Moss, 2011). Adults seem to find it difficult to share or relinquish control in contexts they understand as research. Moreover, children tend to be marginalised from the 'rarefied world' of the academy (Redmond, 2008: 9): a hegemonic 'score-keeping world' where professional adult researchers are privileged (Lees, 1999: 382).

YCAR addressed young children's marginalisation by conceptualising ways in which they *are* researchers and may be considered to be researchers. Participating children were 138 four to eight year olds. This chapter argues that, when young children lead their own play, they sometimes behave in similar ways to professional adult researchers and there are ways in which adults can recognise such behaviours.

Young children's rights to play and research

Disregarding young children's own enquiries disrespects them as rights holders and capable, sophisticated thinkers. Appadurai (2006: 167) argues that research is a 'right of a special kind' to which universal access is not yet secured, so young children's exclusion from being recognised as researchers may be regarded as a social justice issue.

Children's right to play is enshrined in Article 31 of the United Nations Convention on the Rights of the Child (see also Chapter 11). Play seems to be both natural and necessary for children (Moyles, 2010), providing an authentic context for their agency; however, western children's opportunities for free play have decreased significantly in recent years (Witten *et al.*, 2013), resulting in fewer key developmental experiences. Numerous reasons have been suggested for this, including parental concern for children's safety (Refshauge *et al.* 2012), parental time poverty (National Family and Parenting Institute (NFPI), 2009) and the distraction from schooling that free play may cause (Fisher, 2008). Play and learning are thus dichotomised when, in fact, they are often synchronous: young children's constructions of knowledge and understanding emerge through play. Yet increased schoolification in many early childhood settings, and its intrusion into young children's home lives through homework and adult-led activities means fewer opportunities for young children to play freely.

Defining play and research

Defining both play and research seems to present difficulties. Nevertheless, many attempts have been made to do so. In UK contexts, play is often defined as 'freely chosen, personally directed, intrinsically motivated behaviour that actively engages the child' (National Playing Fields Association (NPFA) *et al.*, 2000: 6; see also Chapter 2). Equally, numerous play taxonomies appear in the literature (e.g. Kernan, 2007). Hutt *et al.* (1989) suggest play is constituted of three key elements – ludic play, games with rules, and epistemic play. Social characteristics and benefits of children's play are also widely reported (Broadhead, 2001; Edmiston, 2008), while Ryan (2005) regards play as a serious business: 'Children's play is not a neutral space but rather is a political and negotiated terrain' (p. 112).

Like play, research has no universal definition (Hillage *et al.*, 1998), though copious definitions have been proposed, among which are commonalities. Many research definitions emphasise knowledge generation, while others promote a systematic approach; the role of dissemination in research is also commonly highlighted (REF 2014, 2011). The lack of a universal definition for research in the existing literature meant that securing a definition to underpin the YCAR study was an important initial task. A decision was made to construct empirically a definition of research with professional researchers, which could then be compared with young children's everyday behaviours during later fieldwork. However, rather than a definition, participating professional researchers identified 39 research behaviours, which formed a Research Behaviour Framework (RBF). Moreover, they specified four behaviours that they regarded as 'most important' for research:

1 exploration
2 finding a solution
3 conceptualising
4 basing decisions on evidence.

Each of these was then defined in relation to the extant literature; children's everyday activities at home and at school were recorded in different ways and compared with the RBF behaviours. Later in the chapter, the YCAR study is discussed further, but now some of the ways young children are marginalised from play and research are addressed, together with how their play and research may interweave.

Young children's marginalisation from play and research

The mounting exclusion from free play opportunities has meant children are increasingly denied the benefits play brings (Goldstein, 2012). The reason is partly because children's play remains a nebulous and difficult area for adults to understand, so identifying meanings in children's play often proves challenging. For example, non-verbal social interactions that are manifested in much young children's play can prove impenetrable for adults to comprehend (Bae, 2010). This may explain why adults often want to control children's play; however, such control denies children the authentic satisfaction derived from play experiences children have created for themselves (important experiences, as shown in most chapters of this book).

Adults' inabilities to recognise meanings underlying young children's behaviours may also lie behind young children's marginalisation from research. Young children's abilities to construct knowledge have long been an area for debate. While children's competencies to develop 'a philosophy of what counts as knowledge and truth' are established (epistemology as defined by Strega, 2005: 201), there are views that children's higher levels of knowledge can be constructed over time only through continuous experience. These perspectives present tensions between perceptions of the child as an evolving human and as an expert in his or her own life from birth.

In recent years, however, children have participated in studies addressing their own play (Kapasi and Gleave, 2009); such projects acknowledge children's rights, and include themes of social values, autonomy, risk management, social exclusion and inclusion.

What has young children's epistemic play got to do with research?

Links between young children's epistemic play and research can be identified. The word 'epistemic' has its etymological roots in the Greek word 'epistêmê', meaning knowledge that 'requires that reasons are given as to why something is the case' (Thomas, 2007: 149). Epistemology emerged as a branch of philosophy concerned with the study of knowledge and justified belief; how we know we know. Epistemology underpins many of the protocols that are required by today's academy for contemporary research to be recognised. Hutt *et al.* (1989: 222–224) describe epistemic play as 'the acquisition of knowledge and information ... problem-solving ... exploration ... productive', as well as focused on materials and transformation; in other words, knowledge construction. Children's uses of multimodal expression and communication (see Chapter 20) may also be how they engage in epistemic activity. In these ways, young children generally think and interact with the world through their senses and perceptions so when they reason alongside such sensory experiences, their resulting judgements may be considered robust.

Epistemic play is far more than purely action: bound into epistemic play is the player's consciousness that she is playing in order to acquire knowledge. It can be argued, therefore, that epistemic play requires theory of mind, recognised as a higher-order 'cognitive capacity to attribute mental states to self and others' (Goldman, 2012: 402). Theory of mind is acknowledged as an important indicator for humans' understanding of their place in the world and others' actions, predicated largely on 'our ability to understand the mental states that underlie actions' (Song *et al.*, 2008: 295). Awareness of how we come to know through our actions is one type of theory of mind; it is also an epistemological engagement.

Debate has been voluble regarding the quality of young children's theories of mind; while some suggest that young children have theories, others posit 'commonsense theory of mind ... not the product of scientific theorising' (Wellman, 1990: 130). Interwoven with much of the recent literature and research and children's acquisition of knowledge is Morton's notion of 'theory theory' (1980), which is one explanation for how we acquire, construct and apply knowledge in our everyday lives by developing theories through higher-order thinking such as reasoning, testing ideas, planning, making decisions, inferring and systematically organising information. While 'theory theory' has its detractors (Wringe, 2011), Gopnik and Meltzoff (1997) have been particularly strong advocates of infants' and young children's adoption of 'theory theory' to construct and use knowledge. Their work contributes to a significant, growing and varied body of research recognising that 'children are far more capable (of theorising) than was thought even two or three decades ago' (Whitebread, 2012: 137). These capabilities are sometimes acknowledged in early childhood provision through constructs such as working theories (Hedges, 2014) and characteristics of effective learning (Stewart, 2011).

Taking all this into account, a proposition was framed for the YCAR study. If it could be established that participating young children engage in activity that academy members regard as research behaviour, it could be argued that they engage in research behaviour on the academy's terms.

Young children as researchers in play: some of the YCAR findings

Using varied qualitative methods, hundreds of vignettes were gathered during the YCAR study, featuring participating children engaged in their naturalistic everyday activity at home and at school. Much of their activity was 'freely chosen, personally directed, intrinsically motivated behaviour that actively engaged the child', in other words, play (NPFA *et al.*, 2000: 6). Children, their parents and practitioners helped to gather the data, and they participated in analysing and interpreting the findings. Tables 10.1 and 10.2 show the participants across three primary school settings – Ash, Beech and Cherry Settings (pseudonyms) – and five family homes.

During the YCAR study, 80 epistemological factors presented in children's naturalistic behaviours. These indicated the children's engagements in epistemic play, when they combined sensory evidence with reasoning to explore, find solutions,

Table 10.1 Profile of YCAR participants in three settings

Setting Pseudonym	Number of children	Ages of children	Gender share of children	Number and gender share of practitioners	Most recent OfSTED inspection grade	Predominant pedagogic model
Ash Setting	32	7–8 years	20 boys 12 girls	3 [1M, 2F]	2 [Good]	Formal
Beech Setting	46	4–5 years	23 boys 23 girls	8 [8F]	2 [Good]	Open framework
Cherry Setting	60	4–5 years	40 boys 20 girls	6 [1M, 5F]	2 [Good]	Open framework

Table 10.2 Profile of YCAR participants in five family homes

	Ash Setting		Beech Setting		Cherry Setting
Pseudonym	Annie	Billy	Gemma	Harry	Martin
Gender	Girl	Boy	Girl	Boy	Boy
Age during home fieldwork	8	8	5	5	5
Living with. . .	Mother Father	Mother Father Sister (9)	Mother Father Brother (8)	Mother Father Brother (4)	Mother Father Sister (4)
Description of homes	Modern, detached, 4 bedrooms, garden, on a development in an established English Midlands town				
Home language	English	English	English	English/ French	English
Social Class category (M.R.S., 2006)	A	A/B	B	A	A/B
Family	A	B	C	D	E

conceptualise and base decisions on evidence: the four most important research behaviours, according to academy members.

The 80 epistemological factors fit in to nine categories, appearing across the four most important research behaviours; these are presented as four sets of blocks (Table 10.3). While there were hundreds of examples of children engaging in such activity during the YCAR study, four are presented here, with children's names changed to pseudonyms. Each example includes a cameo of a young child engaging in play, with links to extant literature, and each discusses the meanings of that play as research behaviour. The cameos are followed by a consideration of messages the YCAR study may provide for practice.

Entering a social domain when exploring in play: social encounters

The literature indicates that social encounters can be important contexts for children's epistemic behaviour (Corsaro, 2003) and the research data reiterated this. Equally, physical spaces and objects that the YCAR children encountered seemed to be important factors in both their exploration and social encounters. Furthermore, spaces where children could communicate using varied modalities seemed to relate to their explorations (Bae, 2010).

Cameo 1

In Ash Setting, children engage in semi-independent literacy work with the learning objective 'To be able to understand character behaviour'. They work at tables of four or more children, and Florence (girl, aged eight years) sits next to her friend. After 25 minutes Florence's friend (girl, aged eight years) asks me if my ears are pierced. She gets up to come to look for herself and Florence joins her. Florence and her friend engage in 'freely chosen, personally directed, intrinsically motivated behaviour that actively engage[s]' them (NPFA *et al.*, 2000: 6) – in other words, play. Moreover, Florence is moved to 'examine' my ears for a 'specific diagnostic purpose' through social encounter with her friend.

Here, Florence and her friend were playing socially (Broadhead, 2001). Equally, Florence presented with three key characteristics of epistemic play: acquisition of information, exploration and activity involving materials (Hutt *et al.*, 1989). Florence's behaviour resonates with a view that infants and young children appear 'programmed' to explore (Gopnik *et al.*, 1999) and may be particularly drawn to exploring objects (Garner and Bergen, 2006). Moreover, by mirroring her friend's actions, Florence expresses a desire to be socially aligned, resonating with further literature which suggests that young children communicate their views through non-verbal media which they use as tools for epistemic activity. By making her own 'space' to explore a focus of personal interest that sidelined the teacher's intended purpose, Florence began to develop her own epistemology in a socially democratic micro-context (Hoyuelos, 2004). She became a social agent by constructing her own understanding of the world.

Table 10.3 Four important research behaviours and nine epistemological factors in young children's play

Explore: research as part of young children's everyday play activity

Patterned behaviour	Experiments	Social encounter	Develops own agenda	Shows interest in materials		Seeking	
				Interested in context	Cause and effect	Curious	Focused on task
Applications of prior experience	**Innovation**	**Social domains**	**Autonomy**	**Material contexts**	**Cognitive domains**	**Dispositions**	

Find Solutions: research as part of young children's everyday play activity

Applications of prior experience	Innovation	Social domains	Autonomy	Material contexts	Dispositions	Outliers
		Theory of mind				
Able reader		Employs others to help with finding a solution			Excited by finding solution	
		Shares solution			Motivated by finding solution	
		Resolves another person's problem			Perseveres to resolve problem	
		Solution not shared with or witnessed by others				
Wants to preserve what s/he is doing		Solution not shared with or witnessed by others: unconfirmed				
		Denied opportunity to share solution			Believes s/he has failed	
	Finds own solution	Responding to adult's semi-open questions	Focused on something of personal interest	Inductive reasoning	*Unmotivated*	
	Devises practical method to create solution	Responding to adult's closed questions	Time and freedom to explore, investigate, experiment with something of personal interest	Deductive reasoning	*Has become disinterested*	
Reproducing knowledge s/he already had	*Creates a problem to solve*	*Following adult's direction*	Self-regulates	Exploring properties	*Gives up*	*Solution unconfirmed*

Table 10.3 (Continued)

Conceptualise: research as part of young children's everyday play activity

Applications of prior experience	Innovation	Social domains	Autonomy	Material contexts	Cognitive domains	Outliers
Recalling instructions					Making links – ANALOGY	
Linking prior knowledge to new application	Identifies anomaly				Planning	
					Engaged in symbolic representation	
					Language supports thinking	
Synthesising concepts	Creating an imagined space/persona	Adult stops conceptualisation	Makes decisions based on own criteria		Using imagination	
Thinking tangentially	Developing own idea[s] from external stimulus	Following adult's direction	Autonomously deciding what needs to be done and doing it		Involved in pursuing a train of thought	
Thinking through a problem by applying concepts	Invents a process/method	Works with others to develop conceptualisation	Creating a problem	Creates a new use for object[s]	Predicts	Applies anthropomorphism

Base decisions on evidence (BDoE): research as part of young children's everyday play activity

Applications of prior experience	Social domains	Autonomy	Material contexts	Cognitive domains (Meta-cognition)	Methodological issues
Applies prior experience				Trial and error	Methodological issue
Applies mental model	Values peer perspectives			Thinks strategically	Sampling issue
Extrapolates	Acts on adult opinion	Enacts personal preference	Senses provide evidence for action	Applies human 'reason'	BDoE = research

Adopting a disposition to explore: being curious

YCAR data revealed many incidents of children demonstrating curiosity correlated with epistemic behaviour, which is a finding congruent with the literature. Gemma's mother reported one example that had happened at home (Cameo 2).

Cameo 2

Gemma (girl, aged five years) is playing with a bracelet. She tries and manages to open and close the bracelet, then decides to use the bracelet on her ankle as it is too big for her wrist. Gemma's mother developed this report further during a focus group held later with the family, asserting that 'she was basically playing around with it, asking how to open the bracelet'.

In this cameo Gemma engaged in epistemic play. This focused on the bracelet and its properties (activity involving materials), productivity demonstrated by a novel use for the bracelet and also exploration, characterised by Gemma probing the bracelet as an object and its potential uses. Laevers (2000) categorises curiosity as a disposition, describing it as 'the exploratory drive' (p. 21) and Gemma exemplified this. She encountered new things, asking how to open the bracelet before making a decision to use the bracelet as an anklet. In so doing, Gemma displayed epistemic curiosity. While playing with the bracelet, she studied, examined and investigated it, diagnosed it was too big, then adopted the bracelet as something else. Her behaviour indicated higher-order thinking congruent with deduction.

Adopting a disposition to explore: focusing on a task

We have understood for some time that involvement – another disposition – displayed in young children can be an effective indicator for successful lifelong learning. In the YCAR study, involvement presented itself when children focused on tasks: this seemed to occur when children were engaged in epistemic behaviour.

Cameo 3

One day in Ash Setting, Billy (boy, aged eight years) is sitting on the carpet with his class, listening to the teacher giving instructions for an art activity. While the teacher continues to give instructions, Billy looks down at his sandal and begins fiddling with it, looking intently at it while moving his fingers up and down the straps, flicking the buckle and allowing it to fall back repeatedly. Billy puts his face almost on to his sandal, inspecting it closely. When the teacher has finished her exposition she says, 'Let's see who's sitting beautifully then.' Billy raises his head a little in response but continues to focus his eyes downwards to look closely at his sandal.

Here, of his own volition, Billy developed a personal new focus, which deviated from the teacher's. Nevertheless, Billy's behaviour aligned with the NPFA *et al.* definition of play: a 'freely chosen, personally directed, intrinsically motivated behaviour that (seemed to) actively engage' him (2000: 6). Moreover, Billy's behaviour was characteristic of two features of epistemic play: exploration – 'manipulatory movements', investigation and inspection – alongside activity involving materials (Hutt *et al.*, 1989: 224). In addition to exemplifying play, Billy's behaviour epitomizes 'flow' as his 'attention was completely absorbed by the activity' (Csíkszentmihályi, 1990: 53). As Billy explored his sandal by looking at it and fiddling with it, he exhibited 'concentration . . . strong motivation, fascination and total implication', while focusing 'attention to one limited circle' (Laevers, 2000: 24–25). Furthermore, Billy's close examination of his sandal was behaviour congruent with Stebbins' (2001) four senses of exploration in the context of social sciences research, framed as:

1   to study, examine, analyse, or investigate
2   to become familiar with something by testing it or experimenting with it
3   to travel over or through a particular space for the purposes of discovery
4   to examine a thing or idea for (specific) diagnostic purposes (p. 2).

Engaging with a material context when exploring: interest in context

Some participating children in the YCAR study seemed to combine two aspects of epistemic play when they were interested in their contexts: material contexts and exploration. Moreover, some of the children and their families gathered information about their everyday behaviours at home. Among other resources, they were equipped with camcorders. Gemma (girl, aged five years) acquired knowledge and information as she learned how to operate a camcorder to create a sequenced 'guided tour' of her home. Her behaviour also indicated that, before this event, she had encountered particular objects in her home, and had come to know their names and their uses before filming.

Cameo 4

Gemma focuses the camcorder on different features in her home as she walks through it. She relates the names of the objects as she encounters each one through the viewfinder of the camcorder: 'bin', 'breakfast bar', 'suncream', 'cooker', 'spicy things' [spice rack], 'sugar', 'These are the stairs', 'There's about 1, 2, 3, 4, 5, 6, 7, 8, 9, 10, 11, 12, 13 steps so you can do it whenever you want.'

Gemma trialled her use of a camcorder at home, a space she knew well and to which she may have had an attachment (Spencer, 2004): a physical context in which 'relations, options, and emotional and cognitive situations . . . produced (in her) a sense of well-being and security' (Malaguzzi, 1996: 40). Gemma seemed to value her home for how she could use it and her interest in her context translated to her explorations of the camcorder, her home and the synthesis of the two as she explored as a researcher, travelling through the house to discover more about filming, gathering data and operating the camcorder, examining each physical object or space for the purpose of data gathering.

Here, through epistemic play, Gemma conflated material contexts and exploration. She explored by manipulating the camcorder to inspect and investigate both the camcorder itself and using it as a tool to engage with her material environment. Examples in the literature suggest that Gemma's behaviour is not unusual as young children explore. They may do so to construct actively their own epistemologies (Hoyuelos, 2004). Equally, Gemma's 'tour' appeared to exhibit 'flow' in her thinking – an indicator for young children's optimal development. Gemma had a goal (to use the camcorder to film her home), she was fully involved in filming her home and she personally controlled the process. Gemma's opportunity to explore with a high level of autonomy was likely to be beneficial for her development across physical, cognitive, social and emotional domains.

What are the YCAR messages for early years practice?

The YCAR study raises questions about how play, learning, research and knowledge are defined and recognised, and how value is attached to each. Children's naturalistic behaviours at home and at school were captured in different ways during the study, by adults and children. Many aligned with well-rehearsed definitions of play as well as research behaviours identified by professional researchers at the start of the YCAR study.

While young children are often marginalised from both play and research, the YCAR study found participating young children engaged autonomously in higher-order thinking during research behaviours present in their everyday epistemic play activity. Moreover, the YCAR children sometimes sidelined adults' requirements of them to engage in research behaviours. During the YCAR study, nine epistemological factors emerged in participating children's naturalistic behaviours (see Table 10.3). These factors emerged as characteristics of children's research behaviours, and appeared to act as tools that enabled them to construct knowledge, meanings and understanding. Moreover, it was possible to link the epistemological factors to substantial extant evidence, indicating the children's higher-order cognitive processing and generation of theory of mind.

The YCAR findings carry valuable messages for early years practice, as follows.

- It is unwise to dichotomise play and learning: children do not do so of their own volition.
- Look out for children engaging in the four 'most important' research behaviours in their play: exploration, finding solutions, conceptualising and basing decisions on evidence. Use Table 10.3 to support recognition of epistemological factors in young children's research behaviours.

- Give children time, freedom and space to lead their own play. When children move 'off task', they may construct understanding of higher quality than learning originally planned for them by their practitioner.
- Recognise the value of children's play and research for constructing high-quality understanding. To achieve this, we must link our observations and knowledge of individual children to evidence-based theoretical perspectives on play and research.
- Respect children's right to research in play: this is an ethical approach to research with children.

Conclusion

The YCAR study established that participating young children do engage in research behaviours. This claim can be justified through deductive argument, the academy's dominant methodology:

> Academy members identified particular behaviours as research. Participating children engaged in those behaviours. Therefore, according to the academy members' rubric, the children engaged in research.

Much of the YCAR children's research behaviour was 'freely chosen, personally directed, intrinsically motivated behaviour that actively engaged' them – play (NPFA *et al.*, 2000: 6) – suggesting that play is a medium through which young children may naturally behave similarly to professional adult researchers to construct knowledge. Through the establishment of research behaviours and the emergence of epistemological factors that are visible in young children's natural play activity, the YCAR study increases possibilities for recognising young children as researchers in their own right.

Questions to promote reflection

1   What factors might support young children's research behaviours in early childhood settings?
2   What factors might inhibit young children's research behaviours in early childhood settings?
3   What might the repercussions be for young children who do not have opportunities to lead their own research in self-directed play?
4   How can practitioners support parents to understand the potential value of children's research in play for development and learning?

References and further reading (in bold)

Appadurai, A. (2006) The right to research. *Globalisation, Societies and Education*, 4(2): 167–177.
Bae, B. (2010) Realising children's right to participation in early childhood settings: some critical issues in a Norwegian context. *Early Years*, 30(3): 205–221.

Bailey, A. and Barnes, S. (2009) Where do I fit in? Children's spaces and places. In R. Eke, H. Butcher and M. Lee (eds) *Whose Childhood Is It? The Roles of Children, Adults and Policy Makers*. London: Continuum.

Broadhead, P. (2001) Investigating sociability and cooperation in four and five year olds in reception class settings. *International Journal of Early Years Education*, 9(1): 23–35.

Cammarota, J. and Fine, M. (eds) (2008) *Revolutionizing Education: Youth Participatory Action Research in Motion*. New York: Routledge.

Clark, A. and Moss, P. (2011) *Listening to Young Children*, 2nd edn. London: National Children's Bureau.

Corsaro, W. (2003) *We're Friends, Right? Inside Kids' Culture*. Washington, DC: Joseph Henry Press.

Csíkszentmihályi, M. (1990) *Flow: The Psychology of Optimal Experience*. New York: Harper and Row.

Edmiston, B. (2008) *Forming Ethical Identities in Early Childhood Play*. London: Routledge.

Fisher, J. (2008) *Starting from the Child*. Maidenhead: Open University Press/McGraw-Hill Education.

Garner, B.P. and Bergen, D. (2006) Play development from birth to age four. In D. Fromberg and D. Bergen (eds) *Play from Birth to Twelve*. London: Routledge.

Goldman, A.I. (2012) Theory of mind. In E. Margolis, R. Samuels and S. Stich (eds) *The Oxford Handbook of Philosophy of Cognitive Science*. Oxford: Oxford University Press.

Goldstein, J. (2012) *Play in Children's Development, Health and Well-being*. Brussels: Toy Industries of Europe (TIE).

Gopnik, A. and Meltzoff, A. (1997) *Words Thoughts and Theories*. Cambridge, MA: MIT Press.

Gopnik, A., Meltzoff, A. and Kuhn, P. (1999) *How Babies Think*. London: Phoenix.

Hedges, H. (2014) Young children's 'working theories': building and connecting understandings. *Journal of Early Childhood Research*, 12(1): 35–49.

Hillage, J., Pearson, R., Anderson, A. and Tamkin, P. (1998) *Excellence in Research on Schools*. London: Department for Education and Employment.

Hoyuelos, A. (2004) A pedagogy of transgression. *Children in Europe*, 6: 6–7.

Hutt, C., Tyler, S., Hutt, C. and Christopherson, H. (1989) *Play, Exploration and Learning*. London: Routledge.

Kapasi, H. and Gleave, J. (2009) *Because It's Freedom: Children's Views on Their Time to Play*. London: National Children's Bureau.

Kernan, M. (2007) Play as a context for early learning and development: a research paper. Dublin: National Council for Curriculum and Assessment.

Laevers, L. (2000) Forward to basics! Deep-level learning and the experiential approach. *Early Years: An International Journal of Research and Development*, 20(2): 20–29.

Lees, L. (1999) Critical geography and the opening up of the academy: lessons from 'real life' attempts. *Area*, 31(4): 377–383.

Malaguzzi, L. (1996) The right to environment. In T. Filippini and V. Vecchi (eds) *The Hundred Languages of Children: The Exhibit*. Reggio Emilia: Reggio Children.

Morton, A. (1980) *Frames of Mind*. Oxford: Oxford University Press.

Moyles, J. (ed.) (2010) *The Excellence of Play*, 3rd edn. Maidenhead: Open University Press/ McGraw Education.

Murray, J. (2012) An exploration of young children's engagements in research behaviour. Unpublished PhD thesis, University of Northampton, UK.

National Family and Parenting Institute (NFPI) (2009) Family Trends – British families since the 1950s. Available online at: http://www.familyandparenting.org/familyTrends (accessed 22 October 2013).

National Playing Fields Association (NPFA), Children's Play Council and Playlink (2000) *Best Play. What Play Provision Should Do for Children*. London: National Playing Fields Association.

Redmond, G. (2008) Children's perspectives on economic adversity: a review of the literature. Innocenti Discussion Paper no. IDP 2008–01. Florence: UNICEF Innocenti Research Centre.

Refshauge, A.D., Stigsdotter, U.K. and Cosco, N.G. (2012) Adults' motivation for bringing their children to park playgrounds. *Urban Forestry and Urban Greening*, 11: 396–405.

REF 2014 (2011) Assessment framework and guidance on submissions. Available online at: http://www.ref.ac.uk/pubs/2011–02/ (accessed 27 March 2014).

Ryan, S. (2005) Freedom to choose. In N. Yelland (ed.) *Critical Issues in Early Childhood Education*. Maidenhead: Open University Press.

Song, H.-J., Onishi, K.H., Baillargeon, R. and Fisher, C. (2008) Can an agent's false belief be corrected by an appropriate communication? Psychological reasoning in 18-month-old infants. *Cognition*, 109(3): 295–315.

Spencer, C. (2004) Place attachment, place identity and the development of the child's self-identity. In S. Catling and F. Martin (eds) *Researching Primary Geography*. Special Publication no. 1, August. London Register of Research.

Stebbins, R.A. (2001) *Exploratory Research in the Social Sciences*. Thousand Oaks, CA: Sage.

Stewart, N. (2011) *How Children Learn: The Characteristics of Effective Early Learning*. London: British Association for Early Childhood Education.

Strega, S. (2005) The view from the poststructural margins. In L. Brown and S. Strega (eds) *Research as Resistance*. Toronto: Canadian Scholars' Press.

Thomas, G. (2007) *Education and Theory: Strangers in Paradigms*. Maidenhead: Open University Press/McGraw-Hill.

Wellman, H.M. (1990) *The Child's Theory of Mind*. Cambridge, MA: MIT Press.

Whitebread, D. (2012) *Developmental Psychology and Early Childhood Education*. London: Sage.

Witten, K., Kearns, R., Carroll, P., Asiasiga, L. and Tava'e, N. (2013) New Zealand parents' understandings of the intergenerational decline in children's independent outdoor play and active travel. *Children's Geographies*, 11(2): 215–229.

Wringe, B. (2011) Cognitive individualism and the child as scientist program. *Studies in History and Philosophy of Biological and Biomedical Sciences*, 42(4): 518–529.

PART 3
Playful pedagogies

'Sanctioning play with all its ramifications also means having faith in children, and accepting them as people who need to make mistakes and who must rely on our tolerance when they do so.'

Jenkinson, S. (2001) *The Genius of Play*. Stroud: Hawthorn Press: 138.

11

Re-establishing early years practitioners as play professionals

Justine Howard and Peter King

Summary

Emotional health is paramount to children's development, and play is an important way to support this. There is a growing appreciation that early education should be concerned with the whole child and not just the development of skills and knowledge. Early years curricula that centralise play are consistent with this. The freedom and choice afforded to children in play promotes confidence, esteem and well-being, and as a result it has powerful developmental and therapeutic potential. It is vital that early years' professionals are equipped with a sound understanding as to why, and in what ways, play is such a powerful medium. Rather than seeing play as being qualitatively different across contexts, this chapter suggests that it may be more useful to see this as a spectrum of practice. The role of early years practitioners is a complex one, requiring them to provide for children's rights, care, education and play needs, often concurrently in the same setting. This chapter will consider the literature surrounding the developmental potential of play and the way that playfulness as a disposition promotes development across domains. It will consider the important balance between practitioners understanding play as a beginning, a process and an outcome.

Introduction

Without doubt, when we watch children playing there is evidence that their play affords them opportunities to develop gross and fine motor skills, to interact and converse with others, to explore the properties of objects and to demonstrate problem-solving capacity. Observations of children's play demonstrate it changing in form, content and complexity over time. Children learn in a variety of ways – for example, by rote, observation, modelling and imitation. Do they really need to play in order to learn and develop? As strong advocates of play, we certainly do not wish to question its importance. However, determining *why* play is a unique mode of learning and development for children is a difficult task. Not all of the developmental value inherent in play is easily observed and, as a concept, it is difficult to isolate and so therefore difficult to measure as a causal variable. The following exercise demonstrates this point (see Figures 11.1 and 11.2).

- Observe a child or a group of children engaged in a play activity.

- Write a brief description of this activity and note down the learning or development you think is happening during the play.

- Next, go through your list and ask yourself the following question. Could children develop this skill without being engaged in play activities? The aim here is that you are trying to isolate something that children gain from play that can't be gained elsewhere.

Figure 11.1 An activity to set you thinking (1)

The table shown in Figure 11.2 is an example of what you may come up with.

The play activity: *a brother and sister are playing with the LEGO® blocks. They are each working on individual models (one is building a house and the other is developing a repeating pattern). Both are using the same box of LEGO®.*

Learning opportunity	Area of development	Is this unique to play?
Taking turns with each other	Social	X
Colour recognition by selecting blocks	Cognitive/Intellectual	X
Learning new words	Language/Communication	X
Negotiation about pieces	Social	X
Fine motor skills via picking up and placing blocks	Physical	X

What did you find?

Invariably, there will be no unique learning opportunities left on your list (or at least very few)! Children can develop skills in multiple contexts, including those that are formal. For example, in the play activity above, children can learn to take turns in general conversation and are constantly perfecting their fine motor skills. They will use everyday experiences such as a walk to the shops, to learn about themselves, others and the world around them. Play is not necessarily essential for these things to develop; however, all is not lost and this activity results in deep and critical thinking. My students often become defensive about play and a lot of healthy debate ensues! A common response is "Okay, so children may be able to develop these skills in lots of different ways, but there is something special about learning when it happens in play, something different". Let's start to investigate what this special thing might be and why it might be frequently overlooked.

Figure 11.2 Example of a possible outcome to the activity in Figure 11.1

Cohen (2006) suggests that since the 1950s, our motivation to study play has derived from three perspectives: cognitive, societal and emotional. Cohen associates different professional contexts with these areas. Play from an educational perspective is associated with cognitive development, play therapy with emotional development and the playwork movement with societal development. Traditionally, these perspectives have also differed in terms of whether they tend towards considering play as a way of *being* or as a way of *becoming* (Sturrock *et al.*, 2004). The cognitive approach has been more commonly associated with the way in which play contributes to children *becoming* competent learners. The societal and emotional approaches, however, have tended towards considering play for play's sake and emphasise how *being* is inextricably linked to *becoming*. Their focus has been on the process of play and the qualities that render it valuable for development. Of course, developmental issues are not so easily divided and the boundaries between each of these areas are blurred, particularly if we view play as a disposition rather than as an observable behaviour.

The inherent value of play for promoting child development

An important problem associated with trying to provide evidence for the developmental potential of play is that it is a difficult concept to define (Moyles 1989; Garvey 1991). Without a definition, we have been unable to isolate play in order to measure its impact. It has been argued that previous studies have failed to show that it is specifically play (rather than any other experience) that is influencing children's development. Even studies of children who are deprived of play face problems in this regard as, often, being deprived of play is coupled with other forms of deprivation such as malnourishment, inadequate parenting or poor housing conditions. Significant advances have been made in providing evidence for the developmental potential of play as a result of research that has investigated children's own perceptions of what constitutes play activity (Howard, 2009; 2010).

Research into children's perceptions of their own play has revealed that they define play according to where, when and with whom the activity takes place (Karrby, 1989; Wing, 1995; Howard, 2002), according to how much control and choice they have during their activities (Howard *et al.*, 2006), and according to who they are playing with (King and Howard, 2014). Research also shows that these perceptions are not static. Children develop an understanding of what it means to play based on their experiences. For example, children in early years environments who experience directed activities at the table and free play on the floor, or teacher involvement in formal activity but not often in play, pick up on these cues and use them to categorise future play events (so activities where an adult is present or activities that occur on a table are not considered to be play). Children perceiving an activity as play or not play has a significant impact on how they behave and perform during problem-solving tasks. McInnes *et al.* (2009) have shown that children who practise a task under conditions they define as playful show more purposeful problem-solving strategies, more independence and are far less distracted that those who practise under formal conditions. Playful children also show higher levels of involvement and emotional well-being. Whitebread (2010) also found increased frequency and sophistication of metacognitive events in play where adults are not present (see also Chapter 8). Understanding children's perceptions allows us to maximise on learning via play rather than learning disguised as play: play *as* pedagogy rather than play *for* pedagogy. Adult interaction is of course an important feature of quality early years environments (Siraj-Blatchford and Sylva, 2004). Early years practitioners are pivotal in creating and maintaining the conditions for play and, with careful consideration, can be accepted as play partners (Payler, 2007; Westcott and Howard, 2007; Rogers and Evans, 2008; Howard and McInnes, 2010). Being sensitive to choice and control in play enables practitioners to support children's development in activities that they themselves perceive to be play, while at the same time injecting a sense of playfulness into more purposeful activities. Starting with a fundamental understanding as to the nature of play allows practitioners to maximise on the potential of children's playful disposition. Play serves as a resource pool (see Figure 11.3), and empowers children to meet intellectual and emotional challenge with lower levels of anxiety. This lower level of anxiety leads to an increased sense of well-being, emotional security and subsequent improved task performance.

How the relationship between play resources available and complexity of task determine the level of anxiety/challenge experienced by a child and the potential support required.

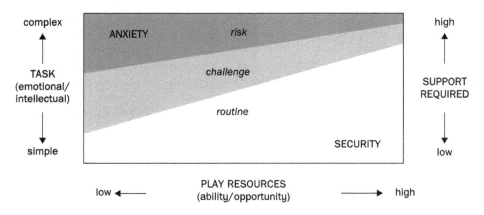

Figure 11.3 The challenge/resource model of play

A play-based curriculum that focuses on emotional well-being builds on the inherent value of play as a disposition. Research evidence clearly demonstrates that supporting children's playful disposition amplifies development in seven key ways:

1 increased confidence and self-esteem
2 increased motivation and engagement

3   effective communication

4   increased self-regulation and metacognition

5   more flexible and adaptable thinking

6   the promotion of healthy attachments and social relationships

7   enabling conflict resolution and anxiety reduction (Howard and McInnes, 2013).

An emphasis on play as a disposition and a process is not articulated well within curriculum documentation, however, which tends to emphasise what kind of play experiences teachers *should* provide, rather than a clear rationale as to *why* play is important. Play is a key way to support children's emotional and intellectual growth, and early years educators are pivotal in the development of playful learning experiences both in terms of the environment they provide and the nature of their interactions with the children (see also Chapter 2). The importance of play and recreation as a restorative behaviour, supporting emotional health and holistic development, is demonstrated by us reflecting on our own recreational activity (Figure 11.4).

- What kinds of activities are you involved in outside of your work or study life? Do you go swimming or to a craft class? Do you love cooking or reading books?

- What are your reasons for being involved in these activities?

- In what ways do you think these activities are important to you?

- How would you feel if you weren't able to do these things?

What did you find?
When asked about our recreational activities (essentially our adult 'play'), we tend to focus almost exclusively on therapeutic potential. Some of the previous responses this activity has provoked include:

"I just find it really therapeutic: it's a release from the pressure of life"
"it's not something I have to do and I don't have to be great at it"
"it provides me with an escape from work"
"it makes me a more balanced person, it reminds me I'm not only a Mum, a wife or a nurse, I am me too"
"it makes me feel good about myself"
"I get rid of all my anger and anxiety"

Figure 11.4 An activity to set you thinking (2)

The complexity of providing for play as a children's service professional

> **Cameo 1**
>
> Hazel arrives at the primary school at 7.55 am and begins to arrange the school hall for the arrival of children who attend the school-run breakfast club where, at 8.05 am, Ben arrives. Ben, who has been assessed to be on the ADHD spectrum, not only attends breakfast club but also goes to the after-school club at the end of the day. At 8.50 am, Hazel has finished tidying up and sets off to the reception class where she works alongside the reception school teacher, acting as a 1:1 with Ben. At break times and lunchtime, Hazel is on playground duty supervising the children playing in the playground, often involving playing a game with Ben. At 3.15 pm, Hazel is back in the school hall waiting for children to arrive who attend the parent-run after-school club. Ben is often the first to arrive and last to leave.

Is Hazel a teacher or learning support assistant? A playworker? A childcare worker? A lunchtime supervisor? A therapeutic play worker? All of these? None of these? How does Hazel interact with Ben in his play across all of these different situations?

The last question is difficult to answer as play is influenced by policy demands and professional practice. Three constructs of children exist in children's early years environments: the play-learning child in early education (Kernan, 2007); the learning-care child in childcare settings (Caldwell, 1989); and the play-care child in play provision (Petrie and Logan, cited in Petrie, 1994). Within early years education, Wood (2013) has identified a tension between how practitioners manage the balance between child-led and adult-led play activities. Difficulties in interpreting how policy should be implemented in relation to the adult role in play are likely to exist across different professional contexts. This can be explored through examining the policies that surround children's rights, play, care and education in the UK and the Republic of Ireland.

Identification of the importance of play as a child's right

In 1989, the United Nations Convention on the Rights of the Child was adopted. This comprises 54 articles outlining children and young people's rights, and is underpinned by the 'three Ps' (participation, provision and protection). There are specific Articles on play (Article 31) and education (Articles 18 and 29). In addition, Articles 12 and 13 are around children having and expressing their views. The ratification of the UNCRC in 1991 (UK), 1992 in the Republic of Ireland (RoI) and 2004 in Wales, following devolution, has enabled subsequent policies around children and young people to have clear links to their rights. In addition, each country recognises children's rights with an appointed children's commissioner or ombudsmen.

The 54 Articles are all specifically linked within a rights-based policy in Wales and Scotland, and form the basis of children's rights in Northern Ireland and the Republic of Ireland. England, which did have five outcomes for children and young people within *Every Child Matters* and was based on the UNCRC, no longer has this policy as, with others developed by the Labour government, it is no longer used by the Coalition government formed in 2010 (see also Chapter 1). In Wales, Scotland, Northern Ireland and the Republic of Ireland, children and young people's rights within the UNCRC are explicitly stated within current education, early years, childcare, and play policies and standards. The only exception is England, where the Early Years Foundation Stage, which has combined early years education and childcare up to five years under the same umbrella, has no mention of the UNCRC. Only Wales and Northern Ireland have a specific focus of play as one aim or theme within their respective children's rights policies.

The natural play of children

In 2002, Wales became the first country within the UK and RoI to have a play policy, supported in 2006 by the publication of the play policy implementation plan (strategy). The RoI followed in 2004, with its play strategy, and in 2010 a teenage recreation policy; England in 2008 with a play strategy, Northern Ireland with a play and leisure statement in 2008, and a play implementation plan in 2010, and Scotland produced a play strategy in 2013. Unfortunately, in 2010, as a result of austerity measures in England, the Coalition government abandoned the country's play strategy. Each play policy and strategy was linked to its respective children's rights policy, with a focus on Article 31, the child's right to play, leisure, sport and cultural activities. The definition of play within these play polices and strategies is based on its being freely chosen, intrinsically motivated for no external goal – or words very much based on this very much used definition. Play is very much focused as a process rather than used as a beginning or an outcome; it is based on a natural thing children do and have a right to do. The right to play, to meet children's health, well-being and learning, is stated within each country's policy or strategy in all areas of children's lives. This includes the home, the community, school and within any form of care.

Play within education policies

The use of play within education policy focuses on the curriculum and learning; however, there is also provision for play outside the curriculum, at children's break or recess. This can be termed non-curriculum play. All countries within the UK and RoI have revised or developed new early years curricula since the ratification of the UNCRC. Some countries have combined early years and primary education (England and Republic of Ireland), while others are separate but closely linked (Wales, Scotland and Northern Ireland). What unites all of these early years curricula is the recognition that play is fundamental in children's learning, health and well-being. It is also recognised that, as children grow older, the use of play moves from being more child centred to more adult directed.

The outcome-based curricula in English and Welsh educational policy clearly have play as a tool for learning, with specific types of play designed to meet educational attainment targets. In the Republic of Ireland and Northern Ireland there is more emphasis on play as a process rather than an outcome within early years education. Each of these countries has produced guidelines on the use of play in early years to support delivery of early years and foundation learning, with more of a focus on the process of play to *support* outcomes, rather than to *meet* outcomes. In Scotland, early years covers birth to eight years; however, the curriculum is within the range of three to sixteen years (no separate foundation stage or phase). Play within their early years framework has a focus on improving outcomes, again an outcome basis for play.

Wales and the Republic of Ireland produced their play policies and strategies prior to their early years Aidstear (Republic of Ireland) or Foundation Phase (Wales). While it is evident that the RoI makes clear reference to its play strategy in subsequent education and childcare-related policies, this is not so in Wales. Scotland did link its early years framework (2008) with play and playwork (which was quite forward thinking as its play strategy was not published until 2013).

Play within childcare standards

Childcare has been a high priority since 1998 with the Labour government's National Childcare Strategy around affordable, accessible and quality childcare provision. This has resulted in the growth of childcare provision in childminding, daycare, after-school clubs and holiday play schemes. In England, since the revision of education within the Early Years Foundation Stage, out-of-school provision (daycare, childminding, after-school clubs) is regulated and inspected by OfSTED if children aged five years or under attend. In Wales, Scotland and Northern Ireland, each of these countries has its own registration and inspection guidelines, which are separate from education. In Wales it is the Care and Social Standards Inspectorate for Wales (CSSIW), in Scotland it is the Care Inspectorate, and in Northern Ireland this is undertaken by Health and Social Service Trust. Currently, only preschool provision is registered and inspected in the Republic of Ireland, but an early years quality framework (Síolta) exists, which is used alongside its early years curricula (Aidstear). Out-of-school provision that has children aged six years or over has to adhere to Children First and health and safety guidelines.

The respective standards and inspection measures set out by each regulatory body clearly demonstrate the importance of planning for sufficient play opportunities and that the play environment is sufficiently resourced. Play, it could be argued, is used more as a starting point for the children, rather than being outcome based (except in England within the Early Years Foundation Stage) or process driven. Although links are made with the importance of play in children's learning (hence education) the planning of play opportunities is not focused to an outcome, just a demonstration the provision has thought about how and what children may play with. What is lacking is the link each country's respective standards and inspection measures have with relevant play policy where the play policy was produced before the standards (e.g. Wales). This is an oversight, particularly as both childcare and play have specific mention in the recent *Children and Families (Wales) Measures (2010)* (Welsh Government, 2010), but the most recent daycare standards in Wales do not mention the play policy for Wales.

How do policy and practice relate?

The dates of publication for policy around children rights, early years education, play and childcare will, or should, influence one another, depending on the date when each was published. The focus of play, whether it is a starting point, a process or an outcome, can be both liberating and constraining for the practitioner when working with children. There is the interpretation from the policy perspective that the provision of play in education focuses on outcomes (assessment) and in childcare as a starting point (planning) and a process (freely chosen). The role of the adult, whether in education, childcare or playwork, will always be involved in play, and the skill is to be prepared to move from starting point, through process and outcome, depending on the context and rationale for play. For example, the play therapist who has a directive approach will focus on play outcomes; the non-directive approach may focus more on process. What can be deduced is that outcomes will always be adult focused if play is being used against adult-generated criteria. From a policy level across learning, care and play, if there were a statutory duty of play, as in the *Children and Families (Wales) Measures (2010)* (Welsh Government, 2010) in Wales, combined with play that is more of a process to support children's learning and development, as in both Northern Ireland and the Republic of Ireland, and that combines early years and learning, as in England, with clear policy links, as in Scotland, this could make the use of play across different professions less of a challenge.

The role of play in education, care and free time will differ in relation to play being predominantly considered a starting point, a process or an outcome. Policy, professional practice and perception will differ in a learning, care and play environment, and how these environments work together (or not) as shown in Figure 11.5 in relation to children's rights within the UNCRC and the three Ps of participation (play); provision (learning); and protection (care).

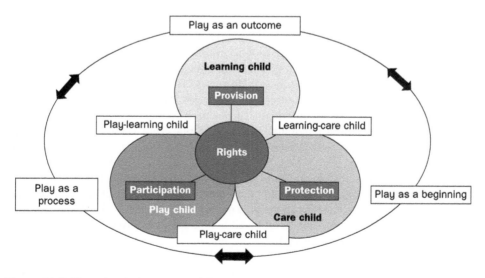

Figure 11.5 The role of play across children's services

Hazel, it can be argued, is constantly working in differing areas within this layout, where professional practice using play will be involved in:

- learning (early years, primary, secondary and tertiary, formal, informal)
- care (childcare, therapeutic care, residential care, lunchtime supervisor)
- play (home, community, school, out-of-school provision)
- rights (right to participation, provision and protection).

The role of play in education, care and free time will differ in relation to play being 'used' as a starting point, a process or an outcome. This has implications for both policy construction and policy implementation, particularly for the practitioner.

Meeting the challenge of providing for play

Wood (2007) suggests that there is a contention between play for the sake of play and play for the purposes of education. However, this contention is fuelled by the fact that classroom practice has largely been driven by accounts that describe the *what* and *when* of play, rather than the *why*. As we have seen, there are qualities inherent in play that render it powerful from a developmental and therapeutic perspective, and these cannot necessarily be isolated. With curriculum emphasis on emotional health and well-being, we are beginning to see a shift away from the *teacher-master* conception to the *teacher-therapist* conception, and it is vital that early years practitioners are treated as play professionals and are afforded the training necessary to prepare them for this role. Despite their spending the most time with the most children, teachers and learning assistants receive markedly less training in the field of play than other professionals.

Soles *et al.* (2009) argue that teachers have such a vital role in supporting children's mental health and identifying when intervention might be required, that training must be amended to include more emphasis on typical and atypical development. Play-based curricula have the potential not only to illuminate such issues but also offer the potential for healing and development. From an educational perspective, to maximise on the potential of play, 'early childhood educators need a sophisticated pedagogical repertoire that is grounded in contemporary theories and research evidence' (Wood, 2007: 318). As we have seen, contemporary research evidence based on listening to children's voices, highlights particular features of play that render it valuable, and these features are those that render it valuable from both a developmental and therapeutic perspective.

Theoretical understanding and levels of training in play, however, have repeatedly been highlighted as a challenge to implementing play-based curricula in the early years (Moyles *et al.*, 2002), and this challenge was evident long before education became so heavily focused on emotional health and well-being. Teachers have faced the dilemma of having to balance their intuitive belief in the value of play with parental pressure towards academic achievement and the need to document learning outcomes (Palmer, 2006). They have felt as though they were driving a curriculum van (Edwards and Knight, 1994), rather than being guided by any real philosophy of learning. It is hardly surprising that many have articulated a lost sense of professionalism (Moyles, 2001). When early years professionals are afforded the opportunity to develop a fundamental understanding as to the nature of play via experiential learning, reflective practice and knowledge sharing, their confidence in dealing with the challenges of their complex role as play professionals is considerably increased.

Conclusion

This chapter has considered the role of play for the early years practitioner across both the UK and the Republic of Ireland. It has also contemplated play across professions: early years, childcare and playwork, considering both policy and professional practice. It has expounded *why* play is important for children's emotional and intellectual development. Identifying the fundamental characteristics of play has highlighted the vital role of early years educators as play professionals and the need for this professional status to be recognised. The chapter suggests that a play-based curriculum promotes resilience, self-esteem and flexibility of thought that can enable children to meet intellectual and emotional challenge as empowered individuals. Focusing on play *as* pedagogy frees practitioners from the constraints of providing activities that simply look like play, and allows them to share in children's activities as play partners. With this freedom, however, comes the need to acknowledge that play *as* pedagogy and play *as* therapy are inextricably linked. Far from suggesting that all teachers must act as therapists or that all children are in need of therapy, the chapter simply asks us to consider whether, if we truly believe in the power of play (defined by children themselves via their perception of freedom, choice and control), we must be prepared for how this might manifest in their play from both a developmental and therapeutic perspective across all professions that use play within their work. It urges us to re-establish early years educators as play professionals and empower them to be driven by a philosophy of play. These issues are not new. Neumann (1971), within her hypothetical definition of play, stated that the act of play is a transaction that has an initiation, enaction and completion, and consists of criteria, a process and objects.

- The criteria of play are intrinsic motivation, internal reality and internal locus of control of the activity (see Endpiece).
- Play is a process that has modes and operation. The modes are sensorimotor, affective, oral and cognitive. The operations are exploration, repetition, replication and transformation. The operations occur in a sequence: exploration, practice and application.
- Play is directed towards objectives: objects, subjects, functions and location.

The early years practitioner (whether this be teacher, childcarer, playworker or play specialist) and even the primary caregiver, needs to consider whether the principle aim of the play opportunities they provide is focused on its initiation (beginning), enaction (process) or completion (outcome) – or, more accurately, how and when they should use all three when working with children.

Questions to promote reflection

1   Do I understand *why* play supports children's emotional and intellectual development?
2   How much freedom, choice and control do children have in their play in my setting? What is the balance between adult- and child-led play?
3   What is my role in children's play? Am I happy with this role?
4   Do I understand the role of play in policies relating to my setting? Is my play practice consistent with policy requirements?

References and further reading (in bold)

Caldwell, B.M. (1989) All-day kindergarten – assumptions, precautions, and overgeneralizations. *Early Childhood Research Quarterly*, 4: 261–266.

Cohen, D. (2006) *The Development of Play*. London: Routledge.

Edwards, A. and Knight, P. (1994) *Effective Education in the Early Years*. Buckingham: Open University Press.

Garvey, C. (1991) *Play*, 2nd edn. London: Fontana.

Howard, J. (2002) Eliciting young children's perceptions of play, work and learning using the activity apperception story procedure. *Early Child Development and Care*, 127: 489–502.

Howard, J. (2009) Play, learning and development in the early years. In T. Maynard and N. Thomas (eds) *An Introduction to Early Childhood Studies*. London: Sage.

Howard, J. (2010) Making the most of play in the early years: understanding and building on children's perceptions. In P. Broadhead, J. Howard and E. Wood (eds) *Play and Learning in Early Childhood: Research into Practice*. London: Sage.

Howard, J. and McInnes, K. (2010) Thinking through the challenge of a play-based curriculum: increasing playfulness via co-construction. In J. Moyles (ed.) *Thinking about Play: Developing a Reflective Approach*. Maidenhead: Open University Press.

Howard, J. and McInnes, K. (2013) *The Essence of Play: A Practice Companion for Professionals Working with Children and Young People*. London: Routledge.

Howard, J., Jenvey, V. and Hill, C. (2006) Children's categorisation of play and learning based on social context. *Early Child Development and Care*, 176(3/4): 379–393.

Karrby, G. (1989) Children's conceptions of their own play. *International Journal of Early Childhood Education*, 21(2): 49–54.

Kernan, M. (2007) Play as a context for early learning and development: a research paper. Dublin: NCCA.

King, P. and Howard, J. (2014) Children's perceptions of choice in relation to their play at home, in the school playground and at the out-of-school club. *Children and Society*, 28: 116–127.

McInnes, K., Howard, J., Miles, G.E. and Crowley, K. (2009) Behavioural differences exhibited by children when practising a task under formal and playful conditions. *Educational and Child Psychology*, 26(2): 31–39.

Moyles, J. (1989) *Just Playing: The Role and Status of Play in Early Childhood Education*. Buckingham: Open University Press.

Moyles, J. (2001) Passion, paradox and professionalism in early years education. *Early Years: An International Journal of Research and Development*, 21(2): 89–95.

Moyles, J., Adams, S. and Musgrove, A. (2002) SPEEL: Study of Pedagogical Effectiveness in Early Learning. Research Report 363. London: DfES.

Neumann, E.A. (1971) *The Elements of Play*. New York: MSS Information Corporation.

Palmer, S. (2006) *Toxic Childhood*. London: Orion.

Payler, J. (2007) Opening and closing interactive spaces: shaping four-year-old children's participation in two English settings. *Early Years: An International Journal of Research and Development*, 27(3): 237–254.

Petrie, P. (1994) *Play and Care Out of School*. London: HMSO.

Rogers, S. and Evans, J. (2008) *Inside Role-play in Early Childhood Education. Researching Young Children's Perspectives*. Abingdon: Routledge.

Siraj-Blatchford, I. and Sylva, K. (2004) Researching pedagogy in English pre-schools. *British Educational Research Journal*, 30(5): 713–730.

Soles, T., Bloom, E., Health, N. and Kargiannakis, A. (2009) An exploration of teachers' current perceptions of children with emotional and behavioural difficulties. *Emotional and Behavioural Difficulties*, 13(4): 275–290.

Sturrock, G., Russell, W. and Else, P. (2004) *Towards Ludogogy, Parts I, II and III. The Art of Being and Becoming Through Play*. Sheffield: Ludemos.

Welsh Government (2010) *Children and Families (Wales) Measures (2010)*. Cardiff: Welsh Government.

Westcott, M. and Howard, J. (2007) Creating a playful classroom environment. *Psychology of Education Review*, 31(1): 27–34.

Whitebread, D. (2010) Play, metacognition and self-regulation. In P. Broadhead, J. Howard and E. Wood (eds) *Play and Learning in the Early Years: Research into Practice*. London: Sage.

Wing, L. (1995) Play is not the work of the child: young children's perceptions of work and play. *Early Childhood Research Quarterly*, 10(4): 223–247.

Wood, E. (2007) New directions in play: consensus or collision? *Education 3–13*, 35(4): 309–320.

Wood, E. (2013) *Play, Learning and the Early Childhood Curriculum*. London: Sage.

12

Permission to play

Kathy Goouch

Summary

The political focus of education seems now to be fixed on establishing narrow policies centred on discrete subject knowledge for young children. This chapter draws on research to support the idea of a pedagogy that is centred on play and playfulness. The varying and complex roles that are required of adults who engage with a pedagogy of play will be identified and explored, and the possibilities and advantages of adults themselves becoming players will be signified. The core principle is that adults can be most useful to children's learning and development if they serve the immediate intentions of children who are playing, rather than focus on pre-set adult agendas. The importance for everyone working with young children to increase their knowledge of play and to understand what children do and learn when they play is considered to be a prerequisite. This will help to avoid the confusion often felt by adults in the company of children playing.

Introduction

In England we are living in times when there are increasing political aims for the education of very young children, and clear and distinct requirements for pedagogy and curriculum in the early years (see also Chapter 1). This situation is combined with a profoundly prescriptive early education discourse, supported by an unrelenting narrative from the national regulator (OfSTED, 2014). Also, while early childhood education and care entitles this phase, it is represented by a rather narrow definition of the academic skills in literacy and numeracy in education that currently dominate political, policy and research discourses in England, with little attention given to 'care'. School readiness, early intervention, affordable daycare, testing, value added and progression towards rather narrow academic targets are the key vocabulary of the moment. Additionally, research into the early years of education has increased across the world which, together with the proliferation of publications from neuroscience in the field, seems to have made this phase of learning rather attractive to politicians and policy makers.

Amid this rather tumultuous situation, adults who do care for and support young children's development and learning (early years teachers, early years educators or teachers with QTS) are tasked with the situation of both contending with the day-to-day care, development and education of young children and of accounting for their activities in terms that will suit the contemporary national regulatory discourse.

The 'teaching' role adopted by adults in the early years needs to be very carefully examined and understood if 'teaching' is not to be misunderstood and used synonymously with 'instruction' (see also Chapter 2). Indeed, cultural understanding of teaching activities is more important than ever as politicians from different continents swap ideas for practice in the hope that they can be simply assimilated into school cultures in home countries (see Cameo 1).

Cameo 1

A Norwegian teacher explained that visiting teachers from England were always surprised to find the lack of any explicit anxiety or concern that very young children were climbing trees in the grounds outside her school. She laughed, saying that they were even more astonished when children climbed down and they noticed the knives the children were wearing on their belts!

An international definition of 'teaching' does not, and perhaps should not, exist. How the child's world is constituted at school and mediated, how opportunities and sites for learning are offered, extended and enriched, are as much a part of the teacher's role as the transmission of information. And this role is culturally constructed and culturally mediated (see Cameo 2).

Cameo 2

A two-year-old child in a nursery class in Hong Kong was individually shaping her pink playdough, alongside other children with other colours. An English visitor tried to touch her dough and to entice her to play. The child was clearly dismayed and guarded her dough fiercely. A Hong Kong researcher explained that sharing such materials was discouraged by teachers as germs and infections travelled quickly in their crowded country, particularly through these kinds of play resources. This two-year-old child had clearly understood the message!

British politicians in recent years have been looking at, for example, China in order to borrow policies, processes and practices in teaching and replace pedagogies with those learned from brief visits overseas. Ironically, at the same time, it has been reported that education authorities in Shanghai are trying to ease the burden of children who spend too much of their childhood on onerous study and that, in spite of high grades, children working through the education system in Shanghai are weaker in applying their skills, solving practical problems, and they lack innovative or critical thinking skills (OECD, 2014; Ren, 2014).

Across the globe, however, there is one aspect that can be part of our international understanding, and that is that people with whom they share their everyday lives matter to babies and children as they grow, develop and learn (David *et al.*, 2003). The idea that, like children, teachers are not all cut from one mould nor shaped to the same cloned pattern in training seems to present a challenge to people outside of the profession. The ability to be responsive to young children and to accompany them in their learning is a skill to be developed, celebrated and enriched in the company of children. The professional nature of teachers, who they are and what they do, is the central theme of this chapter.

There is considerable research evidence that emphasises the social nature of learning (Bruner, 1986; Dunn 2004), the importance of attachment to significant adults (Nutbrown and Page, 2008) and the significance of emotional well-being to children's learning potential (Immordino-Yang and Damasio, 2007). The work of neuroscience indicates the overwhelming contribution that conversation makes to the growth and shape of children's brain development (Gopnik *et al.*, 1999; Greenfield 2000). Additionally, socio-cultural research offers explanations of the subtle and nuanced ways in which moment-by-moment experiences provide ways into learning (Hall *et al.*, 2014). The brain's plasticity in the early years has long been acknowledged and this, coupled with the phenomenal rate at which brain cells proliferate at this stage, reflects the deep significance of this time of life in relation to future development and healthy growth (see also Chapter 3). While neuroscience can provide some information about what the developing brain requires, it is from socio-cultural research that we learn about the nature of the experiences that young developing minds require. These experiences include conversation, interaction and affective engagements with others, which all children, no matter what their material background, need in order to grow, in the broadest sense of that term.

Given what we know, it seems essential that the education of young children in early years settings demands a complex but relational pedagogy. Reconceptualising children and childhood and the meaning of early education is important, and this requires politicians and policy makers to construct children as other than 'defective adults' (Gopnik, 2009: 5) and childhood as a special time 'devoted to learning about our world and imagining all the other ways that world could be' (p. 11). Play is necessary for children's pretence, their hypotheses, possibility thinking, and a place for those possibilities to be tested, mediated and mapped into broader sense-making, world-making patterns, which then serve children in their next steps. Play would seem to offer the physical and conceptual opportunities for children to achieve all of this and it is 'the signature of childhood' (Gopnik, 2009: 14). However, it would be a mistake to think of pretence, hypothesising, creating and playing as a natural incremental and developmental process for all children. Instead it may be more useful to think of children's early learning as a puzzle or a developing picture with experiences, images, language, encounters all being drawn together as children develop an inner life as well as the outer manifestation. This conceptualisation does not discount the need for teachers to provide opportunities to offer new experiences, new images, new vocabulary and languages, and new encounters, but it does also demand respect for culture, communities, and children's creative aspirations. The part, then, that significant, caring and informed adults play is not one of selecting the puzzle pieces but more that of a mediator and guide, helping to ensure the world-making pieces fit together and that the young child is, and feels herself to be, the artist and architect of the design and of the developing product – her world.

A complex pedagogy; complex pedagogues

It is hard to find new language to describe what babies and young children do, the activities in which they engage, without employing the term 'play', however slippery, misinterpreted or politically unfavourable the term itself has become. Play is the best word we have. It is not a new concept but it is becoming better understood as the result of a range of international and national research. Children play to explore possibilities and thus to learn about the world. Young children at play have been described variously as 'scientists', statisticians, systematic experimenters; they are clearly explorers, problem solvers, role takers and dramatists, 'wild pretenders', risk takers and apprentices (Piaget, 1959; Rogoff, 1990; Fei Xu, cited in Gopnik, 2009). All of this world making is undertaken and sometimes accomplished through physical, intellectual and social actions and interactions that can be identified as play. It could also be argued that the same could be accomplished through the direction and instruction by adults, parents and teachers. However, the accompanying behaviour by young children in play is also credited with improved well-being, developing autonomy, self-esteem, and learning the worth of independent and interdependent acts as well as the development of agency. To accompany children in their play is a sophisticated role that can be achieved only by those who know and understand children, who are able to allow the sometimes complex intentions of children at play to take precedence and who will demonstrate respect for such intentionality. Adults working with young children need to be informed, knowledgeable, competent and confident in their engagements in play. For some adults this kind of 'knowing' and 'respecting' is intuitive as they braid together implicit know-how and explicit knowledge (Atkinson and Claxton, 2000: 3).

In the early years of children's lives it is important for the child and adult to form and nurture a special relationship to support development as both biology and culture entwine to create a sense of identity. Although perhaps a natural occurrence between *parents* and young children, in the early years of education and care, such relationships, while not biologically formed, may still be constructed and nurtured by teachers for the purpose of accompanying young children as they make sense of their world. Working with children in this way in nurseries, schools and other settings is sometimes described as organic or intuitive, as above. However, the suggestion of a complex and evolving pedagogy produces something of a dichotomy for teachers as the particular educational climate of the moment, in England and other English-speaking countries, is one of political certainties in relation to education, of robust managerial drives towards prescriptive curricula and tightly controlled levels of accountability. Attention to emotion rather than or in addition to technical or rational acts and involvement can sometimes be considered of little or lesser importance in educational practice, particularly as it is not simply measurable for purposes of accountability. However, some research is now providing new information making closer connections between cognitive development and emotion. An interesting analogy has been made to claim a fundamental role for emotion in education:

> . . . emotions are not just messy toddlers in a china shop, running around breaking and obscuring delicate cognitive glassware. Instead, they are more like the shelves underlying the glassware; without them cognition lacks support.
>
> (Immordino-Yang and Damasio, 2007: 5)

Findings from this work with brain-damaged adults and children indicate that emotion is essential in cognitive development, decision making, problem solving, social interactions and social functioning. Research with 'damaged' patients illuminates 'the nested relationship' between emotion and cognition. The findings from the study confirm that 'neither learning nor recall happen in a purely rational domain, divorced from emotion', and that if educators attempt to create a purely 'rational domain' then they will be encouraging children to 'develop the sorts of knowledge that inherently do not transfer well to real world situations', and further that 'knowledge and reasoning divorced from emotional implications and learning lacking meaning and motivation are of little use in the real world' (Immordino-Yang and Damasio, 2007: 9).

The ability to construct such a 'nested relationship' requires layers of sophisticated professional knowledge: knowledge of children, their development, their lived lives, significant relationships as well as professional knowledge in relation to curriculum and subject knowledge. Influential authors and educators in the field of early education, Froebel in the nineteenth century and Montessori in the early twentieth century (Bruce, 1987; Nutbrown *et al.*, 2008), have particularly emphasised the respectful relationship between educator and learner, and the work of Malaguzzi in Reggio Emilia pursued this idea of a 'pedagogy of relationships' (Rinaldi, 2005). It requires deep commitment and also professional courage to challenge prevailing policy and curriculum doctrine. This kind of professional also needs to understand herself, her own biography, her intentions, values and educational aims. Reflecting upon and understanding who we are, as teachers and as learners, our influences, mentors and professional values, is rarely afforded time in initial teacher training or indeed in practice.

Listening to teachers

Two teachers were provided with an opportunity to take part in a study in order to deconstruct their work with children and to try to establish their intentions. The teachers were asked to consider what they were doing in their professional work and to define their overarching aims, their influences and their intentions in playing with children. Both teachers were systematically observed, both collected video of their practice, interviews were conducted and three-way conversations undertaken. As a result, some conclusions were drawn about the potential for 'teaching' in the early years of education and some defining elements of practice were constructed.

A key founding element of the practice of both teachers was that they subscribed to the view that children cannot be made to play. In both the classrooms the idea of play is completely accepted as the context where children will learn. The nursery classrooms consist entirely of play resources, play areas and ranges of possibilities for the children to play. There are consistent, fixed areas and flexible spaces as well as opportunities for change, resources to be added, moved, transported by the children and adapted. There are routines, but these are also flexible.

In both nurseries, everything – space, resources, routines, time, adults and interactions – is arranged to best fit the perceived day-to-day needs of the children; their physical, social, emotional and cognitive needs. The adults mostly follow the children's lead, their interests and their intentions while at play. One teacher's comment here is significant in understanding her place in children's world of play: 'The more our interactions fit in with the child the more likely that they will be of use to the child in developing and extending, understanding whatever it is they are exploring.' They both, at different times, emphasise that they *help* children. While seeming simplistic, this is in fact a very significant idea and it appears to form the bedrock of their practice; they are both clear that they are there to service children's play. This is not an idle or a passive role, however, although significantly different from the instructive, management role that many teachers of young children adopt. The evidence of the teachers' own words indicate that it is an informed choice, based on experience, information from a range of sources and their deeply reflexive approach to all aspects of their work.

The teachers explained their stance as follows.

J: Children learn best when they're interested and focused and for such very young children that's when they choose what they do themselves . . . and actually the quality of learning is an awful lot better, visibly – you can visibly see their involvement level and their concentration level and even the outputs are so much higher quality and detailed if you don't over-direct them.

M: I think it's important not to have an agenda sometimes when I go to play with children because otherwise I think I start doing and saying things that I want, that's not necessarily what they want . . . I was waiting to see, to give them time to use me if they wanted to, or ignore me if they wanted to – use me to bounce ideas off, tell me something, help them, explain something, be there as another body . . .

J: If they've got you there playing with them then you're there playing and you need to play.

Both teachers felt very strongly that it is often appropriate to wait for the children to lead them, the teachers, into the play action. They were also observed to employ different 'voices' during play, which were variously as follows.

• Narrator of the play (descriptions of the action as it occurred, sometimes together with the children and sometimes as a simple accompaniment). In this case, the occupation of the teacher was in creating an accompanying narrative to function as a bridge in supporting meaning making, giving shape to the event and helping to make connections. In the example in this study, the teacher made no attempt to direct the play or lead it with her narrative voice but saw her role as simply to follow the action, describing the event as it flowed, drawing in children as they approached, helping to solve problems without interrupting the flow of the play.

- Voices within play (participating as actors in the play). In one example the teacher was moving dinosaurs around in the sand tray and speaking as the dinosaur: 'I want my mummy . . .' and 'Help me; I'm lost . . .'. Such examples were frequent and happened either incidentally or through the direction of the children. The teachers were able to tune in to children's play, valuing the children's intentions and the context but also drawing on their professional skills of modelling, observing, interpreting and playing. One teacher commented that 'you see what the child's intention is – you feed into it'.

- The addressee (the opposite of director). During a 20-minute observation of a play period, one teacher made only 17 short utterances, which were all very unobtrusive. The contributions to the play were sometimes barely audible and they served to complement rather than narrate the action. This teacher invariably placed the children in the role of expert. He asked questions of the children and avoided instructional talk. He saw his role as helping children to accomplish their task of the moment. His physical presence was close to the children but not inside their play. He was used by the children to fetch and carry resources, was accepted but not deferred to. He left respectful spaces for the children and observed more than played. His physical presence was nevertheless important to the children. As an addressee, he was 'a listener who can also have a creative role to play in a dialogue, even if sometimes only a silent non-verbal one' (Carter, 2004: 68).

- Their personal voice (born from their own lived lives). When asked if they knew where their practice emerged from, one teacher commented 'my practice comes from a big run of very positive, very committed interactions with people'. She spoke about a range of other influential professionals that she had worked with at the beginning of her career. However, she also spoke about her father as a key mentor and a strong influence on her behaviour with children, particularly in the way that he treated children as 'worthy': 'I don't think about it consciously but when you try and unpick it, I suppose that's what I do, although at the time I don't think, "Oh I must be respectful", but maybe that's where that comes from, you know if children talk you stop and listen just as when a grown up talks. And if they talk over you, you try very hard to say, "Excuse me one minute I'll talk to you in a moment", but you do go back and say, "What was that you were telling me, I couldn't listen properly", rather than the kind of seen and not heard thing. And I suppose that's where that comes from, I don't know.'

- Their professional voice (of accountability to local and national regulators). They were able to reflect seriously on their work with the children and to demonstrate a professional voice that represented their respect for the culture of the school and that of a public servant with statutory responsibilities. They talked about '. . . having high expectations of children and wanting them to achieve as much as they possibly can and more than that'; 'I think about what I do a lot and why I do it and I think about the children a lot, what they're doing and why they do it and how I can support them to do it, what they might need to help them get to where they might want to go . . .'; 'when you're meeting the child's needs, you're meeting your own need to have the child's needs met; that's your need as a teacher isn't it, your professional need'.

In the settings of both teachers it was frequently unclear who led the stories during play, who created them, defined the action or who transformed it. The voices that were heard reflected the joint actions of children and adults together. Adults and children were multi-voicing (Carter, 2004): they were constructing story narratives together; they were 'doing the voices' in the story; directing the play according to the socially constructed narratives of home experiences; and frequently instructing other players. In addition, the teachers were controlling the adult pedagogic narrative, retaining the narrative of monitoring and assessment and sometimes modelling and supplying language. Adults and children in these practices were both inside and outside the play action, inside and outside of reality and fantasy. Voices representing individual consciousness were melded in play, and support was often mutual.

Permission to play

Both teachers played with and alongside children in their classrooms, valuing and enjoying play and commonly accepted by the children as players. However, their value as teachers stretched further. Both teachers' metacognitive abilities were very high. They were able to consider, reflect upon and articulate their practice, their learning, their activities and their professionalism with ease and confidence. The questions and challenges they set themselves were always of a high order and the aims of practice they identified were powerfully expressed:

> Empowerment is the ultimate purpose I think, so that children believe they can do it, take a risk, have a go, be themselves, be creative, use me, not use me. The outcome I expect is that I want children to feel empowered.

> What is important is that children find their place, their space or identity in the world outside their family and are comfortable and competent in it; that they get support, encouragement and affirmation of their own developing skills and understandings. It's the research and enquiry and the disposition to be a learner that I am trying to promote, I think.

The significance of this study's findings rests in the teachers' abilities to value, reflect upon and understand the fundamental importance of three key elements in their work with children: intentionality, narrative constructions and voice. Through their demonstrations of absolute respect for children's expressions of intent and for story narratives in play, the teachers sustained very high levels of motivation in the children, deep concentration and involvement in play. The children trusted the teachers, and this trust was clearly manifested in the children's confidence to collaborate with their teachers and permit the adults to play with them. The teachers recognised play as a site for developing metacognition as children enacted worlds but also explored what the actions could mean. Through the professional voices employed by the teachers they were able to make ephemeral learning become tangible, invisible thinking become more accessible, through narrations of play, creation of bridges in meaning making, and co-constructions and joint interpretations of play acts. This is similar to the work of educators in Reggio Emilia and the 'pedagogy of relationships and listening' (Rinaldi, 2005). The two teachers in this study similarly allowed time, space resources and help for the children to both act and to reflect upon their acts, involving adults and children in metacognition. As children narrated and re-narrated their play narratives they were storying their own understandings, making connections and having those connections supported or questioned by mediating adults (see also Chapter 8).

The teachers are very skilled practitioners, able to intellectualise play, giving it value and status in children's learning. They employ time and energy in understanding the worlds and worlds that children employ in their story narratives so they can co-join in the play and account for it in their professional dialogues, significantly creating a discourse to legitimise children's intentions and their activities. Their insider knowledge of children and of play produced a pedagogy of consistent questioning, such as: What are the children doing? What do they know? What are they demonstrating that they know? What then do they need? What am I doing and why? What else could I do? What do I know about this content? How can I help? In their explorations of their own roles, an activity already embedded in their practice but made explicit in this study, the teachers applied a meta-language to their engagements in play – for example, 'you could see it in his eyes, a connection and a ha ha moment'. Just as children engage in self making through their reflective play acts, so too did the teachers in their thoughtful engagements and their deconstructions of children's learning.

Conclusion

Rather than engaging with 'a state theory of learning' (Alexander, 2009: 307), the teachers in this study demonstrated their commitment to the value of play in children's early learning. The teachers both enthusiastically permitted play but also sought permission to play with the children. Play contexts are risky spaces to inhabit, and occupying play spaces with children demands a level of confidence and trust – in children, in the learning potential of play, as well as in children's own ability to cope with uncertainty, which itself demands strong trusting relationships. Both the teachers and the children felt safe in not knowing potential outcomes but in seeking them in one another's company. Through this engagement the children and their teachers were learning a great deal, not least:

> . . . the importance of the imagination; of dialogue and joint activity which both motivate pupils and capitalises on what is now known about how brain, mind and understanding develop during the early and primary years and of generating that sense of empowerment allied to skill through which learning becomes inner-directed and autonomous rather than dependent on pressure from others.
>
> (Alexander, 2009: 257)

If, as observed in this study, it is possible to achieve even this one powerfully stated aim through permitting children and their teachers to play, then practice that does not embrace play would be questionable at every level.

Questions to promote reflection

1 How does your practice embrace play?
2 What is your pedagogy of play?
3 How far do you trust the children in your setting to learn from their play?
4 How would you enhance your knowledge of play and playful pedagogies?

References and further reading (in bold)

Alexander, R. (ed.) (2009) *Children, Their World, Their Education: Final Report and Recommendations of the Cambridge Primary Review*. London: Routledge.

Atkinson, T. and Claxton, G. (2000) *The Intuitive Practitioner: On the Value of Not Always Knowing What One is Doing*. Buckingham: Open University Press.

Bruce, T. (1987) *Early Childhood Education*. Sevenoaks: Hodder and Stoughton.

Bruner, J. (1986) *Actual Minds, Possible Worlds*. Cambridge, MA: Harvard University Press.

Carter, R. (2004) *Language and Creativity: The Art of Common Talk*. London: Routledge.

David, T., Goouch K., Powell, S. and Abbott, L. (2003) *Birth to Three Matters: A Review of the Literature*. Nottingham: DfES Publications.

Dunn, J. (2004) *Children's Friendships: The Beginnings of Intimacy*. Oxford: Blackwell.

Gopnik, A. (2009) *The Philosophical Baby*. London: The Bodley Head.

Gopnik, A., Meltzoff, A. and Kuhl, P. (1999) *How Babies Think*. London: Weidenfeld and Nicolson.

Greenfield, S. (2000) *The Private Life of the Brain*. London: Penguin.

Hall, K., Curtin, A. and Rutherford, V. (2014) *Networks of Mind, Learning, Culture, Neuroscience*. London: Routledge.

Immordino-Yang, M.H. and Damasio, A. (2007) We feel, therefore we learn: the relevance of affective and social neuroscience to education. *Mind, Brain and Education*, 1(1): 3–10.

Nutbrown, C. and Page, J. (2008) *Working with Babies and Children from Birth to Three*. London: Sage.

Nutbrown, C., Clough, P. and Selbie, P. (2008) *Early Childhood Education: History, Philosophy and Experience*. London; Sage.

OECD (2014) *Pisa Results: What Students Know and Can Do*, Vol. 1 (revised February 2014). Available online at: http://www.oecd-ilibrary.org/education/pisa_19963777 (accessed 22 April 2014).

OfSTED (2014) *The Report of Her Majesty's Chief Inspector of Education, Children's Services and Skills, Early years*. Available online at: http://www.ofsted.gov.uk/resources/130237 (accessed 4 May 2014).

Piaget, J. (1959) *The Language and Thought of the Child*. London: Routledge and Kegan Paul.

Ren, D. (2014) British bid to copy maths excellence doesn't add up. *South China Morning Post*, 22 March.

Rinaldi, C. (2005) Documentation and assessment: what is the relationship? In A. Clark, A.T. Kjorholt and P. Moss (eds) *Beyond Listening, Children's Perspectives on Early Childhood Services*. Bristol: The Polity Press.

Rogoff, B. (1990) *Apprenticeship in Thinking, Cognitive Development in Social Context*. Oxford: Oxford University Press.

13

Developing play pedagogy through critically reflective practice

Sue Rogers and Chris Brown

Summary

In this chapter we discuss the challenges encountered in trying to develop a pedagogy of play in early years settings, drawing on a collaborative project involving 20 early years settings in one local authority in London. The principal aim of the research is to improve outcomes for children from specific disadvantaged groups through practitioner reflection on interactive pedagogic relationships in the context of play. The chapter concludes by suggesting that, when early years practitioners are empowered to identify and address pedagogical issues in a reflective and collaborative way, they are also better able to surface and reflect upon tensions regarding the play/pedagogy nexus.

Introduction

Questions about pedagogy and its relationship to play lie at the heart of current global debates surrounding the nature and quality of educational provision for young children. In relation to play and its role in early learning, there are difficulties facing researchers and practitioners alike in reconciling competing imperatives to meet curricular requirements *and* to acknowledge children's desires and interests (individual and collective). Play, widely endorsed as a leading activity in early childhood, has become subject to increasing attention and scrutiny around the question how and in what ways might play contribute to learning in the early years classroom? (Rogers, 2011). But for anyone working with young children it is clear that developing a play-based pedagogy is not a straightforward matter. Play does not fit neatly into curricular objectives and learning outcomes. It requires a rather different approach, one that allows for the spontaneous, unpredictable and unplanned for outcomes inherent in play. A further challenge is encountered when trying to conceptualise a relationship between two very different imperatives: on the one hand, developing pedagogy, defined largely as something adults 'do' to children in early childhood classrooms, and on the other, developing play, defined largely as a child-led, intrinsically motivated and spontaneous activity (Rogers, 2011). This is particularly challenging as children transition between preschool and statutory schooling, a point that seems to hold true in a range of socio-cultural contexts.

In England, increased government interest, investment and intervention in early years education has brought about a number of significant policy initiatives, not least the development of the Early Years Foundation Stage (EYFS), a curricular framework for children from birth to statutory schools age at five (DFE, 2012). More recently, there has been an explicit endorsement on the part of government that the aim of early years education is principally to ensure 'school readiness', a point that is subject to considerable critique in the early years sector. Further, proposed interventions in the education of disadvantaged two year olds, and rising demand for higher qualifications and skills in the early years workforce, have significant implications for the development of early years pedagogy that can support the complex learning needs and characteristics of young children in the twenty-first century. This challenging policy context is further complicated by the relative lack of focus on and understanding of the term 'pedagogy' when applied to work with young children (Stephen, 2010) and especially to their self-initiated play (Rogers, 2011).

Drawing on data from an ongoing project involving 20 early years settings in one local authority in London, this chapter explores the ways in which an innovative approach to action research and reflective practice can address some of the challenges surrounding play pedagogies. The principal aim of the research is to improve outcomes for children from specific disadvantaged groups through pedagogic change focusing on interactive reciprocal and responsive pedagogic relationships in the context of play. It involves practitioners and researchers working together to improve outcomes for young children through a particular approach to reflection on pedagogy called *Lesson Study*. We will say more about this later in the chapter. One of our interests in the project and in writing this chapter is how best we can make research evidence matter in the context of early years pedagogical practice (see Brown, 2013, for a detailed discussion of this in the wider field of education). Ultimately our concern is to improve outcomes for children, particularly those most at risk of disadvantage. That was a central aim of the project. However, we recognised that improving outcomes through changes in pedagogy is not a simple or straightforward process. It cannot be achieved through the dissemination of research to practitioners alone or in any straightforward way. Nor will change in pedagogy come about without change in thinking on the part of practitioners. Such questions preoccupied us in developing our approach to the project. To move some way towards our goal of 'making evidence matter' (Brown, 2013), we conclude here that shared reflection in professional communities of practice offers a powerful vehicle for effecting change in play pedagogy. Equally, however, we acknowledge the fact that opportunities for reflection in the early years sector are relatively rare due to limited time, funds and commitment on the part of school and setting leaders in spite of the fact that reflective practice is a statutory requirement in the EYFS. From our experience of this research to date, we suggest that when early years practitioners are empowered through a combination of engagement with research evidence *and* opportunities to identify and address pedagogical issues in a critically reflective and collaborative way, they are also better able to surface and reflect upon tensions arising from the pedagogy/play nexus. Importantly they are also more able to tackle these tensions in ways that address both their principles for the education of young children and the statutory requirements placed upon them.

What is critical reflection?

> The deep-rooted values, attitudes and beliefs that a teacher holds about children, childhood and how children learn, directly and profoundly influences the way that they teach and consequently impacts upon children's learning experiences. It has become clear to me that to be a successful [teacher] I must be able to critically examine my own beliefs and recognise the social constructions that inform my own thinking.
>
> (Student teacher, cited in Rose and Rogers, 2012a)

In a study of the relationship between student teachers' principles and practice, Rose and Rogers (2012a) argue for the importance of critical reflection in developing self-confidence and courage to resist the external pressures that inevitably exist in providing rich and meaningful play experiences for children in a culture of 'raising standards'. We can see from this student teacher's comments, expressed in an essay, that critical reflection is an integral part of training for early years practitioners. However, as the study by Rose and Rogers (*op cit.*) showed, the gap between principles on the one hand and practice on the other increased as student teachers entered into school, while the opportunities for reflection rapidly diminished in what was often a heavily timetabled and regulated context.

Internationally, the role of critical reflection is recognised as a vital factor in improving outcomes for young children (OECD, 2006) whether in education, health or policy making. In England, the concept of reflective practice is firmly embedded in the statutory guidance for the Early Years Foundation Stage (EYFS) and in the standards for Qualified Teacher Status (QTS). It is a requirement at all levels of training for practitioners to engage in reflection as a means to improve the quality of provision and outcomes for children.

But what does it mean to be reflective? The work of Schon (1987) has been influential in relation to reflection within schools. However, such work has had influence relatively recently in the early years sector (Hallet, 2013). Schon posits that reflection does not just take place in the aftermath of an action, but occurs *during* it, thus distinguishing between '*reflection in action*' and '*reflection on action*'. Critical reflection requires both. Moreover, critical reflection will not necessarily look for finite answers or solutions but will be interested in deepening self-awareness and understanding of the processes of young children's learning and development in an ongoing process of improving quality of provision, and will be more likely to develop a pedagogic role that is finely tuned in to children's needs and interests. Drawing on the work of Schon (1987), Rose and Rogers (2012b) distinguish between *technical* reflection, thinking in terms of goal achievement and practical issues, and *critical* reflection that they link to two main objectives: first, that pedagogy is socially just and based on a commitment to equality, and second, that pedagogy is appropriately child focused so that practices set within particular political and cultural contexts do not inhibit children's potential or restrict progression in learning and development. How adults view children as learners, as the student notes above, is a social construction informed by our own values, beliefs and experiences. These shape our pedagogical practices and the ways in which we interact with children and hence impact upon children's experience of the early years setting.

Considering the notions of *technical* and *critical* reflection through the lens of expertise it might be supposed that, as practitioners gain experience, confidence and so expertise in their practice, they move more towards critical reflection. This supposition is based on the idea that novices – those low in experience and/or expertise – are keen to learn and achieve in ways that meet the more obvious requirements of peers, line managers and parents. As their level of experience and confidence increases, practitioners are more likely to bring their values and beliefs to the fore, as they relate to new knowledge and greater understanding in terms of pedagogy, into play. They are also likely to feel more confident to do so, believing that children's outcomes will be simultaneously deeper and more meaningful, while also ensuring that external goals are attained (e.g. Flyvbjerg, 2001).

Part of the challenge in providing a play-based pedagogy is coping with the uncertainty and ambiguity of children's play in the learning environment. Providing for play may be threatening for some practitioners because of its difficult-to-measure and potentially difficult-to-manage qualities. By reflecting on this uncertainty in trusting reciprocal relationships with others, practitioners can gather insight into and confidence in their practice, and can be empowered to bring their knowledge of and principles about children into closer alignment with the challenging aspects of their work.

Developing pedagogy through critical reflection

Within this context, the project responded to a specific identified need to support the development of pedagogy in a diverse group of practitioners in relation to newly introduced Characteristics of Effective Learning (CEL). These reflect a notable shift in recent years from 'what' to 'how' the young learn, and provide the pedagogic context for learning in the EYFS, as follows.

- *Playing and exploring* – children investigate and experience things, and 'have a go'.
- *Active learning* – children concentrate and keep trying if they encounter difficulties.
- *Creating and thinking critically* – children have and develop their own ideas, make links between ideas, and develop strategies for doing things (DfE, 2012).

The project was designed to increase practitioners' understanding of and confidence in using the CEL, and enhancing interactive skills in promoting children's *Creating and thinking critically* (i.e. children's ability to 'have their own ideas', 'make links' and 'choose ways to do things'). This focus was informed by research evidence indicating that this characteristic is linked to self-regulation, creativity and motivation (Whitebread *et al.*, 2009). The socio-cultural approach taken in this chapter and in the project more broadly emphasises the role of social interaction in the transformation of interpersonal to intrapersonal functioning (Vygotsky, 1978). Learning is viewed, therefore, as a result of the individual's *active* participation and involvement in situated social practices, and not simply the result of knowledge transmission or acquisition. From this perspective, socially interactive ways of learning such as play are viewed as creating highly effective learning situations. These principles underpin the perspective on early years pedagogy given here and also the approach adopted in relation to reflective practice on the project. In other words, the social construction of knowledge takes place through co-constructed activity where children work with adults or more knowledgeable peers to reach a shared understanding and in the case of the project where practitioners work together in contexts that promote reflection-on-practice. Significant in this research is, then, the renewed recognition that dialogic pedagogies work best for children and adults.

However, this kind of learning has also been identified as an area of weakness in early years pedagogical practice in part due to the limited styles of adult/child or teacher/pupil talk available to children observed in the prevalence of closed questions (Siraj-Blatchford and Manni, 2009), which leaves few opportunities for children to question, expand or reflect on what they have learned. In early years settings, sustained shared thinking has been identified as an effective pedagogic approach, where two or more individuals 'work together' in an intellectual way to solve a problem, clarify a concept, evaluate activities or extend a narrative alongside open-ended questions (Siraj-Blatchford and Manni, 2009). Studies of early years pedagogy show that *co-construction*, where adults and children mutually construct (or co-construct) knowledge and meaning together, is a potentially powerful way for adults and children to exchange ideas and that in this way it can provide a positive interactive frame for adult involvement in child-initiated play. Co-construction is potentially more empowering for children than the more interventionist approach of scaffolding. However, research has shown that co-construction is less commonly used with children aged four and five as they approach statutory school age, scaffolding being the preferred strategy in school (Payler, 2009). A study of children's perspectives of role play (Rogers and Evans, 2008) showed that, while co-constructing learning outcomes is important, it is equally significant for children to co-construct pedagogy with adults, sharing in the decision-making process in how play is organised in the learning environment around dimensions of space, place, time, choice of playmates, and play materials. In adult-determined play contexts, children adopted strategies to overcome some of the rules and routines that inhibited their play and found ways to overcome interruptions from adults, which disrupted the flow of their play activity.

Pre-dating much of this work, the Oxford Preschool Project (led by Jerome Bruner in the late 1970s and published notably in the report by Wood *et al.* (1976)), also endorsed the use of open-ended questions as the most productive form of interaction. However, the research also showed that a range of different adult utterances produced markedly different effects on children's use of language. Among the many speech types employed by educators, the most likely to prompt children's extended utterances were those the authors described as 'phatic' or 'contributions': 'phatic' utterances are short insertions that keep the conversation going ('Really?'; 'Did he?'; 'Oh my!') while contributions are the adult's own offerings ('I really love it when it rains, I like it better than snow'; 'Ooh, you're wearing my favourite colour'). Both these types were found to prompt children to go on talking, much more than being asked questions of any kind. Further endorsements for this approach can be found in a review of research on development and learning in the early years (Evangelou *et al.*, 2009: 76). The review identified key facets of effective learning relationships including the use of talk in building and maintaining such relationships; the recognition of the uniqueness and agency of the child; and the importance of mutually responsive relationships in facilitating pro-social thinking and behaviour.

Establishing a professional learning community

Within the broad socio-cultural and constructivist approach adopted here, the project is informed by the notion of professional learning communities. While there is no universal definition of a professional learning community, they are usually depicted as a situation in which people involved with and concerned about education work collaboratively to learn about how they can improve pupil learning. In the project, the notion of professional learning communities was conceived of as a context in which practitioners and researchers might work collaboratively to bring together knowledge from research and knowledge from practice through a process of joint reflection (Stoll, 2008). The project was designed in such a way as to facilitate partnership between researchers and practitioners through establishing a learning community where research on interactive pedagogies in the context of play, as described above, formed the basis to widen practitioners' repertoire of pedagogic strategies in supporting children's creative and critical thinking (Brown and Rogers, 2014). A knowledge creation workshop was held during the inaugural professional learning community meeting. Following Nonaka and Takeuchi (1995) and Stoll (2009), this involved researchers facilitating a discussion that centred first on current research and knowledge on effective early years practice including play. Practitioners were then invited to share their own practical knowledge in facilitated groups, focusing on information about their settings and current practices.

An action research approach was introduced, drawing on the so-called Lesson Study model of collaborative reflective working. Originating in Japan, lesson study has had widespread international recognition as an effective model of collaborative classroom learning which embodies all the features of effective professional development, although it is less well known as an approach in the early years sector. The approach is deemed to work because it provides opportunities for practitioners to engage in in-depth analysis of the learning and progress made by children and as a consequence, to develop specific pedagogic techniques designed to improve outcomes for children (Dudley, 2011).[1]

Practitioners were asked to identify what they hoped to achieve by the end of the project and how they might do so. Following an approach set out by Earley and Porritt (2013), and 'starting with the end in mind' (the goal they wished to achieve), practitioners were asked how they might use the research presented to them alongside their own practical knowledge, and knowledge provided by others in their study group, to develop their pedagogical approach. Following this initial workshop, practitioners from the partner settings were paired into six lots of three and during each term each setting hosted one visit for their study group. Visits to settings comprised two parts. First, each study group (along with a facilitator) observed an activity, jointly planned by the group members but led by the host practitioner. Second, following the observation the group critically reflected on the activity, analysing children's learning and the practitioner's pedagogical approach. At the end of each lesson study day, all 36 participating practitioners gather for an end-of-day seminar to share reflections with the wider group. This feedback is 'scaffolded' by the facilitators, and related to research and previous learning. Having provided a brief sketch of the approach taken, the final section illustrates some of the ways in which this approach has enhanced the understanding and practices of participant practitioners.

What have we learned?

The project is ongoing but already we are seeing positive signs of its impact on practitioners' work. We give two examples of how reflective practice is helping practitioners to change pedagogy in relation to the CEL.

Learning together

One of the major strengths and positive outcomes of the project is the way in which it has brought together practitioners who work across a range of different settings and age groups. In the lesson study groups reception class teachers work alongside Children's Centre educators, making monthly visits to one another's settings where they engage in a cycle of observations of planned activities, shared critical reflection and shared planning. One Children's Centre educator explained that:

> . . . we all come from different places . . . with different qualifications . . . some have degrees, some haven't . . . but what I have learned is that we're all here for the same outcome, to educate the children with the best practice.

In this way the experience of shared reflection on practice served to build a much stronger sense of community among early years practitioners in the group, breaking down barriers between preschool and school, and between differently qualified staff. For most, participation in the project offered a rare opportunity to observe children outside of their usual age range and setting context. This aspect of the project contributed to a deeper understanding of play development and pedagogic approaches. One reception class teacher commented that visiting the baby room to observe a circle time activity helped her to see how a playful approach could work equally well in her reception class, even in a more structured play activity. Reflective discussion allowed exploration of the idea of playful learning, as an attitude or approach to learning rather than simply a discrete activity.

Similarly, on observing in a reception class, a Children's Centre educator described how the experience had helped her to reflect on her interactions with toddlers, which were sometimes over-managed due to concerns about risk and 'loss of control'. In one carefully planned example of 'washing dolls' in the toddler room in a Children's Centre, the practitioners deliberately stood back to allow children to explore the water freely. The doll washing became a splashing game in which the children explored the effects of their actions on the water. In the reflective feedback session that followed, it became clear that this might have been a challenging and 'risky' activity, liable to foster a perceived need for greater control on the part of the practitioners. The splashing game did not necessarily meet the planned objectives for personal, social and emotional development of 'caring for baby'. However, the group, by this time based on trusting reciprocal relationships, provided a safe context in which practitioners could explore flexibility in planning outcomes and alternative pedagogical approaches.

Standing back and letting the children lead

We know from countless research studies that one of the most challenging aspects of providing for play is the extent to which adults feel able to allow children to follow their own interests in play. 'Standing back' and 'allowing children to take more risks' have been mentioned frequently in project feedback sessions suggesting a shift in pedagogical approaches to play and exploration (see also Chapter 18). Through tuning in to children through observation and listening, practitioners were able to tailor their interactions in much more nuanced ways that supported and co-constructed learning. Practitioners from many of the project settings have expressed the view that a result of the opportunity to reflect on research ideas in the context of practice has been to enable them to feel much more confident in allowing children greater freedom to experiment with materials and space. Many have expressed their surprise in the quality of children's ideas evident in their play and child-led activity (see Cameos 1 and 2).

Cameo 1

Angela works in a Children's Centre as an educator with responsibility for the nursery-age children. After attending the initial project workshop and listening to the research findings she talked about how she found the material challenging and that she felt overwhelmed. She questioned whether the project was the right thing for her and considered withdrawing altogether. Deciding to continue, a few weeks later, she hosted the first lesson study visit and was observed by her project group. This was a turning point for Angela. The feedback she received from the observation of her peer group enabled her to reflect on her style of interaction and on what the children were learning. It affirmed her practice but also helped her to consider alternative ways of working. Later that day, Angela took part in a feedback session to the whole group, presenting her work to 36 practitioners. Following this experience she commented: 'I enjoy my job, but after the first [project] session I had a real sense of achievement from standing up and talking in front of the group.'

A few weeks later she reported that, in spite of feeling daunted initially, she had since extended her understanding through reading research on scaffolding and sustained shared thinking. She now felt more confident and able to see how research and practice related in her setting. She went on to present her research in a staff meeting at her workplace, a move that was both empowering and, as she said, 'really helped me to think about the research'. Angela's progress on the project is an indication of how professional communities of practice and approaches such as lesson study can help to transform in small but tangible and important ways practitioner development and have a positive impact on the experiences of children.

Cameo 2

In this example, the group agreed to focus on 'Thinking critically and creatively' from the Characteristics of Effective Learning in the EYFS. They wanted the children to have the opportunity to find their own solutions to a meaningful 'real life' problem, to rescue a kite that was stuck in a tree. In discussion, the group recognised that one of the main challenges would be to allow the children to take the lead, find their own solutions through trial and error and make mistakes in a safe context. The activity was led by Cath, a teacher working in a Children's Centre, but the planning and discussion that preceded the activity was a shared process as part of the lesson study approach. After introducing 'the problem' to the children, Cath scaffolded children's emergent ideas but allowed them to experiment with materials and, importantly, to get things wrong. The activity, although prompted by adults, was co-constructed between adults and children. Children worked collaboratively and the activity had a playful but purposeful quality. Both children and adults enjoyed working together in this way and the level of problem solving, motivation, concentration and creativity far exceeded Cath's expectations. The reflective approach enabled by the professional learning community had supported risk taking on the part of the adults which in turn had impacted on pedagogical practice and the children's learning experience.

Conclusion

We conclude by suggesting that when early years practitioners are empowered to identify and address pedagogical issues in a collaborative way, they are also better able to surface and reflect upon tensions regarding the play/pedagogy nexus. Importantly they are also more able confidently to tackle these tensions in ways that address both their values and the statutory requirements placed upon them. However, practitioners also expressed a desire to share their 'new' knowledge and experience more widely in their teams. Several participants had shared developments on the project with colleagues in staff meetings and other professional contexts. While this had been positively received the potential to impact on practice more widely in participants' settings was limited because they had not been through the process of critical reflection afforded by participation in the project. To some extent this illustrates the point made earlier that research evidence alone will not change practice. If research is to matter to practitioners we contend that it needs to be related to the reality of work with young children and supported through opportunities for observation and critical reflection in the context of a professional learning community.

Questions to promote reflection

1   What does the EYFS say about reflective practice, and how can this help you to develop play pedagogy?
2   Are you a technical or critical reflector? Give examples of each from your practice.
3   How can research evidence help you to develop play pedagogy in practice?

Acknowledgement

Our thanks to the participants on the project who generously shared their thoughts about young children's learning and to Bernadette Duffy, OBE, for facilitating discussion and project support.

References and further reading (in bold)

Brown, C. (2013) *Making Evidence Matter: A New Perspective on Evidence-informed Policy Making in Education*. London: IOE Press.

Brown, C. and Rogers, S. (2014) Knowledge creation as an approach to facilitating evidence informed practice in early years settings. Paper presented at AERA Conference, Philadelphia.

Department for Education (DfE) (2012) *Early Years Foundation Stage Framework 2012*. Available online at: http://www.foundationyears.org.uk/early-years-foundation-stage–2012/ (accessed 8 July 2012).

Dudley, P. (2011) Online publication available at: http://Lessonstudy.co.uk/wpcontent/ uploads/2012/03/Lesson_Study_Handbook_-_011011–1.pdf (accessed 21 March 2014).

Earley, P. and Porritt, V. (2013) Evaluating the impact of professional development: the need for a student-focused approach. *Professional Development in Education*, 40(1): 112–129.

Evangelou, M., Sylva, K., Wild, M., Glenny, G. and Kyriacou, M. (2009) *Early Years Learning and Development Literature Review*. London: DCSF Research Report 176.

Flyvbjerg, B. (2001) *Making Social Science Matter*. Cambridge: Cambridge University Press.

Hallet, E. (2013) *The Reflective Practitioner*. London: Sage.

Nonaka, I. and Takeuchi, H. (1995) *The Knowledge Creating Company: How Japanese Companies Create the Dynamics of Innovation*. New York: Oxford University Press.

OECD (2006) *Starting Strong II: Early Childhood Education and Care*. Paris: OECD.

Payler, J. (2009) *Co-construction and scaffolding: guidance strategies and children's meaning-making*. In T. Papatheodorou and J. Moyles (eds) *Learning Together in the Early Years: Exploring Relational Pedagogy*. London: Routledge.

Rogers, S. (2011) Play: a conflict of interests? In S. Rogers (ed.) *Rethinking Play and Pedagogy in Early Childhood Education: Concepts, Contexts and Cultures*. London: Routledge.

Rogers, S. and Evans, J. (2008) *Inside Role Play in Early Childhood Education: Researching Children's Perspectives*. London: Routledge.

Rose, J. and Rogers, S. (2012a) Principles under pressure: student teachers' perspectives on final teaching practice in early childhood classrooms. *International Journal of Early Years Education*, 1: 43–58.

Rose, J. and Rogers, S. (2012b) *Adult Roles in the Early Years*. Maidenhead: Open University Press.

Schon, D. (1987) *Educating the Reflective Practitioner*. San Francisco: Jossey-Bass.

Siraj-Blatchford, I. and Manni, L. (2009) 'Would you like to tidy up now?' An analysis of adult questioning in the English Foundation Stage. *Early Years*, 28(1): 5–22.

Stephen, C. (2010) Pedagogy: the silent partner in early years learning. *Early Years*, 30(3): 15–28.

Stoll, L. (2008) Leadership and policy learning communities: promoting knowledge animation. In B. Chakroun, and P. Sahlberg (eds) *Policy Learning in Action: European Training Foundation Yearbook 2008*. Torino, Italy: European Training Foundation.

Stoll, L. (2009) Knowledge animation in policy and practice: making connections. Paper presented at the Annual Meeting of the American Educational Research Association. Available online at: http://www.oise.utoronto.ca/rspe/UserFiles/File/Publications%20Presentations/AERA%2009%20knowledge%20animation%20paper%20Stoll.pdf (accessed 23 January 2014).

Vygtosky, L. (1978) *Mind in Society: The Development of Higher Psychological Processes*. Cambridge, MA: Harvard University Press.

Whitebread, D., Coltman, P., Pino Pasternak, D., Sangster, C., Grau, V., Bingham, S., Almeqdad, Q. and Demetriou, D. (2009) The development of two observational tools for assessing metacognition and self-regulated learning in young children. *Metacognition and Learning*, 4(1): 63–85.

Wood, D., Bruner, J. and Ross, G. (1976) The role of tutoring in problem solving. *Journal of Child Psychology and Child Psychiatry*, 17: 89–100.

Note

1   Lesson study has been described as a process involving groups of practitioners collaboratively planning, teaching, observing and analysing learning and teaching in research lessons. See http://lessonstudy.co.uk/ for further detail.

14

Work or play: how children learn to read the signals

Jan Georgeson and Jane Payler

Summary

In this chapter, we explore how children read the signs available in early years settings to help them determine what is expected of them. This chapter:

- suggests theoretical concepts helpful to framing and understanding research into how children learn about what to do, when and where
- explores what is already known about how children perceive different types of activity that could be construed as work or play
- contributes further to this through findings from two research studies
- invites practitioners to consider how such knowledge may be used to enhance pedagogy with young children.

Introduction and context

Drawing on research evidence and experience, early years educationalists have fought hard to challenge the automatic association made in past decades between 'work' and 'learning' and to foreground the excellent contribution of play to young children's learning (Moyles, 1994; Broadhead, 2006; Ranz-Smith, 2007). During this time, however, the landscape and context of children's services in England have changed dramatically, particularly for children with special educational needs. Services for young children in England aim for effective multi-agency working with initiatives such as Sure Start Children's Centres (referred to in Chapter 1). More recently, education, health and care plans, introduced in September 2014, encapsulate the Coalition government's approach to encouraging education, health and social care professionals to work with families and young people.

Most children under five are educated and cared for by vocationally trained practitioners, many of whom are unlikely to have participated in inter-professional education but, following early years workforce reform, they have more support to implement programmes and interventions. Early years professionals (EYPs) and, since

2013, early years teachers (EYTs) are trained to act as graduate leaders for the Early Years Foundation Stage (EYFS) (DfE, 2012), and national standards for EYPs (2012) and EYTs (2013) both include criteria relating directly to integrated practice. There has, however, been a shift in the language used for play-based approaches to learning and development between the two sets of standards. The EYP Standards made explicit reference to the role of play in children's learning, whereas the EYT Standards focus more strongly on the discourse of 'teaching' and avoid using the word 'play'. Yet the EYFS that early years teachers are to lead *does* retain some mention of 'playing and exploring' as key characteristics of young children's learning.

But how comfortably does the concept of 'intervention' fit within what is still supposed to be a play-based curriculum? And what about children's *perceptions* of the type of activity they are entering into – is it work or play? We already know that perceptions shape expectations, and that expectations influence participation and outcomes (Brooker, 1996; Ranz-Smith, 2007). We will therefore explore what is known about how children perceive different types of activity and how this affects their participation. We discuss findings from two research studies: the first considers how the buildings in which early years provision is offered might shape children's perceptions; the second considers the reality of what children encounter when they enter integrated early years practice, particularly children with special educational needs for whom the challenges around boundaries between work, play, 'intervention' and learning are magnified by the impetus to deliver therapeutic inputs (see also Chapter 11). Exploring perceptions of and participation in different types of activity for young children will help adults to provide the most appropriate pedagogy for children in their care.

Theoretical underpinning

We have found that strands of socio-cultural theory help us to make sense of social interactions. Starting from the Vygotskian concept of the social formation of mind, we consider that every social context is the result of choices people make about what to do and say, and how to manage their surroundings. Everything in any social setting is therefore imbued with meaning and children learn about these meanings in the course of everyday interactions with people, objects and the spaces that contain them. This knowledge builds over their early years so that, by the time that they move into school, children have awareness of when it might be appropriate to play and be playful, and when they should be following instructions and adhering to routines. Everyday practices in the early years of schooling, therefore, introduce children to different pedagogic genres and they become skilled in adopting different ways of talking in different situations, such as circle time and literacy sessions (Christie, 2002).

It is helpful to consider what signals children identify as they learn to distinguish between time to play and time to work. Bernstein (2000: 35) encourages us to recognise that pedagogic discourse will always include both the content of what is to be taught (instructional discourse, encapsulated for most settings in the areas of learning and development) and the regulative discourse of social order, the often tacit understandings about relationships, who is in charge and who can make choices. There are ways that this is signalled in the physical environment and in specialised ways of talking, and children need to learn to recognise these signals. We think it is important to take a multi-modal approach to this endeavour; it is not just verbal interactions that signal what might happen next, but includes sights, sounds, smells, temperature and texture. Practitioners should therefore think about how children and families read the signals from buildings used as early years settings, and how this shapes their understanding about what they can and cannot do in these buildings (Georgeson and Boag-Munroe, 2012).

What is known about how children perceive different types of activity and how this impacts upon their participation?

Previous research has shown that, in the course of their early educational experience, children learn to make distinctions between different kinds of activity, and that this contributes to their developing understanding of the difference between work and play, which they will take with them into adult life (Apple and King, 2004). While it has been shown that young children clearly associate particular objects (paint, blocks, sand, construction materials, board and computer games) with play rather than work (Wing, 1995), other features of the classroom environment (teacher presence, space and absence of constraint) also influence their interpretation (Howard, 2002). Wing concluded from discussions with children that the main criterion for interpreting an activity as work or play appears to be whether the activity is perceived as obligatory or not. This can be signalled by the particular words used by adults when discussing the activity, reflected as 'can do' versus 'have to do' in children's comments. However, distinguishing between the modality, or sense of obligation, of an utterance requires a certain level of language comprehension, which might not be within the receptive language repertoire of some children with special educational needs. Environmental and non-verbal cues to play or work are likely to be more important for these pupils, as well as the recall of or association with feelings of effort and enjoyment (Howard, 2002).

Children, including those with special needs, must learn about the perceptual and physical affordances (Gibson, 1986; Greeno, 1994) of the spaces in which they find themselves. They learn how to respond physically to different physical situations (slopes, steps, wide expanses or constricted spaces) and how to use space socially, in conjunction with other people, taking the movements of others into account and interacting with other people as they move through different spaces. This can shape the way they play and the interactions they feel are available to them (Waters and Maynard, 2010). But they also need to learn about the cultural constraints and affordances of buildings, the movements, behaviour and interaction that are expected in particular spaces.

We should therefore think more about what buildings and spaces signal to children and families. Which particular ways of being/doing/saying are acceptable in that particular space? Should they stay put or move around? Be quiet or sing loudly if they want to? Children will already have experience of places where they can move freely and places where there are constraints, so they need to find out what kind of constraints are operating in early years settings, especially as adults don't all agree about appropriate behaviour; a government minister recently interpreted free-flow play as 'running around with no sense of purpose' (*Daily Mail*, 2013). This sense of freedom versus constraint is at the heart of the distinctions children make between work and play. Considering how the day unfolds, time and space are punctuated by signs of movement, position, objects and sensory stimuli; historically, bells have been used as punctuation to signal different phases of the school day and many settings signal tidy-up time with a particular piece of music; the smell of food preparation signals meal time and the sound of children playing in the school next door signals break time. Signals such as these, by association with particular activities, come to carry meaning and can then be recognised in other situations. They become part of a repertoire of things-we-know-about-places, the multimodal discourse associated with particular activities. This enables us to read buildings as texts, in just the same way that we draw on our knowledge of letters, sounds and writing genres to understand a piece of writing.

The type and purpose of particular activities within settings can be signalled by different discourses; education researchers have noted the specific and characteristic nature of educational discourse (see, e.g., Willes, 1983; Mercer, 1995) and the links between pedagogic discourse and young children's learning (Brooker, 1996; 2002). Roberts and Sarangi (2005) note that, while practitioners' knowledge underpins practice, it is not always evident from what they say. We therefore look to how actions, space, objects and words *together* create and communicate dialogue. Discourse analysis helps to unpick how individuals draw on different systems of meaning in order to make sense of their lives in specific situations and times (Regan de Bere, 2003); the following sections contribute to the body of literature exploring how young children make sense of early years practice.

Examples from our own research

Learning to read buildings for early years provision

Children's capacity to read buildings from their external appearance seems to develop first from recognition of people and objects contained within them, then later responding to generic architectural features. As part of a study into differences in interaction and pedagogy in preschool settings (see Georgeson, 2009), I invited children (aged three and four) to talk about photographs of familiar and unfamiliar preschool settings. Occasionally children might label objects or parts of buildings that they recognised (such as pictures of toys or cartoon characters, or doors and windows), or they might spot and ask questions about children in the photographs, even if these were children they didn't know. When looking at photographs of the outside or approach to an unfamiliar building, children either said they didn't know what it was, or declared it to be a particular place known to them, often trying to connect it to people they knew, for example by commenting 'That is my grandma's house' in response to a photograph of a tall wooden fence with a gate, which they had never seen before.

As soon as I moved on to photographs of the interiors, they readily labelled or commented, sometimes confirming, sometimes changing their initial interpretation from the photographs of the exterior. And some of the older children were able to use features such as doors and windows as signals to the building's use. This sometimes led to a conjecture that the unfamiliar building belonged to a particular class of buildings: 'It's a pub!' (in response to a photographs of heavy double doors covered in notices); 'It's a playgroup' (in response to a hallway with a teddy border above the dado rail, from a child whose setting used a teddy bear in its logo). This influenced their perceptions of what sort of things might happen inside.

The extracts below (in Tables 14.1 and 14.2) illustrate some of the findings outlined above. The first extract is from a conversation with a four-year-old girl who had recently moved into the village from a nearby town (still in England) and attended a playgroup in a village hall. She is looking at photos of two unfamiliar nurseries, one housed in a Victorian semi in a residential street and the second in a large detached Edwardian house set in its own grounds at the end of a drive, with lots of wood panelling and an impressive staircase inside the inner doors. The second extract is from a conversation with two four-year-old girls from a playgroup in an inner-city area, also looking at photographs of nursery two.

Table 14.1 Extract from a conversation with a four-year-old girl who had recently moved into the village from a nearby town

Photograph	Child's comments Researcher's questions (in italics)
Nursery 1: Side of house in street	I've just moved into this country
	Where do you think this is?
	I don't know
Frontage of Nursery 1	England
	Somewhere in England
	It's near David's house
Room in Nursery 1	Look there's the children
	What are they doing?
	They're playing in the water
Inside same room in Nursery 1	What are they called?
	I don't know
	Are they at your . . . your place?
	No . . . [. . .]
Nursery 2: Drive with wrought-iron gates	*Where do you think that is?*
	I don't know
	What sort of place do you think it is?
Frontage of Nursery 2 including car park	I think it's David's house
Front door of Nursery 2 (from outside)	I think it's David's house
Inner double doors, with large brass handles and notices	That's not David's house . . . that's a pub
Hall, stairs and landing, with dark wood panelling	It must be a hotel.

Table 14.2 Extract from a conversation with two four-year-old girls from a playgroup in an inner-city area

Photograph	Child's comments
Nursery 2: Drive with wrought-iron gates	It's the park, it's the park – my daddy took me to the park in the car. Yesterday my daddy took me to the park.
Front door of Nursery 2 (from outside)	It's a school. Look, I see the name. I am going to school . . .
Child with mosaic tiles	What she doing? She do drawing
Messy painting	(*Excitement*) Look, look at them. They do painting!

Both extracts point to children trying to 'read' the buildings by connecting them to people they know – and, when that failed, to me as a possible source of information about the unfamiliar people (in this case children) who used the buildings. Their interpretation of buildings was shaped by the people and places that were important to them, but if they couldn't see a connection to their own experience, they weren't interested.

The children's interpretation of the two nurseries was influenced by the sort of buildings, which were common in their own communities. The design of early years spaces sometimes consciously borrows from buildings in the community of the children who attend; this is particularly true of the municipal infant and toddler centres and preschools of Reggio Emilia, where the idea of workshops around a piazza is reflected in the arrangement of rooms in the preschools and echoes in an approach to activities that combines the seriousness of work with the freedom of play (Rinaldi, 1998). But not all children are sufficiently well embedded in mainstream culture to benefit from cultural references like this and not all children have the same expectations of involvement in work and play, as will become apparent in the next section describing a second example from research.

Examples of different discourses

The research here is a re-analysis of data from a small-scale study into the experiences of four-year-old children with learning difficulties attending both special and inclusive preschools in England (Nind *et al.*, 2007). Payler uses two examples to show that the children were not only required to 'cope' with moving between the three different environments, but also to navigate shifts in communicative environment and different discourses *within* settings. The settings aimed to provide therapeutic input to ameliorate children's needs, as well as providing early years education according to the curriculum of the day. Early years practitioners provided 'therapy' during the usual preschool sessions. Such inputs were designed, planned and intermittently monitored by professional therapists (such as speech and language therapists), most of whom were based elsewhere, but were delivered on a daily basis by early years practitioners to the best of their ability, reporting back to therapists.

Jamie,[1] a four year old attending a special inclusive preschool, had been allocated a place on the basis of developmental difficulties including speech and language delay. Speech therapy took place in a small separate room, lasting eight to ten minutes. The content of the sessions had been planned by a visiting speech and language therapist (SLT), but the sessions were delivered one to one by Jamie's key person, Tom, an early years practitioner. Cameo 1 outlines a session between Tom and Jamie exemplifying the speech therapy and the transition from therapy to usual discourse.

Cameo 1

Jamie sat at the table in the speech therapy room in front of a row of plastic animals of varying size. Tom sat on the floor facing Jamie and asked Jamie to find the 'little elephant'. Jamie pointed at an object on the table, murmuring 'There.' Tom, using a clear voice, gentle tone and Makaton[2] hand signs, said, 'That's the BIG elephant. Where's the little one?' Makaton signs were used to emphasise the words that were the focus of the speech therapy, for example, 'big' and 'little', and to identify the animals. Jamie watched Tom attentively before pointing to another object. Tom praised, 'That's it. Good boy', and made a note of the response in the records. Jamie waited quietly, his hands folded together in front of his mouth, chewing a finger, gazing at the animals. Tom asked Jamie to find the big horse, again using supplementary hand signs. Jamie pointed to one of the animals. Again, Tom praised, 'Good boy!' and recorded the response. This continued for several more minutes, with Tom supporting Jamie with hand signs, praising and recording responses. Jamie was compliant and eager to please. His movements and comments were restricted to the openings provided by Tom within the routine discourse and format of the therapy session.

At the end, Tom asked Jamie to put the animals away. Jamie immediately became more animated, standing up and energetically putting the animals back. Jamie commented on the duck and asked Tom if the gorilla, the largest of the animals, also had to go in the box. Jamie pointed to the pot of bubble-blowing mixture, asking to 'do that', his usual 'reward' for taking part in speech therapy. Tom held the bubble mixture container as Jamie dipped in to it, blew the wand and tried to catch the bubbles. He became animated and engaged. The discourse changed with Tom speaking more naturally to Jamie, 'Ooh, only one! You got it? Caught it? Oh gone! Right, last one, then you can go back into the hall.' As Tom blew bubbles for Jamie to catch, Jamie became even more active, dashing into a space in the room, jumping in anticipation and catching the bubbles with great delight.

Figure 14.1 Jamie in speech therapy with Tom: 'Find the little elephant'

Tom reported that during these moments alone together at the end of the speech therapy Jamie had begun to talk more. It appeared that the time one to one, away from the hustle and bustle of the rest of the preschool, had benefits for Jamie's speech and language beyond the controlled exercises.

Figure 14.2 Jamie's reward at the end: animated and natural interaction

The distinctive features of the speech therapy discourse were:

- controlled use of specific words
- use of Makaton signs to supplement words
- rhythm
- adult-controlled, closed interactive space (Payler, 2007)
- shared understanding developed over time of expectations in relation to discourse and format.

Jamie was making sense of complex tacit rules in relation to expectations of him during speech therapy. The contrast between his communication during speech therapy episodes and immediately afterwards, evident from his actions and words, is striking. During the speech therapy session, he communicated within a closed interactive space determined by the opportunities afforded and shaped by the adult interaction and demands of the exercises. Jamie did not co-construct meanings (Payler, 2009) during speech therapy, initiate contributions or show emotional responses beyond his keenness to provide the correct responses. As soon as the episode was declared over, he began to do each of these, communicating within the affordances now available. Jamie appeared to manage the shift in discourse from therapy to playful exchange with Tom successfully. This highlights the role of the practitioner in understanding the value of providing different types of communicative opportunity. How practitioners create and manage episodes of interaction shapes the possibilities for the ways in which children can interact with them – as partners, as directed participants or as voiceless individuals.

We turn now to another of the case study children, Mandy, a four-year-old girl with Angelman's syndrome. Mandy attended a specially resourced Children's Centre where she had speech therapy, occupational therapy, primarily focusing on feeding herself, and physiotherapy weekly for ten minutes. However, Mandy's routine interaction with the early years practitioners also involved short sessions of physical therapy, particularly walking exercises encouraging her to use a frame for support. The next episode (Cameo 2) exemplifies Mandy's transition from play into 'therapeutic' discourse.

Cameo 2

At the beginning of the episode, Mandy lay on the activity rug exploring a favourite toy with her mouth. She crawled across the room to a worktop to look at and touch the musical toys on display. One of the early years practitioners, Amy, initially supported Mandy in her interest in the musical toys. Amy assisted Mandy to a standing position at the worktop, commenting on Mandy's interest. She, demonstrated how to make a noise with the beater of a toy, then placed the beater into Mandy's hand, praising and encouraging. Mandy participated with interest.

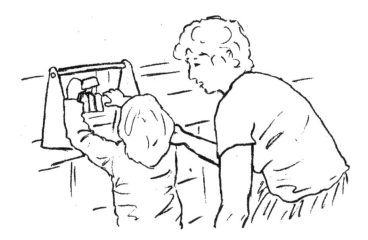

Figure 14.3 From exploring musical toys . . .

Very quickly, however, Amy decided to use this as an opportunity to carry out physical therapy exercises to improve Mandy's walking. Although Mandy showed no indication of having lost interest in the toys, Amy called for Mandy's walking frame and, enlisting the somewhat reluctant help of another child, attempted to encourage Mandy to walk with her walking frame. Amy's discourse changed at this point. Shifting from extending and building on Mandy's interest during which she had used words and actions to facilitate Mandy's fuller participation, Amy adopted a more directive and restrictive discourse. Although Amy still attempted to use a meaningful object (a favourite soft toy) as a focus for joint attention, Amy directed the other child to hold it out of Mandy's reach as a walking incentive.

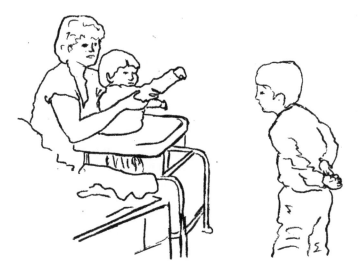

Figure 14.4 . . . to walking therapy; Amy enlisted the help of another child

Mandy was given no choice; Amy used verbal direction and physical guidance, lifting Mandy to hold on to the walking frame in an attempt to ensure Mandy's compliance. The combination of words used as imperatives, 'Got to move you' and 'Walking, Mandy!', the positioning of Amy's body, standing behind Mandy with her arms around Mandy and the use of physical repositioning (lifting Mandy under the arms, repositioning her at the frame several times) ensured that this was non-negotiable. Mandy was presented with a closed interactive space, defined by words and actions, in an attempt to ensure her compliance with the specific objective of the therapy. Mandy's lack of interest in the objective to improve her walking and her consistent desire to move away from the frame back to the worktop were clearly communicated. Mandy finally succeeded in crawling away.

The distinctive features of the physical therapy discourse were:

- tightly focused and exclusive adult-led objective
- strong adult control of child's actions, using body and words
- reduction of Mandy's agency with her lack of involvement clearly communicated
- considerable effort from the adult to sustain the discourse.

For Mandy, the shift from playful exchange to therapy appeared to be unhelpful, causing consternation for both Mandy and Amy.

Mandy and Jamie's experiences of and reactions to shifts between activity type during a preschool session were markedly different, though in quite subtle ways. By examining the similarities and differences, we can begin to unpick the features that may help young children to understand expectations of them during activities and to participate more meaningfully. The similarities included:

- 'closed interactive space' during 'therapy', communicated verbally and bodily (Payler 2007)
- a clear objective tightly controlled by the adult.

The differences included:

- *clear demarcation* in time and space between 'therapy' and 'non-therapy' by the use of a separate room/time for Jamie, but not for Mandy; this may have helped Jamie to know when he could use different forms of interaction – when he could be himself and have a conversation and when he needed to follow instructions; this was further helped by a
- *negotiated* beginning and end to therapy sessions for Jamie, but not for Mandy; it helped to lead to a
- *shared understanding* developed over time between Jamie and Tom with valuable use of a 'reward' time, not evident for Mandy.

Conclusion

We started the chapter by raising questions about how young children read the signs indicating what is expected of them in different circumstances. The examples have shown how contexts are signalled by the choices people make about how they manage their surroundings, organise time, and what they say and do. Effective early years practitioners show awareness of expectations relating to different types of activity, and how these are signalled to – and understood by – children for meaningful participation. These signs include:

* physical and temporal environment – time and space
* social features of the activity – power, control, choice, relationships
* cultural features – the child's prior knowledge of and alertness to 'rules' of games, of control and social exchanges
* potential 'collision' of discourses derived from differing principles – for example, early years practice principles linked to 'play' and therapy principles linked to precise, controlled 'work' towards objectives.

The *nature* of children's participation and their willingness and ability to take part depends on practitioners' understanding of the significance of these often taken-for-granted features of provision.

Questions to promote reflection

1   How might practitioners seek and act upon children's beliefs about what is expected where and when, to enhance children's participation and learning?
2   How might practitioners influence the design, layout and use of buildings, time and space to shape affordances for children and families?
3   How might practitioners become more fully involved in negotiating the nature of therapeutic inputs and activity plans with other professionals to ease children's transitions between discourses and activity types?

References and further reading (in bold)

Apple, M.W. and King, N. (2004) Economics and control in everyday school life. In M.W. Apple, *Ideology and Curriculum*, 3rd edn. New York: Routledge.

Bernstein, B. (2000) *Pedagogy, Symbolic Control and Identity: Theory, Research, Critique*. Lanham, MD: Rowman and Littlefield.

Broadhead, P. (2006) Developing an understanding of young children's learning through play: the place of observation, interaction and reflection. *British Educational Research Journal*, 32(2): 191–207.

Broadhead, P., Meleady, C. and Delgado, M.A. (2008) *Children, Families and Communities: Creating and Sustaining Integrated Services*. Maidenhead: Open University Press.

Brooker, L. (1996) Why do children go to school? Consulting children in the reception class. *Early Years*, 17(1): 12–16.

Brooker, L. (2002) *Starting School: Young Children Learning Cultures*. Buckingham: Open University Press.

Christie, F. (2002) *Classroom Discourse Analysis: A Functional Perspective*. London: Continuum.

Daily Mail (2013) A generation of unruly toddlers: minister under fire for 'ill-judged' claims that nursery children aren't taught manners. Available online at: http://www.dailymail.co.uk/news/article–2312657 (accessed 20 February 2014).

Department for Education (DfE) (2012) *Early Years Foundation Stage Framework 2012*. Available online at: http://www.foundationyears.org.uk/early-years-foundation-stage–2012/ (accessed 8 July 2012).

Georgeson, J. (2009) Co-constructing meaning: differences in interactional microclimate. In T. Papatheodorou and J. Moyles (eds) *Learning Together in the Early Years: Exploring Relational Pedagogy*. London: Routledge.

Georgeson, J.M. and Boag-Munroe, G. (2012) 'Architexture': access and participation. In T. Papatheodorou (ed.) *Debates on Early Childhood Policies and Practices: Global Snapshots of Pedagogical Thinking and Encounters*. London: Routledge.

Gibson, J.J. (1986) *The Ecological Approach to Visual Perception*. Hillsdale, NJ: Erlbaum (originally published 1979).

Greeno, J.G. (1994) Gibson's affordances. *Psychological Review*, 101(2): 336–342.

Howard, J. (2002) Eliciting young children's perceptions of play, work and learning using the activity apperception story procedure. *Early Child Development and Care*, 172(5): 489–502.

Mercer, N. (1995) *The Guided Construction of Knowledge – Talk Amongst Teachers and Learners*. Clevedon: Multilingual Matters.

Moyles, J. (ed.) (1994) *The Excellence of Play*. Buckingham: Open University Press.

Nind, M., Flewitt, R. and Payler, J. (2007) The experiences of young children with learning disabilities attending both special and inclusive preschools: final report for Rix, Thompson, Rothenberg Foundation.

Payler, J. (2007) Opening and closing interactive spaces: shaping four-year-old children's participation in two English settings. *Early Years: An International Journal of Research and Development*, 27(3): 237–254.

Payler, J. (2009) Co-construction and scaffolding: guidance strategies and children's meaning-making. In T. Papatheodorou and J. Moyles (eds) *Learning Together in the Early Years: Exploring Relational Pedagogy*. London: Routledge.

Ranz-Smith, D.J. (2007) Teacher perception of play: in leaving no child behind are teachers leaving childhood behind? *Early Education and Development*, 18(2): 271–303.

Regan de Bere, S. (2003) Evaluating the implications of complex interprofessional education for improvements in collaborative practice. *British Educational Research Journal*, 29(1): 105–124.

Rinaldi, C. (1998) The space of childhood. In G. Ceppi and M. Zini (eds) *Children, Spaces, Relations: Metaproject for an Environment for Young Children*. Reggio Emilia; Reggio Children.

Roberts, C. and Sarangi, S. (2005) Theme-oriented discourse analysis of medical encounters. *Medical Education*, 39(6): 632–640.

Waters, J. and Maynard, T. (2010) 'What's so interesting outside?' A study of child-initiated interaction with teachers in the natural outdoor environment. *European Early Childhood Education Research Journal*, 18(4): 473–483.

Willes, M. (1983) *Children into Pupils*. London: Routledge and Kegan Paul.

Wing, L.A. (1995) Play is not the work of the child: young children's perceptions of work and play. *Early Childhood Research Quarterly*, 10: 223–247.

Notes

1   All names have been changed. Outline tracings of video stills are used to preserve the anonymity of participants.
2   Makaton is a selected purposeful signed vocabulary.

15

Play and transitions: helping 'newly arrived children' settle into school

Hilary Fabian and Aline-Wendy Dunlop

Summary

This chapter explores issues affecting children who join school at times other than the majority. Moving to a new school can be both exciting and cause anxiety because new experiences often bring a complete change of routine and culture, as well as new friends and teachers. Parents, too, need to prepare for change in order to help their child settle well. The chapter identifies ways in which a collective approach to each child's needs, within the context of the family and community, combined with understandings about the role of play and the value placed on curriculum, allow for a personalised approach.

Introduction

A growing number of children move school part way through a phase, not necessarily joining or leaving at the start or end of a year, or the start or end of a term: advance notice to schools is not always possible and some children – for example, refugee or armed forces children – arrive unannounced. Such children are just as likely to move at the end of a week or part way through a year, and may be arriving from another country without speaking or understanding the dominant language. This so-called 'pupil mobility' is defined as 'the total movement in and out of schools by pupils other than at the usual times of joining and leaving' (Office for Standards in Education, 2002: 1).

'The progress made by migrant pupils is influenced by an intricate web of factors that stem far beyond individual schools and classrooms' (Hamilton, 2013: 205), which calls for a transition approach that supports the individuality of children within a shared process, takes account of what each child brings to the classroom community they are entering and, equally, calls upon the receiving community to embrace the newcomer's contribution and wider needs by working responsively with the learner, who at first may be 'on the edge', but who gradually develops changes in their involvement and becomes integrated.

Children vary in the time it takes them to feel comfortable in school. Smith and Pellegrini (2000), when writing about 'situated learning', argue that the degree to which learning may be context-bound is a factor of the links made between prior and present learning situations – from this we can infer that if more is recognisable to children in transition in terms of curriculum, pedagogy and environment, then their learning will travel with them and be available for them to draw upon. Given that we advocate the importance of looking at development in context (Dunlop, 2014) this indicates that receiving practitioners need to work to understand the child's prior experience and contexts as fully as possible in order to help the child bridge into the new. By personalising the process, children's varied interests, contributions and viewpoints can flourish. Play has the qualities that could enable transitioners to participate, to use what they have learned in a previous setting and to integrate and build on their previous experiences as they expand their thinking to embrace the demands of accommodating the new.

Brooker and Edwards (2010), elaborating on a play-based curriculum, consider that play is not a 'laissez-faire' activity and is not necessarily children's natural way of existence, but that 'the teacher has an important stimulating, supporting and cooperative role' (p. 206). Relevant for all learners, this cultural-historical perspective is critical for children whose transitions experience arises from family mobility, migration, additional support needs and complex family situations. For these children, whose experiences position them differently (Harré et al., 2009), play also becomes nurture and a more therapeutic communication approach that supports well-being and positive mental health.

'Nearly a billion people are on the move today across the Earth. We are living through the greatest mass migration our species has ever known' (Salopek, 2013: 37). Changes in family circumstances inevitably affect children and may also bring about educational transitions. Any change in children's schooling heralds further transition for the parent who, like their child, will need to tune in to a shift in culture and identity, new educational models, new curriculum and possibly a different pedagogy. Families who come to school with different experiences risk being positioned by society as 'vulnerable' and lacking competence. It is important that families are met by professionals/practitioners who understand the value of recognising their strengths and support the development of their social capital, which may otherwise be eroded through inequality and social exclusion (Jack and Jordan, 1999). Parents in all circumstances can make a significant contribution to their child's transition through the family continuity they provide, but they also need social supports that can be lost during migration.

Parents from countries where the curriculum is taught in a formal manner may need help to understand the use of 'play for learning' in the classroom. Equally, teachers are likely to find it helpful to be informed about the child's past experiences of learning through play in order to plan their teaching. This raises questions about how to make transition appropriate for each individual child by using a collective, collaborative approach, involving them and their parents, to address their needs and create a personalised transfer. According to the National College for Teaching and Leadership (NCTL, 2013), 'personalised learning . . . creates an ethos in which all pupils are able to progress, achieve and participate. It strengthens the link between learning and teaching by engaging pupils and their parents as partners.' In Scotland the principle of personalisation is a curriculum entitlement and is linked to choice: 'personalised learning which presumes a degree of choice and a stronger role for the learner in making decisions' (Education Scotland, 2012) and means acknowledging children's previous experience and providing individual support.

Personalising school approaches for incoming children means having effective pastoral care, leadership and management of the settling in process, collaboration with parents, and pupil inclusion. However, the main focus throughout each of these issues is the way in which play can be incorporated to make the transition a successful process for each child and their family rather than an event.

Mobility cameos

Some children may arrive with little or no knowledge of the local language (see Cameo 1).

Cameo 1

Patryk was introduced to others in the class but was unable to understand what they were saying or what work he was supposed to do. He said, 'On the first day I sat on the carpet and cried. I spoke to the teacher in Polish but she couldn't understand. Sam and Ben gave me a teddy bear but I threw it on the floor. I felt very sad – I had friends in Poland, but here I had no one. I got five blue tickets for pushing and kicking children at playtime. But one English boy tried to say hello to me in Polish and we played football. Then everyone wanted to be my friend. I stopped feeling scared and thought school was cool.' (Hamilton, 2010)

Patryk not only had little understanding of English when he first arrived but was also frustrated about the lack of friends. However, it is also clear that play – in this case, football – and using his initiative, assisted in making new friendships. What role could the teacher have played in helping Patryk to understand the activities of the classroom, tune in to his interest and help him to make friends?

Trying to adjust to another culture and pedagogy can sometimes provide tensions. Take the following example from a Polish parent (Cameo 2).

Cameo 2

In Poland there is more discipline . . . school is very strict. Children work hard and have a lot of homework. School is a place to learn, not play. Play is done at home. Children just have a desk and chair, no toys. Teachers speak louder. They have a distant relationship with children. Children need to be strong in Polish schools. When I went to school I was scared to go. My children are never scared. School here is colourful and cosy. School here is like a family.' (Hamilton, 2010)

The family in this cameo clearly has expectations of school that do not include play. Their intuitive expectations and preconceptions, based on their own experiences in a different context, might mean that they do not fully understand the processes of learning through play. How are teachers going to persuade parents that play can help second-language children, and that doing things that are fun in a context where they can interact with their peers, makes it easier for them to absorb a new language?

Children who have experienced frequent moves but who may feel relatively secure in the process, because for them transitions are a way of life, may arrive brimming with confidence and capable of quickly assessing what the new situation requires of them, even when they arrive singly and mid-term. Children from service families are such an example, as they tend to be more mobile than most. In Cameo 3, a teacher in the north of Scotland reflects on her experience of service children.

Cameo 3

'We have an army camp in our school catchment area, so families come and go – sometimes staying for several years, sometimes for only a few months at a time. It's not always easy for children who make frequent moves, but I recall one little girl who joined us aged seven-years having already attended four different schools in as many different countries. She was very quick to know the names of all in the class, she watched continuously to pick up on our routines and practices, she asked for help when she needed it and joined in at every opportunity with groups of children in the class. She also picked up the intonation of the local accent and tuned into our local culture. Over the years I have learned to respect such children's experience and to make room for them to share their different experiences with our local children – some of the children have lived in four or five countries before they ever arrive at our school – but not all are such competent transitioners as Susie was.'

In Susie's case her family worked hard to provide continuity. Every time the family made a move her mother made a point of coming into school within a few days of her children starting school to ensure they were placed in an appropriate class and to find out if the particular teacher needed any further information.

Thinking about the curriculum

Curriculum reflects the dominant educational thinking of any particular culture. It influences the teacher and shapes the school experience of the child. Most countries today have their own national curriculum. Children crossing borders will therefore inevitably need to make the journey into new school structures, relationships and programmes. Children moving within countries are subject to differences in local school policies and the way in which the particular school has interpreted the national curriculum. It is helpful to draw out these observable differences with children so they know their own change in circumstances is understood.

Thinking about play: what does it mean for our newly arrived children?

There seems no doubt that children learn through, and are motivated by, play. Learning through play and first-hand experience engages children with others and helps with developing relationships. Children construct social knowledge in social situations and learning is facilitated when they are interacting in meaningful ways with their peers, often through their own self-initiated play. It is the mechanism that helps children to cope with the changes in their world and can be used to provide appropriate frameworks in which children can attempt to work things out for themselves. Play, therefore, becomes one of the most important aspects in helping children to acquire an understanding of the world around them, and how they come to understand themselves as well as build new concepts.

Learning through play provides the conditions for developing confident, strategic thinkers and increased self-belief. One way of developing confidence is to encourage children to play in situations where there is no right or wrong, for example, home corner, sand play, water play and such like. Football helped Patryk in the playground just as Susie quickly learned the Scottish playground games at her new school, but children who are newly arrived are also likely to recognise play equipment in the classroom such as building bricks and have some idea what is required of them. Natalia said that on, 'The first day the English girls in my class came and talked to me. They knew I couldn't understand, so they used their hands to mime and helped me by showing me things to play with' – equipment and games that she knew well from previous experience. Play is about doing and by 'doing' she was able to begin to learn English. So we can see that the curriculum can be designed to incorporate play in terms of resources on offer as well as the context provided by the teacher. However, the setting up of play areas and activities do not, in themselves, produce good language development – they also require the involvement of adults and the planned use of dramatic contexts that make sense to children.

One responsibility of education is to give children the emotional nourishment that will support their well-being. Play is recognised as being healing and calming for children who have faced difficult or negative experiences (Barber, 2008), so opportunities that provide expressive activities such as playdough, role play and messy play are likely to help children work through their feelings and come to terms with their past. Children who are secure, attached and confident are usually more prepared to take risks, which shape the way they face the unknown, and enable children to believe that their world is controllable (Claxton, 1999).

Play is a common childhood experience. Most children have opportunities to play in ways that have been shown to influence learning from social competence to cognitive benefits, including the development of language and imagination, supporting children's emotional well-being and gaining physical benefits. Children usually bring their curiosity, creativity, enquiry, enthusiasm for learning and interest in others with them to school, and demonstrate such dispositions in their play. Some children miss out on this common childhood experience, either through dint of circumstance or because of their additional support needs. These children have more 'complex support needs' – a term that 'acknowledges the challenges faced by families, focuses on the interaction of different problems and highlights ways in which families, with appropriate support, can draw on their own strengths to make positive changes in their lives' (Dockett *et al.*, 2011) rather than stigmatising these differences from the typical. Such children may experience play differently from the typically developing and supported child. There is compelling evidence that engagement in play is a powerful intervention in such groups and has a longer-term impact where parents are involved.

Competent children

The concept of competent children has deep roots but often the nature of transition practice positions children as complete newcomers, rather than as contributors – a necessary shift needs to happen if we are going to be aware of what children bring to school. Ignoring this is ignoring a wealth of previous experience, experience in which children are masters of all that interests them to the level they are capable. To provide well for children in transition, we as adults must try to take their perspective more often, to see the world out of their eyes, to recognise the artist, the mechanic, the seasoned shopper's working maths, the older sibling's social skills and sense of responsibility, the carer, the creator: these are the kinds of competencies we need to be aware of so we make it possible for children to contribute what they know, feel and feel uncertain about.

Building relationships

Supporting children in transition also implies a need to work with parents in order to frame children's educational transitions in positive ways. Parental/family involvement is known to make a difference to children's transition experiences (Dunlop, 2003; Dockett *et al.*, 2011) and is believed to affect children's educational outcomes in the longer term. Furthermore, parents' psychological support and the child's own disposition have been identified as having considerable influence on early academic outcomes. The relationships and complementary roles played by parents and educators shift as children move through the education system (see Table 15.1).

Transitions for children are also transitions for their families. Griebel and Niesel (2002) consider that families co-construct the transition with their child and potentially with their child's educators, and confirm that, because of differences between families, each child will have a personal experience of transitions that differs from that of any other child. How parents feel about the transitions their children make will be influenced by the nature of the relationship with professional staff, commuting across cultures, parental shifts, and teacher responsiveness: 'The way in which school treats parents when they first join has a profound influence on their relationship with the school system for the rest of their lives' (Alexander, 1998: 128).

Table 15.1 Parental/educator shifts

Parents		Educators
Home child	Primary educators and nurturers: 'it's my job'	
Starting preschool	Children learning the new; making new adult non-parental relationships	Settling in/ relationships
Co-construction with child	Anticipating school together	Co-construction with one school educator
Preparation for school: physical, practical, intellectual, emotional	Changing identities. Parent of a school child: 'toughening him up'	Anticipation: preparation of parent and child
Anticipating change	Playing is over, now it's work when school starts	Valuing play as a continuing activity
No longer a nursery child	Letting go	Child as pupil
Parents as carer and supporter	Collaboration; co-construction; co-educators; cooperation	Educator as influential

Recognising the familiar

Starting at another school frequently accentuates differences, but some things, such as play, remain constant, although cultural differences can be found. By taking part in the activities of the classroom, by watching and listening, children will become familiar with the culture and begin to shape their own socio-cultural worlds. However, frame play, in which children and practitioners plan and play together, can create a shared classroom culture in which the newly arrived children are developing the culture alongside their more established peers. In frame play teachers and children plan the play situation and decide the content and context – the frame – for example, by turning an area of the classroom into 'an airport' or 'hospital'. Supported by this physical frame, children and teachers imagine themes, roles and actions, expressing their decisions verbally, in drawings and through paintings, which serve as models to developing a *collective fantasy* (Broström, 2007). Rather than spontaneous play, much is decided on beforehand and because there is a time interval between the formulation of the plan and realisation of the play, the roles, rules and actions are prepared. This results in frame play being more organised and more purposeful than role play, giving it a clear outcome and creating a common understanding of the imaginary play situation.

Most children know what play looks like and are familiar with rules, albeit with other children, in other schools, and sometimes in another language. While they are likely to understand these skills they might not understand how their new classroom works or fully recognise the activities taking place. By being involved in frame play situations, children are listened to and empowered to participate in the classroom, which can help them mediate between the old and the new.

A high degree of contextual support is usually required to help second language learners access the curriculum and understand the classroom. One project that did this involved the use of a computer program designed to help support new children as they made the transition. Photographs were taken of play activities in the classroom and a computer program used to present these, together with a written and spoken commentary in English and voice recordings in other home languages, which were made with the help of parents, children and staff. Natalia gained great pleasure from hearing her first language featured as part of the programme and new opportunities for learning were made possible as she became familiar with the play activities in the classroom.

The place of social and cultural spaces

Creating social spaces encourages play to take place, and thereby develop relationships and understanding of learning. However, space is a complex social construction in which there is a system of expectations and responses rarely articulated because they seem obvious within the culture (Lefebvre, 1991). These spaces have more layers of meaning than immediately meets the eye because this social intersection is not only where learning takes place through play, but also where learning about the culture takes place. Relationships and group cultural values are critical to helping children identify with the school community and gain a sense of belonging during transitions. Spaces contribute to the way in which children adjust to school and gain emotional well-being. Unfortunately, those who do not integrate or acquire the norms of the group, often become marginalised and lose the motivation to succeed. In order to fit in, children need to connect with their environment by detecting and interpreting what is going on, by observing and copying, by drawing on their own experiences, and by interacting with others. Through relationships they not only acquire an understanding of the culture but also construct their own identities within it. Children who migrate across national borders have multiple and intersecting identities, and develop notions of belonging connected to home as a fluid and dynamic place rather than as a fixed geographical location (Laoire *et al.*, 2010).

The place of competent systems

One of the outcomes of the CORe project was identifying the features of competent systems for effective early education and care provision. The report concluded that high levels of systemic competence are required and that individual, institutional, inter-institutional and inter-agency competences and competences of governance are the four ingredients of competent systems. Practices, knowledge and values each surface and are relevant to each layer of the system. The central message in this work is that in competent systems practitioners operate in a reflective way: 'By referring to **practices** instead of skills we intend to distance ourselves from a technical conceptualisation of educational work (*do I do things right?*) to move toward its **intrinsically reflective nature** (*do I do the right things?*)' (Van den Broeck *et al.*, 2010).

Personalising transitions

Children are socially constructed in relationship to others and each will arrive at school with different experiences. For children to gain a positive view of school and feel confident they need:

- a good knowledge of their classroom and some knowledge of the building
- a knowledge of their teacher and the way s/he thinks
- an understanding of the language of the school
- an idea of the nature of the activities that take place in school
- strategies to make friends, and
- a sense of the classroom culture.

In helping children to build a picture of themselves and their place in the world, teachers can involve 'settled' pupils by asking what matters to them and what they think is important for newly arrived children to know about school. Established pupils could then make classroom books to show the play activities using photos, drawings and writing that are specific to the school context. In this way teachers gain an understanding of what is important to the current pupils; the established pupils begin to have an understanding of the needs of newly arrived children and the incoming children are better accommodated by those already in the class.

Conclusion

This chapter recognises that transitions are increasingly a way of life (Brooker, 2009), but draws out atypical transitions, and emphasises the importance of play as a vehicle for supporting children and families when access to new educational settings is not straightforward. Through play, transitions may be personalised: children can draw on their own competence, the contributions they can make in playful situations and instigations of friendship that may fail them in more formal situations if they are unable to communicate conventionally on arrival in school. The power of play in children's culture in itself helps in the crossing of cultures they must make when they arrive in school unexpectedly. The personalising of transitions is a matter of each school developing social practices that enable schools, children and their parents to understand one another and where the play environment affords equality of opportunity for all children in a learning community in which each child can contribute to an inclusive classroom culture.

Each school needs to ensure that it is ready for every child who arrives, whether that is at the beginning of term or midway through the year; on their own or with a group. It is up to schools to make sure that play spaces and opportunities are in place to help children explore their feelings, resolve difficult experiences, continue learning and develop friendships. Children are natural anthropologists and investigators who need to indulge in depth, not just playing with things, but with people. Play and conversation are the main ways by which young children learn about themselves, other people and the world around them. They learn through:

- individualised play activities that build on previous experiences
- emphasis on emotional and social support within the curriculum tasks
- parent-professional collaboration, and
- play activities where goals are co-constructed.

All families may have unexpected changes in family circumstances that may lead to a move during the school year that brings discontinuities for their children. Newly arrived children experiencing atypical transitions need tailored approaches attuned to their circumstances, so allowing a supported transition process. In all transitions play provides a recognisable medium for expressing oneself, being beside others, watching and absorbing, imitating, approaching new friends and instigating contact that allows those involved in the demands of changed circumstances to ease into the new. Play and playful learning each form a bridge into school, into new relationships, into different teaching and learning approaches and into a new life. Play affords the opportunity for children in transitions to belong.

Questions to promote reflection

1   What types of play might help newly arrived children communicate and make friends with established children? What play activities are set up to help new children integrate with established children?
2   How might play be used to help children develop resilience during the transition to a new school?
3   How can parents from countries where the curriculum is taught in a formal manner be helped to understand about learning through play? How can teachers inform parents about the use of 'play for learning' in their classrooms?
4   How can teachers become informed about the child's past experiences of learning through play? How do you use this to plan your teaching?

References and further reading (in bold)

Alexander, T. (1998) Transforming primary education in partnership with parents. In C. Richards and P.H. Taylor (eds) *How Shall we School our Children? Primary Education and its Future.* London: Falmer Press.

Barber, J. (2008) Feeling positive. *Practical Pre-School for the Foundation Stage*, 84: 8.

Brooker, L. (2009) Taking play seriously. In S. Rogers (ed.) *Rethinking Play and Pedagogy.* London: Routledge.

Brooker, L. and Edwards, S. (2010) *Engaging Play.* Maidenhead: Open University Press/ McGraw-Hill.

Broström, S. (2007) Transitions in children's thinking. In A.W. Dunlop and H. Fabian (eds) *Informing Transitions in the Early Years: Research Policy and Practice.* Maidenhead: OUP/ McGraw-Hill.

Claxton, G. (1999) *Wise Up: Learning to live the Learning Life*. Stafford: Network Educational Press Ltd.

Dockett, S., Perry, B., Kearney, E., Hampshire, A., Mason, J. and Schmied, V. (2011) Facilitating children's transition to school from families with complex support needs. Albury: Research Institute for Professional Practice, Learning and Education, Charles Sturt University. Available online at: http://www.csu.edu.au/research/ripple/publications/index.htm (accessed 29 April 2014).

Dunlop, A.-W. (2003) Bridging children's early education transitions through parental agency and inclusion. *Education in the North*, 11: 55–56.

Dunlop, A.-W. (2014) Developing child in society: making transitions. In M. Reed and R. Walker (eds) *Early Childhood Studies, A Critical Companion*. London: Sage.

Education Scotland (2012) *CfE Briefing 5, Personalised Learning*. Available online at: http://www.educationscotland.gov.uk/Images/CfEBriefing5_tcm4–741643.pdf (accessed 25 April 2014).

Fabian, H. (2014) Transitions. In L. Dryden and P. Mukherji (eds) *Foundations of Early Childhood*. London: Sage.

Griebel, W. and Niesel, R. (2002) Co-constructing transition into kindergarten and school by children, parents, and teachers. In H. Fabian and A.-W. Dunlop (eds) *Transition in the Early Years*. London: RoutledgeFalmer.

Hamilton, P. (2010) The inclusion of Eastern European children into primary schools in North Wales: a case study. Unpublished PhD dissertation, University of Wales.

Hamilton, P. (2013) Including migrant worker children in the learning and social context of the rural primary school. *Education 3–13*, 41(2): 202–217.

Harré, R., Moghaddam, F.M., Pilkerton Cairnie, T., Rothbart, D. and Sabat, S.R. (2009) Recent advances in positioning theory. *Theory and Psychology*, 19(5): 5–31.

Jack, G. and Jordan, B. (1999) Social capital and child welfare. *Children and Society*, 13: 242–256.

Laoire, C.N., Carlene-Mendez, F., Tyrrell, N. and White, A. (2010) Introduction: childhood and migration – mobilities, homes and belongings. *Childhood*, 17(2): 155–162.

Lefebvre, H. (1991) *The Production of Space*. Oxford: Blackwell.

Office for Standards in Education (OfSTED) (2002) Managing pupil mobility (reference number HMI 403). Available online at: http://www.ofsted.gov.uk/public/docs2/managingmobility.pdf.

Salopek, P. (2013) Out of Eden. *National Geographic*, 224(6): 36–39.

Smith, P.K. and Pellegrini, A.D. (2000) *Psychology of Education, Pupils and Learning*. London: Taylor and Francis.

Van den Broeck, A., Vansteenkiste, M., De Witte, H., Soenens, B. and Lens, W. (2010) Capturing autonomy, competence, and relatedness at work: construction and initial validation of the Work-related Basic Need Satisfaction scale. *Journal of Occupational and Organizational Psychology*, 83: 981–1002.

Website

National College for Teaching and Leadership (NCTL): https://www.nationalcollege.org.uk.

PART 4
Playful curricula

'. . . the goal is to empower the child by developing his or her skills, learning and other capacities, human dignity self-esteem and self-confidence and this must be achieved in ways that are child-centred, child-friendly and reflect the rights . . . of the child.'

Report of the Committee on the Rights of the Child (2006: para 28)
United Nations Department of General Assembly Affairs and
Conference Services.

16

Engaging playfully with media and materials

Kathy Ring

Summary

Everyday availability of intelligent materials – materials that have transformational properties – will support children in gaining the expertise needed to become fluent and flexible thinkers. Within this chapter, examples of children's transformational activity are drawn from socio-cultural research in early years contexts. This activity is characterised by great absorption, engagement and fulfilment on the part of the children. The experience of children in the preschools of Reggio Emilia is used to support the extension of this approach with children aged between five and seven years.

Introduction

This chapter highlights the power of the decisions practitioners make in relation to the use of space, the media and materials they choose to put into their environment on an everyday basis, and the ownership they allow children to have over how they are used. It recognises the need for practitioners to develop greater knowledge of the properties of these materials in order that they can engage with the representational possibilities they offer to children as they engage in the playful making of meaning.

The child's unique response to experience

The Statutory Framework for the Early Years Foundation Stage (EYFS) emphasises, within its overarching principles, the uniqueness of the child. Through the routines and rituals of everyday practice in enabling environments it is acknowledged that children will learn in different ways and at different rates (DfE, 2012).

One of the key ways in which young children show their uniqueness is through the individuality of their responses to experiences. In environments where children have ownership of the ways in which they respond to the stimuli of well-chosen objects and materials, and where adults are knowledgeable about the possibilities for extension and transformation inherent in these materials, children's representations take the form of personal innovation. They experience the excitement and joy of having an idea or doing or making something new to them, which is valued by themselves and others.

In many settings practitioners have a well-developed understanding of what constitutes creative representation. This has been honed over time and has been part of ongoing staff development. They can recognise it when observing young children and have learned how to extend it without taking away the child's sense of ownership. Many early years practitioners, however, do not feel so secure in their understanding. The following material, adapted from the High/Scope document *Young Children in Action* (Hohmann *et al.*, 1979), offers support and identifies how children use representation to develop understanding of how the world works.

Hohmann *et al.* (1979) describe representation as the process by which children depict objects and experiences through imitation, pretending, building, artwork and written language. The ability to represent indicates that the young child is gaining a more abstract understanding of their world. It emerges from children having the opportunity to:

- explore actively with all the senses
- discover relations through direct experience
- manipulate, transform and combine materials
- choose materials, activities, purposes
- acquire skills with tools and equipment
- use the large muscles and take care of their own needs.

They identify some key experiences that support young children in making links between experience and representation that are cumulative and often take place concurrently.

Recognising objects by sound, touch, taste and smell

A child who has had a wide variety of active experiences can identify many objects from their sensory cues, i.e. a siren being heard calls to mind (stands for) a picture of the whole object, an ambulance. This is an intermediate step between the infant's sensorimotor perceptions and the older child's understanding of symbols.

Imitating actions and sounds

From early imitations of adult actions such as drinking from cups, preschoolers begin to imitate increasingly complex actions, e.g. driving a car. Through imitation they learn to represent with their own bodies and voices what they know about the world. This is the beginning of pretending, or role play, in which children integrate a series of imitations into a recognisable role.

Relating models, photographs and pictures to real places and things

'This truck's like my dad's truck, but his truck is great big and it's blue and I can honk it and I can really turn it on. This one, you have to push it like this.' This kind of experience helps children to make sense of the many representations that occur in their everyday world. Experience in interpreting such representations also gives children the background for the more abstract interpretations that they will be interpreting later, e.g. letters and numbers.

Role playing

Pretending to be someone else by doing and saying what that person does and says, is another way young children represent their experiences and their knowledge about people and situations. Through role play they sort out and use what they understand about events they've seen or taken part in, consolidating and strengthening what they know about their world. Role play helps children make their own sense of things happening in the adult world that they only partly understand.

Making models

Using boxes for filling and emptying, dough for squeezing, rolling and flattening, blocks for stacking and moving from one place to another gives children the opportunity to explore three-dimensional materials. These materials become tools for representation, as they enjoy making models of people and objects. Children's representations vary in the amount and arrangement of details, and in the similarity of the representation to the thing represented. These differences depend on the degree of the children's familiarity with the object represented and their skills with the material being used. A child's clear mental representation of a dog may translate into a primitive-shaped dog at the workbench because she hasn't acquired the skill to saw out the detailed pieces needed. In contrast, her ability in the shaping of clay to fit her internal picture may allow more details to be represented because of skills she has developed in the medium.

Making drawings and paintings

Children use paint or implements for drawing to put down on paper what they can hold in mind about a person, place, object or situation. This might not always be its shape (figurative representation). Boys spend longer than girls, generally, representing action (Ring, 2010), the movement of the brush or pen representing the action of the object/person in time and space (Matthews, 1999). The child's interest at the moment of making the mark will become the criteria for what will be represented.

Observing that spoken words can be written down and read back

The dictation process fascinates many children of preschool age and is a way adults can model for children another way of them representing their experiences. Their dictated stories may be about familiar people and situations, pictures they have made, structures they have built and situations they have enacted in role play. Their stories may be a series of coherent sentences or words or phrases. Through hearing their own words read back, children begin to get a sense of the power of their words to communicate their experiences and ideas, realising they can be makers of stories as well as listeners.

The influence of the socio-cultural context

The socio-cultural context in which young children make meaning ensures that the routines and rituals surrounding the use of materials, e.g. the organisation of time and space, and the modelling of their use by peers and adults, has a significant influence upon the act of making (Anning and Ring, 2004).

Within the culture of the preschools of Reggio Emilia, children's ability to represent knowledge and experience of the world, through what Malaguzzi terms 'one hundred languages' (Edwards *et al.*, 1998) is recognised and prioritised. In stating that young children are rich and competent learners, Malaguzzi (1998) recognises that children do not think and learn in just one way but have many approaches to the world. The interaction between children and children, children and adults, and adults and adults is an essential part of the Reggio experience. Within what could be termed a collaborative curriculum, practitioners tune in to children's interests, developing projects together with the children. Ongoing documentation of the developing process – for example, words, photographs, diagrams, working models, paintings – makes it possible for the teachers to 'sustain the children's learning while they also learn (to teach) from the children's own learning' (Rinaldi, 1998: 120). Slide documentaries, videos and books also support the memory and interactions of teachers, children and parents. By revisiting a project and by looking at the documentation, the children are offered an opportunity to further reflect and interpret their own ideas (Axelsson, 2009).

In the Reggio preschools, playfulness is promoted as a method of learning for children and the adults around them. During a visit to Reggio preschools, children were observed photocopying drawings, to preserve an important stage in their visual thinking. Working with the photocopies offered them the possibility to play with ideas, knowing they could discard them. Malaguzzi (1998) believed that the environment, termed 'the third educator', should enable both the child and teacher to express their potential, abilities and curiosity and would need, therefore, to be flexible.

The atelier, workshop or studio, rich in materials and tools easily accessed by the children, is a space in the Reggio Emilia preschools intended not only as a space of creativity but also as a place of research – a place where the children can test out their theories individually and together with other children, and with professionally competent adults.

This understanding has been supported by projects in England such as 5×5×5=Creativity (Bancroft *et al.*, 2008), and is associated with children being given chances to express themselves through, for example, movement, visual representation, music and words. Adults, both artists and educators, ensure that children are listened to, that their ideas are heard and supported, and that they are offered a creative environment where they can experience a sense of ownership and satisfaction.

Young children's engagement in such extended projects, when driven by interest and supported by skills in the use of materials developed over a number of years, encourages their continuing intrinsic motivation. Csikszentmihalyi (1997) uses the concept of the 'flow state' to describe children who are fully immersed in what they are doing. He sees this state characterised by a feeling of great absorption, engagement and fulfilment, where the whole being is involved and skills are used to the utmost. Intrinsic motivation is supported by an environment that ensures that skill level and challenge level are matched and high.

Alongside developing skills in using open-ended media such as blocks, clay and paint, the importance of children having the freedom to combine resources in many different ways must be emphasised. The powerful ongoing transformations in thinking, which are part of the playful process of, for example, cutting, sticking, marking and layering paper and card or building, rearranging and connecting blocks and plastic crates, can be recognised as part of the young child's free-flowing, multimodal meaning making. The products of such a process are continually changing as children adapt their meanings in mind to the nature of the available resources. These 'in the process of change' makings are both original and expressive. They are often underpinned by fleeting or transitory ideas that cannot always be explained in words but are shown through child-appropriate physical action.

Kress (1997) argues that 'children act multi-modally, both in the things they use, the objects they make, and in the engagement of their bodies; there is no separation of body and mind' (p. 97). He draws on detailed observations of his own young children engaged in multi-modal representations in the home context using:

- found materials to make 'models'
- household furniture and objects mingled with toys to make 'worlds' in which to act out involved narratives in play
- mark-making media such as felt tips and paint to 'draw' elaborate versions of their understanding of the world around them.

He calls these 'the energetic, interested, intentional action of children in their effects on their world' (p. 114).

Kress (1997) feels that the practice of cutting out drawn objects by children has particular significance, and that the affective quality and potentials of the 'cut out' are entirely different from those of the flat two-dimensional object. The cutting out of a drawing enables the child to 'move it about and place it in entirely new environments, with other objects, to form new structures in new imagined and real worlds' (p. 24). It would seem that the cut-out object can 'bridge a gap' for the child between the two- and three-dimensional worlds.

Developing from the work of Kress, Pahl (1999) recognises the need for young children to have time to immerse themselves in their ongoing narratives and to move from one material to another, using what is available to them to shape their sign making. Through their transformations of the materials and objects to hand, their narratives develop and they make new meaning and new forms of representation. Pahl argues that children have more opportunities to utilise fluidity in their meaning making at home. It is within the home context that she feels objects can be freely transformed from one function to another without the 'watchful gaze of an adult' (p. 104) and where children can adapt their meanings in mind to the nature of their resources.

Children's drawings produced in the home, are seen by Pahl (2002: 1–2) to be 'hybrid mixes of influences' and draw not only upon television and video narratives but influences from computer games, fairy tales and visiting grandparents, reflecting 'life as it is lived'. Their artefacts, defined by Pahl as 'pieces of writing, drawing, oral narrations, models and games' (p. 2), are seen to be crucial to their identity formation and sense of self.

The underpinning flexibility of thinking that characterises the breadth, richness and possibilities of young children's multimodal, interwoven responses to their experiences is recognised in approaches to literacy. Genishi and Dyson (2009) see 'learning what to say and how to say it across endlessly diverse situations and where the "saying" could be verbal or nonverbal', as fundamental to becoming literate (p. 9). Within a continuum of children's use of symbol systems the interrelationship of gesture, speech, play, drawing and writing for the young child is highlighted. The importance of speech in allowing children to represent meaning, to share their ideas with other people and to engage in increasingly more deliberate, better-planned and more playful activity is considerable. Literacy is not acquired merely through the mastery of conventional letters, words and sentences but is present in all forms of young children's meaning making: talking, drawing, playing, building, singing, acting and more (see, e.g., Barrett, 2011). Dyson (1990) sees the role of practitioners as helping young children to 'weave literacy from the rich diversity of resources they bring to school with them' (p. 211).

Within preschool and school contexts there is evidence of young children using what is to hand but finding that this is limited in terms of them developing their own ideas and meanings. In a detailed study of 'art making' (Tarr, 1995) many of children's interactions with practitioners were seen to be ritualised. Tarr saw three- and four-year-old children learning to seek out practitioners for validation and acceptance, and in doing so gaining understanding about what was acceptable as 'school art'. When a child completed a piece of work he or she took it to the practitioner and received a comment such as 'Beautiful' or was asked about the subject matter. She recognised this as indirect teaching, which was further supported as the practitioner, in selecting work for display, gave messages to both the children and their parents about what was valued. This practice influenced parent and child interaction about art-work and further shaped children's responses. In offering generalised praise such as 'Lovely', 'Beautiful', there is a failure to extend the child's understanding of art, its language or its skills and, therefore, support the development of the child's self-concept as an artist.

Within Anning and Ring's (2004) longitudinal study of young children drawing across home, preschool and school contexts, there is evidence within a number of settings for drawing being limited. In addition, adult interaction with children who were drawing was over-directed and focused on what was meaningful to adults, i.e. people drawing and name writing – this was combined with a lack of praise and recognition for children's creativity and originality. As children approached their fifth birthday and entered statutory schooling, there was evidence of playful drawing, i.e. drawing instigated and owned by the children, happening during wet playtimes, and 'workful' drawing, i.e. drawing that followed a prescribed adult agenda, happening within a weekly time allocation.

Young children demonstrating flexibility of thinking through ownership of their representations

This small-scale, longitudinal research project took place between 2004 and 2010, and was designed as a response to the findings of previous research (Anning and Ring, 2004). The intention of this action-research programme was to support practitioners in understanding and interpreting their role in supporting young children's use of drawing. It recognised the need for greater understanding by practitioners of drawing as a tool for thinking and as part of the integrated and unique nature of young children's creative representations.

A three-day course was designed where training and action research was intertwined to address both theoretical understanding and pedagogical practices. A total of 60 early years teachers (three cohorts of 20) took part in an interweaving of training, debate and analysis focusing upon data collected as a first phase of action research within their own educational setting. A second, longer phase of in-depth study took place with a smaller number of self-chosen practitioners. In the final third phase of the project, video-taped episodes of meaning making in three of the most visited settings were undertaken, the focus being children or children and practitioners engaged in drawing activity or interaction in relation to drawing activity (Ring, 2010). Within this research project visual methods were foregrounded. The inclusion of video-tapes of children interacting within their environments captured drawing as part of rich episodes of multimodal meaning making.

The images and accompanying narratives that follow are selected from the project data to exemplify, first, the transformations that take place as children engage with the interaction of materials and ideas and, second, practitioner awareness of some of the complexity of what they are seeing.

Cameo 1: Becky, almost three years – mummy

Becky drew a bold shape on paper, which, without being asked, she named 'mummy'. She spent 20 minutes on this creation, carefully colouring it in. She then began to trim off the edges.

Practitioner observation

I thought she would stop there as she then wrote her name on the back of the large cut-out. However, she then started cutting parts of the picture into small pieces, happily cutting across the picture she had made. Finally, with the picture in various-sized pieces, Becky chose one piece to go into the home box and re-wrote her name on the back. The rest of the paper was left behind.

Photograph 16.1 Becky trimming off the edges

Cameo 2: Megan, three years – monster

Megan made circular marks on her paper and said, 'It's a monster.' She then got some scissors and began to cut her picture into several pieces. She said 'I cut 'im up 'cos he's really angry.'

Photograph 16.2 Megan's monster

Practitioner observation

Previously there might not have been scissors readily available or I might have said 'Oh don't cut across your lovely picture. Why don't you use another piece of paper for cutting?', but that would have been me taking over with my own ideas of when something is finished.

Cameo 3: Henry, three years six months – rocket

Henry made a rocket out of various pieces of lined, marked and plain paper, and the 'fire' at the back was stuck on using a glue stick and masking tape.

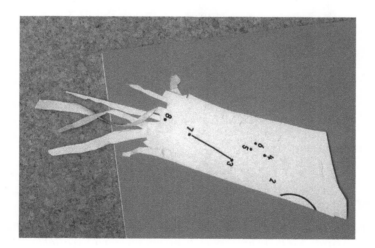

Photograph 16.3 Henry's rocket

Practitioner observation

Other boys were then very interested in how to make one. There was much discussion and the boy helped the other boys to make more rockets. Children individualised them by adding drawn-on windows and pilots. Building on this as a class we looked at making some more rockets and problem solving using 'junk' materials. In the past I had been more directing in my suggestions of what they could make but, by spending more time listening, my contributions were much more subtle and supported them in achieving greater levels of engagement.

Cameo 4: Joshua, four years – pop-out card

Joshua drew what appeared to be a ship, clouds and the sun. He attached to the drawing a worm made from cut, folded and marked coloured paper. He folded his paper in half and on what had become the front cover he drew 'The Power'.

Photograph 16.4 Joshua's 'The Power'

Practitioner observation

Joshua later said, 'It is actually a sea-worm that pops out.' We hadn't been looking at or making pop-up cards but there are a variety of pop-up stories available to the children in the book area. You do need to see the children and know the children and to have followed their interest to really engage and to understand their drawing because they all do it differently. Your environment has to be an enabling environment, bringing children on from where they are rather than setting a goalpost and saying I want you to do this, this and this by the end of the week.

Cameo 5a: Grace, three years five months, inspiring children aged five years

Grace attended the nursery of a primary school. She came in to the F2 classroom to show the class teacher what she had been busy making.

Photograph 16.5 Grace's efforts

Practitioner observation

She had completely independently decided to make a person. It was about a foot bigger than her when finished. The children in my class were very impressed and began to 'build' their own creations. One boy and his friend decided to make a big T-Rex dinosaur. They got four to five sheets of paper and stuck them together with masking tape. They worked across a morning to colour it and to add features. Three other children came over and decided to make a dinosaur of their own. Another child then showed me his creation. It was in a similar style to the dinosaurs but on a very small scale. He said 'It's a robot called Clitch.'

Cameo 5b

Following the visit to school of a blind man and his guide dog, one child created a life-size guide dog.

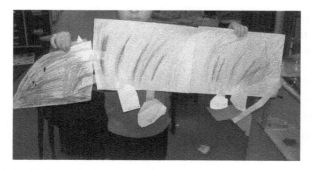

Photograph 16.6 A child's guide dog

Practitioner observation

The children started making different animals, e.g. a tiger, and carried on the building of large-scale shapes into the new class theme of transport, e.g. buses and motorbikes.

Adults tuning in to the playfulness of creative representation

The biggest changes made by practitioners that impacted upon both children's use of drawing and their making of meaning across a range of media and materials, related to them allowing children greater agency in their use of space and materials, and greater ownership of the content of their representations. Starting with one change in practice, standing back, and observing and documenting children's behaviours led to further layers of practitioner decision making. Children's own ability as decision makers was increasingly recognised and prioritised. Giving children ownership caused ongoing ripples of change. For example, the practitioners felt more relaxed in their engagements with children, as the pressure to lead had been taken away and children gained confidence as they worked alongside one another without the interruptions of a constantly questioning adult. This led to greater social interaction, collaboration and sharing, and bonds being built among older groups of children as they worked to common interests or themes. There was a greater playfulness in exchanges among adults and children that came with a shift of power from adults to children.

Over time children's developing confidence in their use of materials led them to take increasing risks. They were experiencing the excitement and intensity of creating something where nothing was before. They were recognising the connection between their actions, the outcomes of their actions in the materials they use, and inner sensations and experiences.

Practitioners discovered the particularly strong interrelationship for young children between drawing and the provision of 'junk modelling' or 'workshop' materials including scissors, glue and tape. The ability to act on and change materials from 'one state of being to another' (Burton, 2000) was intertwined with their creation of physical and verbal layers of narrative as they represented and re-represented transitory versions of real-life and imaginary stories in their play.

Conclusion

Gaining a better understanding of the flexible and multimodal nature of young children's meaning making had led practitioners to:

• put children's well-being at the heart of their practice
• prioritise observation as a tool for better knowing, understanding and making provision for young children's creative representations
• take children forward as meaning makers, rather than fitting them into pre-specified goals
• allow children's fascinations to drive the opportunities they (the practitioners) provided

- recognise and develop understanding of the interconnections and fluency of children's representations across a range of ways of meaning making
- ensure interventions enabled children to access new knowledge, understanding, skills, attitudes, feelings
- bring together children with similar interests
- recognise and support the development of narratives from popular culture
- empower children who communicate most fluently through drawing
- question their taken for granted assumptions as they recognised the richness of children's own meanings.

In moving forward, the practitioners recognised their need and the need of all those supporting young children to know and understand different materials and their possibilities. They wanted to be able to offer more discerning support to children both within and beyond the EYFS, which included what one practitioner called, 'technical language – the words needed to support making things', as used by artists and designers in their engagement with materials. The documentation of children's creative representations in the pre-schools of Reggio Emilia gives many examples of six-year-old children being encouraged to think deeply through the same materials that have been available to them since they were very young. Gambetti (2003) comments:

> In Reggio we have the highest quality kinds of materials we can find, not so the children can become geniuses but so that they and we have many opportunities to discover their learning processes and their abilities to think. I believe that when you give this to children when they are so young, when you empower them in their thinking, it stays with them for ever.
>
> (p. 76)

The provision of intelligent materials, materials valued for their transformational properties, is a key part of the Reggio Emilia pedagogy and philosophy. Providing high-quality materials is not always about expense but is about the knowledge and understanding that underpins decision making about what is made available to young children on an everyday basis.

Questions to promote reflection

1   Which materials do your children become immersed in using on an everyday basis?
2   Why are the children drawn to these materials and how might their use be extended over time?
3   Are there materials you need to know more about, materials you avoid introducing?
4   How can you ensure children's ideas have predominance in your setting?

References and further reading (in bold)

Anning, A. and Ring, K. (2004) *Making Sense of Children's Drawings*. Maidenhead: OUP/McGraw-Hill.

Axelsson, S. (2009) *The Relevance of Loris Malaguzzi in Early Childhood Education*. Available online at: http://interactionimagination.blogspot.co.uk/the-relevance-of-loris-malaguzzi-in.html (accessed 29 March 2014).

Bancroft, S., Fawcett, M. and Hay, P. (2008) *Researching Children Researching the World: 5X5X5=Creativity*. Stoke on Trent: Trentham.

Barrett, M.K. (2011) Educating teachers about the complex writing processes of preschool students (project). *Honorable Mentions*. Paper 1. Available online at: http://scholarworks.gvsu.edu/coeawardhonor/1 (accessed 30 March 2014).

Burton, J.M. (2000) The configuration of meaning: learner-centred art education revisited. *Studies in Art Education*, 41(4): 330–345.

Csikszentmihalyi, M. (1997) *Creativity: Flow and the Psychology of Discovery and Invention*. New York: Harper Perennial.

Department for Education (DfE) (2012) *Statutory Framework for the Early Years Foundation Stage: Setting the Standards for Learning, Development and Care for Children from Birth to Five*. Available online at: https://www.education.gov.uk/publications/standard/AllPublications/Page1/DFE–00023–2012 (accessed 1 April 2014).

Dyson, A.H. (1990) Weaving possibilities: rethinking metaphors for early literacy development. *The Reading Teacher*, 44(3): 202–213.

Edwards, C., Gandini, L. and Forman, G. (1998) *The Hundred Languages of Children*. Greenwich, CT: Ablex.

Gambetti, A. (2003) Teachers living in collaboration. In L.B. Cadwell (ed.) *Bringing Learning to Life: The Reggio Approach to Early Childhood Education*. New York and London: Teachers' College Press, Columbia University.

Genishi, C. and Dyson, A.H. (2009) *Children Language and Literacy: Diverse Learners in Diverse Times*. New York: Teachers College Press.

Hohmann, M., Banet, B. and Weikart, D. (1979) *Young Children in Action*. Michigan: High/Scope.

Kolbe, U. (2001) *Rapunzel's Supermarket*. Byron Bay, Australia: Peppinot Press.

Kress, G. (1997) *Before Writing: Rethinking the Paths to Literacy*. London: Routledge.

Malaguzzi, L. (1998) History, ideas, and basic philosophy: an interview with Lella Gandini. In C. Edwards, L. Gandini and G. Forman (eds) *The Hundred Languages of Children: The Reggio Emilia Approach – Advanced Reflections*, 2nd edn. Norwood, NJ: Ablex.

Matthews, J. (1999) *The Art of Childhood and Adolescence: The Construction of Meaning*. London: Falmer Press.

Pahl, K. (1999) *Transformations: Children's Meaning Making in a Nursery*. Stoke-on-Trent: Trentham Books.

Pahl, K. (2002) Texts as artefacts crossing sites: a multi-modal approach to the home/school transition. Paper presented at BERA Conference, Exeter.

Rinaldi, C. (1998) Projected curriculum constructed through documentation – Projezzione. In C. Edwards, L. Gandini and G. Forman (eds) *The Hundred Languages of Children: The Reggio Emilia Approach – Advanced Reflections*, 2nd edn. Norwood, NJ: Ablex.

Rinaldi, C. (2008) Malaguzzi and the teachers. In C. Rinaldi, *Dialogue with Reggio Emilia: Listening, Researching and Learning*. London: Routledge.

Ring, K. (2010) Supporting a playful approach to drawing. In P. Broadhead, J. Howard and E. Wood (eds) *Play and Learning in the Early Years*. London: Sage.

Tarr, P. (1995) Preschool children's socialisation through art experiences. In C.M. Thompson (ed.) *The Visual Arts and Early Childhood Learning*. Reston, VA: National Art Education Association.

17

In tune with play

Linda Pound

Summary

In this chapter, the term 'playing music' is considered and compared with the language used to describe other playful and creative experiences. The biological functions of play and music are discussed, and their role in learning and development explored. These include a sense of group cohesiveness, supporting memory and the reflection or representation of mood. I discuss the ways in which music can be made more playful and highlight the way in which playful music making supports learning across the curriculum. Playful music has a vital role to play in the development of communication, of physical competence, and in personal, social and emotional growth.

Introduction

In an effort to convince parents and policy makers that play is of value in school, there was a period during the later part of the twentieth century in early childhood education where everything that happened in the nursery or other early years setting was described as work. Children were asked whether they wished to work in the sand, in the home corner or with the blocks. It was hoped that this strategy would give essentially playful activities status and enable them to be seen as serious and productive. It did nothing, however, actually to present play itself as either serious or productive. More recently, the lessons of neuroscience and developmental psychology are supporting educators in seeing not only that, play is often fun, it is of key importance to development. Moreover, play, along with musical elements and social interaction, appears to be part of every child's learning repertoire from the earliest days of life. In essence, play (and, as this chapter will demonstrate, music) is not just fun, but is also of fundamental importance.

The way in which we describe musical activity in everyday life gives some interesting clues to its relationship with play. Our choice of the term 'playing music' contrasts with the language we use in relation to other subject areas or areas of the curriculum. We do not for example suggest playing painting. Although we use the expression 'playing music' in everyday life for a vast range of activities from the efforts of a concert pianist to those of a rap artist creating a new song, we do not generally describe many of the music-making activities that go on in the classroom as playing music. While we talk of children playing instruments, we generally describe other activities simply as singing, dancing or listening to music. We do not generally ask if they would like to play with songs or play dancing. In other areas of the arts, while we may talk to children about playing or (working) with clay, we are more likely to describe their artistic endeavours as painting, drawing or dancing. Artists do not generally talk about playing painting, playing sculpture or playing dance, although we know that engagement in these creative acts involves a great deal of playful activity. Picasso and Mozart, for example, are frequently characterised as essentially childlike in their passionate and creative behaviour.

Perhaps less surprisingly, people rarely talk about playing mathematics or playing physics. Yet it is said that Richard Feynman's Nobel Prize-winning work in physics sprang from playing in the canteen with paper plates. Seymour Papert, inventor of Logo – software that enables children to create their own programs – describes his childhood passion for playing with gears and other rotating objects. He goes on to describe the excitement that underpinned his learning – the exploration and passion being seen as vital components.

Small (1998) suggests that the word music should be used as a verb – musicking – to remind us that being engaged in music (either playing it or listening to it) is an active process that involves others. The term 'playing music' does of course denote action but is not in everyday language applied to all areas of musical activity in the comprehensive way that Small envisages. Although as indicated above we *play* recorded music, we do not play live music – we merely listen to it! Small would describe all such activities as musicking.

What is music for?

Since musicking is a universal feature of human endeavour we can speculate that it has a biological purpose. In all societies, music plays a number of important functions or roles in human living and learning.

Music supports social interaction and group identity

The development of group cohesion through music can be seen in places of worship and at football matches, in armies and in the performance of school songs. It is evident in the way in which educators use song in particular to hold the interest of a group of children coming, for example, to sit on the carpet for story time.

Cameo 1

Three-year-old Joshua found it difficult to leave an activity. Staff found that, having given forewarning of story time, sitting quietly on the carpet and singing familiar songs helped Joshua to join the group. He no longer needed constant reminders but joined in happily, feeling like a member of the group.

Whether in the fiercely defined types of pop music or in the clientele attending the opera house, throughout life music is a matter of identity and of culture. Even very young children recognise and enjoy music that has cultural significance and that they come to associate with their own sense of who they are and who they will become.

The combination of play and music is particularly effective in developing the level of interaction and bonding required to foster the engagement of babies and children in a community. Research indicates that play and music have a number of features in common. In addition to learning through action and exploration, and creating 'self-stimulating fun' (Cross and Morley, 2009: 73), both play and music support the development of the ability to negotiate and cooperate with others.

Music helps to create and express or reflect particular atmospheres or moods

This is evident in everyday life: at funerals and parties, in hotel lobbies or supermarkets, the choice of music helps to put even the apparently passive listener into a particular frame of mind. As adults we are often highly discerning about whether a particular piece of music will suit our mood – either in reflecting it or in helping us to overcome it. We may choose music to relax, revive or rally us. This function is also evident in the universal use of lullabies and soothing songs with young children. Not even babies and toddlers are exempt from the energising influence of music – even before they can move independently, a piece of lively music will have them bouncing and waving excitedly.

In the twenty-first century, music accompanies every aspect of our lives. Apart from individual listening on smartphones or similar devices, music in the form of whistling, singing and piped music fills our waking hours. Inevitably our behaviour is shaped by the music we hear.

Cameo 2

When ten-month-old Layla joined the nursery, to help her get to sleep she needed the familiar lullaby her mother sang to her. Her key person learned and sang the song to her each day. As Layla settled, she began to associate the singing of 'Happy birthday' with a celebration and was eager to join in.

Cameo 3

A Steiner Waldorf practitioner used a small lyre to signal a change of activity for her group. Its gentle rippling sound maintained the quiet calm atmosphere, and enabled children to move into a group activity without any unnecessary rush or disruption.

Music supports memory

Certain pieces of music can conjure up memorable situations – just hear the opening notes of a particular song or piece of music and you are transported to a particular time or place. Advertisers exploit this. The rhythm and cadences of their jingles (whether or not they are set to music) remain lodged in the brain, often to our annoyance when we no longer wish to think about toothpaste or chocolate. But educators are also aware of music's potential – rhymes work because learning a string of apparently unrelated words (one, two, three; Monday, Tuesday, Wednesday) or letters (A, B, C) and being able to recite them in a helpful order is made easier if they are set to music. Most early childhood educators make imaginative use of familiar tunes such as 'Here we go round the mulberry bush' to help children to remember facts, storylines or vocabulary.

Control and discipline

Music can help children to move from one space or one activity to another in an orderly fashion. Many settings use a particular tune or song to signal clearing-up time, for example. Similarly songs can be used to help children to learn social values and behaviours, which might include taking turns or saying 'good morning' to the group.

This emphasis on group management and conformity was openly acknowledged by Robert Owen who, when setting up his innovative and philanthropic venture at New Lanark in the early part of the nineteenth century, gave music a focal place in the curriculum, for children from two years of age. He viewed music and dance as a means of 'reforming vicious habits . . . by promoting cheerfulness and contentment . . . thus diverting attention from things that are vile and degrading' (Donnachie, 2000: 170). All too often, despite the rich potential offered by music the main use made of it is in getting children to conform – all doing the same thing at the same time. That might be all singing the same words or doing the same actions, but it might equally be to do with discipline: all lining up nicely to go out to play or march into assembly. While this has its uses, the expressive and creative uses of music may be overlooked because we are anxious about keeping in time, about getting the tune, words and actions 'right'.

Communication and music

Music eases communication in situations where it would otherwise be difficult.

- Distance may make communication difficult but music can make words or sounds more easily heard and understood. Yodelling, whistling and drumming are familiar examples of this. However, the technique is put into practice in day-to-day situations where the distances are less great but still a barrier to communication. When wanting, for example, to call children from the far side of the playground, adults commonly adopt a rhythmic chant or exaggerate the intonation so that it has a music-like quality.

- Music has a unique role in aiding communication where the feelings expressed would be difficult to put into words (Mithen, 2005). Music can enable us to vent anger, and to describe love, joy or sorrow. The French poet Victor Hugo is said to have suggested that music allows us to express 'that which cannot be said and on which it is impossible to be silent'. Or, as Bowman (2004: 32) aptly writes, 'Music sounds like feelings feel.'

- Music plays a part in supporting the vital and challenging job of drawing in to the culture babies who have not yet learned language. It does this by capturing the baby's attention, developing shared meaning and communicating feelings – effectively reducing the distance between baby and carer by focusing on emotions. Hearing, the first of the senses to develop and the last to leave us, is stimulated before birth by the 'intrauterine symphony' (Bowman, 2004: 37) that surrounds the unborn child.

  The role of musicality in supporting development and learning continues throughout infancy. Adults and even very young children raise the pitch of their voices and use a sing-song melody in their talk with babies. Babies' hearing allows them to differentiate languages and voices – their preferences being their mother's voice and her first language. They also prefer complex sounds with plenty of contrasting pitches and rhythms. The intonations chosen by adults are now known to convey a range of emotions, which show an apparently universal pattern. Thus the tunes and pitch used to communicate, for example, approval, disapproval or comfort show significant similarities whether the language used is English, French or even a tonal language such as Mandarin (Powers and Trevarthen, 2009).

  From three or four months of age, babies and adults engage in playful musical interactions that involve songs, rhymes and chants that may be traditional but increasingly may also be versions adapted from popular music (Trevarthen, 1998). There are many examples from different languages and cultures, adults provoke babies' interest through repetitive songs and rhymes made interesting by slight variations in tempo and pitch. In these 'baby-songs' there is a story-like structure and an invitation to an emotional response, often associated with a delayed climax. 'Walking round the garden like a teddy bear' is a well-known example in English.

- Music is often well used to support communication with those for whom it would otherwise be difficult, namely children with special educational needs. Even children with severe expressive speech difficulties can sometimes join in songs on cue, carried as they are by the rhythm of the music. This has been described by Bowman (2004: 38) in the following words: 'Sound seldom reflects the periphery of the body . . . It circulates in, around and even through us, both individually and collectively.'

  Bond (2009) describes an approach to the education of deaf-blind children, which she calls Dance and Play. She suggests that current practice in this field relies on physical action through which 'the child is encouraged to learn that he [*sic*] can influence the other person: interaction has begun' (Bond, 2009: 405). Adults, as in the earliest effective interactions between young babies and carers, follow the child's lead, and make use of rhythmic movement and sound, which may be perceived for this group of children through vibration.

- Music is also of great value in supporting communication with young children in the early stages of learning English as an additional language. Vocabulary is rendered memorable in song; sounds are often exaggerated and can therefore be more readily identified and actions support the meaning. In common with storytelling, the high level of repetition (which would be unacceptable in everyday conversation) supports the development of understanding.

Creativity and music

Finally, but by no means of least importance, music, together with play, has a role or function in supporting the development of creativity. The early development of individual babies (Trevarthen, 1998) and that of the species as a whole (Mithen, 2005) owes much to music and the physical action that accompanies it. The playfulness of music and dance contributes to human survival since it supports the development of creativity, which in turn shapes our remarkable and flexible brains.

Music and play

Having considered the functions of music it is now important to link music and play. Music is not just important in its own right: it can make a unique contribution to playful learning. The voice is the baby's first plaything and, in the development of humans, dance was probably the precursor or herald of our humanity. It is likely that we were unable to use our voices to sing or our hands to play instruments before we had risen up on to two legs. Humans probably danced on all fours before they stood on their hind legs and walked. Did the playful, emotional excitement and physical exuberance we now associate with dance cause us to rise up on our hind legs?

The publication of the revised Early Years Foundation Stage (EYFS) in England (DfE, 2012) broke new ground by making it a statutory requirement to address children's learning through three main characteristics. Although play, including playful music making, is overtly mentioned in only the first of the characteristics it is integral to all three. This link is explored in Table 17.1.

Table 17.1 Characteristics of effective learning (DfE, 2012) and playful music

Characteristics	Links with playful music making
Playing and exploring	
Finding out and exploring	Finding out requires time to practise and explore sound freely. In addition to whole- or small-group periods of music making, children need time and space to 'play about' with sounds. Like role play or block play, music should be part of continuous provision. All too often the music area gathers dust because adults lack confidence in using the resources. A large area for music making, space to dance and a mirror to see the effect of your movements are essential.
Playing with what they know	When children make up songs, dances and instrumental music, their explorations reflect not only their interests but their knowledge. This will inevitably have a cultural bias – drawing on the music they hear (and see) at home and in the community. Adults have a role to play in introducing children to a wide range of music to encourage sharing of experiences.

Being willing to 'have a go'	In all truly creative play there is an element of risk-taking and children should be encouraged to have a go and to learn to manage risk safely. The traditional emphasis in education on getting it right has led generations of adults to claim that they can't sing, or can't play because they can't read music. It's time to reclaim the play in playing music and to encourage children (and adults) to take musical risks, having a go at picking out a well-loved tune; drumming like the drummer who came to perform; or playing the recorder like your big brother. This in turn will support the cognitive risk taking essential to effective learning.

Active learning – motivation

Being involved and concentrating	Since so much of everyone's time is spent engaging with music, children are inevitably drawn to it. They enjoy listening, especially if they are given opportunities to watch how sounds are made. After just a short amount of times spent observing musicians, young children will imitate many of the actions and mannerisms that they have observed. It's also important to remember that young children listen (and learn) with their bodies. In order to listen well to music they need to be able to move.
Enjoying what they set out to do	Singing, playing and dancing together is fun. Exuberance and joyfulness are essential elements of learning (Pound 2014) and playful music making supports them. Like listening, enjoyment is physical. Excitement makes children move about, but it also changes the chemistry of the brain making learning more memorable and persistent. One of the characteristics of high musical achievers has been found to be that their music making in early childhood is fun (Sloboda cited by Pound and Harrison 2003).
Keeping on trying	Because music can be both joyful and motivational, children will persist, especially when the goals are their own and not driven by an expectation that there must be a right answer or a right way of doing it. The legendary ten thousand hours that are said to be necessary for mastery of anything (including music) cannot be achieved unless the time spent feels rewarding. Children are more likely to keep trying when the activity is enjoyable.

Creating and thinking critically

Having their own ideas Choosing ways to do things	Introducing children to a wide range of types of music gives them material for new ideas. New ideas develop from other people, new contexts and materials. Making up songs and instrumental music allows children rich opportunities to make decisions and choices. These are important strategies for learning and they can be honed or developed in musical play. Which instruments can sound like a car? Do these chime bars sound like a police car?
Making links	Musical play creates opportunities, for example, to make links between:

(continued)

Table 17.1 *(Continued)*

Characteristics	Links with playful music making
	• the different ways that sounds can be made
	• pattern in music, art, nature and mathematics
	• similar patterns or sequences played on different instruments
	• musical and visual representations or places or events (such as music about trains or the sea)
	• different versions of the same tune played at different tempos, in different styles or on different instruments.
	Music making also involves linking with others and this requires self-discipline and negotiation – both important aspects of learning.

How can we make music education in the early years more playful?

The essence of play is its exuberance – music shares this, but often practitioners shy away from allowing playing music to achieve its full potential. Of the many possible or desirable changes, I have selected three as of particular importance. These are musical improvisation, song writing and physical engagement. Renewed emphasis on these three things could transform not only music education but offer an increased focus on creativity in the early years.

1   Improvisation is frequently associated with jazz musicians but in fact it has a firm place in most musical traditions, including western classical music. It fulfils the role of play – in promoting the rehearsal of ideas, exploring boundaries, drawing on and transforming familiar themes. It can be the doodling that leads to the masterpiece, or the transitory chatter. Just as learning to talk involves play, alone and with others, so learning to musick needs to involve playful improvisations – alone and with others. We do not think of spoken conversation as of less value than printed words – different but with different functions. However, the musical equivalent of talk, improvisation, is often described in a disparaging tone as being just 'made up'. In fact we should be encouraging children to engage in musical chatter, cooperating with others to take risks, and to make up songs and music.

2   Singing is widely promoted as making learning easier, and as energising and enthusing learners (www.singup.org). However, although children as young as two years of age can be heard improvising songs as they engage in other forms of play, song writing is often ignored. By statutory school age this spontaneous and creative music making has generally disappeared. Coral Davies (cited in Pound and Harrison, 2003) has identified three types of song produced by children: story songs, songs that follow a known structure (or frame songs), and what she terms secret songs. She believes that, with more active encouragement, children would

continue to make up songs and that creative development would be enhanced. Children's own songs are often overlooked in ways that would be unacceptable in other areas of creative expression – paintings and models, for example, are often lovingly displayed.

Cameo 4

Staff at one Children's Centre began to collect children's invented songs. Sometimes they picked out a song to teach to other children and at other times they typed the words to accompany a display. A number of children, some as young as two, were often creating secret songs. In general these did not follow the normal structure of a song or really tell a story. They were very often a sort of running commentary on what was happening, often sung on a few notes with long-drawn-out phrases and word repetition. Many children made up frame songs – based on known songs or tunes – changing the words. Staff at this centre were particularly good at making up songs of this sort – including children's names or familiar events in known songs – and this encouraged children's own song writing. Small world play was often accompanied by story songs. Sandeep, for example, accompanied play with farm animals with his song:

The horse is in the field
He's eating all the grass
He's treading on the rabbit and
Hitting all the sheep.

3   Physical engagement is an essential part of all learning. Organisms that do not move do not have brains. Sadly, the importance of the body is not always acknowledged. As children move through school there is less and less time for physical engagement in learning. But early years practitioners ought not to be complacent. As Tobin (2004: 111) points out, 'the body is disappearing in early childhood education'. Not only, he claims, has there been a kind of moral but misguided panic about physical contact with children but the emphasis 'on academic over social development' has had the effect of drastically reducing the amount of time that children spend in physical activity, creating 'an imbalance which favors [sic] the brain over the body and skill acquisition over feelings and more complex thinking' (Tobin, 2004: 123).

The recognition of physical development as a prime area of learning (DfE, 2012) underlines the role that physical play has in aligning and gaining control of the body in order to support cognitive development. Music, with its inherent physicality, offers an important mechanism for reclaiming the body in early childhood education. While some educators have embraced Howard Gardner's Multiple Intelligence Theory (Gardner, 1999), not all have understood the importance of the links between physical and cognitive development. In failing to present body, mind and culture holistically, music (and other) educators have missed an opportunity to 'create a model of education in which music's role might be seen as a continuation and enhancement of precisely what makes all our intellectual achievements possible' (Bowman, 2004: 34) – namely the body.

Young children can only respond; it is a physical impossibility to listen to music without moving. Early childhood educators can take two simple steps to re-embody music education, making it more playful. First, we can ensure that music areas have enough space for children to move freely, with or without instruments, and that mirrors are available so that children can see what their bodies look like when they are moving. This is difficult in many classrooms where there is a shortage of space, but we can at least try to make it possible sometimes. Second, we can offer more musical opportunities outside. While physical development does not have to happen outdoors, the space and freedom it can offer make it more likely that gross motor activity will occur. There are, in addition, opportunities to explore loud sounds and natural sounds.

How does music make learning across the curriculum more effective?

While it is vital that music is played for its own sake, it can, as we have seen, contribute to effective learning. The functions of music also give it a key role in effective teaching. Table 17.2 demonstrates ways in which music contributes to learning by supporting development in the prime areas of learning (DfE, 2012).

Table 17.2 The role of music in supporting development in three prime areas of learning (DfE, 2012)

Prime area of learning and development	Contribution of playful music making
Personal, social & emotional development • Making relationships • Self-confidence and self-awareness • Managing feelings and behaviour	Music provides excellent opportunities for young children to express feelings through music. This can help children to become more aware of their emotions and better able to deal with them in socially acceptable ways. Adults can support this by using music to help children anticipate a change in activity or to set a mood. Music-making is essentially a social activity. Gardner (1999) makes clear that musical intelligence relies on awareness of others – a musician who does not watch and follow fellow musicians will not get far. Stage areas for role play and pretend microphones give children opportunities to explore the nature of performance and to develop self-confidence in playful non-threatening ways. Recording musical play enables children to review and reflect on what they have done – and thus increase their self-awareness.

Communication and language • Listening and attention • Understanding • Speaking	As we have seen music has a special role to play in contexts where communication would otherwise be difficult. The rhythm, pitch and speed of speech determine how it is heard and understood. Playful music and musical play enable children to explore the elements of music and thus increase their vocal and physical control. Musical sounds and rhythmic movements, like speech, can act as symbols – representing ideas, thoughts and feelings. In Reggio Emilia, forms of representation are described as languages. In the act of translating ideas from one symbolic language into another understanding is enhanced.
Physical development • Moving and handling • Health and self-care	Physical action is an essential part of young children's learning. Music, like play, allows children to explore what they can do – but although play-based action such as rough and tumble play have much in common with dance, movement in response to music involves higher order thinking (Panksepp and Trevarthen 2009). At a more basic level, songs can be used to help children to remember key routines such as hand-washing, through the use of words set to familiar tunes.

Conclusion

Play is widely described as allowing children to act and learn at their highest level. It seems likely that, in musical play, learning is at an even higher level. Like play, music is of fundamental importance in human development and learning. In particular it offers a bridge between 'physical exuberance and rationality' (Panksepp and Trevarthen, 2009: 112). Early childhood educators have a grave responsibility to ensure that the benefits that playful musicking offers are made available to young children through playful teaching.

Questions to promote reflection

1 What steps do you need to take to make music in your setting more playful?
2 What support do you need to feel sufficiently confident in your own musical ability to intervene successfully in children's musical play?
3 What spontaneous opportunities do you provide for child-initiated 'musicking'?

References and further reading (in bold)

Bond, K. (2009) The human nature of dance. In **S. Malloch and C. Trevarthen (eds)** ***Communicative Musicality: Exploring the Basis of Human Companionship*. Oxford: Oxford University Press.**

Bowman, W. (2004) Cognition and the body: perspectives from music education. In L. Bresler (ed.) *Knowing Bodies, Moving Minds: Towards Embodied Teaching and Learning*. Dordrecht, the Netherlands: Kluwer Academic Publishers.

Cross, I. and Morley, I. (2009) The evolution of music: theories, definitions and the nature of the evidence. In S. Malloch and C. Trevarthen (eds) *Communicative Musicality: Exploring the Basis of Human Companionship*. Oxford: Oxford University Press.

Department for Education (DfE) (2012) *Statutory Framework for the Early Years Foundation Stage*. Available online at: http://www.foundationyears.org.uk (accessed 23 April 2014).

Donnachie, I. (2000) *Robert Owen: Owen of New Lanark and New Harmony*. East Linton: Tuckwell Press.

Gardner, H. (1999) *Intelligence Reframed*. New York: Basic Books.

Mithen, S. (2005) *The Singing Neanderthals: The Origins of Music, Language, Mind and Body*. London: Weidenfeld and Nicolson.

Panksepp, J. and Trevarthen, C. (2009) The neuroscience of emotion in music. In S. Malloch and C. Trevarthen (eds) *Communicative Musicality: Exploring the Basis of Human Companionship*. Oxford: Oxford University Press.

Pound, L. (2014) Playing, learning and developing. In J. Moyles, J. Payler and J. Georgeson (eds) *Early Years Foundations: Critical Issues*, 2nd edn. Maidenhead: Open University Press.

Pound, L. and Harrison, C. (2003) *Supporting Musical Development in the Early Years*. Buckingham: Open University Press.

Powers, N. and Trevarthen, C. (2009) Voices of shared emotion and meaning. In S. Malloch and C. Trevarthen (eds) *Communicative Musicality: Exploring the Basis of Human Companionship*. Oxford: Oxford University Press.

Small, C. (1998) *Musicking: The Meaning of Performing and Listening*. New England: Wesleyan University Press.

Tobin, J. (2004) The disappearance of the body in early childhood education. In L. Bresler (ed.) *Knowing Bodies, Moving Minds: Towards Embodied Teaching and Learning*. Dordrecht, the Netherlands: Kluwer Academic Publishers.

Trevarthen, C. (1998) The child's need to learn a culture. In M. Woodhead, D. Faulkner and K. Littleton (eds) *Cultural Worlds of Early Childhood*. London: Routledge/Open University.

Website

www.singup.org (accessed 11 March 2014).

18

Adventurous play outdoors

Helen Tovey

Summary

Outdoors offers scope for children to be bold, daring and adventurous in their play, to explore new terrains, create exciting and dramatic scenarios, to 'feel life in every limb', and to experience risks and challenges that are not available indoors. Yet the value of such adventurous play is not always recognised, and opportunities can be limited by bland, unchallenging environments and anxiety for children's safety. This chapter considers some key aspects of adventurous play outdoors and argues that, by denying children opportunities for such play, we restrict their opportunities for learning, for understanding and managing risk, and their chances to be bold, adventurous thinkers and learners.

Introduction

Margaret McMillan (1930) argued that children should be able to play 'bravely and adventurously . . . in a provocative environment where new chances are made possible' (p. 78). She created a garden for children where they could climb trees, dig channels for water, make large constructions with open-ended, recycled material, and use real tools for digging and making. The garden included a wilderness area for exploring, and a 'junk heap' of urban scrap materials for building and creating.

Children's play today is increasingly subject to targets and outcomes, constrained by demands for 'school readiness' amid a prevailing climate of risk aversion – what opportunities are there for children to be bold, brave and adventurous in their play and learning?

Why adventurous play outdoors?

Outdoors offers a unique environment for play very different from indoors. It offers the space and freedom to try things out, explore, experiment, push limits, and be daring and adventurous. Being adventurous is about being bold, taking some risks, engaging with the unknown and the uncertain, and being open to new experiences and ideas.

It is about making choices about how to view the world and whether to go this way or that way. It involves intense engagement, speculation and insatiable curiosity – a disposition to be adventurous.

The open space and variety of terrain can offer unique opportunities to be adventurous, to clamber over rocks or fallen trees, to creep through long grass or tangled bushes, to explore nooks and crannies, and to investigate the unknown. Children can engage in expansive, exuberant, 'full-bodied, whole-hearted movement' (Greenland, 2009: 1) as they engage with their environment. Materials can be combined in new ways, offering unexpected challenges and problems to be solved.

The dynamic, unpredictable natural environment, with its ever changing patterns of weather and seasons, offers wonder and surprise, invites curiosity and investigation, and creates exciting play opportunities whether that means leaves to roll in, puddles to splash in, mud and ice to slip on, or shadows to jump on. The sheer variability of the outdoor environment is what makes it unique and contrasts sharply with the more static indoor environment.

The freedom of movement outdoors allows play to flow through space and over time, gaining in complexity. The diverse nature of the outdoor space allows children to find their own level of adventure and challenge. What is brave and risky for one child will be very different for another. Outdoors offers rich potential for children to navigate the risky social world of friendships and relationships with others.

However, outdoors is about *potential*. Adventurous play does not thrive in open, windswept, asphalt-surfaced playgrounds or bland, flat, plasticised, safety-surfaced play areas where children are cut off from the natural world or from authentic first-hand experiences. Nor does it thrive in environments where adults are anxious and fearful about such play, and where they seek to control or curtail it.

Risky, 'dizzy' play outdoors

A distinctive feature of play outdoors is children's propensity to seek situations they perceive to be risky or 'scary' where risk is the central feature of the play. Such play often involves:

- height, motion and speed
- inverting usual body posture – for example, tipping, spinning, rolling and hanging upside down
- joy in precariousness and unpredictability
- deliberately seeking out situations of uncertainty where the outcome is unknown.

The simultaneous experience of risk and challenge, fear and exhilaration, feelings of being 'on the edge' of danger, characterise such play. We can see this in babies' delight in being thrown up in the air, bounced vigorously or tipped backwards by a trusted adult, in young children's joy in balancing along a wobbly bridge, rolling down a grassy slope or swinging on the end of a rope. Typically children increase the challenge or level of risk as they repeat their play, suggesting that it is not just the feelings of joy that motivate children but the desire to experience the very edge of their capabilities.

Such play has some links to what Kalliala (2006) calls 'dizzy play', which often has a freewheeling, spinning, exhilarating quality. Such play is characterised by 'an attempt to momentarily destroy the stability of perception and inflict a kind of voluptuous panic on an otherwise lucid mind' (Caillois, 2001: 23). The phrase 'voluptuous panic' captures the simultaneous feelings of joy and fear that such play can engender. Caillois also noted that such play was important for developing camaraderie, friendship and social cohesion. Greenland (2009) argues that such movement play is central for children's neurological development and vital for later learning. In a 12-year research project on developmental movement play, she noted that, given a choice, 'spin-tip-roll-fall' play followed by 'push-pull-stretch-hang-buffet about' play were the most frequent activities children engaged in and the ones that involved them the most. Such movements stimulate children's vestibular and proprioceptive senses – that is, their sense of balance and awareness of their own body in space. Swinging on the end of a rope provides whole-body experiences of the laws of physics such as speed, momentum, gravity and balance. Similarly, sliding fast down a slope provides experience of speed, energy, forces, friction, cause and effect. Such adventurous play is especially important for children with disabilities, who may be denied such experiences in other areas of their lives.

Gleefulness, giddiness and playing with ideas

Such rumbustious play outdoors is often accompanied with laughter and glee, and children can be literally and metaphorically 'giddy with glee'. Could there be a connection between this giddy, dizzy play where bodies hang upside down, spin fast, travel backwards, forwards, sideways, and do things in opposition to the 'normal course of things' and children's desire to play with other aspects of their expanding understanding of the world?

Chukovsky (1968) observed children's love of 'violating the established order of things' (p. 92) by playing with ideas, turning them around and seeing them from another perspective. This ability to topsy-turvy what is known and examine it afresh is a significant aspect of children's learning, which can enable new connections and contribute to more flexible, innovative ways of thinking.

Play outdoors includes a long tradition and rich culture of rhymes, games, humour and nonsense. Such play often integrates movement – whether clapping, stamping, circling, swaying, falling, skipping, marching, chasing or bouncing – with chanting, rhythm and rhyme. These playground rhymes can be subversive and challenging, and can push out the boundaries of what is permissible or possible, such as this cheeky rhyme from a group of five year olds clapping and singing outdoors as they adapt a traditional rhyme:

Ickety, pickety pop, the dog has swallowed the mop.
Ickety, pickety poo, the dog has swallowed you.
Ickety pickety wee, the dog has swallowed me.
Ickety pickety woo, the dog has swallowed poo!

Such play illustrates children's boldness in playing with the structures of language, their willingness to take risks, interest in the scatological and delight in creating incongruous images. The play is dependent on spotting patterns, following grammatical rules in order to maintain the rhythm and rhyme. It seems that just as children are turning their bodies upside down so they turn ideas and language upside down, deliberately distorting what is known. This allows for new combinations and connections to be made and can be an important part of flexible and innovative thinking. Outdoors offers the freedom, the space and time for such exuberant, risky, dizzy and gleeful play.

Daring dramatic play

Adventurousness and daring can also be seen in imagined play scenarios where children enjoy deliberately scaring themselves by confronting an imagined 'big bad wolf', 'scary monster' or evil character, which often includes chasing, escaping, capturing and rescuing. Corsaro (2003), in his ethnographic study of children's peer culture, noted that tidal waves, earthquakes, falls from cliffs, fires, quicksands and poison were frequent themes in children's play. Bravado, daring and power can also underpin much superhero play in which children venture into new, imagined worlds where they can safely explore universal themes of capture and rescue, being lost and found, courage and fear, power and powerlessness, life and death.

Cameo 1 shows a dramatic adventure outdoors. A group of four-year-old boys used the hollow trunk of a dead willow tree as a prop for their play. They filled the empty space with blue flowers from a nearby bush. First they made poison, then magic medicine.

Cameo 1

Boy A	Let's say this is the cave and the big bad wolf lives here.
Boy B	Yeah and he has POISON.
Boy A	Yeah and he has poison plants which kill people.
Boy B	Yeah and he poisons people, poisons people, poisons people.
Boy A	Yeah and they die like this [gestures with his hand to his throat]. Don't they?
Boy C	But the magic medicine makes them OK again doesn't it?
Boy A	No, we haven't got magic medicine.
Boy C	Mix it. We need to mix it.
Boy A	Yeah we need water don't we. [He fetches a small cup, transforms a piece of bark into a tap and fills the cup with pretend water which is then poured into the tree trunk.]
Boy B	Magic medicine, magic medicine, magic . . .

In this extract from a long episode of exciting play, the boys are exploring good and evil, threat and averting a threat, life and death. They are also developing fluency in using symbols, transforming simple features of their environment into props for their play. The hollow trunk becomes a cave, then a cauldron. The flowers become poison, then medicine; a piece of bark stands for a tap that can produce imaginary water. They step out of the 'play frame' to negotiate at an abstract level, the scene, characters and plot for their story. They enjoy the alliterative power of language in their repetition of 'poison plants' and 'magic medicine'. They are developing an archive of dramatic scripts, characters and plots that can be drawn on later in their play or in story writing.

Rough-and-tumble play

Adventurous play outdoors may also include active physical play, where children engage in running, fleeing, chasing, mock fighting, rolling, grappling and tumbling. Central to this play is the ability to signal 'this is play and is not for real'. Such play signals include exaggerated gestures, laughing and grinning, which are very different from the gestures and expressions used in real fighting such as frowning, grimacing and glaring. Clearly such play is high risk. Players need to exercise considerable self-restraint to control their physical movements to ensure that the playful punch does not have the force of the real punch and that the feigned aggression or fear is not perceived as real aggression or fear. The players have to communicate a complex message that although the pretend actions stand for threat, aggression and hostility in reality, in play they stand for the complete opposite – that is, for friendship and enjoyment. The risk of players misinterpreting the signals is high, although research (e.g. Jarvis and George, 2010) suggests that, in practice, this rarely happens and children develop finely tuned social and communication skills to encode and decode the signals. Jarvis noted that adults were less adept at tuning in to these subtle signals and tended to perceive rough-and-tumble play as aggressive and dangerous. Adults need to tune in to the themes and intentions of the play, and ensure that there are open spaces available for running and chasing and softer, grassed areas for rolling and tumbling, and that such play can take place without disruption to other children's play.

Open-ended construction play

The indeterminate and open nature of the outdoor environment offers scope for large-scale construction play where materials such as crates, planks, ladders, tarpaulins, gutters, pulleys, sand and water can be arranged and combined in many different ways, creating new and exciting possibilities and challenges. Children can design and build their own structures like enclosures, walkways, tunnels, bridges, watercourses, imaginary fires, volcanoes . . . the list is endless. This play can be particularly challenging as materials can be more easily combined together, creating surprise and unexpected problems. It requires a generous supply of 'loose parts': any material that is openended, has no fixed purpose and can be used in a multitude of different ways. The theory of 'loose parts' was developed by the architect Ben Nicholson more than 40 years ago. He made the links between loose parts and creative, inventive thinking, and proposed that 'in any environment both the degree of inventiveness and creativity and the possibilities of discovery are directly linked to the number and kind of variables in it' (Nicholson, 1971, cited in Tovey, 2007: 74). Construction materials such as recycled wheels, planks, crates and wooden ammunition boxes have been long-standing provision in nursery school gardens and in adventure playgrounds.

The outdoor area with its rich supply of 'parts', and space and time for transformation, affords scope for children to develop fluency in using objects symbolically and in developing imaginative ways of thinking. Imagination can generate alternatives to the 'way things are' and therefore expands the range of possibilities. It is important for the development of abstract, symbolic, 'as if' thinking. The transformations also have to be negotiated and agreed with others. Research suggests that the complexity of communication and negotiation increases substantially when children use open-ended resources because they are so ambiguous and many alternative transformations are possible (Trawick-Smith, 1998).

An in-depth study of play in an early years unit (Broadhead and Burt, 2012) found that the outdoor area was a rich context for exciting open-ended play with found and recycled materials. There was evidence of persistence and involvement as children engaged in problem setting and problem solving, and in imaginative transformations. The play was sustained over time, developing in complexity. Interestingly the authors noted that, despite the potentially 'risky' nature of the play, where children would often deliberately seek to increase the level of challenge – for example, by adding obstacles to a bridge made from planks and crates or increasing the gradient of a sliding slope – there was no change in the number of accidents as compared with previous contexts where more traditional outdoor play equipment was in use. Indeed the researchers noted the degree of self-regulation and calculated risk taking as children considered their own levels of confidence and competence before attempting something they considered to be risky. The development of metacognitive and self-regulatory skills is crucial in the development of the higher-order skills involved in learning, thinking, problem solving and creativity.

Adventurous players, adventurous thinkers

Being adventurous and taking risks are recognised as important characteristics of effective learners. The Early Years Foundation Stage guidance, *Development Matters*, states that an effective learner is willing to 'have a go' through:

- initiating activities
- seeking challenges
- showing a 'can do' attitude
- taking a risk, engaging in new experiences, and learning by trial and error (Early Education, 2012).

Tishman *et al.* (1993) identify the 'disposition to be broad and adventurous' and the 'disposition toward wondering, problem-finding and investigating' as the first two of seven dispositions that are characteristic of a good thinker. Indeed risk underpins many of the metaphors we use to refer to creative, imaginative and hypothetical thinking. We 'hazard' a guess, 'dare' to be different, 'venture in the mind' generate 'bold' ideas and take 'imaginative leaps' in our thinking. The oft quoted cliché 'thinking outside the box' implies going outside the defined, enclosed parameters of the known to generate new ways of seeing and thinking.

Adventurous play outdoors can include adventurous thinking such as taking risks, exploring ideas, speculating, imagining, creating and persisting. Research by Robson and Rowe (2012) identified outdoor play and socio-dramatic play as particularly effective contexts for young children's creative thinking. Analysis of observations of children's behaviour identified that child-initiated activities, often in pairs or small groups, featured the highest levels of children's involvement and persistence, and were associated with trying out and analysing ideas, flexibility and originality, imagination and hypothesising. They suggest that outdoors affords the time and space to think creatively and that the opportunity for choice, combination of materials and collaboration with friends may be contributing factors (see Cameo 2).

Cameo 2

A group of four year olds are constructing trenches, bridges, roadways and rivers in the sand pit using planks, crates, pipes, tubes and water from a hosepipe. They are surprised how the water quickly soaks into the sand.

Warren: This flooding's going fast . . . look Quinny . . . going fast. Oh look at all that frost [froth]. Oh where it going? Where that flooding gone? Why it ain't flooding no more? Is it hiding? Is it . . . is it flooding under . . . flooding under . . .? Quinny dig and dig we find the flooding. Oh look, more flooding coming . . . catch it, catch it. Oh, flooding's gone under, all gone. Let's dig and find it. Look, look here's the flooding!

Adult: Boys, be careful with the water, someone's going to slip.

This play is characterised by excitement and surprise. Warren is curious about what has happened to the water. He speculates that it might be hiding, but rejects this in favour of the idea that it might be flooding under the surface. He tests his ideas and adjusts his actions to dig rather than 'catch' the water. There is evidence of reflection, metacognition and self-regulation, as well as considerable involvement and persistence over time. The adult misses the excitement and talk in her concern for safety and an attempt to contain the boisterous play.

Risk aversion

The examples of adventurous, risky play in this chapter can be curtailed by a culture of risk aversion, risk anxiety and restrictions on children's freedom to play outdoors. For many practitioners, risk has become something undesirable to be assessed, controlled and eliminated (Tovey, 2009). There is also evidence that play that is openended and unpredictable, boisterous and fastmoving, or that involves pretend fighting, can be unsettling for adults who urge children to 'play nicely' or curtail the play because of fears for safety. However, although such adventurous play can carry the possibility of harm, it also has positive benefits and any assessment of risk has to be balanced against these benefits.

What is the value of risk taking in play?

Risk is part of being fully alive. Life is full of varied risks and we have to learn how to recognise and manage them. Babies would never learn to crawl, to negotiate steps, to stand up, and children would not learn to run, climb or ride a bike without being prepared to risk, tumble and learn from the consequences.

This willingness to take risks is an important learning disposition. Dweck (2000) emphasises the importance of what she terms a 'mastery' approach to learning – a disposition to have a go, try something out and relish challenge, in contrast to a 'helpless' approach characterised by fearfulness and fear of failure. There is a danger that when we repeatedly say to children 'Mind out', 'Be careful', 'Don't do that!', 'Come down, you'll fall', we can inadvertently develop this 'helpless' attitude to learning by communicating our own anxiety.

Risk taking allows children to push their own boundaries to the limit of their capabilities. It requires some assessment of the degree of challenge involved in the risk as against one's own confidence and capability. Such self-assessments are vital for children's developing understanding of safety, as well as their developing self-regulation in play.

Controlled exposure to some risks also appears to have a positive effect on emotional well-being and resilience. For example, Kloep and Hendry (2007) argue that mistakes, provided that the consequences are not too severe, can offer protection against the negative effects of future failure. Managing fear and uncertainty and holding your nerve are important aspects of emotional well-being and resilience. It appears that risky play has an important role in reducing anxiety about 'scary' situations (Sandseter, 2009), and can help children cope physically and emotionally with unexpected events. The positive emotions of exuberance, confidence, vitality, flexibility, self-esteem and 'being in touch with yourself' are among key indicators of children's overall well-being (Laevers, cited in Greenland, 2009).

Challenging a risk-averse culture

As concern mounts about young children's increasingly sedentary, indoor lives and their lack of freedom to engage in 'everyday adventures' (Gill, 2012) outdoors, there is evidence of a shift in thinking about risk and a challenge to the risk-averse culture.

The UK Health and Safety Executive (HSE) makes it very clear that children need to take risks in play. It states that 'HSE understands and accepts that . . . children will often be exposed to play environments which, while well-managed, carry a degree of risk and sometimes potential danger' (p. 1). It goes on to state that 'HSE wants to make sure that mistaken health and safety concerns do not create sterile play environments that lack challenge and so prevent children from expanding their learning and stretching their abilities' (p. 1). Its key message is clear that 'no child will learn about risk if they are wrapped in cotton wool' (HSE, 2012: 1).

Such statements make a useful starting point for debate between practitioners and parents about the value of risktaking and adventurous play outdoors. Instead of promoting a 'safe environment' we should focus on creating one that is 'safe enough' for children to be adventurous, taking a balanced approach where the benefits of particular experiences are weighed against the possible risks and the likelihood of harm.

Pedagogical implications: the key role of the adult outdoors

As we have seen in this chapter, outdoors can be a source of surprise, wonder and adventure for young children. But if this sense of adventure is not acknowledged or reciprocated by adults then the spark of curiosity, wonder and creativity can be suppressed. Bilton (2012) analysed adult and child interaction outdoors and found that, although children sought out adults to share things of interest and to show things they had done or made, this was not often reciprocated by adults who were more concerned with what she refers to as 'mundane, domestic matters', such as organising turns on the bikes, sorting out disputes or, significantly, telling children to stop doing something. There was little evidence of responses that might extend children's play, thinking or understanding.

In contrast, Waters and Maynard (2010), researching episodes of child-initiated interaction with adults outdoors in a country park, found that when adults responded and interacted in a way that was in tune with children's interests there was evidence of rich and meaningful conversational exchanges. They found that certain features of the environment excited children's interest and afforded rich interactions with adults. These included 'loose parts' in the environment, features of the landscape such as puddles or trees, and imagined places such as 'the elves' home', or 'the dinosaur's hiding place'.

Both studies reveal the potential of the outdoors for rich, cognitive engagement between adults and children and both argue that adults must seize these opportunities by being responsive to children's interests, concerns and talk, rather than imposing a prohibitive or adult-directed agenda.

So how can adults promote adventurous and challenging play outdoors? Possible ways might include those described below.

- *Fostering a positive approach to adventurous play,* seeing risk and challenge as things to be relished, rather than feared. This will involve modelling a flexible innovative approach to situations: 'That's a good idea, let's try it!' rather than 'No, we're not allowed.'

- *Seeing children as adventure seekers and risk takers.* This means tuning in to children's intentions, identifying with the problems they set and supporting them in finding safe ways of achieving what they are trying to do.

- *Providing enough time and space for children to be adventurous outdoors.* Too many children in one play area, too little time outdoors, a poor adult/child ratio, and a bland, unchallenging environment can inhibit play and can create environments where accidents are more likely to happen.

- *Making provision for adventurous play,* ensuring that resources are flexible enough to provide challenge for the most timid as well as the most adventurous. This might include provision of open-ended resources, 'wild areas' with bushes to hide in and trees to climb, opportunities to experience height, speed, varying gradients and terrain, and resources that offer the experience of instability and unpredictability such as rope and swing bridges.

- *Empowering children to keep themselves safe.* This might include teaching safe ways of doing things, such as always using a friend to help carry a long stick or ladder, testing the strength of a branch before climbing, or using a stick to measure the depth of a stream, before paddling. A nature kindergarten involved children in 'risk assessing' a fallen tree before using it for climbing. Children then used loppers, saws and sanders to trim the sharp branches to make it safe for play (Warden, 2014).

- *Replace the narrowly procedural 'risk assessments'* with risk/benefit assessments that weigh up the benefit as well as the risk of an experience. Such a balanced approach can be found in the document by Ball *et al.* (2013), and provides a useful framework for early years settings.

- *Tuning in to children's own play ideas,* recognising that such play can be rumbustious, messy, even chaotic at times, but when supported and allowed to flourish can be sustained, collaborative and complex.

- *Having realistically high expectations of what children are able to do.* This means knowing children well enough to decide when to be quietly watchful, when to be sensitively supportive, and when to actively intervene by joining the play or extending it in worthwhile ways.

- *Encouraging children's adventurous thinking,* for example by nurturing their confidence to pursue new experiences and ideas, to 'venture' in the mind, to wonder, play with ideas, make nonsense, find and solve problems, imagine, represent, speculate, reflect and make unusual combinations and connections.

Conclusion

This chapter has explored some aspects of children's adventurous play outdoors, play that is physical, fastmoving, risky and unpredictable, which adults can sometimes find unsettling, disturbing or unsafe. It has argued that such play offers essential learning experiences for growing bodies and minds. This is not to suggest that all play outdoors should be risky and challenging. Children feel confident to be adventurous from a sense of security. The familiar, the everyday routine, and the calm, quiet spaces are important anchor points. However, if we deny children chances to be bold and adventurous we risk creating a generation of children who may be reckless in their pursuit of thrills and excitement, or risk averse, lacking the essential resilience to take and manage risks for themselves, but also lacking the disposition to be bold and adventurous thinkers and learners.

Questions to promote reflection

1 Do you feel you are an adventurous thinker and learner? How might this impact on your work with children?
2 How can you make provision for children with disabilities to experience adventurous play – for example, the exhilaration of moving at speed?
3 Think about your own environment for outdoor play – are there opportunities for adventure and surprise, risk and challenge? Are there experiences that children find satisfyingly 'scary'?
4 Is there rich provision for 'loose parts' and open-ended play where the direction and outcome of the play is unknown?

References and further reading (in bold)

Ball, D., Gill, T. and Spiegal, B. (2013) *Managing Risk in Play Provision: Implementation Guide*. London: Department for Children, Schools and Families.

Bilton, H. (2012) The type and frequency of interactions that occur between staff and children outside in Early Years Foundation Stage settings. *European Early Childhood Education Research Journal*, 20(3): 403–421.

Broadhead, P. and Burt, A. (2012) *Understanding Young Children's Learning through Play*. London: Routledge.

Caillois, R. (2001) *Man, Play and Games* (trans. M. Barash). Urbana, IL: University of Illinois Press.

Chukovsky, K. (1968) *From Two to Five*. Berkeley, CA: University of California Press.

Corsaro, W. (2003) *We're Friends Right? Inside Kids' Culture*. Washington, DC: Joseph Henry Press.

Dweck, C. (2000) *Self Theories: Their Role in Motivation, Personality and Development*. Hove: Psychology Press.

Early Education (2012) *Development Matters in the Early Years Foundation Stage*. London: Early Education.

Gill, T. (2012) *No Fear: Growing Up in a Risk-averse Society*. London: Calouse Gulbenkian Foundation.

Greenland, P. (2009) *Developmental Movement Play: Final Report and Recommendations*. Leeds: Jabadao.

Health and Safety Executive (HSE) (2012) Children's play and leisure: promoting a balanced approach. Available online at: http://www.hse.gov.uk/entertainment/childrens-play-july–2012 (accessed 17 May 2014).

Jarvis, P. and George, J. (2010) Thinking it through: rough and tumble play. In J. Moyles (ed.) *Thinking About Play: Developing a Reflective Approach*. Maidenhead: Open University Press.

Kalliala, M. (2006) *Play Culture in a Changing World*. Maidenhead: Open University Press.

Kloep, M. and Hendry, L. (2007) 'Over-protection, over-protection, over-protection!' Young people in modern Britain. *Psychology of Education Review*, 31(2): 4–8.

McMillan, M. (1930) *The Nursery School*. London: Dent.

Robson, S. and Rowe, V. (2012) Observing young children's creative thinking, engagement, involvement and persistence. *International Journal of Early Years Education*, 20(4): 349–364.

Sandseter, E. (2009) Children's expressions of exhilaration and fear in risky play. *Contemporary Issues in Early Childhood*, 10(2): 92–106.

Tishman, S., Jay, E. and Perkins, D. (1993) Teaching thinking dispositions: from transmission to enculturation. *Theory into Practice*, 32(3): 147–153.

Tovey, H. (2007) *Playing Outdoors, Spaces and Places, Risk and Challenge.* **Maidenhead: Open University Press.**

Tovey, H. (2009) Playing on the edge: perceptions of risk and danger in outdoor play. In P. Broadhead, J. Howard and E. Woods (eds) *Play and Learning in the Early Years: From Research to Practice.* London: Sage.

Trawick-Smith, J. (1998) A qualitative analysis of metaplay in the preschool years. *Early Childhood Research Quarterly*, 14: 433–452.

Warden, C. (2014) *Nature Kindergartens and Forest Schools.* Auchterarder: Mindstretchers Ltd.

Waters, J. and Maynard, T. (2010) What's so interesting about outside? A study of child initiated interaction with teachers in the natural outdoor environment. *European Early Childhood Research Journal*, **18(4): 473–483.**

19

Playful explorations and new technologies
Nicola Yelland

Summary

In this chapter I extend the notion of *playful explorations* (Yelland, 2011), suggesting that new technologies have an important role to play in reconceptualising play in the twenty-first century. *Playful explorations* that incorporate new technologies enable young children to have multimodal experiences that were not possible in previous times. Such experiences promote engagement with ideas that assist young children to embark on meaning making and enable them to communicate their understandings. These features impact on their self-confidence and autonomy, and encourage them to explore their environments using a range of approaches. Data from an iPad project are provided to illustrate the ways in which learning can occur when engagement with ideas, (multimodal) resources and people takes place.

Introduction

Playful explorations (Yelland, 2011) can be initiated by children or starting points can be encouraged by teachers. They can be extended in multiple or specifically planned directions. They are structured yet flexible and are relevant in preschool settings as well as in early years classrooms in schools. There are pedagogical challenges inherent to designing contexts for playful explorations. The fact that teachers can, and should, create playful explorations in the first instance, or intervene to suggest new directions while the learner is engaged in this form of play, might not align with the views of those who regard play as being initiated by the child, self-selected and voluntary. The change in nomenclature from 'play' to 'playful explorations' is a deliberate one. It denotes a shift in emphasis with regard to notions about what constitutes play and includes contexts of play that can be scaffolded and described in learning scenarios that may be linked to indicators of learning that seem to be a ubiquitous part of early childhood education today.

When young children come to preschool settings they frequently have a broad range of experiences and a high level of enthusiasm about using new technologies. They will probably have used computers, digital cameras, mp3 players, mobile phones and many of the new hand-held devices that are marketed as educational toys. They have already had time for playful explorations with them in the years before they participate in formal settings and have learned how to use them in a variety of ways. For these children, new technologies are resources that they can use to create new things, which can then be shared with anyone beyond their immediate physical space. Making new technologies available alongside traditional materials (e.g. blocks) enables and extends playful explorations. Further, they can be used to document learning scenarios that describe the types of learning that have occurred (Carr, 2001) and also shared with parents.

Photograph 19.1 Girl and iPad

In playful explorations, new technologies form part of a repertoire of experiences for young children's learning that are undertaken in a variety of modes. When scaffolded by teachers, playful explorations enable young learners to participate in multimodal learning using a variety of media. This, in turn, requires a rethinking of the literacies that are required for the twenty-first century.

Contexts for playful explorations

In this chapter, I present learning scenarios with young children using tablet technologies (iPads) in two contexts. The first is in a mothers' group that was formally organised by a local school in a metropolitan area of Australia and the second is in a kindergarten in the same city.

Cameo 1: Two to three year olds (mothers' group)

Every week, the iPads were just one of many activities that were provided in both inside and outside locations for the mothers and their children (aged two and three years old). The activities changed each week and included opportunities for painting, reading, playing with sand and water, craft (e.g. making necklaces, decorating masks), playdough, puzzles and building with blocks.

The activities used on iPads are called Apps. They range in type from electronic books (e.g. *Three Little Pigs*), playing various games with characters from books (e.g. *Angelina Ballerina*) or popular culture (*Dora the Explorer*) and making music, to other activities like making balloon animals, playing with puppets, driving LEGO vehicles, which also exist in the 'real' world.

There was no doubt that the children loved the modality of the tablet technology. This was evident in their faces when they touched the screen in a game or activity. For example, they received an immediate response in some mode (e.g. visual, aural or linguistic) and responded accordingly. Even though the Apps seemed to be somewhat mundane to parents and educators, the observations revealed that the children in this age group seemed to like playing with the majority of them – although, as we expected, they did not play with the Apps for a sustained period of time but rather 'flitted' from one to another and then back again in all the sessions (one hour in duration). The Apps used by this group represented opportunities for them to build foundation skills in mathematics, like sorting, matching, classifying and counting, and they provided contexts to play with music, draw and play with puppets. There were also Apps that required very simple actions (e.g. popping a balloon, pushing a button, driving a LEGO car down a road and making a noise) that usually elicited giggles and laughter from the young children. See Cameo 2 for an example.

Cameo 2: Balloon school

Numbered balloons appear on the screen and the children are asked to pop the number given.

Trina enjoyed popping the balloons, and pressing all of them . . . because even when you get the wrong balloon the App makes a noise . . .

Exploration was possible but often within predetermined constructs that were inbuilt features of the games. The Apps also provided contexts in which the parent and child could interact and talk about the various components of the game being explored, and thus acted as a stimulus for language to be used and practised. One of the most noticeable features of this age group was their characteristically short attention span and their ability to quickly pick up the physical skills necessary to navigate around the salient features of a game or the iPad. For example, they were able to exit the games via the 'home' button, switch games regularly, and turn the iPad on and off.

Typically, two year olds do not share their play materials and play in parallel to their peers when in groups. The observations revealed that when a child was playing with the iPad there were some occasions when another child would come over to see what was going on and they would interact, both verbally and non-verbally. This was unique to iPad play. See Cameos 3 and 4 for examples.

Cameo 3: *Play School* Art Maker

Characters from Play School *can be placed on a selected background scene. Children can move the characters and create a story in movie form.*

Tom saw Trina playing with this App and decided he wanted to play it with her. After a short introduction on how to use the App by the researcher they each chose a character (Jemima and Big Ted), dropped them into the scene, and the researcher showed them how to make and watch a movie of their characters. They thought it was funny when they made Big Ted look like he was sitting on another character. Tom became tired of this game and moved back on to the other iPad. Trina continued playing with this App and then asked Tom if they could swap iPads. Tom wasn't interested in swapping . . .

Cameo 4: Farm Flip

A memory game using farm animals.

Zara and Lisa tried to play this memory game together. This didn't work very well as the game didn't recognise multiple fingers touching the screen simultaneously. After a few minutes, Lisa moved on to the other iPad and started playing the Jungle matching game. While Lisa was playing she was also keeping her eyes on what Zara was doing on her iPad, and would laugh with Zara when her iPad made a funny animal noise.

An interesting observation that highlighted the difference between the pedagogical strategies of teachers and parents became apparent in the observations. While teachers typically let children explore, find out things for themselves and articulate what they were doing, parents were more likely to direct their child to the right answer, or simply show them how to do something. This was evident when Tom was playing with a puzzle game (Cameo 5).

Cameo 5: Underwater scene puzzle

Pieces of puzzles are put together to create an underwater scene. As Tom was trying to do this puzzle, he often tried unsuccessfully to move a puzzle piece into the correct spot. Immediately, his mum showed him the correct placement of the piece or directed him with specific hints. Tom wasn't ever left to think, even for a minute, so that he could figure out how to do it himself.

Photograph 19.2 Underwater collection

Over the six-week period of the study, as we talked with the parents and modelled scaffolding that encouraged the children to explore various aspects of games rather than focus on one and use language to explain their explorations, the parents became more adept at letting their offspring experience the activities with less structure and specific directions. This was especially evident in some of the games where the children would enjoy getting the 'wrong' answer on an App because of the resultant sound effect. Initially, parents would prompt them towards the correct answer in order to achieve the goal of the game, but gradually they came to realise that their children understood it was not meant to happen and were learning in a different way.

What did we find?

The main findings regarding the use of the iPads with two to three year olds were as follows.

- *The children responded to the modality (visual, aural, spatial, oral and linguistic) and immediacy of cause and effect of the Apps.* Being able to interact in a dynamic way with linguistic, visual and auditory stimulation enabled the children to experience success in achieving a goal (e.g. making a balloon pop, matching letters to form a word, completing a puzzle that turned into an animated scene) as well as realising outcomes and viewing the consequences of their actions.

- *The Apps provided a context in which the children could interact with other children as well as with adults who were with them and thus practise language in action.* For example, as Ben was playing *Super Why!*, he was finding letters and following a path in which the letters made a word. As he was playing, his grandmother asked him to identify the letters and say the final words, and she also asked him about how many trees he could see in the wood and what colour the door of the house was.

- *The activities created contexts for learning foundational skills such as sorting, matching, classifying, recognising letters and numerals, and counting.* For example, when playing with *Lunchbox*, Tom was able to identify the range of fruits that are included in the game, as well as sort and count them, identify the odd one out in a sequence, found the first letter of the fruit name, state the colour of the fruit, and he also many found other opportunities to practise these beginning skills. The games that rewarded players with stickers were favourites of this group, and as this particular game stayed at the same level of difficulty despite repeatedly playing it, Tom collected lots of stickers and was very happy!

- *The Apps enabled children to create, read and listen to stories that were animated as well as having the facility to record their voices and innovate on the text.* For example, when Sophia was playing with *Peppa Pig*, her aunt showed her how to use the self-recording option, and together they added a new storyline about the visit to the fair by Peppa and her family.

- *The Apps helped the children to make connections between their real-world experiences (e.g. blowing up balloons) and allowed them to play with characters they had seen in books (e.g.* Angelina Ballerina*), on TV (*Peppa Pig *and* Thomas the Tank Engine*), or in films (e.g.* Cars*), thus helping them understand that things exist in different modalities and locations.* For example, when Tina was dressing Angelina in her ballet outfit in the App, she said she also had a colouring book with Angelina and she made her dress pink the same to match it.

In these playful explorations the adults scaffolded the learning of the young children in a variety of ways (Yelland and Masters, 2007). They supported them (a) technically, about how to use the iPad and the various features inherent to the games, (b) cognitively, as they encouraged them to articulate ideas, and (c) socially, in terms of supporting their playful interactions with other children. This was an important part of the play-based programme since without the scaffolding the initial complexity of using the iPads might have deterred the young children. As it was they were able to play with LEGO blocks in the block corner and on the iPad and talk about how they moved them to 'click' together. Similarly, they could move a truck on the floor and on screen – and exclaim that the one on the screen moved 'much faster!'. They could listen to stories read by the 'teacher' and by a different voice as part of an e-book experience which also enabled them to add their own version of the story to the book (*Peppa Pig Goes to the Fair*).

Cameo 6: Four year olds

The kindergarten had a play-based programme in which the children were able to select an activity from a range of materials that were available, both inside the room and out in the playground area. Inside, this included painting materials, a carpet and book area, a puppet theatre, and a large range of craft materials and plastic items. Outside there was a sand pit, water play, space to run and various forms of climbing frame. The iPads were available on a table inside, since the children were used to selecting an activity and completing it on a table. As the children became used to having them in the centre they wandered outside to use them.

Initially, it seemed as if the boys dominated the use of the iPads but gradually, as the girls saw them having fun, they joined in and asked for their own turn. At first the iPad was the catalyst for a group of four boys to meet. They would generally watch one another play a game and then ask for a turn. Many of them had tablets at home and mentioned that they played with specific games like *Cut the Rope* and *Where's my Water?* These are quite complex games that are enjoyed by adults and children, and we had not included them in the repertoire of games available for the four year olds. In playing with the Apps available to them in the first week the children made (electronic) cupcakes, played with mice in mazes, explored the puppets of *Play School* and 'flitted' around playing with various games because they had a puzzle that they liked, or a 'cool' game that helped them to make words from letters (e.g. *Super Why!*, *Number Train*). They also enjoyed *Brushes* (painting), completing animal puzzles, and playing with a range of counting and literacy-based word recognition games.

They wanted to explore the range of each App's potential, either individually or with a friend, to figure out what it did, and they often formed groups of two or more to take turns playing the games.

All activities in a play-based kindergarten programme afford opportunities for children to select what they want to do and interact with others in conversation or in collaborative projects (i.e. build a garage with blocks). Having an iPad as part of this represents another activity in which children are able to play and explore, and create a variety of contexts for learning about things, people and ideas. The patterns of play were remarkably similar over the different activities. Some encouraged solitary play (e.g. reading, threading) while others were more creative or open ended (e.g. painting and model making with boxes) or physical (e.g. climbing frames, sand and water play). The iPads could be used both inside and outside, and thus enabled solitary and group play, but also provided contexts for the children, and the children with an adult to discuss what they were doing and to make predictions about what might happen next, as well as seeking information on the internet.

The project's observations revealed that, when using the Apps, some patterns emerged as in the following observations.

Solitary play occurred frequently around games that had specific objectives (e.g. completing a puzzle, making a word, counting) (see Observation 1).

Observation 1

When it was Randall's turn he selected the *Angelina Ballerina* App. In the App, Angelina thinks of a flower (e.g. a daisy). The player is supposed to use a finger to pop only the bubbles that appear on the screen containing the daisy. The flower that Angelina thinks of changes and the rate of change is controlled by the success of the player. As they improve, the bubbles appear at a faster rate. When the game started Randall began popping all of the bubbles falling from the sky. I told him that for this game he was meant only to pop the bubbles containing the flower that Angelina was thinking about. He immediately understood this direction and began popping only the correct bubbles.

After one game he left the App (using the home button) and selected the *Counting Train* (the user has to select the correct number – out of three options – to put on the number train). He was able to drag the correct number from the bottom of the screen and place it in the correct position on the number train (e.g. he moved the number 4 in between numbers 3 and 5). He was very pleased when he got the right answer: 'I got it right!' he said excitedly and smiled when the App congratulated him. After playing this App for a while (approximately two to three minutes) he exited by pushing the home button and selected to play *Tally Tots*. In this counting game the player selects a number from 1 to 20 and then counts to that number, as well as completing a task such as putting ten acorns in a squirrel's mouth. He started at the #2 and continued to touch the numbers in order and complete each number task until he reached #10. After he completed a number activity he seemed very pleased with his own efforts – exclaiming 'I did it!' excitedly. After completing the activity for #10 he jumped straight to #20 and completed that activity. At the end of the #20 activity fireflies create the #20 and Rory exclaimed – 'I made the number!' He then counted down from 20 to 16.

The iPad activities can become conversation spots just like other activities (see Observation 2).

Observation 2

While some children were playing with the iPad, others watching would chat to me and more would stroll over from another activity station – simply to chat or show me something marvellous that they'd done. For example, Iris made connection from the *Cupcake Maker* and told me that she cooked with her mummy on the weekend and made cupcakes, just as Rose was doing with *Cupcake Maker*; Randall showed me a drawing he had done while Lucy was creating an iPad sketch; Jane showed me a book she was reading and also shared what she was eating for lunch; Rose and Iris told me about the cubby houses that they had created outside. This form of interaction is useful to stimulate connections in the children's minds, as well as to provide a catalyst for language use and extension.

The four year olds were adventurous and persistent; they were able to share usage of the iPads and demonstrated the capacity to self-regulate their use (Observation 3).

Observation 3

Rose had a lot of other children crowded around her while she was playing *Cupcake Maker*. A few were trying to touch the screen, which she didn't like. She said 'Don't touch . . . it's my turn!' Will suggested she should choose green icing: 'Green, green, green . . .' [he chanted]. Rose chose light pink. Will says despairingly, 'Ohhhhhh, I miss green.' Venus advised Rose that the sweets that she was selecting for the top of her cupcake were not healthy: 'Lollies not good for you because you get sick.' After she said this, Iris started a conversation about how bad lollies are for you and your teeth. . . . When it was time for Rose to hand the iPad over to Randall she did so, but stayed and watched him, and joined in a new conversation . . .

Some children wanted to find out more information about the App. For example, when a group of boys were playing with *Angry Birds*, one of them suggested that they could find out more about the game on the internet as he had done this at home with his parents. We supported their exploration by finding Google in the browser, typing the words in the search box, and then guided their exploration to find a video (on YouTube) about the range of activities possible in the various extended *Angry Bird* games, as well as in finding a short clip of various angry birds having fun flying in space. The teacher (Naomi) indicated that she was much more interested in the potential of the iPad for exploration and discovery rather than just using it to play with Apps. She envisioned this to include internet searches for information, such as the time when the children expressed an interest in how a butterfly emerges from a cocoon, after discovering one in the playground. She realised that there was the potential to use the iPad to record digital photos and movies that could then be made either into books or movies, and subsequently watched by the whole group to stimulate conversations.

Naomi (the teacher) told us of a scenario that took place one day in which having the iPad made a positive difference to the learning of one boy (Cameo 7).

Cameo 7: Naomi's reflective notes

Owen arrived at kindergarten today with a plan for a project he wanted to complete. 'I really want to make a *General Grievous* costume today,' he told me. Unsure as to who General Grievous was, I asked Owen what he looked like. Owen shared that General Grievous was (a character) from the Clone Wars and that 'he has four arms which he uses to hold light sabres'. I asked Owen if he could draw a picture of General Grievous for me so I could have a better understanding of what he looked like, which would then help with the plan to create the costume. Owen didn't want to draw the picture, and continued to describe the character to me. He had very specific instructions about what he wanted it to look like. I then suggested we use the iPad to Google an image of General Grievous to assist us with the creation of the costume. Owen thought this was a great idea, so we did. Owen was pleased to find an image and we set about creating the costume . . .

In this instance the iPad was a valuable resource in supporting Owen to achieve his goal/plan. He arrived at kindergarten eager and enthusiastic to be able to follow his interest through to completion (which took about two hours in total), which was very rewarding!

The main findings regarding the use of iPads with the four-year-old kindergarten group can be summarised as follows.

- *Using the iPads with the selected Apps provided contexts and opportunities for solitary and social play.* The iPads did not isolate children from interacting with their peers but rather gathered children together. Children were often peer-to-peer educators, supporting and helping one another to engage with the Apps and navigate their way around the iPads, showing each other the volume control, changing screens, going back to home page, etc.

- *Playing with iPads enabled opportunities for conversations between children and between adults and children.* The iPad connected children through a common interest or focus. When engaged together children enjoyed having conversations about their play. For some children it was a lovely way to build peer interactions.

- *Activity on the iPads was characterised by self-regulation and persistence.* We noticed that when children were engaged with the iPad they displayed intense concentration and focus on the task at hand. Children who often had difficulty sustaining concentration on a specific task, appeared to have no difficulty when engaged with activity on the iPad.

- *Playing with the Apps provided an opportunity to encounter and use foundational skills for (school) learning.* There was lots of exploratory play as children discovered which Apps they liked playing, often revisiting these in later sessions, consolidating their learning and understanding. This is not dissimilar to children revisiting a theme in imaginative play or building towers with blocks – with each visit they acquire new learning and/or deeper understanding.

- *Children were able to experience multimodal learning.* The iPads provided children with choice as to how they wanted to engage in particular learning experiences. Many children enjoyed using the iPad to complete puzzles as well visiting the 'puzzle table'. They said that they liked the iPad puzzles better because they were 'more fun'!

Conclusion

In thinking how we might reconceptualise play in the twenty-first century – and make explicit claims about learning in planned and spontaneous activities – we need to go beyond just making statements that play is inherently good and automatically linked to learning. I have suggested (Yelland, 2011) that playful explorations with new technologies, which may include interactions with adults including teachers, constitute dynamic opportunities for teaching and learning in the early years. We need to provide contexts so that young children can experience different modes of representations, which, in turn, afford them the opportunity to formulate new understandings about their world.

The challenge for parents and educators is to maintain a balance between the real and virtual worlds (Yelland, 2007). Parents have often expressed their concerns that new technologies take away from their child's 'real'-world experiences. It is up to them to ensure that this does not occur. Children should be given opportunities to self-select, but parents and other adults should be able to encourage diverse contexts for playful explorations that give them a range of learning opportunities with a variety of materials. Often it would seem that parents think that, because they have purchased a toy or software, their child will spontaneously want to play with it without adult intervention. This may be the case, but it is also evident that the new toy can be a shared learning context in which parents or other adults can interact with the child, with a variety of positive outcomes emanating from the conversations. For example, an adult can provide the context to broaden the language or vocabulary base of the child as well as by asking probing questions that will facilitate the learning of specific concepts and hopefully enable the child to make the appropriate abstractions that lead to higher levels of thinking and knowing.

The examples provided here illustrate the notion of playful explorations to elucidate the ways in which learning can occur when engagement with ideas, (multimodal) resources and people takes place. New technologies provide scenarios that are very appealing to children and have the potential to broaden the range of play experiences. They can act as a catalyst for interactions, either with another child or with adults, enabling children to make connections between representations. This in turn facilitates greater in-depth understandings about concepts and experiences.

Playful explorations can be supported by adults and extended in new scenarios and investigations, depending on those things in which children show interest. These new play worlds afford contexts in which young children not only acquire new conceptual understandings but also think more deeply about identities and how to interact with one another. This type of learning complements and extends three-dimensional playful explorations in the 'real' world. Early childhood educators can enable and support children's meaning making via interactions and resources that encourage them to make connections between the different modes of representations with new technologies.

Questions to promote reflection

1   What playful technological explorations do you provide in your setting?
2   How do you provide a range of different, technological experiences for children in your setting?
3   How comfortable are you with probing questions that will facilitate the learning of specific concepts that enable children to make the appropriate abstractions that lead to higher levels of thinking and knowing?
4   What ways have you found to support playful technological explorations?

References and further reading (in bold)

Carr, M. (2001) *Assessment in Early Childhood Settings: Learning Stories*. London: Chapman.

Yelland, N. (2007) *Shift to the Future: Rethinking Learning With New Technologies in Education*. New York: Routledge.

Yelland, N. (2011) Reconceptualising play and learning in the lives of children. *Australasian Journal of Early Childhood*, 36(2): 4–12.

Yelland, N. and Masters, J.E. (2007) Rethinking scaffolding with technology. *Computers and Education*, 48(3): 362–382.

20

Mathematics and the ecology of pretend play

Maulfry Worthington

Summary

Social pretend play is acknowledged as the highest form of play, enabling children to connect cultural experiences with imagination and supporting symbolic understanding. In contrast academic subjects can sit uneasily in early childhood education, and often result in play, mathematics and literacies that are effectively separated into unconnected terrains.

High-quality, spontaneous pretend play affords a potentially rich social-ecocultural niche where social and cultural learning can flourish and revealing the origins of children's cultural mathematical knowledge and emergent processes. Free from adult objectives and goals, children's pretend play is found to be always meaningful, and often rich and intellectually challenging.

Introduction

Play, mathematics and literacies have long been at the centre of research and debate by educators; however, in England teachers are under continual and growing political pressures to provide 'evidence' of narrow skills, and the importance of play can be overlooked. These pressures are reflected in ever changing curricula guidance and a narrow testing culture. Empirical evidence shows that in schools this has resulted in increasingly formal contexts, with 'cognitive tasks' regularly privileged over play (Brooker, 2011: 156). Formal contexts of adult-led lessons and 'skills based' teaching disembedded from meaningful contexts lack social and cultural meaning for children: this leads to superficial understanding disconnected from the use of mathematics in the real world, and alienation towards mathematics (van Oers, 2012).

Whereas the 'early years' in England are deemed to extend from birth to five years, an early childhood culture and ethos effectively ends when children move from home or nursery into school at the very premature age of four years. The language that teachers use also changes, from a focus on children and their play and learning in nursery, to the language of curriculum targets and planning in school (Carruthers, 2014). For many children, play in school serves little more than a brief respite from adult-directed tasks, and when it does occur it is often interrupted for the serious business of 'work' or curtailed by the demands of school routines (Moyles and Worthington, 2011).

Ecocultural influences

'Ecology' refers to the relationships and interactions that organisms (including humans) have with their environment, the nature of these clearly influencing children 'in real-life settings with real-life implications' (Bronfenbrenner, 1994: 38). According to Bronfenbrenner, engagement with cultural knowledge allows 'progressively more complex reciprocal interaction between an active, evolving . . . human organism and the persons, objects and symbols in its immediate environment' (1994: 38).

Brooker argues that, often, 'knowledge and skills acquired in the home are derived from that particular culture, which may bear little resemblance to the school culture, so that the "cultural capital" children bring with them is invisible' (2010b: 34). A similar concern triggered research by Moll *et al.* (1992), who acknowledge the significance of children's home cultural knowledge or 'funds of knowledge' for their school learning, and for their play (Riojas-Cortez, 2000).

Taking an ecocultural stance to pretend play (often referred to as 'role play'), contrasts with a utilitarian perspective in which play is *pedagogised* to serve specific learning goals, 'an "instrument of learning for future competencies" which Drummond refers to as a "cognitive learn as you play regime"' (1999: 53, cited in Rogers, 2011: 5/15). This is evidenced by several research studies that looked for, but found little evidence of, mathematics in planned pretend play (see Worthington and van Oers, 2014). In contrast, the research findings described in this chapter show that *spontaneous* play can work *in support of* children's interests, motivations, thinking and mathematics. Children's integration of cultural knowledge within socially collaborative contexts such as play avoids dichotomies between academic and social learning, and is related to high-quality learning and positive outcomes for children (Siraj-Blatchford, 2010).

Wood (2010) emphasises that the meaning of play for children 'can be seen as an "inside-out" perspective, which derives from the emergent/responsive approach, and privileges children's cultural practices, meanings and purposes' (p. 11). Rogers proposes that rather than simply viewing play 'as a vehicle for delivering the curriculum, under the guise of "play-based learning"', the starting point should be to view play from the children's perspective (2010: 163). This can be described as 'relational pedagogy', which

> . . . allows for uncertainty and possibility, remembering that for children, a principle reason for participating in play is to be with people you like and are interested in, and to make relationships . . . play that prioritise[s] the child rather than the curriculum, [that is] more concerned with the creation of democratic, culturally inclusive classrooms, rather than with cultural and behavioural conformity.
> (Moore, 2004: 121, cited in Rogers, 2011: 14)

Social pretend play and cultural learning

Social pretend play provides a potentially ideal context in which social and cultural knowledge intertwine: it is acknowledged to be the 'leading activity' in early childhood, paving the way 'for the child's transition to a new, higher level of development' (Leont'ev, 1981: 369). According to Leont'ev, by approximately three years of age, 'A need to act like an adult arises' (1981: 372). Van Oers refers to participation in cultural practices as a ' "lived role" or *imitative participation* . . . Imitation through a lived role opens agency that requires involvement with the activity' (2012: 144–145, original emphasis). Göncü *et al.* (2007: 161) highlight the extent to which young children's activities 'reflect common cultural practices' – for example, Ayaan, one of the children in this study, was observed by her teacher as she played with a large quantity of tiny shells and water in a builder's tray (Cameo 1).

Cameo 1

> Ayaan appeared to be preparing rice in a traditional way for her family, putting it into small amounts of water to wash the grain: this takes some time and, according to Ayaan's Auntie, helps to clean out any undesired 'bits' from the rice. In the UK this is actually not necessary as machinery does this during the manufacturing process, but many African (particularly Somali) families may still do this as part of tradition and habit.

Enculturation of mathematics and symbolic languages

A significant aspect of pretend play is semiotic mediation – using one object to signify another that underpins children's own symbolic representations – such as drawing, maps, writing and children's informal mathematical signs and texts – in ways that are meaningful, and will always make personal sense.

Leont'ev (1981) observed, 'The central content of a child's development is its appropriation of the achievements of mankind's historical development, including those of human thought and human knowledge' (p. 311) such as mathematics. Munn and Kleinberg (2003) emphasise that whereas children can readily 'be taught the mechanics of arithmetic, if they lack any wider sense of purpose of these activities then their spontaneous learning will be hindered' (p. 52). These cultural rules concern 'how to use a system, and what its role is in our culture . . . [They] are possibly the most important things that children learn': without understanding them children 'risk becoming stranded in a sea of meaningless activity' (Munn and Kleinberg, 2003: 51/53).

Building on the concept of emergent writing, and following Hughes's (1986) seminal work, Carruthers and Worthington have conducted extensive research into children's informal mathematical signs and representations to evolve the educational concept of *children's mathematical graphics*. Their research has charted children's developing mathematical understanding through their signs and representations in various contexts (e.g. 2005; 2006; 2011; Worthington, 2009) and in play (e.g. Worthington, 2010; Worthington and van Oers, 2014).

Home social and cultural practices

This chapter explores ecocultural influences within naturally occurring niches of home and nursery, the ways in which they impacted on the pretend play of young children, and the mathematics and graphicacy they spontaneously embedded in their play in the nursery. Longitudinal data on which this chapter draws were collected in a nursery within a Children's Centre in a large city in the south-west of England. The ethnographic case studies focus on the children's pretend play and mathematics, and their spontaneous use of signs and visual representations to communicate. The transcripts of the children's play in this chapter are taken directly from the teachers' written observations, recorded in each child's learning diary.

The seven case study children were three to four years of age and in their final year in nursery. The play episodes of three of the children featured here suggest what Engel (2005) describes as *'what is'* (or *'as if'*): as the children engage in pretend play selling ice creams, take orders in a cafe and play safes, their talk, signs and meanings are elaborations of what happens in real life. The mathematical concepts the children explored included all aspects of the curriculum, with number, quantities and counting, and money featuring most often in their play, suggesting that these are aspects they most frequently meet at home. Time, length, distance and direction, speed, weight, temperature, shape, space and capacity also featured in their play episodes.

Ayaan's home culture

Ayaan's family comes from Somalia: she lives with her mother, father and four siblings. At home Ayaan spends time with her mother, other female relatives and friends of her mother. On their sitting room wall many Koranic texts are respectfully displayed high up on the walls. When not at nursery Ayaan is involved in activities including watching television, shopping, food preparation, going to the park and caring for her younger sibling, experiences that are woven through her days. Ayaan is keen to learn Arabic like her older brother and in one corner of the living room is a large blackboard where Ayaan's aunt teaches her Arabic letters. Her father drives a taxi, and when he comes home Ayaan and her siblings clamour to help count his takings for the day.

Pretend play: Ayaan's ice creams

The following episode is an example of pretend play rooted in a home activity; it combined shopping and the use of money. Playing ice cream shops was Ayaan's favourite pretend play activity, and repeated many times throughout the summer term. Ayaan was learning to speak English at this time and experiments with 'minutes' and 'pounds'. Her teacher believed that frequently initiating this play supported both Ayaan's spoken English and her growing confidence.

Cameo 2

For two weeks Ayaan has been playing in the gazebo, offering pretend ice cream through the window to children. Today when a child replied 'Yes', Ayaan answered, 'No left', adding 'I make more.' Collecting stones and pretending to make ice cream, Ayaan asked Tariq if he wanted any. She passed him an imaginary one, then pressed buttons on the till saying, 'It's 50 minutes.' Shortly afterwards Ayaan drew dashes in a notebook without comment.

The next time Ayaan played ice cream shops she asked '50 minutes please.' When a child offered '£1.00', Ayaan replied, 'That's £50 please.'

Photograph 20.1 Ayaan selling ice creams

In educational settings around the world, the widespread practice is for adults to plan and resource an area of the classroom for pretend play that is established for several weeks. In this model adults decide the focus of the play (such as a hospital) where children are expected to do hospital things. However, while many young children will be familiar with hospitals, post offices, shoe shops or doctors, they seldom relate to the genuine, immediate and personal interests and experiences of young children. In contrast, the play narratives of the children in this study revealed authentic aspects of their recent lived experiences that they had shared with someone close.

The children's play narratives included car park access, entry registers, postal workers, delivery men, grocery shops, restaurants, builders and camping. Because of their direct involvement in these experiences the children understood *if* (and *when*, and *why*) to include mathematics or graphics, using talk, marks and signs to communicate their thinking in ways that were relevant and specific to their narrative. None of these was planned or suggested by teachers. Brooker proposes that such play is dependent on adults' view of children 'as competent individuals who are capable of making sense of their experiences of the world, in collaboration with others and with the support of cultural tools' (2010a: 44).

Children's use of symbolic languages in pretend play

Vygotsky asserted that, 'Writing should be meaningful for children . . . an intrinsic need should be aroused in them . . . writing should be incorporated into a task that is necessary and relevant for life. In the same way as children learn to speak, they should be able to learn to read and write . . . writing should be necessary for her in her play. Writing should be *taught* naturally . . . and that writing should be "cultivated" rather than "imposed"' (1978: 118, original emphasis). The same can be said for the symbolic 'written' language of mathematics in early childhood. The difficulties young children face when the language and graphical representations of 'school' mathematics fail to match their existing understandings is well demonstrated in Hughes's (1986) research. Rather than using pretend play to serve specific curriculum goals, the model discussed in this chapter shows how open and spontaneous pretence in a democratic learning environment supports their cultural, mathematical and literate knowledge.

Home and nursery cultures

Cameo 3: Shereen's home culture

Shereen's family is from the Philippines. She enjoys watching children's DVDs, dancing to music and playing with her younger brother at home. In Shereen's family, shopping for food, preparing, cooking and eating at home and in restaurants are significant practices. The central role of food in Shereen's family was emphasised when, during a home visit, Shereen's grandma (who was visiting from the Philippines) gave the author a dish of the noodles she had cooked. Shereen has a mature proficiency in drawing and writing, activities she is proud to show.

Pretend play: Shereen's café

The graphical signs and symbols children choose to use to communicate are central to *children's mathematical graphics* and their developing understandings of mathematics, clearly illustrated in the example in Cameo 4.

Cameo 4

Shereen had decided to play cafés in the nursery garden; in her role as 'waitress' she noted down orders and explained what items were available. Shereen approached her friends and teacher Emma for orders, drawing wavy lines on her paper. Later she returned to ask Emma, 'What you want: rice, chocolate, cake and chicken?' Emma said she didn't want chicken and Shereen wrote a mark for 'chicken' and drew a cross by it, clarifying, 'It says "x" [cross] no chicken.'

Later, and after several further requests from Shereen, Emma said she would have chicken. Pointing to the 'x' she had written earlier Shereen said 'Look! No chicken!'

Shereen referred back to where she'd drawn the cross and reminded Emma what it signified, asking 'You want mushroom?' Then pointing to her drawing of a mushroom explained 'Look. A tick, that mean we got some', adding, 'you want ice cream? It's 3, 4.'

Photograph 20.2 Look! No chicken!

For the children in this study, communicating ideas through graphics is natural and frequently chosen – for example, the seven children in the larger study used graphics to communicate in almost half of all their pretend play episodes during the year. They freely used a range of informal marks (scribble marks); signs for symbolic languages (such as zigzag lines to represent writing); letter and numeral-like signs: they used standard symbols such as arrows, crosses and ticks (as Shereen did). Moreover, their texts showed a range of genres including (in addition to those featured in this chapter) entry cards and signs for a car park, writing persuasive letters, cheques, receipts, registers, bookings for a campsite, shop, car park and cinema 'open' and 'closed' signs, maps and plans, receipts and shopping lists (Worthington and van Oers, 2015). Many of these arose through the mathematical ideas the children explored in their play narratives.

Isaac's home culture

Isaac is an only child. He has often watched and been involved in his father's joinery work and in converting their house, work that has included extensive use of tools and mathematical talk such as calculating and measuring timber, marking out squares and angle cuts, and the use of a spirit level. At home Isaac has his own tools and workbench in the kitchen alongside his father's.

Isaac is highly interested in and knowledgeable about a wide range of technologies including security gadgets such as cameras, padlocks and safes, and for more than two years his favourite book for bedtime reading has been a builders' trade catalogue. Isaac and his father share their interests in camping, motorbikes and trains, and Isaac's cultural learning is embodied in their diverse shared projects. Isaac's father now runs a local microbrewery, work that involves deliveries, invoices, payments and counting cash, all literate and mathematical activities in which Isaac is involved.

In all societies young children's cultural knowledge will naturally include aspects of their family's daily routines and tasks such as preparing a meal or caring for a baby, and sometimes children will watch or be involved in a parent's work, such as carpentry or working in the fields (see, e.g., Göncü and Gaskins, 2007). Some of the children's experiences will be peripheral (observing, noticing) and in others they will be involved as apprentices (Lave and Wenger, 1991). John-Steiner proposes:

> Learning by being with a knowledgeable partner is a more effective method of developing a particular language of thought than learning from books, classes, or science shows. The crucial aspect of these informal or formal apprenticeships is that they provide the beginning with insights into both the overt activities of human productivity and into the more hidden inner processes of thought.
>
> (1985: 200)

According to Göncü et al. (2007), young children's wealth of home cultural knowledge implies that 'theories of play should be situated in children's context, taking into account unique dimensions of children's specific communities' (2007: 175, emphasis added).

Pretend play: Isaac, Jayden and the safe

Isaac's teacher, Emma, bought a small safe into the nursery to support Isaac's interest and for the other children to investigate. A few days later she observed the following play narrative, rich in mathematics (Cameo 5).

Cameo 5

Jayden and Isaac moved a small cupboard to create a safe, placing a keyboard and clipboard on top. They transported wooden blocks on the trolley and when another child removed one, Jayden wrote wavy lines on his clipboard. Taking his paper he placed it in the safe, tapping several keys on the keyboard and repeating this each time a child removed a block.

Isaac announced, 'This is the safe. There's a key, only one – you press it here and it opens. It has a number and no one else knows it, "one, one, eight, seven, zero, six". It's rather difficult to remember.'

Jayden put some real coins and play cheques in their safe, and Isaac stuck the calculator on the cupboard door, adding: 'You need to press the buttons to get in the safe . . . it's four, nine, seven, nine.' Jayden pressed some numbers making 'beep, beep' noises as he opened it, then closing the doors asked, 'What's the closing number?', saying 'one, nine, five, two' as he pressed buttons on the calculator.

Later Jayden said, 'you need to give me "one, nine, five, two"' and when Emma explained that she didn't have enough cash but could write a cheque, Isaac replied, 'I need hundreds of pounds!' Emma managed to find a selection of coins in her purse and Jayden responded: 'OK! We need to fill the box: you need to give me 15 hundred and 60 pounds.'

After several days playing with their 'safe', Isaac decided to write down the number of blocks being taken from the block areas, 'one, two, three, gone! Gotta write it down and put it in the safe.'

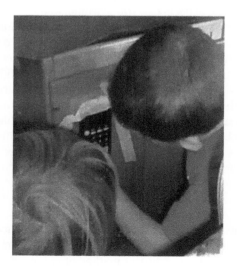

Photograph 20.3 Entering figures to open the lock on the safe

Rogoff emphasises that, in communities in which children have access to many aspects of adult life, 'children learn ... through their observation and participation in ongoing mature activities' (2003: 301). Access and involvement vary according to the characteristics of individual children: 'what they have the opportunity to observe differs greatly depending on whether they are included in the full range in their community's activities' (Rogoff, 2003: 298–299), although as Smith (2010) emphasises, children in some cultures have many more opportunities to observe or participate in adults' work than others.

The learning environment

The word 'environment' refers to so much more than the physical environment and resources, embracing the philosophical values and shared beliefs of the head teacher and teachers (MacNaughton, 2005; Dahlberg, *et al.*, 2007), and contributing to the ethos of a setting. Williams, *et al.* (2014) have drawn on Bronfenbrenner's work to examine the interrelationship between teachers' work and children's learning in preschools. They found that teachers either emphasised children's learning of social knowledge, or learning as an integration of social and cognitive knowledge, 'an integrated learning approach' (2014: 1). Those who took a 'social pedagogic [integrated] orientation' avoided direct 'subject content that can be experienced as pre-primary learning', placing 'higher value on the learning of social competencies and play . . . For these teachers, it is not a question of one or the other, but more of creating conditions for children's holistic learning in a variety of areas' (Williams *et al.*, forthcoming).

The teachers at the nursery in this study take a holistic view of learning, in which collaboration and communication are significant features, encouraging children's self-initiated ideas and supporting their complex thinking through rich dialogue, rather than anchoring practice in curriculum goals (Worthington and van Oers, forthcoming). Play has a high profile, and children's own graphics and mathematics are valued, their writing, drawing, maps and *mathematical graphics* visible everywhere. Teachers are knowledgeable about these aspects of early learning, and experienced in documenting children's play and learning, their written observations providing valuable tools for reflection and shared learning. There is no designated area for pretend play in this nursery: the children play wherever they want, indoors or out, and collect artefacts and tools as (and if) personal needs arise within their play. Adults support children's pretence through taking an interest, through providing resources to support children's personal interests, through creating mathematically and graphically rich environments and through modelling graphics for authentic purposes each day. Kamp highlights that 'the freedom for innovation allowed by certain types of play may have a definite cultural advantage, particularly in societies where adult roles are rather open-ended (Sutton-Smith, 1976)', characterising this aspect of play as 'adaptive potentiation' (Kamp, 2001: 19).

Discussion

In England many of the policies relating to early childhood education contrast sharply with what young children need to support effective mathematical understandings, particularly regarding children's cultural mathematical knowledge and the abstract symbolic graphical language of mathematics. The situation is particularly acute for children of four to six years in school, especially regarding early 'written' mathematics. Brooker argues that, in order to take children seriously:

> We might conclude on the basis of these observations that, rather than prescribing and structuring play activities directed towards learning objectives of the curriculum, we need only to offer children spaces in which they can undertake activities which are important and meaningful to them, and resources which enable them to fulfil their intentions, in their own way, and in their own time.
>
> (Brooker, 2011: 162)

Rather than disembedded tasks, high-quality pretend play can support mathematical (and literate) learning by providing a powerful means of enculturation in which children can develop the everyday concepts that underpin school instruction and the 'scientific' concepts of school knowledge (Vygotsky, 1978).

The findings discussed here raise an interesting paradox: where play is free from adult planning and goals, and where children's participation is spontaneous, pretend play is often rich, sustained and intellectually challenging, providing meaningful contexts that support cultural knowledge, such as mathematics. More than any curriculum goals, targets or skills practice, a setting's ecosystem impacts on the quality of play and on children's thinking and learning, offering exciting futures for pretend play and mathematics.

Conclusion

There appear to be several important ecocultural features that influence children in choosing to explore mathematics and communicate through *mathematical graphics* within their play. First, a direct relationship exists between the children's cultural knowledge at home and within their pretend play. Second, open opportunities for pretend play (and children's *ownership* of their play) support high-quality and sustained pretend play, promoting exploration and elaboration of cultural knowledge. Third, the incidence, sustainability and success of pretend play is dependent on the values, beliefs, knowledge and practices of head teachers and staff members in early childhood educational settings.

Questions to promote reflection

1. What do you know of the children's existing home cultural knowledge?
2. To what extent are the children free to initiate and develop their pretend play, and how sustained are children's pretend play episodes?
3. What range of mathematical talk and graphics can you document in children's pretend play during one week?
4. What might you *deliberately* do to support high-quality pretend play?

Acknowledgements

The author is grateful to the children, families, staff and head teacher of Redcliffe Children's Centre in Bristol for sharing the children's rich play and learning.

References and further reading (in bold)

Bronfenbrenner, U. (1994) Ecological models of human development. *International Encyclopedia of Education*, Vol. 3, 2nd edn. Oxford: Elsevier. Reprinted in M. Gauvain and M. Cole (eds) (1993) *Readings in the Development of Children*, 2nd edn. New York: Freeman.

Brooker, L. (2010a) Learning to play or playing to learn? In L. Brooker and S. Edwards (eds) *Engaging Play*. Maidenhead: Open University Press.

Brooker, L. (2010b) Learning to play in a cultural context. In P. Broadhead, J. Howard and E. Wood (eds) *Play and Learning in the Early Years*. London: Sage Publications.

Brooker, L. (2011) Taking play seriously. In S. Rogers (ed.) *Rethinking Play and Pedagogy in Early Childhood Education*. Abingdon: Routledge.

Carruthers, E. (2014) The pedagogy of children's mathematical graphics. PhD thesis, University of Bristol.

Carruthers, E. and Worthington, M. (2005) Making sense of mathematical graphics: the development of understanding mathematical symbolism. *European Early Childhood Education Research Association Journal*, 13(1): 57–79.

Carruthers, E. and Worthington, M. (2006) *Children's Mathematics: Making Marks, Making Meaning*, 2nd edn. London: Sage.

Carruthers, E. and Worthington, M. (2011) *Understanding Children's Mathematical Graphics: Beginnings in Play*. Maidenhead: Open University Press.

Dahlberg, G., Moss, P. and Pence, A. (2007) *Beyond Quality in Early Childhood Education and Care*. London: Routledge.

Engel, S. (2005) The narrative worlds of *what is* and *what if*. *Cognitive Development*, 20: 514–525.

Göncü, A. and Gaskins, S. (2007) An integrative perspective on play and development. In A. Göncü and S. Gaskins (eds) *Play and Development: Evolutionary, Sociocultural and Functional Perspectives*. Abingdon: Taylor and Francis Group.

Göncü, A., Jain, J. and Tuermer. S. (2007) Children's play as cultural interpretation. In A. Göncü and S. Gaskins (eds) *Play and Development: Evolutionary, Sociocultural and Functional Perspectives*. Abingdon: Taylor and Francis Group.

Hughes, M. (1986) *Children and Number: Difficulties in Learning Mathematics*. Oxford: Basil Blackwell.

John-Steiner, V. (1985) *Notebooks of the Mind*. New York: Harper and Row Publications.

Kamp, K.A. (2001) Where have all the children gone? The archeology of childhood. *Journal of Anthropological Method and Theory*, 8(1): 1–34.

Lave, J. and Wenger, E. (1991) *Situated Learning: Legitimate Peripheral Participation*. Cambridge: Cambridge University Press.

Leont'ev, A.N. (1981) *Problems in the Development of the Mind*. Moscow: Progress.

MacNaughton, G. (2005) *Doing Foucault in Early Childhood Studies*. London: Routledge.

Moll, L., Amanti, C., Neff, D. and Gonzales, N. (1992) Funds of knowledge for teaching. *Theory into Practice*, 31(2): 132–141.

Moyles, J. and Worthington, M. (2011) The Early Years Foundation Stage through the daily experiences of children. *TACTYC Occasional Paper* No. 1.

Munn, P. and Kleinberg, S. (2003) Describing good practice in the early years – a response to the 'third way'. *Education 3–13*, 31(3): 50–53.

Riojas-Cortez, M. (2000) Mexican American pre-schoolers create stories: sociodramatic play in a dual language classroom. *Bilingual Research Journal*, 24(3): 295–307.

Rogers, S. (2010) Powerful pedagogies and playful resistance: role play in the early childhood curriculum. In L. Brooker and S. Edwards (eds) *Engaging Play*. Maidenhead: Open University Press: 152–165.

Rogers, S. (2011) Play and pedagogy: a conflict of interests? In S. Rogers (ed.) *Rethinking Play and Pedagogy in Early Childhood Education*. Abingdon: Routledge.

Rogoff, B. (2003) *The Cultural Nature of Human Development*. Oxford: Oxford University Press.

Siraj-Blatchford, I. (2010) A focus on pedagogy: case studies of effective practice. In K. Sylva, E. Melhuish, P. Sammons, I. Siraj-Blatchford and B. Taggart (eds) *Early Childhood Matters: Evidence from the Effective Pre-school and Primary Education Project*. London: Routledge.

Smith, P. (2010) *Children and Play*. Chichester: John Wiley and Sons.

van Oers, B. (2012) Meaningful cultural learning by imitative participation: the case of abstract thinking in primary school. *Human Development*, 55: 136–158.

Vygotsky, L.S. (1978) *Mind in Society: The Development of Higher Psychological Processes*. Cambridge, MA: Harvard University Press.

Williams, P., Sheridan, S. and Sandberg, A. (2014) Preschool – an arena for children's learning of social and cognitive knowledge. *Early Years: An International Journal of Research*, 34(3): 226–240.

Wood, E. (2010) Developing integrated pedagogical approaches to play and learning. In P. Broadhead, J. Howard and E. Wood (eds) *Play and Learning in the Early Years*. London: Sage Publications.

Worthington, M. (2009) Fish in the water of culture: signs and symbols in young children's drawing. *Psychology of Education Review*, 33(1): 37–46.

Worthington, M. (2010) Play is a complex landscape: imagination and symbolic meanings. In P. Broadhead, J. Howard and E. Wood (eds) *Play and Learning in Educational Settings*. London: Sage Publications.

Worthington, M. (2011) Coomuniceren in rekentaalo: noodzakelijk voor kinderen in hunspel (Communicating mathematically – 'necessary' for children in their play). *Zone*, 1: 12–15.

Worthington, M. and van Oers, B. (2014) Pretend play and the cultural foundations of mathematics. *European Early Childhood Education Research Journal*, 24(3). In press.

Worthington, M. and van Oers, B. (2016, forthcoming) Children's social literacy practices in pretence.

Website

Children's Mathematics Network: http://www.children-mathematics.net

21

Play, literacy and language learning

Helen Bradford

Summary

This chapter outlines the crucial nature of play experiences in supporting the development of vital language and literacy skills during the earliest years of children's lives. It is further based on the premise that children will arrive at their early years settings with idiosyncratic degrees of language ability and literacy knowledge and understanding already established. The chapter incorporates discussion in the following areas:

- children's early language and literacy experiences
- the role of the adult in early language and literacy development
- exposing children to quality language and literacy experiences through playful contexts.

Introduction

International interest in early childhood education has grown in the last decade. An important part of this interest has been early language and literacy development, which is a priority for most societies because of an established correlation between acquired language literacy skills and later educational success (Sylva *et al.*, 2010). Early language and literacy development has therefore become a declared priority for most governments, and changes to early years curricula have reflected such lines of thinking. The Early Years Foundation Stage (DfE, 2012) in England places communication and language as a core tenet of its developmental approach, for example. Language development should be a fundamental goal of all early years' curricula for two reasons:

1 the early childhood years are a critical period in the development of linguistic competence
2 linguistic development provides access to future learning through equipping the child with an essential communication tool.

All languages have their own sound systems and children tune in to the ones they hear around them from birth; language development is a gradual process that must be appropriately supported in order to optimise a child's future outcomes. By the age of five, provided they do not have language difficulties, all children have acquired the adult grammar for the main constructions of their native language (Peccei, 2006). This is true across all cultures and in all languages. All children must learn to talk, however, and the development of language must be scaffolded through interaction with more experienced language users. It is therefore important to support, plan for and encourage age-appropriate dialogue in the early years setting.

Language is central to children's learning and development, not least because competence in using the spoken word impacts on early reading and writing skills. Teale and Sulzby (1986) defined children's early reading and writing behaviour as emergent literacy. Superseding the view that literacy developed only in response to systematic instruction, emergent literacy concerns 'children's individual literacy learning trajectories and the stages they go through as they progress towards conventional literacy' (Makin, 2006: 267). Emergent literacy can be described as a set of practices that young children who have had relatively little experience of reading and writing engage in. Two important concepts underpin this perspective:

1   young children are literate beings from birth
2   it incorporates an element of growing metacognitive awareness in young children, perceiving them to be active enquirers into the nature and purposes of literacy (Wray, 1994; Jacobs, 2004).

In this respect literacy development is to do with learning about the functions and forms of literacy. Indeed, research built on socio-cultural theory shows that children's earliest discoveries about literacy are learned through active engagement with both their social and cultural worlds (for example, Compton-Lilly, 2006). Literacy development will therefore occur wherever literacy practices are occurring; thus children begin to learn about reading and writing initially in their homes and communities through interacting with others in reading and writing situations. It follows, then, that children arrive at their early years setting with at least some knowledge and understanding of the function and purpose of literacy.

The role of the adult in early language and literacy development

Language

The role of the adult in expediting children's language development using appropriate strategies is well documented in research. Vygotsky (1978) described the young child as an apprentice for whom cognitive development occurs within social interactions. In other words, as language ability becomes more sophisticated, children are guided into increasingly mature ways of thinking and communicating through interacting with more capable others and through interactions with their surrounding culture. More capable others can include a range of people who are part of the child's immediate social and cultural network, such as family members (parents, grandparents, siblings), as well as their playmates and peers. Children's language development is likely to be stronger if they are encouraged to become active participants in conversation, if they are encouraged to be questioning, to hypothesise, imagine, wonder, project and dream out loud, and to hear stories and to tell stories to others.

The role of the adult is a feature of more recent developments in neuroscience, which explore both the potential and vulnerability of a child's brain from birth. Brain development is remarkably rapid and responsive during the first five years of life. Neuroscientists have defined the brain's activity in terms of connectionist networks. At birth there are billions of brain cells but they are not wired up together. The brain is therefore a work in progress, with early language experiences defining language ability. Evidence from longitudinal studies and from population studies, for example, provides information that early childhood is the period when the child responds to the environment with potential susceptibility; it is the quality and type of language experiences that shape the brain's developing architecture, critically shaping who they are as teenagers and adults (Gammage, 2006). Brain-based research therefore supports connections between what neuroscience tells us about the crucial role of the adult in supporting language development. The social and cultural aspects of language development are equally important at this time, as children learn, through talk, to place themselves within a specific social context, and in this way the development of language and of identity are closely linked.

Developing a meta-language for reading and writing

Britton (1970) suggested that a working knowledge of the structure and function of talk serves as the basis for reading and writing growth. First, children show extensive communicative abilities, even before the onset of the second year of life and before the utterance of conventional words. Makin (2006), for example, looked at language interactions during shared book reading between ten babies aged eight to twelve months and their mothers. The babies in Makin's study were defined as being in the 'prelinguistic stage', communicating through paralinguistic gestures such as vocalisations, body language and gestures, and facial expressions. Makin (2006) also found that mothers used literacy-related terms such as 'book' and 'page' with their babies. Babies were encouraged to help with page turning; some mothers would talk about 'the last page' or 'the end'. Second, social interaction with another human being is important in relation to the developmental process of language (Vygotsky, 1978; Kuhl, 2004), thus key adults such as parents and early years practitioners have the potential to scaffold children's language learning. Oral feedback acknowledges children's efforts and encourages continued practice, for example, including filling in many details about the structure of language and organising these into more coherent communications.

Dyson (1983) looked at the role of oral language in the early writing achievements of kindergarten children. She states that, 'to write *conventionally* [italics added] children must be able, not just to talk, but to conceptualise words which will represent their thoughts' (Dyson, 1983: 3). Bracewell, *et al.* (1982) argue that spoken and written discourse production call upon many of the same component cognitive processes, thus typical development reveals similar patterns of performance for both modalities. For example, written discourse shares a similar but later-emerging sequence in vocabulary and sentence construction to spoken discourse (Scott, 1991). Aram (2006) suggests that parent interventions throughout the day such as identifying printed words or talking with a child as they attempt to write words at home may foster children's understanding of the nature and functions of writing. This may happen even when writing is not the focus of attention – for example, a parent saying to a child that they will be able to go shopping as soon as they have finished writing a shopping list. Here, the parent is not teaching their child to write, nor are they intervening in a child's own attempts to write. However, they are conveying the idea that writing serves a definite purpose.

Development of reading and writing skills is therefore influenced by verbal interactions with adults that support a child's understandings of the power of reading and writing; what they do. In this way developing a meta-language to support children's emerging understanding of the uses and formats of reading and writing can be developed.

Literacy: reading and writing

Participation in reading and writing practices represents an important phase of literacy learning for children. It is through such participation that they gradually learn important concepts about how reading and writing work. Children come to understand that print is meaningful through understanding that written text conveys a message – for example, that writing in books and in the environment is made up of separate words that correspond to spoken words, that those words remain the same every time they are read, that words are made up of individual sounds and letters, and that in English, texts are read from left to right. Research has pointed to the advantages for young children of family involvement in their literacy development. Teale and Sulzby (1986) argue that the home environment can be the source of three broad categories of literacy experience: those in which adults interact with children in reading and writing situations; those in which children explore print on their own; and those in which children observe adults modelling literate behaviours.

While many studies, such as that of Teale and Sulzby (1986), have focused on the social class dimension of family literacy practices as a major influence on young children's literacy development, current research suggests that it is the quality and frequency of literacy-related actions and interactions that children experience at home rather than assuming a deficit model (Sylva et al., 2010). All parents have the potential to provide their children with experience of a rich variety of home and community literacy activities, and patterns of relationship can be established between home literacy practices and children's emergent literacy knowledge. Children's understanding of the intentionality of print is related to both the frequency of literacy events in the home and to their personal involvement in these – for example, being read a story or writing a birthday card. Children know more about the alphabetic code and the specific forms of written language in homes where literate members read and write for their own entertainment and leisure. Children of preschool age who have begun to construct knowledge about the forms and concepts of print will therefore begin formal literacy instruction with a distinct advantage over their peers who might not yet have begun this learning. It is important to understand that all children will arrive at their early years settings with some literacy knowledge and understanding.

Language, literacy and playful strategies

Knowing that early experiences can impact on long-term literacy outcomes, it is important to expose children to quality language and literacy contexts; play is one way of doing this. Play experiences can be created to support and scaffold children's developing language and literacy skills and understanding in one of two ways: first, by the children themselves as they independently test their hypotheses of the functions and purposes of reading and writing within the world in which they inhabit; second, by adults responding to both known and expressed interest, developing scenarios sometimes with, or on behalf of, the children they are responsible for. It is important to know every child as an individual, and to respond appropriately to optimise their learning and development.

Play is important for early learning for many reasons (see also Chapter 2). All of us learn best when we want to do something, and are least likely to learn when we are being made to do something that does not interest us. Children are naturally drawn to play experiences and many concentrate for long periods in their self-chosen play. Play, therefore, offers children the chance to explore and learn at their own pace and stage of language, or reading, or writing development; it offers children the chance to be in control and to feel competent within relevant, meaningful and open-ended experiences – for example, writing with a real purpose and without fear of 'getting it wrong'. Through play, children are able to meet their own needs and make sense of their world. Play can provide children with opportunities to mark make, effectively laying foundations for the later use of symbols such as letters and numbers, to represent ideas. Play encourages creativity and imagination; it offers children the opportunity to consolidate learning. Finally, children's play enables early years practitioners to observe them at their highest level of competence and to see, understand and accommodate their ideas, concerns and interests.

Play is an important vehicle for providing meaningful contexts through which children can explore print independently. Bromley (2006: 7) argues that, 'in play children mimic adults' writing habits for their own ends'. One of the challenges for early years practitioners is therefore to arrange the most appropriate physical environment to support and include writing experience, including maximising opportunities to incorporate writing into play. Neuman and Roskos (1997) investigated young children's literacy activity within play settings specifically designed to reflect authentic literacy contexts for them. The study further acknowledged the role peers can play in a child's literacy development. From observations and taped conversations, evidence was found to suggest that more expert play partners, through their more capable demonstrations of 'pretend' play such as how to post letters in a post office, appeared to teach their less skilled peers, increasing their knowledge of the environment.

The value of role play

The early years practitioner must focus on language development as a priority to ensure that children know how to communicate successfully. Social interactions should be an embedded element of practice in the early years and beyond. Role-play areas support and encourage collaborative talk and provide good opportunities for children to learn how to communicate together in a range of situations. Learning through play in this way provides a 'no risk' environment in which children learn to express themselves, alongside others, through language. Role-play areas can be the province of children only – and sometimes it is important for the children to play alone. However, there are times when the practitioner could enter the fantasy situation and play alongside them – for example, having their hair done at the hairdresser's. Knowing when and how to intervene constructively without the children feeling that the practitioner is intruding takes sensitivity and watchfulness.

Role-play areas provide generous and varied opportunities for incorporating reading and writing opportunities within play. One early years practitioner created a Jack and the Beanstalk-themed role-play area with her reception class, for example. The area was the giant's castle at the top of a beanstalk that wound around the top of the castle. The children wrote letters to Jack on green beanstalk leaves in role as Jack's mother, asking him to collect specific items for her from the castle such as the golden eggs. The children put the letters in a post box in the role-play castle. The early years practitioner then attached the letters to the beanstalk after school each day for the children to find and read the following morning. This provided opportunities for discussion and acknowledged the credibility of the children's writing, encouraging others to write knowing that their letters would be valued in the same way. Another role-play area created that year was based on the story of *Handa's Surprise* (Eileen Brown). The role-play area became Handa's home in her village and included her basket with all her fruit. Dressing-up clothes were provided so that the children could role play Handa's journey to see her friend Akeyo. They were able to go outside to do this in the reception outdoor area, having been taken on the journey initially by the early years practitioner who strategically placed the animals in the story along the way. The children then drew maps of their journey once back in Handa's home, labelling the animals encountered on their journey and the types of fruit they had taken from her basket.

Language skills and becoming a fluent reader

Prosodic reading, or reading with expression, is considered one of the hallmarks of fluent reading (Schwanenflugel *et al.*, 2004). Their study highlights the key role of word decoding speed in reading prosodically. When a child is reading prosodically, oral reading sounds much like speech with appropriate phrasing, pause structures, stress, rise and fall patterns, and general expressiveness. To read in this way children must be able to do more than decode the text and translate punctuation into speech. They must also incorporate the ordinary rise and fall of pitch in ordinary conversation. Without appropriate language skills, there will therefore be a negative impact on reading ability. Becoming a skilled reader takes time, however; it is important to note that in the early years young readers begin with an emerging decoding speed. They will read with lengthy, sporadic pauses between sentences, marked with a hesitant start-stop quality. Young readers may also read with long pauses in the middles of sentences where none is needed. They are developing their reading skills, however. It is important to support young readers as the overriding aim should be to nurture a love of books and reading, rather than to dent enthusiasm.

Children should be encouraged to see books as part of everyday life from birth, and books should be incorporated both at home and within their early years settings as an integral element of everyday practice. Books can come alive with visual aids, with strong intonation and with an enthusiasm for what they entail. It is important to remember that there are now some very sophisticated and appropriate interactive books for babies and toddlers. Children begin at the role-play stage of reading where they show an interest in books and the print they see around them. They will develop favourite books. They imitate the behaviours they observe in adults, such as holding a book carefully, turning the pages and talking out loud as they do so. They are soon capable of retelling stories they have heard as they read the book for themselves. Reading story books aloud to children and asking questions will enhance their understanding of the text. Talking with them about what they think is happening in the story, asking open-ended questions such as, 'What do you think is going to happen next?', will encourage predictive skills. Playful rhymes, action songs and poems should always be included as part of a child's reading repertoire.

The importance of story and reading with children

Children who are read to are more likely to possess a greater understanding of the difference between the conventions of written and spoken language. Wells' seminal (1986) longitudinal study investigated the influence of the home during the preschool years on children's long-term literacy development from the start of speech to the end of their primary education. The main focus of the study was an investigation of language development in the years prior to school entry; however, Wells also looked at what was required for children to be able to extend their command of language in relation to reading. One of his main conclusions was the importance of being read to. He argued that listening to stories being read aloud gives children experience of the organisation and structures of written language, and that through listening to stories children are able to develop their mental model of the world and a vocabulary that enables them to talk about it. Listening to stories also leads to the opportunity for collaborative talk between children and adults; children can relate to the stories and understand the significance of the events recounted within them in the light of their life experience, and vice versa.

What happens when an adult shares a book with a child? What are children learning from the experience and what is the adult doing to support that learning? The adult reads, holds the book the right way round, talks about the story, turns the pages, perhaps points to the illustrations. Through sharing books, children learn that:

- books are meaningful and exciting
- books are about discovery
- books provide an opportunity to hear spoken language
- books provide an opportunity to learn about the conventions of language, how verbal and non-verbal skills are required for successful communication
- books provide an opportunity to respond to spoken language.

When we read with children, we use strategies to build language and cognition, such as labelling and modelling sentence structure. Children return to favourite books and should be encouraged to choose a book to be read to them. Sharing books is important, at any age. The early years practitioner should understand that reading with young children is not something that should be rushed or done out of a sense of duty; they should understand that they are helping to develop a lifelong love of books and of learning, fostering engagement and supporting children's active participation. They should also see sharing books as a valuable way of scaffolding children's language development.

Language skills and beginner writer behaviours

Children begin to explore the features of writing from a very early age. They do so with the intention of creating meaning before understanding of the alphabetic principle has developed, and despite the fact that the writing produced is not conventional in that it cannot be read by an adult (Bradford and Wyse, 2012). Intentionality is a characteristic of the writing process, which recognises that children are already making planned organisational decisions about their writing, and that they write with an expectation that the graphic signs they make will make sense. Harste *et al.* (1984) discovered that children as young as three display intentionality within their early attempts to write. Goodman (1986), and more recently Lancaster (2001), argue that children as young as two engage in writing tasks for a wide variety of reasons and that most have begun to use symbols to represent real things.

Clay (1975: 15) argued that, by examining children's earliest attempts at writing, we are provided with a 'rich commentary on [children's] ... learning about print', learning that is 'encapsulated in their accumulated attempts to write'. Analysis of children's unconventional texts suggests that young children's authoring processes are not qualitatively different from those used by older writers. Several studies make a case for adults and children alike using similar cognitive processes in terms of the decisions they must make when confronted with a writing task. Writing involves choosing from a range of possible actions, which in turn implies a degree of conscious awareness of potential alternatives. Pahl (1999) argued that children will interpret things according to the information and resources to which they have access at the time and according to what is currently salient in their thinking. In other words, children will simply make use of what they know. In this respect it is inexperience that determines their ability to write conventionally, rather than the strategies they use when they approach a written task. Jacobs (2004: 18) describes such strategies as 'temporary scaffolds', which will be gradually refined as children begin to understand more about the writing process.

Examples of play and contexts for language and literacy learning

This chapter has argued that all of us learn best when we want to do something, and are least likely to learn when we are being made to do something that does not interest us. Note how the following three vignettes emanate from the children's self-initiated desire to incorporate language with reading and writing skills through the creation of meaningful contexts.

Cameo 1

Alastair, aged two years and four months, was observed as he played outside in the garden of the Children's Centre he attended for 15 hours a week. An activity had been set up for all children to access involving finding eggs hidden in straw, placing them in a basket and counting them. The early years practitioner who had set up the activity had also provided a large whiteboard positioned at child height with an egg number line from 1 to 20 attached to the outer edge, and large, thick whiteboard pens. Children who came to explore the activity were encouraged to record on the whiteboard the number of eggs they had found once they had counted them. The early years practitioner supported the children to find the corresponding number on the egg number line, modelling one-to-one ordination from left to right. Alastair was intrigued by the activity and observed it from a distance for about 15 minutes. Then, as soon as he saw an opportunity, he went straight to the whiteboard and counted out loud to seven, while simultaneously (albeit randomly) pointing to eggs on the number line with his left hand and making a mark for every number he spoke out loud with the pen he held in his right. The numbers that Alastair had written as he counted appeared on the board as no more than a series of regimented, squiggly lines. In his own mind, however, and from the perspective of the observer, Alastair had written his own set of numbers from 1 to 7. He wrote them from left to right on the board.

Note how Alastair has found a meaningful, playful context within which to display his knowledge of emergent literacy, including counting out loud, number representation and recording.

Cameo 2

This is Oliver playfully writing at home about what he knows and what is meaningful to him. One Saturday morning, with no prompting, he gathered paper and pencil and wandered into his parents' bedroom while they were still sleeping, sat on the floor and began to write. When his parents awoke, he carried on writing. Figure 21.1 shows what he produced.

Figure 21.1 Oliver's playful writing

Oliver was just shy of four years old when he wrote this piece. He has dedicated it to his sister Esther, and to his mum and dad. He began by writing the numbers 1 to 10. Then he revised his plan as it made him think of the rhyme, '1, 2, 3, 4, 5, once I caught a fish alive'. To this end he has inserted 'wns I cut a fish aliv' between numbers 5 and 6. He has completed the rest of the rhyme after number 10.

Cameo 3

Edward, aged five years, wrote this piece alongside his father who was concentrating on work-related issues writing on his laptop. They were doing their 'homework' together on a Sunday afternoon. Sometimes writing just has to be done! For his homework, Edward had to write a sentence about what was special to him – see Figure 21.2. Note how Edward's father would have been modelling purposeful writing, albeit on a laptop, for his son. Edward's father is British, but he has a French mother, which is why he calls his father 'papa'. He is taught cursive writing in his reception class.

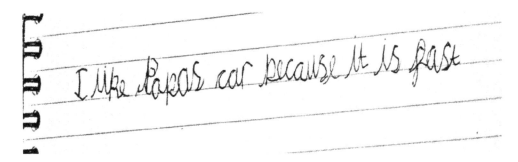

Figure 21.2 Edward's cursive writing

Conclusion

Language and literacy development should be a fundamental goal of all early years curricula for two reasons:

1   the early childhood years are a critical period in the development of linguistic competence, and reading and writing skills
2   language and literacy development provides access to future learning.

Children learn in environments that facilitate and enable meaningful, purposeful and playful contexts both at home and in their early years settings. Understanding how children learn through play helps us to understand how children develop their own developmental trajectory in becoming competent literate beings.

Questions to promote reflection

1   In what ways do play and fun have roles in the early years curriculum and children's early language and literacy development?
2   How can we incorporate meaningful, playful language and literacy contexts for children to flourish as developing language and literacy experts?
3   How can we make sure that planning incorporates appropriate playful responses for individual language and literacy learners?

References and further reading (in bold)

Aram, D. (2006) Early literacy interventions: the relative role of storybook reading, alphabetic activities, and their combination. *Reading and Writing*, 19: 489–515.

Bracewell, R., Frederickson, C. and Frederickson, J.D. (1982) Cognitive processes in composing and comprehending discourse. *Educational Psychologist*, 17: 741–751.

Bradford, H. and Wyse, D. (2012) Writing and writers: the perceptions of young children and their parents. *Early Years: An International Research Journal*, 33(3): 252–265.

Britton, J. (1970) *Language and Learning*. Miami, FL: University of Miami Press.

Bromley, H. (2006) *Making My Own Mark – Play and Writing*. London: Early Education.

Clay, M.M. (1975) *What Did I Write? Beginning Writing Behaviour*. Portsmouth, NH: Heinemann Educational Books.

Compton-Lilly, C. (2006) Identity, childhood culture, and literacy learning: a case study. *Journal of Early Childhood Literacy* 6(1): 57–76.

Department for Education (DfE) (2012) *Statutory Framework for the Early Years Foundation Stage*. London: DfE.

Dyson, A.H. (1983) The role of oral language in early writing processes. *Research in the Teaching of English*, 17: 1–30.

Gammage, P. (2006) Early childhood education and care: politics, policies and possibilities. *Early Years*, 26(3): 235–248.

Goodman, Y. (1986) Children coming to know literacy. In W. Teale and E. Sulzby (eds) *Emergent Literacy: Writing and Reading*. Norwood, NJ: Ablex.

Harste, J.C., Woodward, V.A. and Burke, C.L. (1984) *Language Stories and Literacy Lessons*. Portsmouth, HA: Heinemann Educational Books.

Jacobs, G.M. (2004) A classroom investigation of the growth of metacognitive awareness in kindergarten children through the writing process. *Early Childhood Education Journal*, 32(1): 17–23.

Kuhl, P. (2004) Early language acquisition: cracking the speech code. *Nature Reviews Neuroscience*, 5(11), 831–843.

Lancaster, L. (2001) Staring at the page: the functions of gaze in a young child's interpretation of symbolic forms. *Journal of Early Childhood Literacy*, 1(2): 131–152.

Makin, L. (2006) Literacy 8–12 months: what are babies learning? *Early Years: An International Research Journal*, 26(3): 267–777.

Neuman, S.B. and Roskos, K. (1997) *Handbook of Early Literacy Research*. New York: The Guildford Press.

Pahl, K. (1999) *Transformations: Meaning Making in a Nursery*. London: Trentham.

Peccei, J.S. (ed.) (2006) *Child Language: A Resource Book for Students*. London: Routledge.

Schwanenflugel, P.J., Hamilton, A.M., Kuhn, M.R., Wisenbaker, J. and Stahl, S.A. (2004) Becoming a fluent reader: reading skill and prosodic features in the oral reading of young readers. *Journal of Educational Psychology*, 96: 119–129.

Scott, C.M. (1991). Learning to write: context, form and process. In A.G. Kamhi and H.W. Catts (eds) *Reading Disabilities: A Developmental Language Perspective*. Boston, MA: Allyn and Bacon.

Sylva, K., Melhuish, E., Sammons, P., Siraj-Blatchford, I. and Taggart, B. (eds) (2010) *Early Childhood Matters: Evidence from the Effective Pre-school and Primary Project*. London: Routledge.

Teale, W. and Sulzby, E. (1986) *Emergent Literacy: Reading and Writing*. Norwood, NJ: Ablex.

Vygotsky, L. (1978) *Mind in Society: The Development of Higher Psychological Processes*. Cambridge, MA: Harvard University Press.

Wells, G. (1986) *The Meaning Makers: Children Learning Language and Using Language to Learn*. London: Hodder & Stoughton.

Wray, D. (1994) *Literacy and Awareness*. London: Hodder & Stoughton.

22

Children's fantasy role play: why adults should join in

Neil Kitson

Summary

This chapter highlights the importance of fantasy role play and socio-dramatic play in the cognitive, social and emotional development of young children. Socio-dramatic play offers substantial learning potential for those working with young children. Facilitating the play enables practitioners to extend and enhance children's learning through creating situations that motivate and encourage children to behave and function at a higher cognitive level. This is most effective when done through sympathetic and interactive interventions. Only when educators acknowledge and recognise the importance of their role in children's fantasy play will they feel able to intervene and begin to develop its true potential.

Cameo 1

In the corner of the nursery is a 'shop'. The adults have been successful in getting real objects for the children's play. Indeed they are proud of their success and consider this to be a rich and valuable environment for the children to develop role play. Kisha, Ashok and Michael have been in the 'shop' for some time now. Kisha is singing on the phone, while Ashok and Michael are repeatedly putting money in and taking money out of the till. The children are all busy and are engaged, but these superficial activities have little of the promise of dynamic role play. Enter the adult in role as a confused older person who can't remember what she came in for and needs help getting home. At once the 'play' takes on a perceptively different quality. No longer are the boys playing tag with the money but as shopkeepers working out what is needed. Kisha uses the phone to call the person's home to confirm the order, to arrange a lift home and to tell off the family for sending the older person to the shops on her own. The children use language in sophisticated ways, have a developed understanding of morality and display an ability to solve complex problems.

Introduction

I don't know if you have ever watched young children like Kisha, Ashok and Michael when they are involved in role-play games; I mean really *watched* and not just seen them while they're playing. What they are able to do is quite amazing. One of the most fascinating things for me is the way that they are able to negotiate the rules of the game without ever seeming to formally agree on them. The game just rolls and turns, and they all seem to instinctively understand. Now, clearly there is more to it than that and as we go through this chapter we'll look in a bit more detail as to what these things might be. But seeing that the children appear to be able to do this so effortlessly, wouldn't it be great if we, as educators, could use this ability to help *us* to teach *them*? There are a number of ways in which this could be done. We could just let children get on with it by themselves, as Kisha, Ashok and Michael were doing because they can do pretty well by themselves, but from all that I have seen they can get even more out of the experience if we as adults join them in the game. We can shape the game, as in the example above, help give it structure, reinforce areas of learning as we go along, challenging them without ever having to formally teach.

We need not be up there directing, telling children what they should be doing. If this form of play is so valuable that we encourage children to do it, why don't we get involved as well? In my experience the reason has nothing to do with the children but has much more to do with the adults who seem to find it hard to join in.

Over the next few pages a few reasons will be given as to why we should sit on the floor and pretend that the bus is late or hide in the corner pretending that the Gruffalo is coming. For me it is analogous to encouraging children to read and enjoy books. What we do is share books with children, we talk about what has happened and what might be going to happen; we model good practice by allowing them to see us reading. We would think it very strange if people tried to develop reading solely by giving the children lots of books to look at. Sharing and participation are good practice and yet, when it comes to fantasy play, at worst (and I know this is a bit of a cliché but I have seen it), we tell the children to go into the corner and make up a story.

People have always been intrigued by the way children play, but over recent years this has become more formalised and people have thought it worthy of academic study. There has been growing interest in the way that young children use fantasy play within their basic strategies for learning (Edgington, 2004; Wood, 2004). It is seen as a powerful and dynamic tool to engage children in the learning process (Kitson and Spiby, 1997). Moreover, it is instinctive and a basic activity that children already 'know'. Independent of educational environments, they appear to develop the ability to engage in fantasy play by themselves. While it is accepted that these activities are a 'good thing', what is less widespread is the study of the practitioners becoming part of that learning process.

There is the belief among some adults working with children that we should view children's play as sacrosanct and that fantasy play, even more than other forms of play, allows children to operate without adults almost as a form of therapy. Indeed I am not opposed to this notion entirely. It would be daft to think that, as an adult working with young children, every time they headed for the dressing-up box an adult should be the first one in there. Clearly engaging in such activities allows children a sense of intellectual freedom – it is their story played out to their evolving rules. My concern is that children will frequently repeat very similar if not identical forms of play, engage in very similar role-play activity, model the same if not identical behaviours, and resolve similar problems repeatedly. I can remember as a child sitting with my older brother at the top of the stairs at home with our legs sticking through the banisters playing our own invented game called 'Fred Brodie and Fred Brodie's mate'. As the younger sibling I was, of course, the 'mate'. I have no recollection of what we did but we were content (and quiet) for hours. Our parents must have looked on delighted that we were so quiet for so long. There is no doubt that if we hadn't been enjoying ourselves we wouldn't have continued the game. But this game didn't develop or extend and, as a result, our thinking and skills didn't develop or extend. If playing the same fantasy game, children will have only a limited cognitive area in which to develop and grow their thinking, their skills and their imagination (Hendy and Toon, 2001).

Effective intervention can channel children's learning, helping them construct new problems and challenges, encouraging and supporting individuals, and extending and motivating language performance and ability. Perhaps we should learn to see this as engaging in their learning rather than intervening. By engaging, we are offering them a scaffold around which they can explore intellectually (Parker-Rees, 2004; Dolya, 2009). This, then, is the crux of my argument – this is the case for adult intervention.

So what do we mean by fantasy play?

Children engage in a wide variety of play activities, which can be seen throughout the chapters of this book. Fantasy will occur at differing levels within individual children's play and games and at different levels of maturity. Socio-dramatic play is, for the most part, concerned with the nature of role and of social interaction, while other types of play involve bodily activity or the use and exploration of objects

In socio-dramatic play children demonstrate a growing awareness of their social surroundings, consciously acting out social interactions and experiencing human relationships actively by means of symbolic representation. The key difference between socio-dramatic play and dramatic play is that in the latter children can pretend on their own. They can act out a situation to the exclusion of others, while the more higher-level socio-dramatic play requires interaction, communication and cooperation. Dramatic play is imitative and draws upon first- or second-hand experiences, and uses real or imaginary objects (Hendy and Toon, 2001; Rogers and Evans, 2008). This play becomes socio-dramatic play if the theme is elaborated in cooperation with at least one other person and the participants interact with one another in both *action* and *speech*.

Smilansky and Shefatya (1990: 22) suggest six elements necessary for fantasy play, as follows.

1   *Imitative role play:* the child undertakes a make-believe role and expresses it in imitative action and/or verbalisation.
2   *Makebelieve with regard to toys:* movements or verbal declarations and/or materials or toys that are not replicas of the object itself are substituted for real objects.

3   *Verbal make-believe with regard to actions and situations:* verbal descriptions or declarations are substituted for actions or situations.

4   *Persistence in role play:* the child continues within a role or play theme for a period of at least ten minutes.

5   *Interaction:* at least two players interact within the context of the play episode.

6   *Verbal communication:* there is some verbal interaction related to the play episode.

The first four of these apply to dramatic play but the last two define only socio-dramatic play. This difference can be illustrated with a couple of examples.

Cameo 2

Three year old Joseph puts a cape on his shoulders and runs around the nursery saying, 'I'm Batman. I'm flying and I'm getting the baddies.'

This behaviour has elements of 1 and 3 present, so it can be defined as dramatic play.

Cameo 3

Two girls are playing 'hospital' in the doctor's surgery. They are wearing white coats and are giving each other instructions such as, 'I'll go and use the phone.' Questions like, 'Can I have the listening thing now?' and statements such as, 'I've got the medicine spoon' suggest elements of imitative role play are present – they are acting but not *interacting*: merely informing each other what is going on.

These girls are engaging at the very basic level of socio-dramatic play. Contrast these with two children pretending to build a house together for a pigeon using make-believe tools, talking and acting as if they are doing the job, sharing their ideas and developing the story together: this would be an example of higher-level socio-dramatic play as elements 2, 3, 4, 5 and 6 are present. It could be argued that this is a richer, more involving form of play offering the children who are playing more opportunities to learn by testing things out. All socio-dramatic play and drama is a metaphor for the children's lives and it is the function of the teacher to help the children to reflect on the significance of their play in order to learn from it. What better place to reflect than from within the drama as part of the story?

Why is socio-dramatic play important?

Through their fantasy play, children create new pretend situations. These can contain within them a wide range of seemingly unconnected elements all drawn from the child's previous experiences. Fantasy acts as a way of unifying experiences, knowledge and understanding, helping the child to discover the links between the individual components. Moreover, as children are able to control the fantasy play, they are also able to control its components. The manifestation of the fantasy element (the play) develops as the child grows older. Children bring to the fantasy play existing knowledge, skills and understanding of the world, which they then assimilate within existing schema or create new and novel interconnections (Wood, 2004).

What is needed in the early years is the development and extension of fantasy play, the legitimising of it, so that children themselves can come to understand the value of it; through this activity considerable learning about people's lives, human interactions, the workings of society and the individual's role within it can take place. Through play, children can begin to learn to cope with life, and with a range of complex social issues such as failure, loneliness and disappointment. Educators need to move children beyond these immediate horizons so that they can begin to look at the deeper level of 'role' and the greater complexities of life. For this to happen, children need to be challenged.

Socio-dramatic play in action

There is a sound argument in both psychodynamic and cognitive developmental theories for the specific benefits to be had by encouraging children to engage in fantasy play. The advantages of assimilation and role learning are clear, but how might these be developed in an early years context?

The potential benefits to be gained from fantasy play are difficult to quantify but we can discuss them in general terms. Singer and Singer (1990) identify three areas where the benefits of fantasy play can be seen:

1   actual spontaneous verbal output (around 50 per cent) in socio-dramatic play
2   a corresponding increase in social interaction
3   a significant improvement across a range of cognitive skills after 'training' in imaginative play.

Socio-dramatic play can influence the creativity, intellectual growth and social skills of the child. This provides a useful basis for what might otherwise be seen as abstract constructs. Among generalised notions of the benefits of socio-dramatic play are the following points relating to children's potential learning:

• creating new combinations out of experiences
• selectivity and intellectual discipline

- discrimination of the central features of a role sequence
- heightened concentration
- enhanced self-awareness and self-control
- self-discipline within the role context (e.g. a child who is playing a special role within a game might inhibit crying because the character in the game would not cry)
- the acquisition of flexibility and empathy towards others
- the development of an intrinsic set of standards
- acquisition of a sense of creativity and capacity to control personal responses
- development of cooperative skills since make-believe games in groups require effective give and take
- awareness of the potential use of the environment for planning and other play situations
- increased sensitivity to alternative role possibilities so that the notion of father need not be one's own father but may include many kinds of behaviour associated with the broader concept of fathering
- increased capacity for the development of abstract thought by learning first to substitute the image for the overt action and then later a verbal coding for both the action and the image
- heightened capacity for generalisation
- a step towards vicarious learning and a greater use of modelling (Smilansky, cited in Singer and Singer, 1990: 224).

Clearly not every child engaged in fantasy play will automatically develop these abilities, nor will the children *not* engaged in fantasy play fail to have these areas of learning available to them. Rather, fantasy play provides an opportunity for the child to gain ready and enjoyable access to these opportunities.

It is important to highlight the role that fantasy play has in the development of morality (Winston, 2000). Children test out their ideas and attitudes in a number of different situations and practise what will happen in real life but within the safety of the enactment. The success that results contributes towards building self-confidence and self-esteem. Furthermore, socio-dramatic play aids the development of the social dimension within the child: children develop the social skills they will need later in life.

Media representation and superhero play

There are a number of studies that show the increasing amount of screen time that young children are consuming (Marsh, 2000; Singer and Singer, 2007). This may come in the form of cartoon representations of the real world, of narrative dramas designed for young children or in the form of computer games. It is not surprising, therefore, that young children will incorporate these into their role play. This integration can vary from simple reinterpretation and re-enactment of the narrative through to the incorporation of the concept of superpowers into more mundane forms of narrative.

One of the limitations for young children is that such play has many of the attributes of 'magical' play: solutions to problems created in the drama can magically be summoned up through the use of the superheroes' powers. This can have a limiting effect on the dramatic value of the role play as the children are engaging in the play through the interface of the superhero. There is a distance created. The children are not engaged in dramatic activities; rather they are engaged in playing the superhero. I have a very strong image of a young boy running round the nursery with his anorak flapping around his back but buttoned at the neck. His arms were out and he was swooping in and out of other children. Intrigued, I took to joining him in his 'game' in an attempt to understand more about what he was doing. He patiently arranged my coat in a similar fashion to his own and instructed me in the correct way to move about the space. We were Superman (as represented by the coat) and we were flying (as represented by the coat). When I attempted to develop the play through narrative challenges, all attempts to deepen the fantasy were solved instantly with the superhero powers as other children in the past had used magic. I have observed this type of play on many subsequent occasions and have witnessed many similar results. This is not to say that such play is any less valuable to its participants.

A report from Islington Primary Strategy Early Years Team (2007) on the role of superhero play showed how children engaged in such play were among the least aggressive at the nursery, yet the process of daily sword making with Construct-a-Straws© gave them the confidence to play at nursery, cemented their strong friendship, and led them to explore a wealth of books and stories. For another child, making a red Sticklebrick© gun seemed to be a transient but important form of comfort that helped him settle in to the new environment. Children find it easy to access superhero play: they are able to participate in the chase and the excitement, and be part of a group. They see it as offering positive opportunities for developing cooperative skills – it is, by its very nature, a cooperative activity as it's difficult to have a capture-and-rescue game on one's own. It encourages children to express their feelings in a safe and secure environment, and helps them develop negotiation skills that they are able to transfer to everyday situations.

That said, I have noticed a gender imbalance with superhero play: boys traditionally gravitate more readily to this type of role play than girls. There is a significant amount of research to show that girls, given the right circumstances, will readily engage in superhero play (Marsh, 2010; see also Chapter 5). Boys will often choose to engage in superhero-type play rather than less structured and informal role play. There have been many theories put forward as to why this should be the case (Jordon, 1995). It could perhaps be culturally related in that there are many more strong positive male role models available within the canon of superheroes. It could also be that, as adults, we are more comfortable with boys being superhero roles and so subconsciously reward their play (Jones, 2008).

So why should adults join in?

If children use fantasy role play so naturally why should adults become involved? One of the most valuable contributions that adults can make to fantasy play is their own involvement. All too often adults tend to restrict their involvement in socio-dramatic play to a very superficial engagement. Skilful interaction can stimulate and act as a catalyst (Moyles, 1989), help focus the children's attention and set up challenges, all of which enhance and deepen the child's experiences. Adults are able to create learning areas appropriate to the needs of individual children. Dolya (2009) has indicated that, if we push children to *excel* today, then tomorrow it will become their *norm*. The significant factor is the active engagement of the adults in encouraging children to struggle with ideas, concepts and morality.

Interfere or intervene?

As with most forms of play, socio-dramatic play has a structure and rules, although at first glance this structure may not be apparent. Social play needs rules that we all understand in order for the interaction to take place. Interventions do not mean taking over: the adult becoming part of the play can facilitate the implementation of the rules as well as act as a behavioural model for the children to copy. Part of this is helping the children differentiate between fantasy and reality. It is useful to identify clearly for the children when socio-dramatic play is taking place. This can be done very effectively by the adult working with the children saying, 'We are going to make up a story.' In this way the children are clear about the expectations of the activity and also have a much clearer idea of when they are, and are not, involved in the fantasy. It is equally important for the adult to make it really clear when the socio-dramatic play is over. This is merely the formalisation of what children do for themselves.

Any episode of socio-dramatic play entails the exercise of shared imagination and the shared development of the theme of that particular play episode. Young children are naturally egocentric and find it difficult to share. By selective interventions, sensitive adults can monitor the negotiation of the children's ideas and act as facilitators. They can help the children remain consistent within their role and aid the development of the story. The adult working within the fiction is able to set problems and keep the children on task, so making them confront the challenges.

Intervention in socio-dramatic play enables the participating adult to keep the activity going by motivating the children to persist. While some children engage in such play readily, others need to be guided and encouraged to play a full part. The adult can help to refocus the story in order to bring the group together and generate excitement by introducing tension into the story. These are both essential to the development of socio-dramatic play but difficult for young children to attain for themselves. Inputs or interventions into socio-dramatic play become the subtle tools of the adult working with children. Within the play, the adult is able to enrich and deepen the play, and open up new learning areas for the children; intervene and structure the learning from within, without significantly reducing the children's ownership.

Although the adult can guide and shape the socio-dramatic play, essentially the play and action must belong to the children: their ideas must be used. The words spoken must be their words, expressing their thoughts. It may perhaps be that the adult simply joins in an existing 'game' with the children without the intention of simply being in the group but rather of moving the children's learning on, placing obstacles in the way of their story so that, by overcoming these obstacles, learning opportunities are created.

Another way of doing this is to construct the story with the children: 'What shall we make up a story about today?' Feeding from the children's ideas, both children and adult construct the fantasy. The adult's role is again that of facilitator, stretching and extending the children while maintaining interest and excitement. This adult participation legitimises the play and encourages the children to see what they are doing as something valuable. By setting up stories about, say, post offices, the children are involved with maths, language, social skills, manipulative skills, and so on. If such pretend areas become a garage or a desert island, then a new set of learning potentials is created. By selecting appropriate themes for the children's needs, the adults can then give access to appropriate areas of learning.

Is fantasy role play for all children?

Fantasy play and socio-dramatic play transcend normal barriers of learning as perceived in traditional learning settings. The ability to participate in the activity is not governed by other abilities; rather it is governed by a willingness to participate. Although this idea has been widely explored (Peters and Sherratt, 2002; Rogers and Evans, 2008), it took me a long time working with skilled practitioners to really understand it. Being part of a group who were working with a number of children with severe learning difficulties showed me that these children still benefited by being part of the role play even if their participation is restricted. With children in mainstream education who find accessing aspects of the curriculum difficult, fantasy role play is often very liberating. Coming from a position of not succeeding, role play can enable them to achieve. Fantasy role play must never be seen as a panacea for learners. Rather it offers a different way of learning, focusing on different sets of skills that allow young children to develop a different kind of world around them.

Conclusion

In this chapter, I have argued that adults should not be frightened about participating in children's fantasy role play; not all the time but as a means to develop learning. We looked first at the development of fantasy play, at the evidence supporting the need for adult intervention in such activities, and opportunities for cognitive development. The role of superhero play was briefly touched upon, and links were made to learning development and accessibility for all children. It was emphasised that adult intervention has to be sympathetic to the needs of the children and operate within their fantasy. The adult's role is to provide a structure within which the children can interact and set up problems to be solved, to encourage children to test out ideas and, perhaps more importantly, to open up personal learning strategies to the children. At the end we returned to the basic idea that the resistance to engaging in this form of learning, this form of teaching, lies within our reluctance as adults to join in with the fantasy play – if we allow this to happen a unique learning opportunity is lost.

Questions to promote reflection

1   If you don't do so already, what stops you from engaging with the children in fantasy and socio-dramatic play? If you do engage in fantasy play with the children, what do you feel are the benefits?

2   Do you have particular children in your setting who might be able to 'shine' through involvement in role-play contexts?

3   What is the potential within your setting for developing socio-dramatic/ fantasy play areas? What might these be? What are the possibilities for learning?

4   In which of Smilansky and Shefatya's six elements of socio-dramatic play do children in your setting engage?

References and further reading (in bold)

Dolya, G. (2009) *Vygotsky in Action in the Early Years: The Key to the Learning Curriculum*. London: Routledge.

Edgington, M. (2004) *The Foundation Stage Teacher in Action – Teaching 3-, 4- and 5-year-olds*. London: Paul Chapman.

Hendy, L. and Toon, L. (2001) *Supporting Drama and Imaginative Play in the Early Years*. Buckingham: Open University Press.

Islington Primary Strategy Early Years Team (2007) Engaging boys in the early years: the experiences of three Islington settings. Available online at: http://www.islington.gov.uk/publicrecords/ library/Education-and-skills/Information/Leaflets/2011–2012/(2012–03–03)-Engaging-Boys-Leaflet.pdf (accessed 22 April 2014).

Jones, D. (2008) Superheroes v. demons: constructing identities of male student teachers in the early years: conversations. *Perspectives in Education*, 26(2): 125–130.

Jordon, E. (1995) Fighting boys and fantasy play: the construction of masculinity in the early years of school. *Gender and Education*, 7(1). Available online at: http://www.tandfonline. com/doi/pdf/10.1080/713668458 (accessed 22 April 2014).

Kitson, N. and Spiby, I. (1997) *Drama 7–11*. London: Routledge.

Marsh, J. (2000) But I want to fly too! Girls and superhero play in the infant classroom. *Gender and Education*, 12(2): 209–220.

Marsh, J. (2010) *Childhood, Culture and Creativity: A Literature Review*. Creativity, Culture and Education Series. Newcastle-upon-Tyne. Available online at: http://www. creativitycultureeducation.org/childhood-culture-and-creativity-a-literature-review (accessed 4 May 2014).

Moyles, J. (1989) *Just Playing? The Role and Status of Play in Early Childhood Education*. Buckingham: Open University Press.

Parker-Rees, R. (2004) Moving, playing and learning: children's active exploration of their world. In R. Willan, R. Parker-Rees and J. Savage (eds) *Early Childhood Studies*. Exeter: Learning Matters.

Peters, M. and Sherratt, D. (2002) *Developing Play and Drama in Children with Autistic Spectrum Disorders*. London: David Fulton.

Rogers, S. and Evans, J. (2008) *Inside Role-play in Early Childhood Education*. London: Routledge.

Singer, D. and Singer, J. (1990) *The House of Make Believe*. Cambridge, MA: Harvard University Press.

Singer, D. and Singer, J. (2007) *Imagination and Play in the Electronic Age*. Cambridge, MA: First Harvard University Press.

Smilansky, S. and Shefatya, L. (1990) *Facilitating Play: A Medium for Promoting Cognitive, Sociocultural and Academic Development in Young Children*. Gaithersburg, MD: Psychosocial and Educational Publications.

Winston, J. (2000) *Drama, Literacy and Moral Education*. London: David Fulton.

Wood, E. (2004) Developing a pedagogy of play. In A. Anning, J. Cullen and M. Fleer (eds) *Early Childhood Education*. London: Sage.

PART 5

Play is universal

'Children's play generates a "culture of childhood" from games in school and in the playground to urban activities such as playing marbles, free running, street art and so on. Children are also at the forefront of using . . . virtual worlds to establish new means of communication and . . . cultural environments.'

(Convention on the Rights of the Child (2013) *General comment No.17 on the right of the child to rest, leisure, play, recreational activities, cultural life and the arts* (article 31). UNCRC.)

23

Play with children from diverse cultures

Karen Barr and Penny Borkett

Summary

This chapter discusses some of the challenges of, and opportunities for, developing inclusive practice with children from diverse cultures within early years play and learning environments. It highlights the importance of children taking agency over their play and discusses how this may be achieved using the Mosaic approach. This chapter also examines what is meant by the term 'culture', and considers some of the socio-cultural theories that relate to working with children from diverse communities, with discussion of how practitioners can plan activities that are inclusive to all children. The role of effective communication with parents in understanding children's home cultures is emphasised as a key component in developing inclusive practice to support all children.

Introduction

In western culture, play is extolled as an invaluable vehicle for young children's learning and development. It provides an excellent means for children to gain first-hand experience of life by exploring how things work, and fostering their imaginations by enabling creative and critical thinking through problem solving, experimentation and pretend play. Play-based curricular policies are founded upon research and theory and have been developed over time to take account of new findings and new understandings of how children learn. There are numerous ways in which children learn through play as well as non-play activities. Western pedagogies influence beliefs and practices within early years education and care contexts in Britain, and those working in early years settings have to work within the parameters of national and local policies (see Chapter 1). Nevertheless, it is essential to consider wider views on what appropriate play provision might encompass in order to facilitate an inclusive approach to working with children and families. Children from a wide range of backgrounds attend early years settings and if an ethos of respect for diversity is to be cultivated, a culture of openness to others' perspectives is crucial.

This chapter considers some key issues in developing appropriate provision. These are:

- acknowledging our own assumptions and challenging dominant discourses
- curriculum requirements
- children's 'agency' within early years contexts
- what is meant by the term 'culture'
- socio-cultural theory
- the risk of 'silencing' families
- children's transitions between cultural settings.

Acknowledging our own assumptions and challenging dominant discourses

Our personal views of what play should look like and how best to make effective provision for children to benefit from play experiences depend upon our values and beliefs. These are developed throughout our lives and are influenced by our interaction with the world around us, including our own childhood experiences, relationships with friends, family, colleagues and other professionals, what we have read, and what we see in our lives and in the media. Our personal histories as well as current life experiences impact on the way we think. Dominant discourses of what constitutes 'good practice' in providing play experiences shape the way in which curriculum policy is developed and implemented. It is important for those working with young children to acknowledge how their views have been formed and how they influence practice (see Preface), particularly as those views might differ from those of the families who access early years provision. In order for equitable practice to be developed it is necessary to be open to new ideas of what appropriate practice might be and to act responsively to new research and our own and others' lived experiences. It is easy to assume that our views are shared by others, but reflection on others' beliefs and values can enrich and deepen our knowledge and understanding of different perspectives and thus enable new theories to be formed that inform professional judgement (see also Chapter 2). Regular dialogue with children and families facilitates renegotiation of practice to ensure fairer, respectful and inclusive approaches to pedagogy and the curriculum that value the diverse cultures of all children accessing the services offered.

Curriculum requirements

The Early Years Foundation Stage (EYFS) is built upon the view that young children learn best through play (DfE, 2014), and recommends that appropriate play and learning experiences be provided through a cycle of observation, assessment and planning, in order to take account of children's interests, needs and past experiences of play. Although the EYFS asserts that children are all unique, and adopts the view that children's cultural lives should be respected, it gives no indication of how this should be achieved (Ang, 2010). This means that practitioners, through reflective practice, have a responsibility to cultivate an ethos of respect within early years settings in order to tailor approaches to practice that are inclusive to all children who attend.

Children's 'agency' within early years contexts

The term 'agency' focuses on children's ability to have their voices heard regarding the kind of provision to which they belong. This term can be used to extol the view that children should be valued and respected as they are integral to the lives of their community. The early years setting can be seen as a community within a child's home community. In order for children to have true 'agency' in their setting, practitioners need to view children as members of society whose voices truly count. When children have agency they might, for example, have a say in the resources and environment of the setting, what is provided at snack and meal times, what they play and whether they play inside or outside. To an extent, the free-flow environment and continuous provision suggested in the EYFS allows for this as children can move freely within the environment and choose the resources that they access. The requirement for planning to be centred on the interests and needs of children further endorses the agency of the child. When practitioners observe children they can gain an insight into what is important to them in order to plan for relevant experiences that engage them. However, involving children in the planning of resources is perhaps a challenging issue. In many primary schools children are invited to have their say in the way school is led, through regular consultation meetings known as school council; however, there is little evidence to suggest that such opportunities have, as yet, become practice within early years settings.

It is essential that practitioners involve children in the planning of activities on a regular basis. This can be achieved, in part, by focusing on what has been discovered through observations. Conversations between parents and practitioners are opportunities in which to share information about the child's preferences at home, which can further inform planning. Enabling children to have agency over their lives, settings and play affords them the opportunity to act out situations, develop new skills and knowledge, and to experiment with play and resources within a safe community in the early years setting. This, in turn, offers children autonomy, self-confidence and the opportunity to feel valued for who they are. Moreover, when children take ownership of the activities offered to them and how they use resources, they can become autonomous learners, which can raise their self-esteem and self-confidence.

One tool that can enable children to 'have a voice' and gain agency over their lives in early years settings is the 'Mosaic approach'. Developed by Clark and Moss (2011), this multi-method approach enables children to share their views, particularly about changes to childhood environments both inside and outdoors. Children from the Thomas Coram Early Childhood Centre were the first to investigate this way of gathering information, and it has been further developed in order to ensure that even the youngest children are able to have a say in what resources are made available, where and with whom they choose to play. A range of methods of listening to children are used within the Mosaic approach in order to capture children's perspectives as fully as possible. These methods include observing children, child conferencing, children photographing elements of the environment that are significant to them, and discussion with parents. In using this approach, practitioners gain insight into what is important to them in order to enable children's agency within the culture of the setting.

What is meant by the term 'culture'?

There are many definitions of the term 'culture'. Broadly speaking, this encompasses the ideas, customs and social behaviour of a particular people or society. The term culture relates to something that is organic and dynamic: it is constantly evolving and changing, and is an important and integral element in a child's life. The cultural background of a person is very much tied up with their own identity. It is vital that early years practitioners embrace the cultural knowledge and background of families and children if children are to gain a positive self-image. Kenner (2000) asserts the view that:

> Children live in simultaneous worlds. So a child is a member of a cultural group of her family but is also actively creating the cultural group of their setting, thus viewing the child as an active creator and transformer of culture.
>
> (p. 235)

For various reasons families may live in different countries around the world now more so than in the past. For some this can be very positive in cases where families make a choice to live in different places, but for many others this can be negative and the decision may relate to political issues in countries from which they have fled for reasons of safety. When the latter happens it can be very strange for parents, who may have left partners in a country where their lives are at risk and moved to a country where their cultural heritage is not valued. It is therefore vital that practitioners are welcoming and understanding, are prepared to embrace the culture of others and recognise the importance of valuing this in all children's lives. Some families will find the westernised view that children learn through play to be a strange concept.

While visiting Ghana, Africa, one of the authors, Penny, was involved in a conference that set out to encourage practitioners in Ghana to embrace a new curriculum that was built upon the value of play. This was seen by politicians as the best way to educate young children. However, during her visit it became apparent that, although the country is developing fast and new streams of industry are coming into it, there is still a great deal of poverty, particularly in rural areas. For many of the practitioners and parents the most important issues in education are that children learn to read and write. She returned to the UK wondering whether a play-based curriculum is as important for children in Africa, as issues within different cultural contexts require further understanding when considering this view.

Brooker (2002), in her work with Bangladeshi parents in London, noted that some parents did not view play as a tool for learning. Instead they, in a similar way to the African parents, expected children to be taught to read and write at nursery. Issues like these can be challenging for practitioners who are being advised by government that they need to plan the curriculum according to EYFS, while also having to discuss children's learning with parents who would prefer a more academic approach to learning.

The Te Whāriki approach used in New Zealand (see Chapter 24) employs the metaphor of a woven mat to demonstrate how the curriculum for young children views all aspects of a child's life as interwoven. While the individual elements of the curriculum are similar to the EYFS and the 'characteristics of learning' (DfE, 2014), the New Zealand curriculum policy places more emphasis on the cultural and spiritual lives of children and families. Although the UK Government accepts the significance of a child's cultural life, it rarely comments on the spiritual element of young children, which can be viewed by some as an essential aspect of their lives. Much of the writing about the importance of valuing children as spiritual beings focuses on the need for practitioners to recognise awe and wonder as being part of a child's development, and to accept that this is a vital part of children's development. Recently, Hay and Nye (2006) have viewed spirituality as being something that is 'biologically built' (p. 63), which may not necessarily pertain to any particular religion. Hyde (2004) follows this view, and extols Ranson's (2002) assertion that religion and spirituality are not disparate elements of humanity but interconnected. Holmes (2002) continues in this vein, suggesting that places of worship should foster children's beliefs; however, she has a word of warning for the educational system, which she believes can crush or sabotage children's burgeoning spirituality by not recognising it as an essential part of their development. It is essential for practitioners to be proactive in finding out about families' spiritual and cultural feelings in order to understand how best to ensure that their views are taken account of in order to develop provision that respects and values children's home culture as part of partnership working with families.

Cameo 1

A few years ago, a practitioner working in a multicultural area of a city in the Midlands carried out a piece of research that began with the question: 'Is it appropriate for a Sure Start programme to be offering a westernised approach to play, in a community where the majority of parents come from different cultures?' The Sure Start team struggled, when running parent and toddler groups, to engage children and parents in play activities with toys. Also families receiving home-based support for children with special needs did not engage with toys provided, and at times refused to have certain toys in their homes due to religious reasons. This became a real issue for staff. A member of the team was, at that time, studying for a higher degree course and decided to focus on this issue in her research.

The results of the research indicated that some parents did not value westernised toys because of the financial cost. Many of these families were asylum seekers or refugees, who were used to making their own toys and whose children, in their native environment, were more used to playing outside in large open areas with wider family members. Other families expected their children to look after younger siblings, and to help their parents to prepare food or to go to the Madrasa for Islam lessons, which meant that they did not have a great deal of time to play. Others were happy for their children to be enjoying books and playing outside with cousins and other relations, but were worried about crime figures associated with young children playing outside in the UK. Further research indicated that there had not been much difference in murder statistics compared with 20 years previously, but reports in the media can frighten parents, particularly those who are new to the country.

At the same time that this research was being carried out there was increased interest in the value of treasure baskets and heuristic play in early years settings (Goldschmeid, 1994). Educationalists also began to see the value of using open-ended resources with young children as such resources offer them a multitude of play options. As soon as these were introduced into the centre the children and their parents became more involved in their children's play. One afternoon was spent making treasure boxes with the children so parents and children worked together to make something that could be used in the home to recall special times in the families' lives. The children seemed better able to play with toys that had no predetermined outcomes than to play with some of the commercially developed toys that were available to buy. The researcher now values far more the use of natural ingredients in play that children can make into whatever they want and encourage children to be more creative in their play. The research enabled her to develop practice and demonstrated that families' home cultures and perspectives on play were valued within the setting.

Socio-cultural theory

In order to consider why a child's cultural identity should be acknowledged and developed it is prudent to consider what some of the child development theorists have to say about a child's cultural identity. Some theorists recognise strongly and advocate the need to recognise the cultural element of who children are. Bruner (1996), for example, championed the view that the cultural element of all families and children needs to be recognised. Furthermore, Vygotsky (1978) views children as cultural participants both in their own families and in the communities in which they live. Other theorists go on to suggest that children's view of themselves is socially constructed, both through the experiences of the child and more subtly through suggestions that the child may pick up from the media, their peers and siblings, and through activities in which they engage. Bronfenbrenner (cited in Cole and Cole, 1996), through his theory of ecological systems, views children and families as being part of a much wider set of systems that all relate to and impact on one another.

This theory is often depicted as a series of concentric circles to demonstrate the multi-layered nature of a child's relationships with immediate and wider community systems (see Figure 23.1). This theory of systems locates the child at the centre with the relationships that the child makes with the important people in their early life, which are known as the *microsystem*. The next layer relates to the *mesosystem*, which comprises educational settings, the community and the faith organisations to which families belong. It is interesting to note here the role of faith within this system; this may be because the theory was developed at the end of the twentieth century when the role of faith was a little more prominent in people's lives, or perhaps it is that

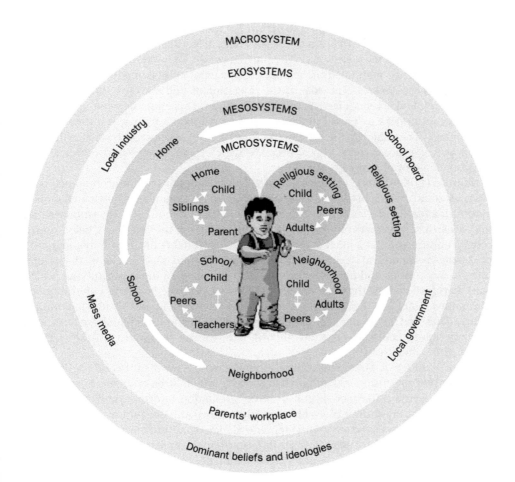

Figure 23.1 Bronfenbrenner's theory: the multi-layered nature of a child's relationships with immediate and wider community systems
Source: Cole and Cole, 1996.

Bronfenbrenner believes that children are spiritual beings and that faith is an important element in families' lives. The third element, the *exosystem*, explains the effects of wider organisations such as local government, media and parents' workplaces on the family. Finally, the *macrosystem* relates to the dominant beliefs and ideologies of society that permeate families' lives. Each of these systems is seen as being reciprocal and interrelated, thus each system has an impact on the family and the development of children within the family.

To illustrate how this theory might work we can consider the effect of redundancy on a family. A parent, who has previously been working, might suddenly spend more time at home. This parent may become depressed as a result of losing their job. Due to financial issues they might struggle to afford for their child to attend an early years setting, which, as well as affecting the parent may affect the emotional well-being of the child (micro- and mesosystems). The partner might be looking for new work and claiming benefits, so may need the support of the local authority and services in the community (mesosystem). The role of the government and society's differing views on the unemployed is recognised as the macrosystem. This example demonstrates the need for practitioners to view families as groups of people with specific needs and requirements. The majority of families will need little support but some will need the support of practitioners who appreciate their circumstances and their cultural background and offer support.

Bourdieu (1930–2002), a French sociologist, philosopher and anthropologist, uses the term 'capital', which in the main usually relates to economy, as in how much money and wealth a family has, as well as their home and all that they own. He espouses that families also have access to cultural capital, which relates to the benefits of belonging to a certain culture and the impact of that culture on the family's life. He further suggests three elements of cultural capital: the first of these relates to mind and body; the second relates to institutions and the effect of government policy on those institutions, which would therefore include the curriculum; and the last element relates to cultural goods that families may have in the home in relation to books (holy and secular), paintings and artefacts that may speak of the history of families and their cultures. As with Bronfenbrenner's ecological systems theory, here we see recognition of the spiritual element of families' lives.

Rogoff (2003), a socio-culturalist, expounds the views of Bronfenbrenner in suggesting that practitioners, rather than viewing all children as being homogenous groups, should view differences in culture as being exciting, informing and enlightening. She suggests that practitioners should value the history and the culture of the past, yet also that practitioners need to extend their knowledge of culture by embracing the view that society is made up of people from different backgrounds, faith and educational systems; this adds variety and excitement to society. Rogoff strives to encourage people to move from ethnocentrism, whereby someone sees a person's own ethnic group as being superior, to being more open to the differences in our society and the enrichment that this can bring to our communities. Furthermore, she asserts that the process of human development relates to all of society being part of cultural communities in which they interweave, suggesting that it is this involvement that transforms people to become members of society. This would also suggest that culture is organic and constantly evolves, bringing together new ideals and changing them in the light of new understandings.

The risk of 'silencing' families

In order to develop inclusive practice with children from diverse cultures, it is essential that no family is excluded from participating within the setting. In order to avoid marginalising cultural perspectives that are different to majority views, particular attention should be paid to including those whose backgrounds differ to our own. Often, unfair power issues can prevail within early years settings if practitioners' views are privileged over those of parents and children. Sometimes professionals are seen as the experts, whose knowledge and understanding is more significant or important than parents' perspectives. MacNaughton and Hughes (2009) carried out research with parents and staff in Australian early childhood settings, which highlighted the risk of unfair thinking habits or practices that can exclude some families' views. Through a series of focus groups, they found that it is easy to unwittingly 'silence' particular families who might find it harder to approach staff or when communication is a challenge, so their views are not heard. Often in settings time is at a premium, and some parents in the study found it more difficult to make the most of snippets of time with practitioners if their home language or cultural background differed. Sometimes practitioners spent more time with parents with whom they had more in common or with whom they found it easier to get along, even though this was not deliberate. In order to address these issues, consideration needs to be given to how time is distributed equitably between families, and how the views of all families can be actively sought in order to inform understandings of every culture within the setting.

It is important to recognise that cultures are not homogenous but heterogeneous. In other words, a group of people associated with a particular culture may have different views and beliefs even though they may have much in common with others who relate to the same culture. Life experiences and particular family views shape the way in which individuals see the world and develop their own unique set of values. This means that practitioners need to avoid making assumptions that, for example, a family with a particular religion feels exactly the same about an issue as another family belonging to the same faith. Moreover, many children belong to families with mixed heritage, and thus family traditions and values can be quite varied and might change over time as new people join families. This highlights the necessity to engage with each family within an early years context to develop understandings of each member's feelings in order to take account of this to promote inclusive practice.

Children's transitions between cultural settings

Practitioners need to understand children's home cultures in order to provide effective support when children make transitions between the home and early years setting. For some children, this can be an emotional time as they adjust to different environments with potentially differing expectations of them. In cases where a different language is spoken at home to that spoken in the early years setting, particularly if the language is unknown to the child, this can be even more unsettling. The way in which children are allowed or expected to use resources in different contexts can mean that they have to understand a different set of rules, which can cause anxiety. For example, a child who is allowed to bounce on the sofa at home but not in nursery might feel confused as to why this is a problem in one context but not another. Sensitive feedback with gentle, clear reasoning (and an alternative play experience offered with similar thrills and opportunities for emotional and physical development!) may be needed to avoid negative impact on the child's self-esteem.

For all children there is potential for the transition from home to school or nursery to be stressful, particularly when a child first joins the setting (see also Chapter 15), but this is much easier for some to cope with than others. There are various reasons for this, including the child's previous experience of change, which may have enabled them to build up resilience and confidence in new situations; prior opportunities for social interaction with peers and adults; and general well-being that could depend on a range of external influences on the child's life. However, the transition for a child whose home culture, social background and ideology is more similar to that of the practitioners and other families within the setting is likely to entail fewer adjustments in their thinking and behaviour. Additionally, parents of these children are more likely to gain more from limited opportunities for dialogue with practitioners as there may be more shared understandings of what an appropriate early years curriculum might be. It is essential to be aware of the potential for some children to be disadvantaged by a culturally biased curriculum and that children whose home cultures vary from accepted forms of play and interaction expected within the setting have additional transitional issues to deal with. This emphasises the need to engage with all families to understand children's backgrounds, and how to ensure that these are valued within early years education and care contexts.

When children enter a setting that, as well as differing in expectations of them, is quite different in terms of the physical environment and play and learning resources, this may feel very strange. It is important that resources reflect the cultures of the children accessing the setting for several reasons: this makes provision for children to engage in experiences that are relevant to their own lives; it enables celebration of the richness that diversity affords all children from a range of backgrounds; and it promotes a sense of belonging in children from diverse cultures. Children of all backgrounds can enjoy music from a wide range of cultures, either played through an audio system or playing musical instruments. Clothing, special artefacts and everyday objects from children's home cultures included in the setting can help to demonstrate that diverse cultures are valued and promotes positive attitudes of receptiveness as part of the curriculum. Cooking, stories and art techniques from other cultures can be included as part of everyday planning, and often parents are willing to share and demonstrate these so that authentic experiences can be enjoyed. Involving parents in planning relevant experiences, and seeking their expert knowledge on their children's well-being and development is an essential means of supporting transitions into the setting. Effective relationships between a child's key person and family are likely to ease the transition as well as ensuring that provision is continuously beneficial for the child.

Conclusion

Culture is fluid and dynamic, as are children's interests and needs at different times in their lives; thus practice and provision need to be responsive to change. In order to understand how best to respond, practitioners can draw on a range of information from the children and their families, and share decision making with them. Inclusion is not something that, once achieved, can be put to one side – rather it is by a continuous process of reflection and development that inclusive practice can be maintained and improved. Receptiveness to new ideas, and commitment to involving children and families in shaping the culture and practice of early years settings is needed in order for everyone to feel valued and to benefit from the richness of multicultural communities.

Questions to promote reflection

1   How do you enable children's agency as part of your professional role?
2   How do you find out about the home cultures of children with whom you work?
3   How does your practice ensure that children from all cultures develop a sense of belonging within the setting?

References and further reading (in bold)

Ang, L. (2010) Critical perspectives on cultural diversity in early childhood: building an inclusive curriculum and provision. *International Research Journal of Early Years*, **30(1): 41–52.**

Brooker, L. (2002) *Starting School: Young Children's Learning Cultures*. **London: McGraw-Hill.**

Bruner, J. (1996) *The Culture of Education*. Cambridge, MA: Harvard University Press.

Clark, A. and Moss, P. (2011) *Listening to Young Children: The Mosaic Approach*. London: National Children's Bureau.

Cole, M. and Cole, S.R. (1996) *The Development of Children*, 3rd edn. New York: W.H. Freeman.

Department for Education (DfE) (2014) *The Early Years Foundation Stage: Setting the Standards for Learning, Development and Care for Children from Birth to Five*. London: Crown Publications.

Goldschmeid, E. (1994) *People Under Three: Young Children in Day Care*. London: Routledge.

Hay, D. and Nye, R. (2006) *The Spirit of the Child*. London: Jessica Kingsley.

Holmes, T. (2002) Children with time and space to explore spirituality. Available online at: http://www.lexisnexis.com.lcprosy.shu.ac.uk/uk/legal/auth/bridge.do?rand (accessed 5 November 2013).

Hyde, B. (2004) Children's spirituality and 'The Good Shepherd Experience'. *Religious Education*, 99(2): 137–150.

Kenner, C. (2000) *Home Pages: Literacy Links for Bilingual Children*. Stoke-on-Trent: Trentham Books.

MacNaughton, G. and Hughes, P. (2009) *Parents and Professionals in Early Childhood Settings*. **Maidenhead: Open University Press.**

Ranson, D. (2002) *Across the Great Divide: Bridging Spirituality and Religion Today*. Sydney: St Pauls.

Rogoff, B. (2003) *The Cultural Nature of Human Development*. Oxford: Open University Press.

Vygotsky, L. (1978) *Mind in Society: The Development of Higher Psychological Processes*. Cambridge and London: Harvard University Press.

24

International dimensions of play and transitions

Sally Peters

Summary

This chapter considers the role of play in supporting children as they move from early childhood education to school. It will draw on a number of the author's New Zealand studies that look at children's learning journeys as they move between early childhood education (ECE) and school contexts and curricula. The ideas will be located within some of the international discussions on this topic, and also introduce some of the strategies teachers have utilised to enhance the role of play in transitions and the research findings associated with this approach.

Cameo 1

Joe discusses with his teacher how he felt about starting school: 'I wanna stay at day care 'cause you have to be in clothes, not a uniform . . . you had to be in clothes . . . and you can do anything.' Asked if there's anything specific he misses he reflects 'I, I, I miss that . . . um, the big playground because on the playground is a slide, it's pretty fast.' Later he adds 'I, I, I miss about those bikes because I know bikes . . . and, and I know bikes and go really fast and we have a slide for bikes and they go really fast.'

Introduction

One can't help but wonder what school holds in store for Joe, who 'knows bikes', and plans to be a 'dinosaur catcher' when he grows up. He's interested in speed (on bikes and slides), and likes rugby and basketball. What can the stories of Joe and his classmates tell us about the experiences of children as they make the move to formal schooling? How might supporting their transitions so they have a positive start influence their achievement later? Although New Zealand has a generally high level of educational attainment there is concern about the gap between the highest and lowest performers, and regular comment about the 'tail' in achievement data (see, e.g., New Zealand Treasury, 2008; Clark, 2013). However, as Macfarlane (2014) notes, perhaps it is time to focus more on the tales rather than the tails. This chapter draws on a number of the author's studies exploring stories of children's learning journeys as they transition between ECE and school settings, and through this offers a perspective from New Zealand on play and transitions. While the unique features of the New Zealand context help to shape the data, the ideas resonate with international literature on this topic.

This chapter briefly outlines the New Zealand context in which the studies have taken place. It then touches on pre-transition play, explores ways of connecting the learning journey across the transition, play in the early weeks at school and some of the practical strategies our teachers have been exploring with transition pedagogies and play.

New Zealand context

In New Zealand the transition from ECE to school, in terms of both the context and curriculum, almost always occurs as children turn five. Earlier in this volume, Dunlop and Fabian consider play and transitions with a focus on what they call 'atypical' transitions where children join an established class. In New Zealand, because children start school on or just after their fifth birthday, joining an established class is typical for 'new entrants' here, raising some specific challenges for both children and their teachers.

Peters (2010) provides some background about the context and a review of New Zealand research on transitions. (Curriculum documents for ECE (Ministry of Education, 1996) and school (Ministry of Education, 2007; 2008) can be found online.) When thinking about early years curriculum planning, one problem is 'making the selection of the most important aspects of culture for transmission to the next generation. The crucial cultural question is 'What is worthwhile?' and the crucial political question is 'Who makes the selection?' (Lawton, cited in Mutch, 2001: 75). With differing views about what is worthwhile, and about how to achieve what is deemed worthwhile, curricula for young children can be experienced as 'sites of struggle' between ideas about what early years education is for, and what are appropriate content and contexts for learning and development (Soler and Miller, 2003). Often this struggle intensifies at the point of transition between early childhood education and school, and ideas about the role of play are often located within this struggle.

Pre-transition play

This section touches briefly on some of the benefits of play pre-transition to school. There are many aspects that could be considered here and this is by no means intended to capture them all, only to highlight two possibilities. The first relates to play about school as a preparation or priming activity (Broström, 2005; Hartley *et al.*, 2012). The second considers the development of children's 'working theories' as a foundation of learning on which to build.

Play as preparation

It has been suggested that some aspects of play can act as valuable priming events for school (Hartley *et al.*, 2012), and Broström (2005) wrote about the possibilities of play to be a transitory activity, which helps the children involved to be active, rather than passive learners.

In our recent study (Peters and Paki, forthcoming) some early childhood services include school uniforms in their dressing-up corners and visits to school provide opportunities for children to explore and discuss what school will be like. Videos on the school website (led and narrated by children) also introduce early childhood children to school life. At one centre the five year olds also came back to their early childhood centre to talk to the older four year olds about school and to answer their questions. ECE cooking activities focused on making food for lunchboxes and on Fridays the children ate from lunchboxes as if they were at school. In another ECE setting that was located on a school site the ECE children regularly spent time at school, and siblings and friends in both contexts could converse through the fence.

Having some first-hand knowledge and props to explore understandings of school through socio-dramatic play seemed beneficial preparation. Within this, as Dockett and Perry (2006) recommend, teachers can prompt 'what-if games' to work through possible problems and strategies. One of the teacher researchers on our *Learning Journeys* project commented:

> It means that our kids are . . . 'Hey I can actually go to school and I'm confident to go to school.' . . . If you go into preschool room, not one of those kids is scared to go to school, 'I'm going to turn five and I'm going to school'. But before that I don't think we'd set them up enough. So I definitely think you've got to set your kids up to win. Otherwise they are going to fail. And then you're going to wonder why they've failed.

Joe's mother commented on how well Joe's early childhood centre had been 'exposing him to school. A lot of interaction, sports day, school days that they are invited to. It makes it easier'.

The development of working theories

Within a pedagogy of play in ECE there has been interest in fostering the development of children's working theories (Davis and Peters, 2011; Peters and Davis, 2012; Hedges, 2014). The New Zealand early childhood curriculum, *Te Whāriki* notes that:

> . . . in early childhood, children are developing more elaborate and useful working theories about themselves and about the people, places, and things in their lives. These working theories contain a combination of knowledge about the world, skills and strategies, attitudes, and expectations . . .
>
> (Ministry of Education, 1996: 44)

In a project exploring working theories (Davis and Peters, 2011) we were surprised at the astonishing depth to many children's theorising and thoughtful practitioners explored ways of supporting and extending this thinking. For example, showing children photographs and videos of their play led to the children extending their original ideas and also gave the adults chance to reflect on the ways they were tuning in to spoken and unspoken theories.

During the research we noticed how easy it was for adults to assume knowledge of the child's interest and meaning, and hijack the direction of the activity or conversation, rather than taking the time to adapt and fit with the child's thinking. As discussed in Peters and Davis (2011), supporting children's working theory development and intervening where appropriate (or even judging when is appropriate) is not easy. Earlier work in the Effective Provision of Pre-School Services (EPPE) project in England found that sustained adult–child interactions, which they called 'sustained shared thinking', although associated with high cognitive outcomes for children, occurred infrequently in the participating early childhood centres. Siraj-Blatchford and Manni (2008) noted that, even in the EPPE settings that were identified as good or excellent, only 5.5 per cent of questions asked by early childhood staff were open-ended and encouraged speculation or trial and error, and/or provided potential for sustained shared thinking.

Our research suggests that, even when there's sustained interaction and working together, the occasions where adults genuinely work with the child's theory, rather than hijacking the direction may be even less common. However, play does offer a rich context for thinking to develop and such dialogue to occur. Children's working theories are often more sophisticated in areas of interest/expertise than in aspects of more fleeting interest, and sensitive families and teachers know when it is appropriate to engage with this thinking (Crowley and Jacobs, 2002). If a new entrant teacher was aware of the child's current theories he/she would be more able to build appropriately on these to support children's learning.

Connecting learning journeys across the transition

The New Zealand Curriculum for school includes the requirement for school learning to 'build on the learning experiences the child brings with them' (Ministry of Education, 2007: 41). However, teachers are still exploring ways of identifying the richness of that prior learning, and finding ways to recognise and extend it. Our Education Minister recently stated, 'I dare to imagine a world where all teachers formally handover their young charges to the next sector with a meeting, a discussion between professionals about each child, a passing on of their learning story and so on' (Parata, 2013). However, the chance for professionals to discuss individual children's learning at transition points is not happening yet, although many families do share the child's early childhood portfolio with school (see Hartley et al., 2012, Chapter 3, for an example of using the portfolio as a transition tool). Some early childhood centres create special 'transition' portfolios for the families to pass on to school. The portfolios generally capture valued aspects of learning within narrative Learning Stories (Carr, 2001; Carr and Lee, 2012), often with photographs as well. This provides some insights into the child's play, interests and friendships.

Play in the early weeks at school

Some schools use Learning Stories, too. In a resource for school teachers that includes an example of how to write a Learning Story, the example is based on a child's play on the flying fox at school and highlights behaviours associated with the key competencies evident in her play (Davis *et al.*, 2013). Overseas, some teachers have experimented with more playful pedagogies at school (e.g. Martlew *et al.*, 2011; Reynolds *et al.*, 2011). Some exploration in this direction is evident in New Zealand, too. As noted earlier, opportunities for play can provide a permeable space for children's interests to be included in the curriculum. It has been shown to be valuable for learning dispositions too. Carr *et al.*'s (2009) research studied children's learning dispositions of reciprocity, imagination and resilience as they moved from early childhood to school. They found that 'children's learning dispositions are fragile in the onslaught of any school curriculum that is packed with compulsory tasks, tight scheduling and summative assessments – and does not recognise learning dispositions in practice or in documentation' (p. 220). However, although many new entrant teachers may value play and a more open approach to curriculum, for the majority of children there's often a change in the nature of play once they get to school. Like Joe, they find play at school very different to prior-to-and out-of-school play.

The nature of play at school

One marked difference between play in ECE and school is that school entry often introduces distinction between 'work' and 'play', with work being prioritised by teachers, even though much learning occurs also through play. Times to play also change, with play often restricted to moments in class when work has been completed or to lunchtime and playtime. Looking back on his transition, Steve reflected on this change, noting, 'At kindy you could just play and everything but at school you have to do what you had to do. At kindy you could really choose.' At school he had felt he would have liked to 'go out to play when I had to stay in and do work and everything. Sometimes when I was out to play I actually wanted to go in and do some work.'

Play in the playground

The context for play is also different at school. Steve commented, '[At school] there was lots of big people there and the playgrounds were much bigger, and better, and there was no really small people there except a few new people.' Although the playgrounds were better he felt 'lonely' and 'bored 'cos you've no idea what to do'.

Like Steve, Joe and his peers did not particularly enjoy school 'playtime':

Teacher:	OK, now we've got the tricky bit. What don't you like about school?
Mere:	Playtime.
Teacher:	Tell me why you don't like playtime.
Mere:	'Cause we don't do any learning.
Teacher:	OK – interesting.

Joe:	The same, same.
Teacher:	Mandy, what don't you like at school?
Mandy:	Playtime.

Joe's explanation linked back to his comment in the opening paragraph of this chapter where he said he preferred wearing his own clothes in ECE rather than the uniform at school. 'I don't like playtime 'cause we get hot and I take off my jersey then I get cold and I put on my jersey and I took off my jersey and I get cold.' Mandy agreed, 'Sometime when it's cold when I don't have my jersey, I don't feel hot, I'm cold.' While it might be tempting to see complaints about jerseys as trivial, underpinning this is the fact that for New Zealand children, school is often the first time when they have been required to 'play' outside for a set period of time whether they want to or not, regardless of temperature. In addition, as one teacher noted 'There's a gazillion children with the same clothes', so managing not to lose a jersey if you take it off is an added responsibility for a five year old who is already negotiating a new environment. No wonder some new-entrant children express a sense of relief when it is raining and they can stay inside.

No one to play with

Distress at not having anyone to play with during lunchtimes and break can also be an issue, and in some case lead to a dislike of school (Peters, 2004; 2012). Some of our recent data reflected the same concerns as children in Peters (2004) had expressed a decade earlier:

Teacher:	How were you feeling when you started school?
Brian:	Angry.
Teacher:	Why?
Brian:	Because no one's going to play with me and I wanted to go on my iPad.
Teacher:	What made you think no one was going to play with you?
Brian:	Because I was trying to find someone to play with me . . . I can't even find anyone.
Teacher:	OK. Is that why you played with your brother?
Brian:	Yeah.
Teacher:	What about the buddies you were put with in class?
Brian:	[Pauses] . . . They, I didn't like them, they didn't want to play with me.
Later in the conversation . . .	
Teacher:	What don't you like about school Brian?
Brian:	[Pauses] . . . Not having friends and not playing with them or walking around who won't wait for me.

There's the big space and lots of children that make it difficult to find a familiar face. There's also the challenge of gaining entry into peer groups, perhaps made more difficult by the New Zealand system of children joining existing classes. Even previous friends from the same early childhood centre may have made other friends by the time a new child arrives. Others join classes where they don't know anyone.

Findings from earlier research still seem applicable to playground observations today. For example, Corsaro's (1981) research with nursery-aged children found that young children do not readily accept new playmates, and requests to play were greeted with rejection about half of the time. Howes (1988) found that being rebuffed was more common for children without friends than for those with friends. However, Corsaro (1981) noted that initial resistance did not always result in permanent exclusion. Unfortunately, some children do not appear to have discovered that initial resistance could be overcome and spend much of the break time wandering, waiting for the time to pass. ECE settings that help children develop strategies for social interaction are assisting children with valuable skills for school entry.

Having something to play with

Although social skills are important, friendships do not rest solely with the child. Contextual factors play a key part, too. In an earlier study (see Peters, 2012) it appeared that including more resources to play with at school could be helpful in facilitating entry to social groups for children who found it hard to gain access by other means. This can be particularly important for children who do not share the dominant language of the school setting. For example, when Yuka, who could speak almost no English at all when she started school, brought a doll from home, she became engaged in sustained family play with a number of other girls in her class over the lunchtime period. From then on she often took her dolls to school. Her mother noted, 'Once she realised that she could bring her dolls and she could play with other children with dolls she was very happy.' Gregory (2005) also found that play at school was valuable for bilingual children who used home language in their socio-dramatic play, gradually inserting English words and experimenting with language. The ways in which resources supported communication between children with different languages, and how in meaningful play contexts mime and gesture were used along with increasing vocabulary to develop shared understandings was also been noted by Long (1997).

Transition pedagogies and play

With all of the points raised in this chapter in mind, teacher researchers in our Learning Journeys project (Peters and Paki, forthcoming) have been exploring a range of transition pedagogies. Play can offer an important context for learning in school. It can reveal important attributes and understanding that are more difficult to gain through other activities.

Addressing the challenges of play in the playground has also proved a valuable context for learning within the class. Prompted by playground observations showing changes in the children's play from preschool to school, and awareness of the possible challenges for new children when preschool children and teachers experienced the rush of children coming out to play when the bell rang, teachers sought children's views about play.

First steps after listening to the children were to create quiet places to play near the new entrant classrooms, with trays of toys to play with. This small step had a big impact for new children, providing an alternative to the noise and bustle of the larger playgrounds. Later, quiet places to meet friends were also identified, but the tray of toys by the classroom meant children were less dependent on others to play with, while also having resources to aid interaction.

The children's initial ideas also formed part of a DVD to share with new children and parents. The children and teachers then went on to co-construct large books about the playground. These included photographs of what the children saw as important and narration of the text by the children. In the books, children identified the duty teacher, what happens on rainy days, and the meaning of symbols (such as flags showing that an area is too wet to play in after rain). They highlighted the areas they enjoyed playing in, including ones they felt new children needed information about such as 'the back field' and 'the big hill', and all the quieter places to play. This book could then be shared and discussed with new children as they arrived.

Teachers took seriously the difficulties children experienced in joining groups of peers, and worked with the children on the kind of approaches they might use if they wanted to play. They also discussed with the children what they might do if a child was trying to join their play. This work aligned closely with the key competencies in the curriculum. The curriculum also notes the importance of taking account of the child's whole experience of school (Ministry of Education, 2007: 41). Listening to and supporting children's concerns about their thoughts and feelings created more personalised transition pedagogies.

This has been noticed and appreciated by parents and caregivers too:

> . . . it's really changed this year, the whole transitional process has . . . yeah . . . is amazing . . . With having a second [child starting school now], which has been really interesting to be able to compare. Completely different . . . Just being able to put strategies into place straight away before things get out of hand, you know. 'Cos once they get out of hand, it's a bit late then. I think this study has been what has helped both sides [ECE and school] put in the kind of strategies and procedures to help the kids out.
>
> (Parent interview)

Conclusion

While there appears to be widespread support for the benefits of play, there is much to be considered in relation to the role of play and the transition to school. This fits within a bigger picture of understanding children's whole experience of school and taking seriously their concerns. This chapter has shared some of the work of teachers who have been focused on the subtle nuances of pedagogy that can adapt to support the diverse range of children who join their classes, with the aim of enhancing their learning over time. However, this is part of a learning journey for the adults, too, and the work is continuing. As for Joe, so far so good. His mother notes, 'He comes home very excited about his achievements . . . He's progressing really well . . . He seems to enjoy school . . . He's socially secure and everything out of that will follow. That belonging and stability and acceptance.' We hope to be able to achieve that for all children starting school.

Questions to promote reflection

1   How has paying closer attention to the stories (tales) of children's experiences at school provided you with insights when considering their achievement (both successes and 'tails')?
2   What strategies can adults use to avoid 'hijacking' the direction of children's thinking during their play?
3   In what ways might teachers support children's play in the school playground?

Acknowledgements

I am very grateful to the New Zealand Teaching and Learning Research Initiative (TLRI) for the funding to support a number of research projects cited here. I also appreciate the work of my colleagues (both university and teacher/practitioner researchers) in these studies, and the willingness of children, families and other teachers to participate in the research.

References and further reading (in bold)

Broström, S. (2005) Transition problems and play as transitory activity. *Australian Journal of Early Childhood*, 30(3): 17–25.
Carr, M. (2001) *Assessment in Early Childhood Settings*. London: Paul Chapman.
Carr, M. and Lee, W. (2012) *Learning Stories: Constructing Learner Identities in Early Education*. London: Sage.
Carr, M., Smith, A.B., Duncan, J., Jones, C., Lee, W. and Marshall, K. (2009) *Learning in the Making: Disposition and Design in the Early Years*. Rotterdam: Sense.
Clark, J. (2013) Inequality of school achievement: why the events of 2012 will not fix the problem. *NZ Teacher*. Available online at: http://www.educationreview.co.nz/nz-teacher/january–2013/inequality-of-school-achievement-why-the-events-of–2012-will-not-fix-the-problem/#. U1t7U62Sz1t (accessed 27 April 2014).
Corsaro, W.A. (1981) Entering the child's world – research strategies for field entry and data collection in a preschool setting. In J. Green and C. Wallot (eds) *Ethnography and Language in Educational Settings*. Norwood, NJ: Ablex.
Crowley, K. and Jacobs, M. (2002) Building islands of expertise in everyday family activity. In G. Leinhardt, K. Crowley and K. Knutson (eds) *Learning Conversations in Museums*. Mahwah, NJ: Lawrence Erlbaum.
Davis, K. and Peters, S. (2011) Moments of wonder, everyday events: children's working theories in action. Teaching Learning Research Initiative Final Report. Available online at: http://www.tlri.org.nz/moments-wonder-everyday-events-how-are-young-children-theorising-and-making-sense-their-world/ (accessed 25 April 2014).
Davis, K., Wright, J., Carr, M. and Peters, S. (2013) *Key Competencies, Assessment and Learning Stories*. Wellington: NZCER (DVD and PD resource book).
Dockett, S. and Perry, B. (2006) *Starting School: A Handbook for Early Childhood Educators*. Castle Hill, NSW: Pademelon Press.

Gregory, E. (2005) Playful talk: the interspace between home and school discourse. *Early Years: An International Journal of Research and Development*, 25(3): 223–235.

Hartley, C., Rogers, P., Smith, J., Peters, S. and Carr, M. (2012) *Crossing the Border: A Community Negotiates the Transition from Early Childhood to Primary School*. Wellington: NZCER.

Hedges, H. (2014). Young children's 'working theories': building and connecting understandings. ***Journal of Early Childhood Research*, 12(1): 35–49.**

Howes, C. (1988) Peer interaction of young children. *Monographs of the Society for Research in Child Development*, 53(1).

Lange, S. and Thomson, B. (2006) Early identification and interventions for children at risk for learning disabilities. *International Journal of Special Education*, 21(3): 108–119.

Long, S. (1997) Friends as teachers: the impact of peer interaction on the acquisition of a new language. In E. Gregory (ed.) *One Child, Many Worlds: Early Learning in Multicultural Communities*. London: David Fulton.

Macfarlane, A.H. (2014) Ngā tapuwae o mua, mō muri: challenges and promises of tribally-based research. Paper presented at Te Kōhao o te rangahau Indigenous Research Conference, University of Waikato, April.

Martlew, J., Stephen, C. and Ellis, J. (2011) Play in the primary school classroom? The experience of teachers supporting children's learning through a new pedagogy. *Early Years: An International Research Journal*, 31(1): 71–83.

Ministry of Education (1996) *Te Whāriki. He Whāriki Mātauranga mō ngā Mokopuna o Aotearoa: Early Childhood Curriculum*. Wellington, New Zealand: Learning Media.

Ministry of Education (2007) *The New Zealand Curriculum*. Wellington, New Zealand: Learning Media.

Ministry of Education (2008) *Te marautanga o Aotearoa*. Wellington, New Zealand: Learning Media Limited.

Mutch, C. (2001) Contesting forces: the political and economic context of curriculum development in New Zealand. *Asia Pacific Education Review*, 2(1): 74–84.

New Zealand Treasury (2008) *Working Smarter: Driving Productivity Growth Through Skills*. Wellington: New Zealand Treasury. Available in: Nusche, D., Laveault, D., MacBeath J. and Santiago, P. (2012) *OECD Reviews of Evaluation and Assessment in Education, New Zealand, Main Conclusions*. Available online at: http://www.oecd.org/education/school/49681563.pdf (accessed 28 April 2014).

Parata, H. (2013) Speech to the NZ OECD conference on ECE. Available online at: http://www.beehive.govt.nz/speech/speech-nz-oecd-conference-ece (accessed 24 April 2014).

Peters, S. (2004) Crossing the border: an interpretive study of children making the transition to school. Unpublished PhD thesis, University of Waikato, New Zealand.

Peters, S. (2010) *Literature review: transition from early childhood education to school*. Report commissioned by the Ministry of Education. Wellington: Ministry of Education. Available online at: http://www.educationcounts.govt.nz/publications/ece/78823 (accessed 29 April 2014).

Peters, S. (2012) 'I didn't expect that I would get tons of friends . . . more each day': children's experiences of friendship during the transition to school. In L. Miller, R. Drury, R. and C. Cable (eds) *Extending Professional Practice*. Maidenhead: Open University Press.

Peters, S. and Davis, K. (2011) Fostering children's working theories: pedagogic issues and dilemmas in New Zealand. *Early Years: International Journal of Research and Development*, 31(1): 5–17.

Peters, S. and Davis, K. (2012) Working theories and learning dispositions in early childhood education: perspectives from New Zealand. In T. Papatheodorou (ed.) *International Debates on Early Childhood Practices and Policies*. London: Routledge.

Peters, S. and Paki, V. (forthcoming) *Learning Journeys from Early Childhood into School*. Teaching and Learning Research Initiative Project.

Reynolds, E., Kidd, E. and Stagnitti, K. (2011). Play, language and social skills of children attending a play-based curriculum school and a traditionally structured classroom curriculum school in low socio-economic areas. *Australian Journal of Early Childhood*, 36(4): 120–130.

Siraj-Blatchford, I. and Manni, L. (2008) 'Would you like to tidy up now?' An analysis of adult questioning in the English Foundation Stage. *Early Years: An International Journal of Research and Development*, 28(1): 5–22.

Soler, J. and Miller, L. (2003) The struggle for early childhood curricula: a comparison of the English Foundation Stage Curriculum, Te Whāriki and Reggio Emilia. *International Journal of Early Years Education*, 11(1): 57–68.

Endpiece
Tina Bruce

Through their play, children become partners with their future, but they need adults who are informed advocates, promoting, protecting and tuning in to their free-flow play (Bruce, 1991). The socio-cultural environment is important in establishing individual children's sense of agency in developing their play. Research into brain development is showing that nurture triggers, shapes and influences nature (see Chapter 3). Our environments – social, cultural, physical and material – serve as an extension of our brains, it seems.

Observing free-flow play in action

Tom, aged two years, spent an afternoon cracking a bowl of nuts with two types of nutcracker: a corkscrew model and a pincer model. He was involved in forces, holes and broken parts. He shared this experience with his mother. By the age of three, he was making paper aeroplanes. He was completely fascinated when shown by an older child that he could cut bits off the wing to make flaps, which speed up and slow down flight and vary the direction of the aeroplane. Vygotsky (1978) has emphasised the importance of children spending time with people who are more skilled than they are if learning is to be effectively developed.

During his play, Tom loved to throw sticks into bushes in the garden and into water. He, in Europe, is doing what a group of three children (aged two, four and seven) are doing on the banks of the River Nile in Egypt. They are making boats that will sail in particular directions and float with cargoes. Tom is playing with forces, crashes and splashes, just as they are as they throw sticks and stones into the Nile around the boats that they have made. Free-flow play is happening all over the world. There is a common core of play, which has a universal dimension.

Hannah, at 14, is choreographing a solo dance for her GCSE course. This is the culmination of the dance play she has maintained from the age of ten months, when she began the 'knees bend' swaying to music indulged in by children in cultures throughout the world (Davies, 2003). At six she danced for hours on end with her four-year-old friend, Ming, using dressing-up clothes, music on a tape recorder and homemade instruments, playing at dancing and using everything she knew about dance.

In Cairo, a different mixed-age group comprising three boys (one 12 year old and two 15 year olds) free-flow play-dance on a patch of park between two busy roads. They have brought a ghetto-blaster, play Arabic music and all do their own thing. Gradually, one echoes what another does, and their movements coordinate more and more until they are dancing together. In free-flow play, one of the features is that the players are sensitive to one another's personal agendas as well as a feeling of group sensitivity emerging.

At an international conference in England, Nigel Kennedy spoke of the way musicians found they could improvise and literally 'play' music together, which was of a high standard and respected the different cultural backgrounds from which they came. They found they could allow one style of music to emerge and subside, letting another form become dominant at different points. This kind of free-flow playing respects individuals and encourages group sensitivity. There are resonances with the processes involved in creativity here, since improvisation and making connections are key aspects of creativity.

Seven-year-old Chris spends a week on a boat holiday on a river with William (11) and Ayo (13). Mixed-age groups are untypical in schools. Here the older children teach him to work a lock, tie a knot, move safely on to land, light a barbecue, put up a tent, strip a stick, make an arrow, make a bow from willow, fish, swab the deck and sweep the stairs. He is learning in a very practical way key elements of science and technology as well as geography and history. He sees the older children settle to an hour's homework each day, and spends that time choosing to sketch, play, read and practise, becoming, for example, skilled in lighting his own barbecue. As he plays, he wallows in using the bow and arrow, and celebrates his skill in shooting at a target of his making.

Chris, like William, loves to 'play' scientifically. His imagined world is to do with alternative hypotheses for what will happen to the arrow when he does this, that or the other. Adults are around, but he can take responsibility and is proud of himself. When he needs help, he asks, or an adult notices and comes to offer help. He is told (or read) a story each evening sitting by the camp fire. In particular he loves King Arthur stories. There is no competition with other seven year olds. He is the only one. He goes at his own speed and sets himself high standards, encouraged by the admiration of others, but influenced to learn by the leadership of the older children.

Play is a concept that embraces diversity, and is inclusive.

Daniel, from the age of three, thoroughly enjoyed dressing-up clothes. It was a tradition at family gatherings to play charades, which involved one group acting out words – titles of books, films or famous names – while the others tried to guess who/what they were. Because of his disabilities, Daniel had great difficulty in reading, writing and breaking words down into components. For years, the joy of charades for him was in choosing his dressing-up clothes and trying to get the group to act a story he told. The rest of the family group worked gently around his play agenda, acting out phrases like 'Footballers' Wives'. By the time he was about 12, he was thinking about the costumes others would wear, rather than simply planning his own. He began to join in thinking about what roles they would adopt, although the storyline and characters still revolved around him. Everyone felt the effort was for him and respected his hard work in trying to do this.

Suddenly, at the age of about 14, he made a huge step forward. He saw that a phrase like 'Footballers' Wives' could be acted out in four parts, according to the number of syllables. He realised, in a quantum leap forward in his thinking, that the group could then make a story out of the whole phrase. He no longer needed to be the centre of attention. The first syllable had a hospital operating theatre with people with bad feet having surgery. The second was a football match with the ball going into the goal. The third had children in a lesson at school not knowing the answer to a teacher's questions, saying 'Erh' all the time. Then came a party and he needed to introduce his wife. The whole word was then acted out, echoing a scene from the programme on television. He was now participating in group free-flow play.

Play in a social context has made a phuge contribution to his development. We often see a slower development in children with special educational needs and disabilities, but this helps to illuminate and show clearly why play is so important in developing learning as a whole person.

The bedrock principles of early childhood practice

The great pioneer educators were aware of the delicate balance between what is universal to being human and the unique way in which every individual is human. For example, Froebel (1782–1852) was constantly aware of certain aspects that human beings have in common, which bind them together as a species across the world. He considered free-flow play to be an important one of these, seeing every child as a unique individual who needs sensitive and appropriate help in order to develop and learn optimally. In this way, we can see that play is an integrating mechanism in a child's development, and perhaps into adulthood, too.

In Bruce (1987), ten principles were extrapolated from the literature, as follows.

1 Childhood is seen as valid in itself, as part of life and not simply as preparation for adulthood.
2 The whole child is considered to be important. Health, physical and mental well-being, is emphasised, together with the importance of feelings, having ideas, thoughts and spiritual aspects.
3 Learning is not compartmentalised, because everything is linked.
4 Intrinsic motivation, resulting in child-initiated self-directed activity, is valued.
5 Self-discipline is emphasized (4 and 5 lead to autonomy).
6 There are especially receptive periods of learning at different stages of development.
7 What children can do (rather than what they cannot do) is the starting point in the child's education.
8 There is an inner structure in the child, which includes the imagination and emerges especially under favourable conditions.
9 The people (both adults and children) with whom the child interacts are of central importance.
10 The child's education is seen as an interaction between the child and the environment the child is in – including, in particular, other people and knowledge itself.

Because there is widespread confusion about what play is, 'free-flow play' was adopted as a term because it expresses a view of play supported by 12 features extrapolated from the literature. The features are increasingly used by practitioners to inform their observations and to identify and locate play in the child's learning.

Twelve features of free-flow play (Bruce, 1991)

1   It is an active process without a product.
2   It is intrinsically motivated.
3   It exerts no external pressure to conform to rules, pressures, goals, tasks or definite direction. It gives the player control.
4   It is about possible, alternative worlds, which lift players to their highest levels of functioning. This involves being imaginative, creative, original and innovative.
5   It is about participants wallowing in ideas, feelings and relationships. It involves reflecting on, and becoming aware of, what we know – metacognition.
6   It actively uses previous first-hand experiences, including struggle, manipulation, exploration, discovery and practice.
7   It is sustained and, when in full flow, helps us to function in advance of what we can actually do in our real lives.
8   During free-flow play, we use technical prowess, mastery and competence we have previously developed, and so can be in control.
9   It can be initiated by a child or an adult, but if by an adult he/she must pay particular attention to 3, 5 and 11 of the features.
10   Play can be solitary.
11   It can be in partnership or groups, with adults and/or children who will be sensitive to one another.
12   It is an integrating mechanism, which brings together everything we learn, know, feel and understand.

Commonalities and differences in free-flow play across cultures

It is helpful to begin studying how play develops in children (and adults) by looking at the ubiquitous aspects such as the features common to play. It is also important to look at socio-cultural differences in the way that children play in different families and communities trans-globally, if we are to respond to and value the uniqueness of each human being and the rich diversity of different cultures, and to consider the ways in which children with disabilities and complex needs engage in play, providing for their particular needs in a spirit of inclusion.

Free-flow play is found among children in all parts of the world, as well as in ancient civilisations. It is part of being human. However, those who study play view it through a variety of different lenses, which result in it being encouraged, discouraged, constrained or valued in widely differing ways, which have a great impact on the child's access and opportunities for free-flow playing.

There is a tendency among some to see free-flow play as a privilege enjoyed mainly by middle-class children in Europe and North America and yet, in reality, this is unlikely to be so. It is 'misguided to characterize the middle classes as historical pinnacles of indulgent concern for children's needs' (Konner, 1991: 196). It may even be that those in the 'fast lane' of complex industrialised societies are in danger of losing, or at least damaging and seriously eroding, aspects of traditional childhood that are in fact central to being truly successful human adults.

In complex industrialised life there is so much that children need to know. In the UK since the late 1980s there has been slippage into the earlier introduction of formal schooling with an emphasis on direct teaching and the transmitting of a particular culture. This is typically presented to children through highly pre-structured experiences in a predominantly 'tell and write' mode (see Chapter 1). However, this may not produce the kind of adult who can survive the future nearly so well as the adaptive intelligence, imagination and creativity required of children brought up to actively experience and learn in real-life situations, with opportunity and access to free-flow play.

As Brazelton (1969: 281) points out, young children 'show a resistance to being pushed into habits that are not sympathetic to their style, a resistance backed up by all the strength inherent in a well-organized personality, infant or adult'.

It is not a question of those in complex industrialised societies trying to return to a romantically perceived view of the hunting and gathering or agricultural community, where children play, socialise and learn from being with adults as they work each day. It is much more a question of not discarding what is central to humanity by throwing the baby out with the bath water in an attempt to keep a place in the 'fast lane'. Those who study children free-flow playing do not see romance but a highly effective mechanism giving access to symbolic and physical functioning of a high level, crucial for the future of humanity both as individuals and as participants in their communities and cultures.

Children's play is sometimes used and taken over by adults as a way of gaining access to guiding and structuring children's learning so that they are, it is argued, adequately prepared for adult life and helped to learn in ways that are appropriate to childhood. This 'preparation for life' view of play is supported by modern theorists such as Bruner, and has gained great influence in England and North America, although not so much in the Nordic countries and other countries of western Europe (Moyles, 2010).

It is interesting to examine figures produced by Whiting and Whiting's *Six Cultures Project* (Konner, 1991). Five agricultural societies in Kenya, Mexico, the Philippines, Japan and India were studied together with a town called 'Orchardtown' in Pennsylvania, New England, USA. The children in Orchardtown were involved in household and garden chores for 2 per cent of their time. They were engaged in casual social interactions, watching adults, chatting and so on, for about 52 per cent of the time. Formal school-type learning took up 16 per cent of the time. From these figures, we could perhaps argue that these urban children are playing for a healthy and appropriate part of their day. However, there is more to this, as we shall see later.

We know from Donaldson's (1978) pioneering studies that children perform better on embedded tasks that make what she calls 'human sense' to them. When the tasks are in the context of their own everyday lives, and have purpose and function, and when children are able to learn through their senses with freedom of movement, they learn with more breadth, depth and permanence. Their well-being and sense of self is stronger. They are more confident. They are more engaged and take pride in what they do. They want to participate and make a good contribution. They have the dispositions needed for lifelong learning (see Chapter 2).

We have seen a massive switch in developed industrial societies so that children are now in compulsory schooling in contrast to performing compulsory chores or labour. In agricultural societies children tend to work at chores for their parents for 17 per cent of the time, in fields or in the home. They play for 44 per cent of their time. They are involved in casual social interactions, chatting, watching adults and so on for 34 per cent of their time, and in formal learning for only 5 per cent of the time (Konner, 1991: 309).

When we speak of child labour being an abuse of children's rights, we need to be clear what we are talking about. Putting children to work in coalmines and factories with the growth of industrialisation is not the same as children helping in the home or on the family farm. Konner argues (1991: 309) that 'Despite their hardships, chores give children skills they are proud of all their lives, and can bring parents and children closer together.'

In hunting and gathering societies, children learn through watching, socialising, playing and slowly doing, with virtually no formal teaching. In agricultural societies children are required to do more of the essential chores that arise through living in one place rather than moving on. Pretty Shield (in Niethammer, 1977: 27), a member of the Crow tribe, remembering her childhood at the turn of the century, describes the 'chores' element in her education:

> Indian girls were gently led into the art of motherhood, and their introduction to other womanly tasks was gradual, too, at least for the littlest girls. They accompanied their mothers and big sister while they gathered foods, weeded gardens, and went for water and wood. As the girls grew older more was expected of them. A Fox woman, living in the area of what is now Wisconsin and Illinois, told how she was encouraged when she was about nine to plant a few things and to hoe the weeds. Then she was taught to cook what she had raised, and was lavishly praised for her efforts.

Pretty Shield also remembers the importance of free-flow play during her childhood (Niethammer, 1977: 25):

> Learning the role of woman by playing was the pervading method of education for young girls, and mothers often took pains to see that their daughters had accurate miniatures of real household equipment to use in playing house. In some of the Plains tribes such as the Cheyenne, Omaha, Arapaho and Crow, daughters of the more well-to-do families even had their own skin tents as play-houses, and when time came to pack up camp to follow the buffalo, the girls got their own household – tipe, toys and clothes – packed and ready to move.

Children in hunting and gathering societies and agricultural societies learn through watching, playing, socialising and slowly doing according to an apprenticeship model. Children do not have to tell or write what they learn. They have to show their learning by doing (for example, weaving in the context of everyday life). In their play, they reflect on these active experiences and wallow in them, demonstrating the technical prowess they have been struggling to master. Play is about wallowing in what has been experienced and dealing with mastering, facing, and controlling what is experienced emotionally, socially, bodily, in movement, thoughts and ideas. Play is, in the main, about the application of what is known, using the skill and competence that has been developed.

This contrasts with industrial societies, in which household chores are replaced with child labour in factories and mines, or with formal schooling with children following adult-set and led tasks for long hours of the day. Konner argues (1991: 310) that school 'attempts to turn children into a workforce with skills that society needs. In these senses it exploits children just as much as work does.'

Conclusion

Both the traditional philosophical principles supporting play, with its emphasis on experienced intuition and practice wisdom handed down from generation to generation, and the theories giving high value to childhood play and beyond into adulthood remain important. Play needs committed adult advocates.

Societies that neglect their infrastructure are likely to hit problems, producing adults who are not able to problem solve, persevere, concentrate, be imaginative or creative, make connections, improvise, be flexible and adaptive, read the body movements and language of others, see things from different points of view, or tune in to the thoughts and feelings of other people or situations. Free-flow play is part of the infrastructure of any civilisation.

Play often has to function in a hostile environment, but when it is encouraged, supported and extended, it makes a major contribution to, and sophisticated impact on, the development of individuals and humanity as a whole.

References and further reading (in bold)

Brazelton, T. Berry (1969) *Infants and Mother: Differences in Development*. New York: Delacorte Press.

Bruce, T. (1987) *Early Childhood Education*. Sevenoaks: Hodder & Stoughton.

Bruce, T. (1991) *Time to Play in Early Childhood Education*. London: Hodder & Stoughton.

Davies, M. (2003) *Movement and Dance in Early Childhood*, 2nd edn. London: Paul Chapman.

Donaldson, M. (1978) *Children's Minds*. London: Fontana.

Konner, M. (1991) *Childhood*. Boston, MA: Little Brown.

Moyles, J. (ed.) (2010) *Thinking About Play: Developing a Reflective Approach*. Maidenhead: Open University Press.

Niethammer, C. (1977) *Daughters of the Earth: The Lives and Legends of American Indian Women*. New York: Collier/Macmillan.

Vygotsky, L. (1978) *Mind in Society: The Development of Higher Psychological Processes* (trans. M. Cole, V. John-Steiner, S. Scribner and E. Souberman). Cambridge, MA: Harvard University Press.

Author index

Subject index

active participation, 19, 49, 56, 63,76, 77, 78, 95, 96, 107, 110, 111, 117, 119, 151, 152, 188, 202, 207, 217, 252, 257, 269, 288, 300
adult/child co-construction of knowledge, xix, xx, 21, 25, 28, 31, 37, 45, 76, 81, 145, 146, 152, 156, 179, 198, 221, 236, 263, 269, 270
accountability, 81, 141, 144
adults:
 advocates for children, 12, 109, 126, 297, 303
 and child relationships, 28, 52, 77, 95, 96, 141, 142, 146, 149, 152, 153, 155, 160, 178, 246, 280, 284
 and control, 9, 32, 33, 34, 82, 90, 108, 128, 145, 154, 167, 169, 204, 214
 intervention, 11, 12, 35, 42, 44, 87, 88, 134, 152, 160, 199, 221, 225, 253, 255, 262, 264, 269, 270, 289
 roles, xxi, xxiii, 12, 50, 76, 138, 178, 246, 298
art(s), 4, 8, 45, 71, 87, 188, 190, 192
assessment:
 children's self-assessment, 220
 credit model, 42, 43
 deficit model, 42, 46, 253
attachment, 27, 28, 30, 66, 70, 117, 129, 140
attention span, 228
attitudes, 16, 46, 77, 150, 154, 199, 218, 220, 267, 284, 288
attunement, 27
autonomy, 7, 26, 108, 112, 118, 141, 223, 227, 299
awe and wonder, 279

baby rooms, 64, 66, 67, 72, 154
biological determinism, 55
borders/border crossing, 176, 180
boundary/ies, 10, 49, 67, 78, 100, 127, 160, 208, 215, 220
brain
 development, 8, 25, 26, 27, 33, 34, 36, 140, 252, 297
 neuroscience, 20, 34, 138, 140, 201, 252
 neo-cortex, 30
 plasticity, 27, 29, 140

challenge(s), 10, 14, 15, 16, 17, 19, 21, 29, 32, 36, 43, 47, 50, 55, 77, 81, 88, 94, 95, 96, 98, 104, 128, 134, 135, 140, 145, 148, 151, 156, 178, 191, 213, 214, 217, 218, 220, 221, 222, 223, 225, 235, 254, 264, 268, 269, 275, 287, 292
characteristics of Effective Learning, 109, 151, 156, 206
childhood innocence, 56
child-initiated experiences, 11, 15, 82, 86, 95, 152, 211, 219, 221, 299
children
 as researchers, 106, 109, 119
 being/becoming, 42, 49, 50, 51, 55, 58, 59, 65, 127
 constructing epistemologies, 108, 110, 111, 118, 119
 in poverty, 6, 36, 46, 107, 278
children's
 agency, xix, xx, xxii, 51, 52, 107,141, 152, 159, 169, 198, 239, 275, 276, 277, 285, 297

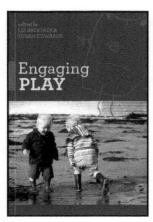

ENGAGING PLAY

Liz Brooker and Suzy Edwards (Editors)

2010
978-0-335-23586-5 *(Paperback)*

eBook also available

This insightful edited collection brings together the perspectives of leading and emerging scholars in early childhood education and play from within Europe, the UK, Australia, New Zealand and the USA.

The chapters cover a wide range of contexts, from child-led activity in informal settings to the more formal practice of school-based learning. A range of theoretical viewpoints of play are considered and related to the experiences of today's families, children and educators across different educational settings.

Engaging Play offers an insight into the pedagogical play discourse of twenty-first century early childhood education, and in doing so offers an informative reading experience for students, researchers and policy makers alike.

www.openup.co.uk

OPEN UNIVERSITY PRESS
McGraw - Hill Education

A-Z OF PLAY IN EARLY CHILDHOOD

Janet Moyles

9780335246380 (Paperback)
2012

eBook also available

This indispensable guide uses a unique glossary format to explore some of the key themes in play in early childhood, many of which regularly arise for students, tutors, parents and practitioners. As well as covering key concepts, theories and influential figures in the field, the book considers important aspects of each construct and highlights the complexity of play in early childhood.

Key features:

- Split into a comprehensive glossary running through elements of play from A – Z, it is a useful, fun and unique companion to understanding children's play
- Original thoughts from well known early years people including Tricia David, Carol Aubrey, Angela Anning and Lilian Katz

www.**openup**.co.uk